Walt Kuhn, Painter

Plate 1. Drawing of
Walt Kuhn, by
Jules Pascin

Walt Kuhn, Painter

His Life and Work

By Philip Rhys Adams

Ohio State University Press: Columbus

Copyright © 1978 by the Ohio State University Press
All Rights Reserved.

Excerpts from *The Story of the Armory Show,* by Milton W. Brown,
are reprinted by permission of Joseph H. Hirshhorn Foundation;
Copyright © 1963 by Joseph H. Hirshhorn Foundation, Inc.

Library of Congress Cataloging in Publication Data

Adams, Philip Rhys, 1908–
  Walt Kuhn, painter.

  Includes index.
  1. Kuhn, Walt, 1877–1949. 2. Painters — United States — Biography.
I. Title.
ND237.K8A84   759.13   78-3502
ISBN 0-8142-0258-6

TO BRENDA

CONTENTS

LIST OF ILLUSTRATIONS

Preface

Almost every night for the three spring weeks that Walt Kuhn spent in Columbus, Ohio, in 1942, he poured out a flood of reminiscence and recollection whose purpose could be interpreted only as biographical. Years later that intent was confirmed when a letter turned up that he had written to his wife Vera in New York on 15 April, 1942: "Probably the best results of the trip are my private talks with Adams. He drives me to appointments and we usually wind up in a booth in some joint or other." That may not be the commission or the authorization for this book, but it is at least the license under which it was started. Unfortunately there was no one of even vaguely Boswellian inclinations present on those April evenings to write down the recollections as soon as they were recounted, so a fallible but stubborn memory will have to be relied on to fill the gaps in the artist's own story. And it is largely his own story; few painters have written in such detail of their work as Walt Kuhn did, in collaboration with Paul Bird, in *50 Paintings by Walt Kuhn* in 1940, and few have left so voluminous a correspondence. Also, as many other writers as possible have been quoted extensively in a deliberate attempt to give a rounded picture of the exciting context in which he lived and worked. After all, his productive life missed covering exactly the first half of the twentieth century by a scant two years, and Kuhn was often at the storm center of artistic events. So this publication can be considered merely the frame of the painting; it is the painting that counts, but the frame can concentrate attention on the painting and protect it somewhat from outside distractions.

The help of many people must be gratefully acknowledged, and those whose names may be unintentionally omitted are no less sincerely thanked. First of all comes Miss Brenda Kuhn, the artist's daughter, who patiently waited from the time of the Cincinnati Art Museum's Memorial Exhibition in 1960 until the author's retirement from the directorship in December 1973 made it possible to begin active work. She stayed in constant touch with Miss Betty L. Zimmerman, assistant director of the museum, who correlated the material Brenda sent on and hearteningly reassured her that the idea was not dead but merely lying fallow. Sincerest thanks to Miss Zimmerman, and thanks again to Brenda, who, when work at last began, unhesitatingly turned over restricted but invaluable medical, legal, and other private documents and never by so much as a question tried to affect the nature of the book or its direction. On the contrary, she urged complete frankness in discussing some delicate and personal matters. It is equally hard to thank properly the Amon Carter Museum of Western Art in Fort Worth, Texas, and its director, Mr. Mitchell Wilder, who volunteered a financial grant for preliminary research. This made possible the most amiable collaboration with Mrs. Gregory H. Doherty, née Marna Spaeth, a trained art historian who knew Walt Kuhn herself as well as through her parents, Otto and Eloise Spaeth. Special thanks go to Marna. And it is impossible to imagine a study of American art without that indispensable institution the Archives of American Art, whose New York, Detroit, and Washington offices, under the leadership of the chief archivist, Mr. Garnet McCoy, were unfailingly obliging and helpful. The entire staff of the Cincinnati Art Museum Library, with Mrs. Patricia Rutledge at its head, went out of its way to help by arranging inter-library loans, giving stack privileges — not necessarily the perquisite of a director emeritus — and even a carrell for the seemingly endless hours of microfilm reading. Mrs. Katherine K. Ryder, executive secretary to the director, is also thanked for many kindnesses. Governor W. Averell Harriman and his staff are sincerely thanked, as are the staffs of the Kennedy Galleries, the Hirschl and Adler Galleries, Mr. Maynard Walker, Mr. Harold A. Ley, Jr., who furnished recondite information on Brooklyn geography, and Miss Helen Pernice as well as Ms. Ermalou Rotta and Miss Gretchen Mehring for their typing.

Of course, the illustrations would not have been possible without the generous cooperation of the public and private owners of Walt Kuhn's works, and since a book about a painter without illustrations is unimaginable, adequate thanks are difficult to express. Nonetheless, they are most sincerely given. The photographers are too numerous, and in some cases unidentifiable, to acknowledge individually; but special thanks go to Mr. C. W. Bostain and Mr. Frank van Houten Raymond of Cincinnati, and above all to Mr. Ben Klein of Young and Klein, Inc., also of Cincinnati, whose skilled staff accomplished literal resurrections of vanished or unlocatable works from old catalogues and magazine reproductions.

Though it may be a wifely duty to listen for months to a monorail monologue, Rosan Adams deserves thanks for a performance above and beyond. Probably only the fact that she too knew Walt Kuhn slightly and is a steadfast admirer of his work made it endurable.

January 1976

Walt Kuhn, Painter

Plate 3. Walt Kuhn, age 17.
Courtesy of the Kuhn
Estate

another matter, cultivated and hospitable people who saw the young student through several bouts of homesickness, especially at Christmas, the one exception being a failed artist cousin who had attached himself to Walt in Paris when he was on his way to Munich. Both father and son agreed in correspondence that he was a tedious bore to be rid of as soon as possible.

Walt continues writing of his father: "Being keen and self-reliant he saw a future in this country, and the following year travelled back to his home town and returned with his bride, his junior by a year. She being the orphaned daughter of a Spanish Consular Attaché [in Munich], both her mother and father having died in a sudden local epidemic. He drifted into the shipping supply business, and through hard work and in possession of a personality well suited to the times gathered many influential friends and prospered. He and his wife, the former Amelia Barbâs, raised a family of nine children of which Walt Kuhn was the only survivor. He was born on [there is an erasure at this crucial point]."

A few corrections of fact are needed here; after all, Kuhn was not writing with vital statistics and naturalization papers at his elbow. Actually his father was born in Würzburg in 1843 and was sixteen when he joined his sisters in New York in 1859. Also, his wife, whose adopted name of Hergenhan Walt Kuhn does not mention, was born in 1845 and hence was two years younger than her husband. It is technically true that by 1927 Walt was the only survivor of the Kuhn children, since his sister Margaret had died in March 1920. She was six years younger, grew up to marry Herman Grimm, a skilled mechanic, and have a son, but he does give the impression that he was the only one to survive childhood.

Also, it might be wise to clear up some of the confusions still surrounding his birth date. To begin, the Kuhn infant listed in the 1877 baptismal records of the Roman Catholic Church of the Visitation at 98 Richards Street, Brooklyn, was christened William; but Walt was called Walter Francis from early childhood and signed his first San Francisco cartoons "W. F. Kuhn," changing to the crisper "Walt Kuhn" in 1900. There were no little Kuhns christened Walter Francis, at least at the family parish Church of the Visitation however. But it is not unheard of for children's names to be changed; sometimes the children do it themselves for their own obscure reasons, without notifying the keepers of the records.

In December 1911, during the run of the Pastellists exhibition at the Madison Gallery, he wrote to his wife Vera that Archer Huntington had seen and been greatly impressed by his work, remarking to a member of the gallery staff, "If he can paint like that at 34 what will he be doing at 44?" Thirty-four subtracted from 1911 is 1877. More significantly, when his medical crisis of 1948 required accurate dates, Vera gave 27 October 1877, and it is so recorded on his death certificate. He gave the same date to the standard reference books, including the

American Art Annual, until 1931 when the date 1880 appears, and then is repeated in the 1935 edition. It is 1880 in Mallett's *Index of Artists* in 1935, and still stubbornly goes on. His wife and daughter Brenda tried to correct the error in the well-documented chronology they drew up for the 1960 Memorial Exhibition in Cincinnati, without noticeably slowing its momentum; it is very hard to dislodge things from standard references.

Plate 4. Vera Spier, age 17. Courtesy of the Kuhn Estate

Brenda's credible recollection of the birth date change, as told by her father at the time, is that in the late 1920s the Downtown Gallery was handling Walt's work and that its gifted but capricious impresario, Edith Gregor Halpert, on her own impulse announced his birth date to the press as 1880. Walt Kuhn shrugged it off and went along. Show business is show business, and many people in their early fifties do not mind being thought three years younger. Besides, although he was a self-styled "late bloomer," he didn't want to appear too late, or to be associated in the public mind with the slightly older members of the "Ashcan School" of 1908, whose grip on American painting he had helped to loosen with the Armory Show of 1913.

The question of the name of Walt Kuhn's mother and the degree of his Spanish birthright is more complicated. The "sudden epidemic" that killed her parents was one of the ordinary hazards of life in the mid-nineteenth century scarcely remembered today, but the Hergenhans who are said to have adopted her lived in Hammelburg between Fulda and Würzburg on the northern border of Bavaria, a long way from Munich. Perhaps a general appeal went out to succor the orphans of some unusually severe epidemic, or one of the Hergenhan sons might have married a Spanish wife, which is hardly more probable, and the fact that no baptismal record can be found for her in Hammelburg is a kind of inferential evidence of her adoption. She entered this country, was married, was naturalized, and died as Amelia Hergenhan. It is interesting, though, that her marriage license spells it Amalia, a more Spanish usage.

In spite of having entered the maiden name of Walt's mother as Amelia Barbâs on his death certificate in 1949, his widow and daughter began to doubt that she was wholly Spanish. They could find no mention of a Barbâs attached to a Spanish embassy in Munich, and later search showed that neither the Archivo Nacional de la Historia nor the library of the Foreign Ministry in Madrid had any personnel lists for Munich from 1823 to the late nineteenth century. The Carlist Wars following on the heels of the Napoleonic disruption had demoralized even the record-loving Spanish bureaucrats, though there certainly had been a full Spanish Embassy to the Kingdom of Bavaria before Bismarck and the German Empire, with a consular attaché needed if only to clear papers for the cork trade. Finding a regional locale for the name Barbâs is not a hopeful prospect either; and even if it were, equally disorganized tax and sporadic census records are not much more promising. Accordingly, on the basis of his family's uncertainty and doubtless striving for scholarly rectitude, the catalogue of the 1960 Memorial Exhibition says that Walt Kuhn was only one-quarter Spanish.

Nevertheless, some light is thrown on the problem by a family legend that Walt's blond Brünnhilde aunts were a bit wary of their exotic sister-in-law, calling her "the little black one," which does not sound as if her father had been a Bavarian. Walt's own positiveness about his mother's birth and name also must be weighed. Theatrical in temperament and secretive by nature, he might not have minded a hint of mystery about his origin, and in the fashion of show business did drop three years off his age; but it is unlikely that any man would deliberately invent a maiden name for his mother out of whole cloth. So a current review of the evidence and the unmistakably Spanish elements of his mature painting incline toward a reversal of the verdict, and Amalia Barbâs is here accepted as his mother's proper, if not legal, name.

All this genealogical concern might seem beside the point, since it has not been established, and may never be, that an artist's genes make him an artist or even shape his style, except that Walt Kuhn took ethnic factors seriously. In 1931, for instance, after a session with André Derain, he wrote to his wife from Paris: "Picasso and Matisse you see are really not natural and Derain is only getting better because he is coming back to his own native natural [*natural* is underscored in both instances]. So for me my own native natural, with the flavors racially contributed." Recommending an exhibition for his gifted pupil-protégée Lily Cushing in 1948, he wrote, "Being purely Anglo-Saxon she shines as a draughtsman." It may be difficult to determine what Anglo-Saxon draughtsmen he had in mind, but he was more to the point in a 1938 letter to another talented pupil, Frank di Gioia, who with the characteristic misgivings of a second-generation New York-born Italian was unsure about his admiration for his dynamic fellow Italians in California. He wrote to di Gioia: "It is perfectly OK for you to admire them, your race is one of your greatest assets. Whatever there is in my own work is also supported by my racial background." And with eloquent simplicity he wrote to a friend in 1935: "I would like to talk to you about some of the journeys I have made — several to Spain, to my mother's country."

When he saw ethnic factors, whether hereditary or environmental, affecting national cultures instead of individuals, Kuhn was on firmer ground. In resentment of Parisian domination over the painting of his time, for example, he said: "How much better it would have been if American art could have grown out of Dutch painting instead of our having to fit ourselves into a French frame, which no American can ever do. And he isn't fooling anybody but himself if he thinks he can." And again, "No country has everything, the Germans are better musicians than the French, and God knows the English can write." It is also known that the Spanish can paint.

Plate 5. Walt Kuhn, ca. 1904–1905. Courtesy of the Kuhn Estate

Francis and Amalia Kuhn became American citizens on 15 November 1871, and from the mid-eighties to the mid-nineties they owned and operated the International Hotel as a profitable extension of the ship-provisioning business. It was at the foot of Dwight Street on the Erie Basin waterfront, directly opposite what was originally called the Erie Basin Dry Dock Company, later Robbins Dry Dock, and finally the Todd Ship Yard. Its garden was the only green spot in sight. An 1877 Currier and Ives lithograph shows a panoramic view of Manhattan, Brooklyn down to Red Hook Point, and the colorful variety of shipping, some steam, some steam and sail, but mostly windjammers of all riggings and sizes. Brooklyn then was as many-masted as Walt Whitman's Manahatta.

Amalia Kuhn managed the food service of the International Hotel, and very well by all accounts. There was an occasional French chef to keep a close watch over, and only one class distinction on the generous menu: wine for the officers' dining room and beer for the seamen's. Newspapermen and importers were regulars. Her daughter-in-law Vera, who knew her only from 1909 to her death in 1914, remembered her as

short, with no stomach, "flat as a board." Amalia had piercing black eyes and hair, which never turned white. In the hotel kitchen, over which she presided, if things went wrong she could have a furious temper, it was not uncommon for pots and pans to go sailing through the air. But she was kind to men injured in street brawls, she would run out with her "sweet oil" (olive oil?) to sooth wounds. By 1909 she was worn out, slept half the day and bossed her daughter Margaret who did most of the work. Though Francis bought Amalia beautiful clothes, she let them hang in the closet and just wore "wrappers" and men's shoes. Amalia was enthusiastic about art and loved the theatre, but in her retirement never got enough interested in books to learn to read them easily. How well she learned to speak English I do not know, except that between themselves, around home, a sort of pidgin German-English was spoken.

The International Hotel was a setting almost too good to be true for an impressionable boy. Every tide brought a flow of sailors bearing gifts, tall tales from far places, bagpipe and guitar music on winter evenings. Walt especially remembered this from the blizzard of 1888 when a whole ship's crew was marooned in the hotel. He recalled a sailor from the eagerly watched-for S.S. *South America* who regularly brought presents only an indulgent mother could put up with — a monkey, live tropical birds or dried fish, a shark's jaw, baby alligators, and once, for a brief stay, a baby anaconda.

Dockside life had its own diversions; roustabouts would sometimes settle grudges with knives or fists, bringing out Amalia with her sweet oil. Walt remembered two Irishmen stripped to the waist going thirty-five bare-knuckle rounds under his window until a firehose stopped the match, if it could be called that. He told how drivers used to race their empty drays from the docks back to the warehouse, often taking a shortcut across a corner of the hotel grounds and knocking down the flagpole. His father was not a patient man, but said that he was "no clever Irish boxer." One time too often, though, when the flagpole went down again after fair warning, he grabbed the two drivers and bashed their heads together. A good landlord must be able to keep order in his house, and grounds.

Walt remembered many more things, like helping his father drape the hotel in black for General Grant's funeral in July 1885. From the roof next year he saw the Statue of Liberty unveiled on Bedloe's Island. About that time, at the age of eight or so as he recalled it, he began to illustrate some of the sailors' yarns in pen and ink. In the manner of mothers, Amalia kept a few; one was a battle with Eskimos, another a portrait of George Washington, with a prophetic attention to the details of his uniform.

He gives his own condensed account in his sketch for the 1927 press release: "Walt Kuhn's development as an artist began early. His constant meeting with men of the sea with their stories of adventures abroad stimulated his imagination with the result that at the age of fifteen he sold a drawing to a magazine for the then enormous sum of fifteen dollars. That was the one big moment that decided his career.

His education, entirely in private schools [Katherine S. Dreier, whose Société Anonyme Collection at Yale was one of the pioneering ventures in modern art, was a schoolmate at one of them] was interrupted considerably by just about every known children's disease. At sixteen he was fed up with schools, and went out to make a living." The last of the schools was the Brooklyn Polytechnic Institute, where he spent part of 1893.

Plate 6. Walt Kuhn, 1928. Courtesy of the Kuhn Estate

2

His father had hoped for West Point or the law, but Walt pointed out that Francis had made his own decisions at the age of sixteen, and proceeded to try his hand at commercial photography, selling real estate with some success, and a job in a sporting goods store whose sideline was renting theater costumes. Walt delivered them and picked them up, spending more time backstage than back of the counter. This was only natural; his mother had exposed him to the theater almost as soon as he could walk. Amalia was an actress at heart, and once exclaimed, "Just think, if it weren't for all this [meaning her husband, children, and household duties] I could have been a Duse!" The inoculation took. He claimed that by the age of fourteen he had seen not only Duse and many of the classics but also every act that played variety in New York. Show business — chiefly vaudeville, revues, and the circus — was to be a second and gainful career; and more importantly, it supplied him with a limitless fund of artistic ideas.

The press release goes on to its early end: "Finally taking advantage of the bicycle craze, he for a time conducted a bicycle sales and repair shop [at 9 Liberty Street] on his own — with the money earned he next joined a life class for one winter evening [a week] and made his first attempts at art — finally in 1899 he travelled all the way to California by day-coach, and took a job cartooning on the old San Francico Wasp for $5.00 a week — and lived on it. One day he found a man who had just built himself a house and induced the latter to let him decorate the walls, which he did — eleven rooms [and a mermaid on the bathroom ceiling] for $100, including meals for the artist. (The hundred dollar contract is one of his prized possessions.)" Such narrative compactness is admirable, but the bare facts need a little fleshing out.

Possibly to promote his bicycle business, he barnstormed county fairs as a professional bicycle racer. The purses were hardly worth mentioning, but he ate, learned some of the dirty tricks of the trade, saw a lot of people and sideshows, and slightly bowed his long legs. In the process he may have also sharpened his already marked competitive instincts. Walt Kuhn started his western odyssey with a straw suitcase, enough food from his mother's kitchen for at least three days, and a new revolver. He never used it except for target practice, but to go West without one was almost indecent exposure. Everything west of the Hudson was fascinating new country; if the outskirts of a town looked interesting, he would get off the train, find some odd jobs, then journey on. In Salt Lake City, the real West at last, he talked the contractor for the new Salt Palace into letting him "decorate" the interior walls.

He reached San Francisco with sixty dollars cash in his pocket and no modesty at all. He soon began a series of "the worst drawings ever made for any publication" for the *Wasp* (for five dollars a week). If one glances at a few of the cartoons, this seems a fair assessment, on both counts. His pictorial comments on the Boer War, however, produced a raise in three months. The *Wasp* was a weekly of political commentary and satire, literary criticism, and poetry. In its time it was distinguished, in San Francisco at least, for its design and illustrations, which is somewhat hard to believe today, unless perhaps its competition were to be considered. But the contributions of Ambrose Bierce, who may have been one of its founders, were its real distinction.

Bierce was Ohio-born, fought through the Civil War in the Ninth Indiana Infantry, was wounded twice, cited for conspicuous gallantry, and breveted major. He began his abrasive career with gossip columns in several San Francisco journals, taking three and a half years off between 1872 and 1876 for more serious writing in England. His best remembered works are *The Devil's Dictionary* and the short stories assembled under the title *In the Midst of Life*. Some references say that Bierce left San Francisco for Washington, D.C., in 1899, others say in 1897. The latter seems more probable, since Kuhn never mentioned meeting him, and he was not easily forgotten.

Ambrose Bierce had an almost Spanish *apetencia de muerte*, literally an appetite, a longing, for death, at its best an assertion of life in the face of death. The violence he had known at firsthand in the Civil War stayed with him all his life, till in 1913 he disappeared into

Plate 7. Christmas Card, 1936. Courtesy of the Kuhn Estate

revolution-torn Mexico, perhaps at last finding "the good, kind darkness." Kuhn felt a special affinity for his macabre short stories, more than once recommending "An Occurence at Owl Creek Bridge" with its frozen instant of mortality.

After a year at the *Wasp* Kuhn left, with a contract to paint hotel signs up and down the coast. It did not pay much, but it included meals. He rode up into the High Sierras, drove a ten-mile stagecoach run for a while, filled in at guitar with small bands, registering every impression a young and virile country could make on a young and virile sensibility. These western years colored a good part of his life. He returned to the West as often as possible, visiting Colorado and California again as late as April 1948. Even his Christmas cards, which have been seriously collected, were hand-colored line cuts of ink drawings of cowboy celebrations of the season — real unwashed, unpicturesque cowboys, not the Hollywood variety. The 1936 card catches three square-dancing cowboys in a ballet pose years before *Oklahoma!* and Agnes De Mille. With the *Imaginary History of the West*, twenty-nine small oils painted from 1918 to 1923 (numbers 32–60), he summed it up and took his leave, as far as his formal painting is concerned. It had been a glorious adventure, with deeper meanings. Kuhn felt that he had experienced a basic America, un-machined, tough to the point of hardness, independent, masculine, but not incapable of feeling.

He had also learned something about his own artistic abilities. The appraisal of his *Wasp* cartoons came years later, but even in 1900 he was beginning to develop a drastic self-criticism, ultimately almost equal to Paul Cézanne's. He then wanted to become no less than "the best damn caroonist alive." By 4 December 1901 he had raised his sights a little, sending his address home as "Herr Walt Kuhn — *Illustrator*, (italics mine) Schleissheimer Strasse, München."

Getting to be the best damn cartoonist alive would take some doing. He came back to New York in the fall of 1900 wearing a beard and a cowboy Stetson. The beard did not last long, but he always wore a wide-brimmed hat, not wide or floppy enough to suggest Bohemia but more like a campaign hat, definitely western. Several months, or about as long as his western savings lasted — living at home stretched them a good deal — were spent in plans for formal training and in persuading his father to finance at least a year's study abroad, in Paris, of course, the goal of all budding artists at the turn of the century. Francis Kuhn was not ungenerous, but he was skeptical about the whole art business; he wanted to be assured that it was "honest." Making money was a man's duty, and he correctly assumed that an artist's career was a risky way of going about it. He finally agreed, however, stipulating that his son not turn into a European and that a second year would depend entirely on the success of the first. Walt's early letters show his true gratitude, but later on he rarely spoke of his father's help, wanting to give the impression that he had always been self-supporting, as indeed he was from 1903 on.

3

After a rough second-class crossing and an equally rough boat train, Kuhn reached Paris at two on an early March morning in 1901. He had no trouble at customs with his trunk or bicycle, and settled into a comfortable bed-and-breakfast room at the Grand Hotel de la Haute Loire on the Boulevard Raspail, recommended by the "American Artists' Association." Kuhn was never so cautious in the West, but this was strange new territory, soon to be a bit overpowering. His first letter, of 13 March, brims with the excitement of a first crossing, two days of seasickness cured by taking his meals from a tray at his deck chair or in the smoking room; avoiding the overcrowded dining saloon; officious "German grocerymen" trying to organize everything in second class, even to collecting two dollars a person for the ship's orchestra, which Walt had thought execrable; a Russian engineer friend returning to his government job in Saint Petersburg, who later explored Paris with Kuhn for two weeks; "the 'ladies' of rather loose character in much demand among the 'gentlemen.'" As for Paris, he goes on: "By the way, I am agreeably surprised at my success with the French language. So far I have had no trouble at all in finding out everything I wanted to know and find myself improving every hour almost." Not so at a variety theater:

> I didn't expect much of a performance as it was a little dirty hole of a place. I was well pleased with the show however, the music was fine and the costumes were gorgeous. . . . I understood very little as they spoke so rapidly and I lost the point of the jokes entirely excepting those which were explained by action. I enclose the seat checks for Margaret.
>
> My art school is only about a five-minute walk from here so you can see I am pretty well fixed. . . . I will probably get to work before Monday next as I don't care much for this roaming about. This is at the entrance of the Latin Quarter and one sees nothing but long-haired artists and other freaks.

By 22 March he had enrolled and started his first class at the Académie Colarossi, a kind of unregimented congress of students, monitors, and models where one might or might not ask for a teacher's criticism, getting it at two-week intervals. When it came, it was unsparing; there was no solicitous nursing of the tender young plant. Young independents would drop in to work from the model and proselytize in favor of their new movements. It was not at all what Kuhn wanted or needed; he was desperate for fundamentals — the almost elementary training that his contemporaries seemed already to have had, whether or not they had been professional cartoonists. Kuhn felt out of place.

Nor had the charms of Paris cast too strong a spell; they were wearing thin. "Things are too expensive too. A cup of coffee costs more than in America, sometimes six cents, sometimes 12 cents, and then the waiter wants a 2 cent tip." He went to Munich in May, ostensibly to visit relatives but actually to spy out the land. It may not have been flowing with milk and honey, but Kuhn had already decided Munich would be better for him than Paris and promptly moved. It was cer-

Plate 8. *Nocturnal Landscape.*

Courtesy of the Currier Gallery of Art, Manchester, New Hampshire

tainly more congenial; he wrote on 15 May, "I think I am getting along very well in the art of exterminating beer."

His father was disturbed, thinking the whole enterprise a failure, and urged him to come home. He was afraid Walt was turning into a European, and on his scale of values the only thing worse was to be a German. Walt wrote back, "Don't worry. I will paddle my own canoe and come out on top." Later on in the fall of 1902 Walt further reassured him that in spite of all that he learned in Munich and some good friends he had made there, "I really hate Germans."

Short though the Paris stay had been, it had given him enough of a start, including a salutary self-analysis, for him to begin working hard and steadily on his own through the Munich summer and early fall. At last on 15 November 1901 he could write triumphantly, if a little incoherently:

I have been admitted to the Royal Academy. I am now under the best painter in Europe. . . . There are only twelve [in the entering class] and only [one] other American beside myself. There were about 20 [in the whole academy] that wanted to get to him, and only four were taken. I am one of the four.

My professor's name is Zügle [*sic*], he is famous for his horses and cattle which he has painted. . . .

I worked pretty hard all summer, made some pretty good things and got in on the strength of my work. Our relatives were surprised when I told them. They didn't think I could do it after being here only six months. Especially as Zügle is the hardest man to get to. There are 22 proffesors [*sic*] on the Academy and Zügle and Franz Stuck are considered the best.

Well, Governor, when your birthday comes I am going to drink a whole liter of beer to your health, so give my love to the ladies and remember me as your affectionate and happy W.

13

"Yes, he was such a high flyer in his youth that now he has the gout in his wings."

Plate 9. Cartoon from "A Little Bird Told Me." Courtesy of the Kuhn Estate

(The calligraphic "W" with its slight flourish on the final stroke was already his official cipher.) In view of the fact that it was quite unusual for the Royal Academy (now the Academy of Creative Arts) to admit anyone with as few — in fact, no — academic credentials, Kuhn's euphoria is understandable, and his pride at having justified his father's reluctant gamble rather touching.

Nowhere but in Munich would Heinrich von Zügel have been called "the best painter in Europe." Franz von Stuck had much more of an international reputation, but hardly that much, and was a leader in the little-remembered Munich "Secession." Heinrich von Zügel (1850–1941) was a kind of Barbizon painter with an overlay of Germanic thoroughness, or a Barbizon overlay of Germanic thoroughness. Some of his titles give a fair picture of his work: *Flock of Sheep, Shepherd Dog, Calves in the Water, Spring Sun, The Return, End of Day.* He became professor at the academy in 1895.

He was a classroom martinet, and the discipline was precisely what Walt Kuhn needed. None of von Zügel's students were allowed to paint for the first six months, they drew and redrew the most painstaking studies of animal anatomy. Sketches of the whole animal were an occasionally permitted dessert. It sounds more like a first-year course in veterinary surgery than an art school. Architectural sketches of equally conscientious exactness were also occasional diversions. Professor von Zügel even took the whole class to Venice for a month in the early spring of 1902, where Kuhn found the Italians "a mean set of robbers."

He wrote home on 12 March: "You see when we leave Venice we all go to Wörth-am-Rhein for the summer, as Professor Zügel transfers the school to that place during the summer months. . . . I am very hopeful as regards the future and am very thankful that I got under such a wonderful master. I hardly think I shall study under any other man, for when I go home I will know enough to continue study by myself."

By now Kuhn had definitely decided another year was necessary so as not to lose what he had learned; he wrote from Wörth on June 26: "What I studied at home was all play along side of what I do now. From the way my Professor speaks to me I have every reason to believe that I will not be a failure." His father evidently agreed, worrying chiefly about his son's health and the danger of overworking himself. In confirmation Walt had written on 2 March: "Since I have been abroad you have shown great confidence in me and my doings. A fact which I respect and appreciate, and for which you will not be sorry."

The impression Walt Kuhn later gave, perhaps unintentionally, that his father was unsympathetic to, or at best indifferent to, his artistic ambitions is belied by many similar letters. His daughter had been sufficiently persuaded by it, however, to find on rereading them that her father was simply "buttering-up" his grudging paternal patron. At this remove they seem genuine enough, sometimes movingly so. On 12 January 1902 he wrote, "I received your two first letters of the New Year and thank you very, very for the sincere sentiment and affection which you expressed in them." From Würzburg on his way to Holland he wrote on 24 September 1902: "You certainly picked out a fine old city for your birthplace, and I wish you were here to tell me all about it, to show me where you walked as a boy. You were only a boy when you left home, were you not? How often you told me about this town and still how little." He had seen the name August Kuhn in big letters on a butcher shop, and "was very sorry that I promised you that I would not go near any of our relatives." On 29 December 1901 he had written: "Now that I am getting along as I want to, I feel a little selfish in getting all the benefits. I hope and sincerely wish that you are doing as much for Margaret as you are doing for me. In fact I would not be satisfied unless I thought so. She is entitled to just as much as I am." It must have been a close-knit family.

"Oh, hubby, look ! Baby has just got its first feather !"

Plate 10. Cartoon from "A Little Bird Told Me." Courtesy of the Kuhn Estate

When the summer session ended in Wörth, he spent a month painting and sketching in Holland, to discover that the Dutch landscape had invented its seventeenth-century masters. "Everything is arranged for you, all the colors are in tone, and the clouds compose themselves in receding planes." He was "painting canvases now," with Maasluis near Rotterdam as headquarters.

Back in Munich he wrote on 27 October 1902, "Yesterday I took my Holland sketches to my professor and he gave me such a good criticism and such a big future that I could hardly believe him, a thing he seldom does." And he may not have done it then. Years later Kuhn told a very different story, again and again, especially to young artists he suspected of taking their work too easily, to the effect that when he showed von Zügel only one completely finished painting he had thought the best, von Zügel asked for others. Kuhn answered that there were none, one good one in a month was enough, there was plenty of time. "Time? With your puny talent do you know what time it is? It's a quarter to twelve!" It may have been the most important lesson Munich taught him. The historic truth probably lies between the two accounts; but the latter one is more telling, and was much more often told.

Work at the academy went on at its accustomed pace. In "Presse-Fest," 14 January 1903, Kuhn wrote: "I am at school from 9 to 12 and 2–4 o'clock every day. In fact we work as long as there is daylight. You need not worry that I will overwork myself. I got so used to going through the same thing every day that I don't mind it anymore. Everything is so much easier than last year."

But it was not all work; Walt Kuhn was a lusty, energetic young man, almost greedy for every experience he could crowd into his days. He took his mandolin with him everywhere, and there were plenty of riotous student evenings. One night, he boasted, three of them polished off a whole bottle of "Old Crow"; American rye and bourbon were rare treats, whereas Munich beer flowed on.

The end drew near, coming on 6 May 1903. "Frau Kübles senior took a tearful farewell. I got to like her very much. She is the only one of the family I can really say I like. . . . I left Munich with a

15

heavy heart. I learned a lot there and I think it will stay in my memory as the pleasantest time of my life." He paused for a last summer session at Wörth, writing on 15 May 1903, "We have all nations represented, Germans, Italians, Russian, Hungarian, English and American. . . . I am the only born American that ever studied under Zügel."

The von Zügel story has a sad ending. When Kuhn was assembling the Armory Show in 1912, he saw some of his old professor's paintings again at a dealer's gallery in Berlin, and wrote to his wife on 8 October: "Zügle looks to me like a man with a lot of knowledge and hardly anything else. It was another shock. It showed me that I hadn't spent the last years in vain, anyway. Zügle's color today looks to me like mud, and even the drawing is mechanical and simply clever. That settles the old man for me, although he was just the one to rough-house me into learning how to plug. I guess after all artists are born not made, for if they were, Zügel would be a Christ. I'm sorry now that he was invited to our show." Nevertheless, he looked him up in Munich, giving him entry blanks and shipping instructions. No von Zügel canvas is listed in the Armory Show catalogue. Probably none came. Professor von Zügel may have seen behind a loyal pupil's gesture, or perhaps he did not feel that he belonged, or wanted to belong, in such company. Matisse was not Millet, and Henri Rousseau was not Théodore Rousseau.

4

The Francis Kuhns had moved east in the spring of 1903 to the "country" at Freeport, Long Island, with the pleasures of a vegetable garden and a horse Walt rode on weekend visits. They were now operating the Kensington Hotel on Ocean Parkway and Avenue D in Brooklyn. It was primarily a residential hotel in what must then have been a rustic suburb. Walt soon found studio and living quarters at 119 East Twenty-third Street in Manhattan, where he kept at his painting and started the rounds of magazines and newspapers with his cartoons. The results were meager at first, but there was plenty of leftover wanderlust; so in the late fall he went south with the weather to Savannah, Georgia, and Boynton, Florida, seeing a new part of the country and living on three dollars a week by catching fish or trapping ducks to vary his diet. His cash income came from selling small souvenir paintings to tourists at ten dollars each, unsigned, sometimes with an alligator or a crane, but always with a palm tree and indigo water. It is still an active winter industry practiced rather more by wistful has-beens or might-have-beens than potential Walt Kuhns.

In the summer of 1904 he could manage a return trip to Munich, Wörth, and Paris. Back in New York his circle of friends steadily widened. He joined the Kit Kat Club, founded in 1884 and claiming some tenuous spiritual descent from its illustrious but differently spelled London predecessor. Its chief occupation besides conviviality was giving an annual Artists and Models Ball, proudly advertised as the "oldest traditional costume ball" in the country; the proceeds went to scholarships in the School of the National Academy of Design. Kuhn was soon enlisted to help plan the balls, devising amateur vaudeville numbers and painting decorations, an innocent pastime that delighted him for years. The Salmagundi Club on lower Fifth Avenue, founded in 1871 and less pretentiously named after the humorous pamphlets launched by Washington Irving in the early nineteenth century, was exclusively an artists' club, with a few lay members; it presented seven members' exhibitions a year, one of the few chances a young artist had to show, and then only if he had been tentatively admitted to the

Plate 11. *Mr. & Mrs. Barnyard Fowl Give a Reception*

17

fraternity. There in the 1905 season Walt Kuhn probably first exhibited his paintings in New York. One was bought, by the director of art education in the Brooklyn Public Schools; it is now in the Currier Gallery of Art in Manchester, New Hampshire, along with its brilliant later sister *Lancer* (number 389) of 1939. The lady donor's parents had been friends of the Francis Kuhns, and her 1959 letter fondly recalls: "This being his first picture to be exhibited in New York, Walt was very happy about it. I was in a party of young people he got together to 'celebrate' on that occasion." There seems to have been an element of family and parochial loyalty in this first purchase, not unusual for young artists. *Nocturnal Landscape* (number 2) is a small oil panel showing a team of plow horses heading toward their barn; its colors are the Munich "mud" he deplored in 1912. Of course, by then he was a full-blown impressionist, and the color has been more kindly called "brown sauce" in the case of Frank Duveneck and other Munich-trained painters.

All his life Kuhn yearned for the "country" as only a born city-dweller might, and he spent the summer of 1905 in Cherry Hill, New Jersey, now North Hackensack. In the fall he moved to 232 West Fourteenth Street, and his cartoons began to sell, first to *Life*, then to his dreamed-of goal *Puck*, *Judge*, the *New York World*, and a comic strip to the *New York Sunday Sun*. More important though was the regimen of life drawing he began in the Artists' Sketch Class, an informal group of artists who pooled their money to pay for models. He felt that he must strengthen his drawing, and he eventually turned out over three thousand studies of the figure.

A mere handful of these early drawings was kept, and with only another handful from the ruthlessly edited later years they reveal a draughtsman of the absolute first rank. It is still a mystery that he only once in his lifetime allowed an exhibition of his figure drawings by themselves. He knew they were more than good, must have intended some of them to be seen, and frequently gave them to friends. Perhaps he felt that they gave away too many secrets of his private artistic evolution. He often said that Cézanne's inability to pull a cloak of surface finish over most of his paintings told too much of his agonizing struggles, quoting a discerning European connoisseur's description of the monumental *Still Life* in the Bliss Collection (now in the Museum of Modern Art) as "Nothing but a lot of corrections! But *what* a picture!", in contrast, for example, to the Samuel Lewisohn *Pot of Geraniums and Fruit* now in the Metropolitan Museum.

The fourteen to twenty dollars he was paid for each cartoon brought a little more economic freedom, and they were in fact his financial mainstay until 1914. He spent the summer of 1906 in Fort Lee, New Jersey, a center of the infant movie industry, as was Astoria on Long Island, until the more dependable sunlight of southern California removed it to Hollywood. Much as he loved all things theatrical, he had little to do with these primitive film activities in Fort Lee. For him the

Plate 12. *Self Portrait of the Artist*

Courtesy of Kennedy Galleries, Inc.—Kuhn Estate

town was a quiet retreat on the brink of the Palisades, far enough away from brawling hectic Manhattan, where he went only when business required. A few other artists felt the same way, and in-town friends would join them there for a weekend or an evening at Albig's, as amiable a resort as any in Greenwich Village. Furthermore, the food was good and simply cooked, a necessity for Kuhn throughout his life.

In the winter of 1906 he moved his Manhattan base to West Sixteenth Street near Union Square, and then in 1907 to 120 East Twenty-third Street, spending a few winter weeks again in Savannah,

19

Plate 13. *Polo Game*

Private Collection

where the living was easy. The summer classes of the New York School
of Art moved out to Fort Lee in 1908 and Kuhn joined the faculty,
moving back with the school to continue teaching through the winter of
1908–9. The New York School of Art originated in 1896 on Fifty-seventh
Street as the Chase School, named for its founder William Merritt
Chase, the brilliant impressionist technician and influential teacher,
friend of Whistler, J. Alden Weir, Duveneck, and John H. Twachtman.
It expanded into the New York School in 1898, and Chase continued
teaching in it for ten years. Walt Kuhn never liked teaching except on
his own private terms; American students would not submit to the
Germanic discipline that he thought was basic, and the energy teaching
used up was better conserved for his own painting.

    Not many paintings from these early years can be found to-
day, and those few only because they escaped his control. In later years
he bought back as many as he could, or traded for them, often as not
destroying them. He thought most artists' beginnings were best forgotten, and once observed that Vincent van Gogh's fumbling starts up to
and including the *Potato Eaters* would be of no interest except for the
occasional flickering light they shed on his mature work. Of Walt
Kuhn's few, *The Eye-Opener* (number 4) is little more than a painted
cartoon in his western mode, and *Albig's* (number 5) shows a Robert
Henri influence that he would gladly have disavowed. Or perhaps it is

20

an echo of John Sloan, whom he respected more, if only for his subject matter. It brought quite a good price at Sotheby Parke Bernet in 1974.

The *Life* cartoons are something else. They are much more sophisticated than the early paintings, and are a far cry from the amateurish mixture of Thomas Nast and A. B. Frost in the *Wasp* cartoons. They show a skilled sureness of drawing that catches the birds of their subjects with almost ornithological precision. Of course, the birds are symbols of human foibles, and hardly need their sadly dated captions, as proved by the uncaptioned small vignettes on a few blank facing pages. The four-flusher, the hypocrite, the addled housewife and plodding husband, the social climber and the hobo, can be instantly recognized; they sting a little while they amuse. *Life* copyrighted seventy-four of them in 1906 and published them in 1908 under the title *A Little Bird Told Me*. As late as the summer of 1910 Kuhn was receiving royalty checks, one on 7 July for twenty-three dollars.

Framed by a laurel wreath in the frontispiece, a crow wearing a jester's cap and smoking a bull-dog pipe perches on the helmet of Pallas Athena. The inscription below reads, "Dedicated to a lot of people who take themselves too seriously." If he ever sent a copy to von Zügel, it would have been a fitting nod of thanks for those veterinary years in Munich.

Plate 14. *Bathers on Beach*

Courtesy of Hirschl & Adler Galleries, Inc.

21

Plate 15. *Tragic Comedians*

Courtesy of the Hirshhorn Museum and Sculpture Garden, Smithsonian Institution

NOTES TO CHAPTER ONE

WALT KUHN'S BIRTHPLACE was sought out and briefly inspected in May 1975.

Kuhn's AUTOBIOGRAPHICAL DRAFT for a press release was probably connected with his first large-scale exhibition at the Grand Central Galleries in 1927. It is a three-page penciled holograph in the Archives of American Art, Smithsonian Institution. This invaluable resource for all studies of American art is hereafter referred to as "Archives." All quoted letters, unless otherwise specified, are in the same repository, where over twenty thousand items are preserved in the Walt Kuhn files. The Kuhn family threw away very little, keeping even a few shopping lists.

The history of Walt's CHANGED BIRTH DATE can be traced through the irrefutable Thieme-Becker's *Algemeine Lexikon der bildenen Küntsler* (Leipzig , 1928), 22:84, which gives 27 october 1877, as does the earlier but often refutable Bénézit, *Dictionnaire critique et documentaire des peintres, sculpteurs, dessinateurs & graveurs* (Paris 1924), 2:818. Mallett's *Index of Artists* was published in New York in 1935. *The American Art Annual*, published by the American Federation of Arts, Washington, D.C., gives 1877 in the 1915, 1917, 1919, and 1921 editions, then skips to the 1931 and 1935 editions, both of which give 1880. Brenda Kuhn's account of the change comes from a letter of 20 June 1975, not in the Archives. The death certificate is in the Archives.

SPANISH BIRTHRIGHT: Señorita Carmen Guzmán, secretary of the Archivo Nacional, is sincerely thanked for her investigation of the Foreign Service records. It was no help that the name Sarbâs was mistakenly given her at first; but she is not without hope, and the search goes on.

Kuhn's concern with ETHNIC FACTORS: the comment about Anglo-Saxon draughtsmanship was made in a letter of 23 October 1948 to Walter Heil, director of the De Young Memorial Museum in San Francisco. Its oddity derives from the fact that Walt Kuhn never showed much interest in William Blake, and Constable, who was a great influence on him, was a famously weak draughtsman in the usual academic sense of the word; Turner was noted in the School of the Royal Academy as "impenetrably dull" in drawing, possibly because he could not or would not draw like Flaxman. Augustus John, whose work Kuhn knew well in the John Quinn collection, but did not necessarily admire, was insistently Welsh and even hinted at gypsy affinities.

The letter to FRANK DI GIOIA is dated 18 June 1938, and the mention of his SPANISH JOURNEYS is in a letter to Toby Freeland of 13 February 1935.

All other direct quotations throughout come from the writer's memory, sometimes committed to print. The FRENCH FRAME was published in the Catalogue of the Memorial Exhibition presented by the Cincinnati Art Museum in 1960 (hereafter to be referred to as "Memorial Exhibition, 1960") on page 3; as is the NO COUNTRY HAS EVERYTHING. Kuhn saw many national traits in military uniforms, a lifelong study of his: the square-shouldered German, with coal-scuttle helmet and clumsy boots; the operatic Italian, complete with sashes and cock's feathers; the poilu, sloppy but with a certain Gallic verve; the Englishman, always the well-dressed gentleman; the American a poor copy of the Englishman, with a civilian hatband under the corps colors of his campaign hat. He may not, like Miniver Cheevy, have "missed the medieval grace of iron clothing," but he often deplored, during his postwar travels, the growing monotony and colorlessness of military costume. This was a time when political philosophies, as well as anthropological theories, were being built on the premise that "Nordic" peoples were genetically superior to "Meridional" or "Mediterranean" peoples, much less Slavs and Semites. It was, of course, a Nordic assumption, with even Rembrandt and Shakespeare cited as evidence, and is now almost wholly descredited; but few escaped its vicious influence: witness, among other things, the continued misuse of the work *Aryan*.

The PANORAMIC LITHOGRAPH is listed in Frederick A. Conningham, *Currier and Ives Prints: An Illustrated Check List* (New York: Crown Publishers, 1949), as number 4434, H. 20.14″ W. 32.14″, under the title "New York and Brooklyn/with New Jersey and Hoboken Water Front," 1877, Parsons and Atwater on Stone.

VERA KUHN'S MEMORIES OF HER MOTHER-IN-LAW were faithfully transcribed by her daughter in a letter of 7 May 1975, not in the Archives. Amalia also had a wayward sense of humor; Walt told of how the two of them, under her direction, once dipped a stick into the peculiarly evil-smelling excrement of some tropical cat and rubbed it on the insides of the guest room doorknobs.

Many of his REMINISCENCES OF WALT KUHN'S CHILDHOOD were told to the author. More are gratefully quoted, almost directly, from an unpublished manuscript in the Archives by Eloise Spaeth (Mrs. Otto L. Spaeth), a close younger friend and attentive listener. The FLAGPOLE INCIDENT was published in the Catalogue of the University of Arizona's Kuhn exhibition, *Painter of Vision* (Tucson, 1966), p. 14.

AMALIA KUHN'S THWARTED THEATRICAL YEARNINGS comes from her granddaughter Brenda; it was apparently an often-told family story.

Information about the WASP comes from the rare book librarian of the San Francisco Public Library. Some pages with cartoons can be found too in the Amon Carter Museum of Western Art, Fort Worth, Texas.

Data on AMBROSE BIERCE can be found in *The New Century Cyclopedia of Names* (New York: Appleton-Century-Crofts, 1954), and in *The Oxford Companion to American Literature*, 4th ed. (New York: Oxford University Press, 1965), from which the direct quotation is taken.

The APETENCIA DE MUERTE is defined by Arturo Barea in *Lorca, the Poet and His People* (New York: Harcourt, Brace & Co., 1949), pp. 113-14. In 1934 Walt Kuhn wrote to Marshall Field: "No doubt you have already read 'In the Midst of Life' by Ambrose Bierce. If you haven't, be sure to do so soon. I know you will enjoy it. It is one of my favorites."

The WESTERN TRIP, including Kuhn's interest in Ambrose Bierce, is mentioned in Memorial Exhibition, 1960, pp. 3-4, as is the Académie Colarossi.

An Imaginary History of the West was given to the Colorado Springs Fine Arts Center by Walt Kuhn's widow and daughter in 1950 as an appropriately placed memorial.

The DUTCH LANDSCAPE remark is published in Memorial Exhibition, 1960, p. 4.

A QUARTER TO TWELVE is published in Memorial Exhibition, 1960, p. 4, and the University of Arizona catalogue, 1966, p. 15.

NOCTURNAL LANDSCAPE'S LETTER OF DONATION was graciously furnished by the Currier Gallery of Art. The writer was Miss Esther Crockett, of Keene, New Hampshire.

The BLISS CÉZANNE is number 736 in Lionello Venturi's *Cézanne — son art — son oeuvre* (Paris: Paul Rosenberg, 1936), and the LEWISOHN STILL LIFE is number 599. To avoid further confusion of titles, they are taken from Venturi.

The EUROPEAN CONNOISSEUR was Marczell von Nemes, the well-known Hungarian collector-dealer and one of the rediscoverers of El Greco. The quotation from von Nemes occurs in Walt Kuhn's article "Cézanne: Delayed Finale," *Art News*, April 1947, p. 16.

Thomas Craven, in *Cartoon Cavalcade* (New York: Simon & Schuster, 1943), published five *Life* cartoons on pages 32, 49, 53, 63, and 74, three of them not included in the 1908 book. On page 13 he also says, " . . . And Walt Kuhn, now a modernist painter of all things, made charming little sketches of misbehaving animals, and naughty birds peering into Ladies' bath houses."

The *New Yorker* magazine must be thanked for modernizing CARTOON CAPTIONS, in the late 1920s. It considered them a minor art in themselves, and only James Thurber is said to have been allowed to write his own.

Courtship and Marriage

The curtain rises on a genteel rooming house at 120 East Twenty-third Street in New York. It is evening in the fall of 1908. A young artist on the top floor finds that his lamp does not work. The obliging landlady borrows one from a young lady on the second floor. The second scene opens late on the following afternoon with a knock on the young lady's door. She opens it to find a gangling young man with a mop of dark hair leaning against the door jamb. He looks to her like "a cross between Mephistopheles and Abraham Lincoln." He asks if she is the young lady who so graciously lent him her lamp, and if so may he take her to dinner that night? They exit to a Hungarian restaurant whose sauces they both enjoy. The orchestra swells to a paprika theme that can be heard faintly for the next forty years.

1

The dramatis personae were Walt Kuhn, age 31, and Vera Spier, age 23. Vera Spier was gently born and raised in Washington, D.C. Her father had come as a young man to America from Buckeberg, Germany, near Hannover, and her mother, Olga Maria Hesselbach, was native-born. A maternal uncle was a noted surgeon, and her brother, LaSalle Spier was a distinguished composer-pianist who played with the Lenox, Rich, and National String quartets, and gave recitals in Europe as well as in America. He and Walt Kuhn for many years shared a mutual respect, not always to be expected between brothers-in-law of notably different temperaments and backgrounds. Kuhn often worried over "Salle's" spending too much time and creative energy on his piano students that he should have saved for his voice, chamber music, and orchestral compositions. In return LaSalle often worried about Kuhn's health.

Vera was a skillful jewelry designer in the prevailing art nouveau mode, but painting was closer to her heart. She had left the nest of her comfortable and affectionate family in the summer of 1908 to work at the artists' colony in Woodstock, New York, moving to East Twenty-third Street in the fall. After the somewhat operatic meeting with Kuhn, their friendship rapidly matured into an engagement, as Vera dutifully told her parents, who somehow never managed to meet their prospective son-in-law. On his side Kuhn took no chances: Amalia Kuhn was a fiercely possessive mother who had already broken up one engagement, so she first met Vera as a daughter-in-law in being. Furthermore, he had completely broken with his Roman Catholic upbringing.

This accounts for the wedding's taking place on the neutral ground of Hoboken, New Jersey, in the rectory of St. Matthew's Lutheran Church, 57 Eighth Street, on 6 February 1909. The young couple moved to a house on Hudson Terrace, Fort Lee, their home for ten years to come.

Kuhn must have felt some proper compunction at not having gone to Washington to meet the Spiers, and wrote apologetically to Vera's father, saying that he deserved and would "submit to any righteous wrath" that might descend on him. The answer was most gracious: "Our home is at your disposal and any 'righteous wrath' will disappear as soon as you enter the door." Vera's mother wrote even more warmly: "You already had my forgiveness before the asking. After seeing Vera so extremely happy I could not possibly be angry with you."

The summer of 1909 was spent in Blandford, Nova Scotia, where Kuhn began a transition from Munich mud to the scintillant open air blaze of impressionist color. It did not happen overnight; the first move was away from the rigid draughtsmanship of the academies, both European and American, toward Edouard Manet's early figure impressionism, so largely learned from Velasquez and Hals. *Albig's* (number 5) hints at this direction, already taken by William Glackens, John Sloan, George Luks, and Everett Shinn of The Eight. They had all been at one time or another pictorial reporters for the *Philadelphia Press*, and on moving to New York had continued to support themselves as illustrators for magazines and newspapers. In the days before speed cameras a newspaper's demand for rapid, almost instantaneous drawing to be rushed immediately to the engravers required not only a simplified style but answered to Delacroix's definition, "If you can't *see* a figure falling from a fourth floor window before it hits the ground you are not drawing." It was a far cry from the labored exercises of Munich anatomy classes. Winslow Homer had undergone the same journalist's discipline while covering the early years of the Civil War for *Harper's Illustrated Weekly*; it stood him in good stead all his life.

Tow Team (number 11), shown by Walt Kuhn in the April 1910 "Exhibition of Independent Artists," is another step along this path,

Plate 16. *Summer Interlude*

Private Collection

but not free of Munich's dark monochrome. Robert Henri praised it somewhat perfunctorily for its "vigor" and reproduced it in his review of the exhibition in the 10 May issue of *Craftsman*. The "Independent Exhibition" was held in a store and loft at 29 West Thirty-fifth Street, between Broadway and Sixth Avenue, in the spring of 1910; and the *New York American* credited Kuhn with originating the show, which Robert Henri helped to organize, lending a prestige much enhanced by the *succés de scandale* of The Eight. In fact, the "Independent" was a similar defiance of the National Academy's conservative tyranny, and it was there that, most significantly for the future of his own style and American art in general, Kuhn first met Arthur B. Davies.

The jury of the Academy in 1907 had rejected the paintings of Robert Henri's friends Glackens, Luks, and Sloan, but accepted his. In protest Henri withdrew his own works. Meanwhile, Arthur B. Davies had been showing at the Macbeth Gallery, founded in 1892 and the first dealers in the country primarily concerned with contemporary American art. In 1908 the Macbeth Gallery asked Davies to arrange an exhibition of some promising younger artists of his choice. It was a mixed lot; the reportorial group of Luks, Sloan, Henri, Glackens, and Shinn was joined by Davies himself, whose idyllic reveries have often been compared to the French symbolists; Ernest Lawson, a pure impressionist following in the distant footsteps of Alfred Sisley; and the already postimpressionist Maurice Prendergast of Boston, a decorative echo of Georges Seurat. Lawson was born in Nova Scotia and Prendergast in Newfoundland, but both spent their creative lives in the United States.

Eight painters exhibiting together for the first and only time in 1908 were naturally called The Eight, though almost immediately labeled "The Ashcan School" by a hostile, or an at least amused, press. More serious champions of sweetness and light, the true and the beautiful, fulminated against these apostles of deliberate ugliness. It is a strange indictment to return against the gentle Prendergast or Davies, or even Lawson, and Glackens who was soon content to be a disciple of the late Renoir, while Shinn continued his futile emulation of Degas's fascination with theater subjects. However they all, even Prendergast as can be seen in his sketchbooks, had been influenced to some extent by Manet, who had not been unscarred by far more savage denunciation in his own time and in another country.

Their name may even have been suggested by an earlier group of The Ten: "Ten American Painters" from Boston and New York who had banded together in 1895 to form what became a kind of "academy of Impressionism," as Edgar P. Richardson calls them. They were Thomas W. Dewing, Edmund C. Tarbell, Frank W. Benson, Joseph De Camp, J. Alden Weir, John H. Twachtman, on whose early death William Merritt Chase was elected as a replacement, Willard L. Metcalf, E. E. Simmons, Childe Hassam, and Robert Reid. They first exhibited at the Durand-Ruel Gallery and continued showing together for about twenty years.

Many of these once-bold innovators are forgotten or only half-remembered for what at the end seemed to be only a "a predeliction for exquisiteness in painting." But there were others. Theodore Robinson of Vermont and Wisconsin had painted in Giverny close to Claude Monet from 1887 to 1892, and brought the master's full style back with him to New York. George Inness's Boston dealers financed a stay in Italy from 1870 to 1875. In this unlikely setting Inness, after the expected canvases of umbrella pines and Roman aqueducts, developed his late style of misty but intense refracted color with few if any clearly drawn contours. Homer Martin had also grown up in the Hudson River School tradition; an eight-year sojourn in Brittany and Normandy, however, where he discovered Eugène Boudin, converted him to a luminous impressionist palette, and earned him great applause when he brought it home in 1887.

The most momentous event in the story of impressionism in America was Paul Durand-Ruel's exhibition at the American Art Association galleries in New York in 1886. The association had invited the Paris dealer, whose daring and often financially hazardous support of the impressionists had begun in 1871, three years before their first group show, to present a cross-section of his protégés. "Works in Oil and Pastel by the Impressionists of Paris" opened on 10 April 1886. It was a tremendous show in size as well as impact; there were over three hundred works, forty-eight by Monet, twenty-three by Degas, seventeen by Manet, forty-three by Pissarro, thirty-eight by Renoir, fifteen by Sisley, and three by Seurat. Boudin, Caillebotte, Mary Cassatt, Forain, Guillaumin, and Berthe Morisot were also represented.

It was the first time New York-bound artists and collectors could see the new movement at its inclusive best, and Durand-Ruel wrote: "The exhibition was an immense success, for reasons of curiosity, but, as opposed to what happened in Paris, it provoked neither uproar, nor abusive comment, arousing no protest whatsoever. The general public, as well as every amateur came, not to laugh, but to learn about these notorious paintings which had caused such a stir in Paris." It was in fact so popular that it had to be extended for a month, moving to the National Academy's large galleries on Twenty-third Street. As a result, Durand-Ruel opened his own New York gallery in 1888.

There had been a few earlier and tentative efforts to introduce the controversial new style; Durand-Ruel had sent a handful of Manets, Monets, Renoirs, and Pissarros to Boston for "The Foreign Exhibition" held at the Mechanics Building in September 1883. And in the fall of the same year William Merritt Chase and Carol Beckwith presented in the National Academy galleries an exhibition that they had organized to raise funds for the architectural pedestal of the Statue of Liberty. It was opened by General Grant, an adequate if improbable celebrity. All the acceptable Barbizon masters were there, along with Géricault and Courbet. Chase, however, not only slipped in but starred four Manets including *Lady with a Parrot* and *Boy with Sword*, the first Manet owned in America, and *Little Ballet Girls in Pink* by Degas. Private collections were forming in Boston and Chicago as well as in New York, with the urging of Mary Cassatt of Philadelphia and Paris. Of course, she herself was one of the original Parisian impressionists, accepted by the French today as one of their own.

2

These happenings and names are called out of the past to show how solidly established impressionist style was in America by 1909. It was beginning to be taught in the schools, certainly in Chase's New York School of Art. Perhaps that was one cause of Walt Kuhn's disillusionment with teaching. Among too many of its provincial practitioners, impressionism was not built on a firm foundation of drawing and formal composition, but it is still surprising that Kuhn came to it so late. Undoubtedly he had been "observing and investigating," and continued to do so through the summer and fall of 1909. It can be inferred that he also did a good deal of experimenting, but kept no single painting that can be definitely attributed to that year or to the first half of 1910.

On 21 June 1910 Kuhn and Vera started off again for Blandford, arriving by night boat in Boston for a two-day stay. Vera's journal is the sole source for the developments of the summer, telling how on 23 June they visited Boston's Museum of Fine Arts, where there were "no Germans — a dozen canvases by Monet, several by Sisley — Monet easily leads them all." There were "2 Manets, one large sketch for the execution of Maximilian that has no right in a gallery." The judgments of the young are absolute altogether.

That night they boarded the S.S. *Prince George* and landed at Yarmouth on the morning of 24 June, taking a train for Chester, the railroad stop nearest to Blandford. On the evening of the twenty-fifth they were settled in, and she "could not resist making a color sketch of the harbor in the evening glow." On 5 July they met "Glackens & wife out walking." The weather was not too good, and on 10 July she remarks, "We are reading too much Ibsen and heavy stuff." Heavy stuff chiefly meant James Gibbons Huneker, who was soon to become an important friend of Kuhn's. From 1900 to 1912 he was music, drama, and art editor of the *New York Sun*, later writing for the *Times* and the *World*. He evidently had a wide range of interests on which he wrote voluminously, lushly, and with some authority. His *Promenades of an Impressionist* was published in 1910, its title taken from a line of Stendhal, "Let us promenade our prejudices." It was probably part of the Kuhns' heavy reading.

Vera enters a wifely complaint on 13 July: "How can I take interest in all he does & do myself justice too? . . . He is working too

Plate 17. *Vera Reading by Seashore*

29

hard." On 28 July comes a revealing remark: "Walt painted in barn — is finding that he gains great experience by this indoor painting — is going to do more of it on bad days. Is coming along fine on figures." And about this time she makes the arresting statement that he spent a bad day in the barn "laying out Cézanne's pallette."

That Kuhn had mastered the impressionist technique can be seen in the nine paintings he kept from 1910, but where had he seen Cézanne? He could well have heard of him — in Huneker, for example, and from several others — or seen a few reproductions, but he must have seen at least one Cézanne oil in the flesh to try to lay out his palette. Alfred Stieglitz's dedicated partisans insist that the first Cézannes exhibited in America were shown by him at the Photo-Secession Gallery, 291 Fifth Avenue: a small group of lithographs in 1910 (one or two of them colored lithographs perhaps) and a group of watercolors in 1911. Two Cézannes had almost furtively crept into the Luxembourg Museum in 1895 with the remnants of the Caillebotte Collection, and it may be that Kuhn was observing and investigating shrewdly enough in Paris in 1904 to have spotted them, "skied" as they probably were, if shown at all. Vollard was showing Cézannes then, but Durand-Ruel had not yet exhibited any in New York. Nevertheless, the conclusion is inescapable that by 1910 Walt Kuhn had already seen beyond impressionism to the larger world that lay ahead.

Although Stieglitz deserves all honor for his pioneering ventures, including the first one-man Picasso show anywhere, in 1910, it was simply not in his nature to produce the seismic shock of the 1913 Armory Show. He preferred a small circle of the chosen, who almost literally sat at his feet, to the vast Philistine herd, but he could not help feeling cheated. Later, in 1913 Kuhn wrote of Stieglitz's plaintive repetition, "But I started it all!"

Home life back at Fort Lee that fall was not all smooth sailing. There were money troubles, as might be expected; no details are available or needed. Kuhn mentioned them only once, in a September 1911 letter. Although his cartoons were selling well, if unpredictably, to *Judge* as well as *Life* and various newspapers, there was no steady income, however small, from the teaching he had found personally irksome as well as professionally distracting. Neither was there any money for domestic help, and the young couple learned in November that a baby was on its way. Fort Lee was much more isolated in those days, and Kuhn found it necessary to spend more and more time in the city at night as well as day, since his growing circle of professional friends was in some ways as important to his creative life as his hours at the easel. He had met Frederick James Gregg, dynamic and prolific art critic for the *Sun*, who introduced him to J.G. Huneker, and he tried to see as much as possible of Arthur B. Davies.

Walt Kuhn often said that Davies was the most vital formative influence in his artistic life, which calls for some elaboration. Arthur Bowen Davies was one of the most enigmatic personalities in American art. He was born in 1862 and raised in a utopian community near Utica, New York, where he began studying under a landscape painter at the age of fifteen. Moving to Chicago with his family in 1878, he continued studying art and worked as an engineering draughtsman in Mexico for two years. He came to New York in 1886, where he made his living as a magazine illustrator and continued study at the Art Students' League. Benjamin Altman, the merchant prince and collector of old masters, Chinese porcelain, and Persian rugs, sent him to Europe for independent study, chiefly in Italy. He returned for his first one-man show in 1896 and immediate success as a painter of romantic landscapes with friezes of dancing, elongated figures, most often set in the Apennines even when they purported to be the Mohawk and Delaware valleys. He liked obscure and poetic titles for them. Bryson Burroughs, artist-curator of painting at the Metropolitan Museum, wrote that Davies gave himself "to precise and dainty design and to pearly tints diaphonously spread."

No one could possibly guess that underneath lay a profound interest in, and understanding of, the most advanced tendencies in European art, as well as a more evident grounding in the classic Renaissance past. He was somewhat professorial in appearance, with impeccable manners, and strangely secretive. Some aspects of his professional as well as his private life are still mysteries. In the 1920s after some unsuccessful experiments with cubism, which consisted largely of building his floating figures with rectangular planes, he designed tapestries to be woven by the Gobelins works in Paris. He died in Italy in 1928. There was a vein of poetic mysticism in Davies that Kuhn, with his interest in ethnic factors, might have ascribed to his Celtic-Welsh ancestry. On 11 November 1912 Kuhn wrote Vera from Paris, where he and Davies were in the frantic midst of assembling the Armory Show, "Davies in all his delicacy is always masculine."

Davies's range of artistic interests and self-taught scholarly knowledge was extraordinary, opening Kuhn's eyes and those of many others to Archaic Greek sculpture and the Egyptians, to Chinese scroll painting, pre-Columbian and African art. Kuhn's close friendship with Davies was his one exposure to academic learning, no matter how informal, and he never forgot it. It was "observing and investigating" of a slightly different kind, but it was no less valuable.

Kuhn spent the latter part of the fall preparing for his first one-man show. It opened late in 1910 at the Madison Gallery, 305 Madison Avenue, near Forty-first Street, and ran through the early weeks of 1911. The Madison Gallery was part of the Coventry Studios, an interior decorating shop run by Mrs. Clara S. Davidge, the daughter of an Episcopalian bishop, who could lay some claim to being the "first interior decorator" in America. Mrs. Gertrude Vanderbilt Whitney shared her enthusiasm for the younger American artists, and was probably the financial backer of the gallery. It was managed by the painter Henry Fitch Taylor, who after 1913 also experimented, not un-

31

successfully, with cubism. Taylor's few remaining paintings recall Jean Metzinger rather more than the founders of the movement. He sat on the inner cabinet of the Armory Show, and Mrs. "Clarissa" Davidge, as Mabel Dodge called her, was one of its most ardent fund-raisers. When Taylor and Mrs. Davidge were married in 1913, they spent their honeymoon arranging the Armory Show's Boston exhibition.

Several of Kuhn's paintings stayed at the Madison Gallery, where John Quinn discovered them in the spring of 1911. He bought *Salt Mists* (number 9) for two hundred dollars and *The Frozen River* (number 7) for three hundred. Even if Kuhn sold no others, this is a good sale for a first one-man show, considering the dollar's far greater purchasing power in those remote days; and John Quinn was to be almost as important in Kuhn's life as Arthur B. Davies.

It can be assumed that all of the nine paintings he kept from 1910, including, of course, the two bought by John Quinn, were in the show. *Tow Team* (number 11) may have been painted in 1909, since it is the least impressionistic of them. They are quite creditable and stand up fairly well today. Their titles suggest their composition and style: *Houses on Street* (number 6), *Rowboat at Shore With Houses* (number 8), *Walking along the Seashore* (number 14), and *Summer Interlude* (number 10), showing Vera leaning against a rock and Kuhn sprawling on the sun-drenched grass under a beach umbrella by a rocky inlet, with two small square houses on the horizon. They are very much the kind of canvases that sprout like mushrooms along the Atlantic coast every summer to this day, and very much like others being painted then and before, except for their bold color and incisive drawing. It would be more interesting to see some of the figures Kuhn was "coming along on fine" in the barn studio. There is no mention of any models for them, even local types, so Kuhn may have been developing the figures from sketches. In any case they fell to his executioner's torch or scraping knife at some later time.

The late Aline Saarinen, who knew Walt Kuhn quite well, wrote a lively chapter on John Quinn in *The Proud Possessors* of 1958, but it is more timely to introduce him through B. L. Reid's massive Pulitzer Prize-winning and definitive work of 1968, *The Man from New York: John Quinn and His Friends*. Mr. Reid, of Mount Holyoke College, came to his subject by way of authoritative works on William Butler Yeats and Gertrude Stein. He says in his preface:

When he was identified at all, it was some such hurried and uninstructive tag as "John Quinn (1870-1924), American lawyer and patron of the arts." I was baffled and curious. Why did he show up in so many different places? one wondered; why was he not back home practicing the law? Why would W. B. Yeats pose so complacently with this man standing at his shoulder? Why would Yeats write so many letters, such witty, serious, and circumstantial letters to an American lawyer, addressing him apparently as a cultural equal? What is John Quinn doing posed in a stiff white wing collar in a Paris studio garden with Ezra Pound, Ford Madox Ford, and James Joyce? (Do they know he is there? Did they invite him in?) What was such a man doing in possession of the manuscript of *Ulysses* or *The Waste Land?* Was he the same man who owned Brancusi's *Mlle. Pogany,* Matisse's *Blue Nude,* Picasso's *Three Musicians,* and

Plate 18. *Four Boats*

Courtesy of Mr. & Mrs. Brenwasser, Wyckoff, New Jersey

Rousseau's *Sleeping Gypsy?* One was astonished to discover how many of the capital works of the modern movement in art turned out to have been owned, and owned early, by John Quinn.

Mr. Reid might well ask such questions and, fortunately, answer them.

John Quinn was indeed an astonishing, not to say unique, man. Born to Irish immigrant parents in Tiffin, Ohio, and raised in nearby Fostoria, he founded his own New York law firm in the "heroic days" of 1906. He was at the very heart of the Irish literary renaissance, as friend, financial patron, and legal champion in America, where Synge and Joyce later badly needed one. He collected Irish painters, including the poet-mystic George Russell, and had what amounted to a standing order for Augustus John's major output, paying in advance.

By 1911 his taste began to change. Reid writes:

The year 1911 was to be a critical one in the definition of Quinn's taste and in sharpening his appetite. Though he had not met Gwen John [Augustus John's reclusive painting sister] he had begun to write confidentially to her, charmed by the candor and naive grace of her letters. To her on January 5 he made a critical pronouncement: "I like to be a man of my own day and time." He did not have and did not expect to have the kind of fortune that allowed one to collect the famous art of the past. What money he had would go farther, and do more good, if he confined his view to recent work, more especially to strictly contemporary work. He could not afford Old Masters, and anyway their ground was already tiresomely travelled over by generations of connoisseurs and moneyed men. "There is more real pleasure in the recognition and appreciation of a contemporary who is doing fine work", he wrote to

Gwen John. The choice was multiple, and perfectly conscious: the money bought more; there was more sport, more raciness, more "vigor" in the game of contemporary art. Furthermore one could feel the warming sensation of taking part in art, helping it to be born, in some sense *making* it, when one bought the work of living men.

About American art too Quinn had made up his mind, as he said to Gwen John: it was inferior to European art and interesting at all only in landscape. So he bought Lawsons [with his "palette of crushed jewels," as one rhapsodic critic wrote] and when he discovered the work of Walt Kuhn at the Madison Art Gallery [*sic*]in the spring, what he bought first was *Salt Mists* for $300 and *Frozen River* for $200. Quinn's ideas about art were coming clear, he thought, but in fact his taste wavered now for some time, and his purchases tended to lag behind his theory. He still felt more comfortable and safe with landscapes, with a homely element.

Kuhn soon became a close friend and confidant, especially on masculine retreats to the Adirondacks, and Quinn began almost immediately to rely on his judgment of American and European moderns. Walt Kuhn has been called John Quinn's "Art Secretary" and "Art Adviser"; he probably never had, or wanted, such titular rank, or a retainer's fee. Quinn's purchases of his work were his financial return. Reid writes that by 1920 Quinn's "list of American enthusiasms had dwindled to a single name, Walt Kuhn . . . To Kuhn he was loyal both publicly and privately."

Aline Saarinen says, "Augustus John's American counterpart in Quinn's life was Walt Kuhn. Quinn met Kuhn through Frederick James Gregg, the art critic of the *New York Sun*, an Irishman as redoubtable as Quinn himself, who was making American art *his* crusade.

Kuhn painted circus folk and apples in a tough, objective way. Quinn bought so many of these paintings that some of the less favored artists called him 'Kuhn's milk-cow.' Quinn liked the man as well as the art. Kuhn's hard-boiled lust for life appealed to him." Mrs. Saarinen's facts are a little off here; there are thirty-seven Kuhn paintings and drawings and nineteen small sculptures listed in the catalogue of the 1927 Quinn sale, and there were only two circus subjects and one still life, of flowers.

She continues: "The two tall figures — one dressed in artist's tweeds, big-featured, with high, broad cheekbones, the other with his fine ascetic head rising like a statue from the pedestal of his stiff collar — were a familiar, almost conspiratorial pair. Quinn usually lunched at the Banker's Club, but he would sit late into the night at the Round Table at the artists' hangout, Mouquin's. He and Kuhn drank beer under the pearly nudes of Bouguereau and Correggio [*sic*] in the old Hoffman House bar and smoked ten-cent perfectos from the Hoffman House box . . . They appeared as pirates at the Kit Kat Klub [*sic*] balls."

Obviously, Arthur B. Davies and John Quinn were keeping Kuhn away from Fort Lee much of the time. But what a comment it is on the thirty-three-year-old Walt Kuhn that two such men had singled him out. Neither of them would live to see his artistic fulfillment in the late twenties and early thirties, but their prescience had not failed them.

Brenda Kuhn was born on 13 June 1911 at the Hahnnemann Hospital in Manhattan. Walt enthusiastically proclaimed, "I am a papa." in many letters, and passed out the ceremonial cigars. She was not a strong infant, however, and as soon as mother and child could safely travel, Vera left for the help and comfort of Washington. Kuhn went up to Ogunquit, Maine, with his brother-in-law, LaSalle. The pattern of daily letters to Vera during long absences from her had not yet been set, and except for a few postcards there is little record of what Kuhn did other than recuperate. Finally in September he wrote a long letter, mentioning "reconciliation" and the money troubles that he hoped would soon be over. He said: "I can only work after long rests, otherwise I tire before I get half way down a canvas. As regards the work I am all up in the air. Don't know what's good or what's bad — just the same as usual. . . . Don't ever talk to me again about summer art schools or colonies, Woodstock included, of all the brainless bunch of weak-minded humans they are the climax."

Jacques Lipchitz, the eminent Parisian-American sculptor, once said that the only artist he had known who physically spent himself on a canvas was Chaim Soutine, who would literally collapse from exhaustion after finishing one. Walt Kuhn was much the same, though always giving the impression of boundless energy. Weeks of preparatory thought, drawings, and sometimes watercolors preceded each major work with its strain of execution. This as well as his remorseless self-criticism may account for his relatively small corpus of paintings. He often accused the French of inventing "mass production" in painting, beginning with the Barbizon masters and continuing through Monet and Renoir to Picasso and Matisse. Renoir was quite frank about it, telling Albert André that he was a "painter, not an artist" and that except for *force majeure* he had never missed an artisan's daily work. Time eventually edits, but Kuhn preferred to do it himself at a costly physical and nervous price.

He returned to Fort Lee in October to get ready for his part in the Pastellist show at the Madison Gallery. None of his Ogunquit landscapes were sold, — in fact, none of them survive — but he got a very good press, especially from Huneker. Early in November he wrote to Vera again in a conciliatory vein: "If we can sustain a strong love and confidence which I am vain enough to think I deserve, in spite of everything, we must succeed and we will both look back on these days with a feeling that they have not been in vain."

He was in better spirits now, and wrote on 2 November 1911, "Gregg has just left here — Have hopes for getting Mr. Q. out to F. Lee Sunday — so I will postpone bringing in the pictures till next week." And on 21 November he wrote, "Gregg said a fine thing the other day, viz — 'In your two exhibitions, last year and this, you had not a single potboiler.'"

Kuhn was beginning to have his own labor pains, writing Vera on 11 December, "From what I hear it is quite likely that there will be a revolution this winter and that a new society will form." On 12 December he wrote: "We certainly made good this time [in the exhibition], but what we need now is publicity. The stuff is there but everybody must see it. Beginning the first of January I am going to organize a new society. The plans are still in embryo state but clear enough in my mind's eye to spell positive success. No one is on it but Gregg and he's 'mmmm' and the best adviser I could get . . . As soon as I have it thoroughly planned we are going to give it all to the papers and they will jump at it. Of course Henri and the rest will have to be let in — but not until things are chained up so that they can't do any monkey business."

Actually three others were in on it, but Kuhn went on to tell Vera that he did not want to be president of the new society; a better-known figure would be needed there, and he could have more real control in the less conspicuous role of secretary. In his 1938 pamphlet *The Story of the Armory Show*, he says: "Three of the exhibitors, Elmer MacRae, Jerome Myers and myself, together with Mr. Taylor, the director, would sit and talk of the helplessness of our situation. Finally on December 14, 1911, we agreed to take action. Additional artists were invited. On December 16th the group had grown to sixteen members." Milton Brown's 1963 *The Story of the Armory Show,* its title taken with due acknowledgment from Kuhn's pamphlet, says:

> The first official meeting of this society took place at the invitation of Henry Fitch Taylor at the Madison Gallery on December 19 . . . At that first meeting thirteen artists were present—D. Putnam Brinley, Gutzon Borglum, John Mowbray-Clarke, Arthur B. Davies, Leon Dabo, William J. Glackens, Walt Kuhn, Earnest [*sic*] Lawson, Jonas Lie, George B. Luks, Elmer L. MacRae, Jerome Myers and Taylor, and by proxy Karl Anderson, James E. Fraser, Allen Tucker and J. Alden Weir. The minutes of the meeting along with that of January 2, 1912, exist in a notebook in the Kuhn Papers. Taylor opened the meeting in the following words: "You have been asked to meet here this evening to take active steps toward the formation of a national association of painters and sculptors — an association of live and progressive men and women who shall lead the public taste in art rather than follow it.
>
> "The National Academy of Design is not expected to lead the public taste. It never did and never will, and as no such organization as the one contemplated exists in this country today, we must all, I think, admit the very positive need of forming one.
>
> "Recognizing the need for such an organization, the only effective way of meeting that need is to set to work and form it. The matter is now before you and open for discussion; we shall all be pleased to listen to any gentleman present who has anything to say for or against the movement."
>
> After this short welcoming speech Taylor was elected temporary chairman and Kuhn temporary secretary. The first order of business was the drafting of a platform, and in the simple and forthright one-sentence statement of principle is the foundation of the organization and the Armory Show itself. Proposed by Borglum and seconded by MacRae, the meeting accepted the following as its platform:
>> For the purpose of developing a broad interest in American art activities, by holding exhibitions of the best contemporary work that can be secured, representative of American and foreign art.

A name for the organization was discussed, and it became the Association of American Painters and Sculptors when it was incorporated. J. Alden Weir was elected president, in his absence; Gutzon

Plate 19. *Morning*

Borglum, vice-president; Kuhn, secretary; and MacRae, treasurer. Weir, an Academician, was sympathetic to the younger generation, but when he learned in the press the following day (Walt was correct in predicting that the papers would jump at the release he had drawn up in advance) that the motive of the new association was basically anti-Academy, he resigned in an open letter to the *Times* and in a formal note to Henry Fitch Taylor. Arthur B. Davies then accepted the office.

Brown cogently explains the matter: "His reputation was unassailable, his art was unique and unconnected with any of the more recognizable tendencies in American art, and he stood aloof from cliques, yet was identified with liberal artistic movements. The problem seems to have been to convince this essentially retiring and apparently unaggressive individual to accept the job." Kuhn probably played a major part in this persuasion and seems to have been reasonably sure of

37

its outcome. Brown continues: "And it may have been a good many of the members thought they were getting a new figurehead to replace Weir and that then they could simply go ahead with their own plans. Subsequent events led many to regret the choice, for they had picked a tiger. This man of fastidiously aristocratic bearing, a painter of poetic sensitivity bordering on the ephemeral, this shy, reticent and coolly formal person, whom his closest co-workers continued always to call Mr. Davies or 'the Chief,' turned out to be a creature of driving energy, incisive command, organizational ability, and authoritarian attitude. Once in the seat, he drove with unswerving directness and amazing control. His was truly a hand of steel in a suede glove."

Among other things Davies immediately recognized comparable abilities in Walt Kuhn. Kuhn had written to Vera on 15 December: "Expect that Quinn will be our legal adviser (gratis) when the time comes . I've shown that I can paint; now I'll show them that I can fight [last three words underscored]." He would soon have ample opportunity.

This highly charged atmosphere had a stimulating effect on his painting that summer even though only four were kept — possibly only three unless the vigorous *Work Horses* (number 19) can be assigned to that year. His two oils in the Armory Show were painted in 1912 in Nova Scotia, and John Quinn bought both of them, *Morning* (number 17) for six hundred dollars and *Girl with Red Cap* (number 16) for three hundred and fifty. The Quinn Catalogue of 1927 reproduces the latter and describes it as "A young woman [Vera]) in a white gown, adorned at her breast with a large black bow, is seated on a moss-grown cliff, facing the spectator. Behind her an inland creek, and beyond the opposite shore crested by a few scattered houses." It shows that Walt was coming along fine with figures, but he destroyed it in 1929, presumably having bought it back from the Quinn sale. That was the year of the *White Clown* (number 248) when he felt that at last he had reached his mature plateau. The Quinn Catalogue describes *Morning* with modified rapture, "Luminaristic view of landscape with cattle grazing, flooded with brilliant light from the rising sun; in the middle distance a vista of opalescent water, and graceful sailing craft." There is a seated woman's figure in the left foreground and a man standing at the right. Everything is boldly, sketchily drawn, and the explosion of the sky over the sailboats and rocky cliffs definitely recalls Van Gogh,whom Walt could have known only from reproductionsiin 1912, except for a self-portrait in John Quinn's collection.

Vera and Walt had taken Brenda with them to Yarmouth, Nova Scotia, in the summer, and Vera's journal has few entries other than those dealing with the care of a one-year-old. On 2 August she notes, "He paid a call on Prendergast," in Boston on their way up; and on 12 August, "Painted me lying on a rock."

Vera Kuhn Reading by Seashore (number 18) is a successful figure painting with a gentler, fully impressionist palette. Sentiment may have saved it from destruction, but it is gratifying that Kuhn kept it.

Plate 20. *Bar Room Fight*.
From *An Imaginary History
of the West*.

Plate 22 (above). *The Commissioners.* From *An Imaginary History of the West*

Plate 23. *Bareback Rider*

Plate 21 (opposite). *Harlequin (Masked Clown)*

Plate 24. *Flower Still Life*

Courtesy of Kennedy Galleries, Inc.,—Kuhn Estate

NOTES TO CHAPTER TWO

The circumstances of VERA MEETING WALT KUHN are well remembered by Brenda Kuhn from her mother's telling. The paprika theme was one of those mild, arcane jokes such as every family knows. The author begs indulgence for the first paragraph; the incident does recall the first act of *La Bohème*, and anyway, it was exactly O. Henry's New York.

Several of Vera Spier Kuhn's JEWELRY DESIGNS are preserved in the Archives.

HENRI'S REVIEW in the 10 May issue of *Craftsman* reproduces *Tow Team* on page 165.

The account of The Eight and The Ten is taken almost bodily from Edgar P. Richardson, PAINTING IN AMERICA: THE STORY OF 450 YEARS (New York: Thomas Y. Crowell Co., 1956), for which thanks are most sincerely given. Dr. Richardson is especially skilled and perceptive in his discussion of the American impressionists, though his later comments on Walt Kuhn are hardly those of an enthusiastic admirer. However, even Homer is said to have nodded, and further almost limitless thanks must be given for Richardson's having brought the Archives of American Art into being, as well as the *Art Quarterly*.

Details of the FRENCH IMPRESSIONISTS' INTRODUCTION TO AMERICA come almost *in toto* from Richard J. Boyle, *American Impressionism* (Boston:New York Graphic Society, 1974), pp. 51-54. Mr. Boyle is sincerely thanked, although since the writer contributed the Foreword he may be excused for claiming some proprietary privileges.

MARY CASSATT'S AMERICAN ORIGIN and loyalties are apparently unknown to the French authorities, who habitually single out Whistler's *Mother* as the only American painting in the Louvre, often lending it for diplomatic purposes to the United States, while proudly exhibiting several Mary Cassatts in the department it houses in the Musée du Jeu de Paume.

Manet's BOY WITH SWORD and the LADY WITH A PARROT were bequeathed by Irwin Davis to the Metropolitan Museum of New York in 1889. The present administration of the Metropolitan was about to "deaccession" it when the *New York Times* discovered the proposed desecration and led a successful public protest.

WILLIAM AND EDITH GLACKENS were lifelong friends of both Walt and Vera Kuhn. After William's death in 1938 and Walt's in 1949, the relationship between the families continued.

J. G. HUNEKER was born in Philadelphia and studied piano in Paris. Kuhn may have figured dimly in his scandalous *Painted Veils* of 1920, a prematurely explicit novel about artists, critics, and dilettantes in New York's Bohemia. His *Ivory, Apes, and Peacocks,* a compilation of essays published in London in 1915, was dedicated to John Quinn.

THE STIEGLITZ CHRONOLOGY comes from *America and Alfred Stieglitz: A Collective Portrait* (Garden City, N.Y.: Doubleday, Doran & Co., 1934), p. 314.

Information about the PUBLIC VISIBIITY OF CÉZANNE can be found in John Rewald, *Paul Cézanne: A Biography* (New York:Simon & Schuster, 1948), pp. 179-88.

The source for the MADISON GALLERY and MRS. DAVIDGE, born Clara Sydney Potter, is Milton W. Brown, *The Story of the Armory Show* (New York: Joseph H. Hirshhorn Foundation, 1963), pp. 29, 63, 71–72, 186. This invaluable work will be much referred to as Brown, *Armory Show,* 1963.

WALT KUHN'S DEBT TO ARTHUR B. DAVIES has been published in Memorial Exhibition, 1960, p. 7, and University of Arizona, 1966, p. 18.

THE BRYSON BURROUGHS QUOTATION concerning Arthur B. Davies, as well as other biographical data, comes from the article by David W. Scott, formerly director of the National Collection of Fine Arts, Washington, D.C., in *The Britannica Encyclopedia of American Art* (Chicago: Encyclopedia Britannica Educational Corp., 1973).

One of HENRY FITCH TAYLOR'S few surviving post-Armory Show cubist paintings, with a still clearly recognizable human figure, is in the collection of the Cincinnati Art Museum in the city of his birth.

JOHN QUINN'S DISCOVERY OF WALT KUHN is mentioned in B.L.Reid, *The Man from New York: John Quinn and His Friends* (New York: Oxford University Press, 1968), p. 93. This monumental work will also often be referred to as Reid, *The Man from New York,* 1968.

The HEROIC DAYS of New York law is a quotation from Aline Saarinen, *The Proud Possessors* (New York: Random House, 1958), p. 209. Her DESCRIPTION OF KUHN AND QUINN comes from pages 212--13.

QUINN'S LOYALTY TO KUHN is from Reid, *The Man from New York,* 1968, pp. 466-67.

WALT KUHN'S PAMPHLET, *The Story of the Armory Show,* 1938, was published in facsimile together with his translation of excerpts from *Noa Noa,* by Paul Gaugin, and other pertinent documents concerning the Armory Show, under the title *The Armory Show: International Exhibition of Modern Art* (New York: Arno Press, 1972), 3 vols., with an Introduction by Bernard Karpel. The pamphlet facsimile is in volume three. The first volume reproduces the Catalogues of the New York, Chicago, and Boston exhibitions; the second volume, pamphlets, including Walt Kuhn's translations from *Noa Noa;* and the third volume contains "Contemporary and Retrospective Documents."

Milton Brown's account of the FIRST MEETING comes from *The Story of the Armory show,* 1963, pp. 30–31.

JOHN QUINN'S PURCHASE of *Morning* and *Girl with Red Cap* is mentioned in Reid, *The Man from New York,* 1968, p. 149; and in Brown, *Armory Show,* 1963, p. 258.

Chapter Three : 1913

The Armory Show

In the early months of 1912 Walt Kuhn had to support his family by his comic strips and cartoons, then selling with dependable regularity to *Life* and *Judge*. A large one, *Mr. and Mrs. Barnyard-Fowl Give a Reception,* is possibly his best, with its acute observation of the society ceremonials he was gradually becoming more exposed to, if only through exhibition openings and benefits. The greatest amount of his time, energy, and thought was obviously going to the Association of American Painters and Sculptors.

On 9 January its constitution was adopted and trustees were elected; they were Davies, Borglum, Kuhn, MacRae, J. Mowbray-Clarke, Myers, Henri, and Taylor. One salient feature of the constitution provided that no juries were to select any association exhibitions. This pious resolution was soon to be overlooked in the assembling of the American section for the one exhibition the association ever presented. However, it, like all other pronouncements of the new group, was applauded by the press, thanks to Kuhn's carefully written and placed releases. His news sense and timing were already thoroughly professional, acquired by osmosis, perhaps, from newspaper friends.

That one exhibition, and it was enough to end all other exhibitions, came to be known as the Armory Show, and its story has been told many times.

The two chief sources have been mentioned: Kuhn's own account in a quarto-sized pamphlet of twenty-five pages plus three pages listing the three hundred exhibitors' names, privately printed in 1938 on the twenty-fifth anniversary of the "International Exhibition of Modern Art given under the auspices of the Association of American Painters and Sculptors, Inc.,"as it should correctly if ponderously be called; and Milton W. Brown's comprehensive and authoritative work published on the fiftieth anniversary in 1963. They will be much quoted here in a kind of counterpoint, not necessarily with pages cited, even in the notes.

Brown takes up his story after the 9 January meeting, "Dedicated as it was to exhibition, the Association's first problem was to get a place to show. But this was no simple assignment. After all, the complaint [and excuse] of the Academy had been that New York had no adequate exhibition building for a large show. The earlier Independent show had been a failure partly because of the inadequacy of the loft in which it was presented." The academy was actually trying at that time to have a building of its own put up in Central Park, one of the many such efforts by worthy institutions which, as urban planners like to point out, would in a few years have obliterated the park.

Kuhn goes on:

. . . The old Madison Square Garden was discarded as prohibitive in size and cost. All other places seemed too small or otherwise unattractive. Some of the members mentioned casually about the possible availability of an armory, several of which permitted tennis playing for a fee. With this hint I visited several armories, talked to their respective colonels and finally found after a conversation with Colonel Conley, then commanding officer of the old 69th Regiment, N.G.N.Y. (The Irish Regiment), now the 165th Regiment Infantry, that his armory, Lexington Avenue at 25th Street, would possibly lend itself to our purpose.

In the meantime my friend, John Quinn, who until long after, thought the whole scheme a crazy one and had up to then shown no interest in the new art manifestations, agreed to take over all legal matters. So at last, with borrowed money, the president, vice-president and myself, signed the lease with Colonel Conley, $1,500 down, balance of $4,000 to be paid before the opening of the show on February 17, 1913, the exhibition to continue for one month. Most of the members, knowing that the thing was on its way, and no one aware as to how in the world it was to be accomplished, retired to their various studios and hoped for the best.

"An undertaking of this importance usually calls for underwriters. Some of the better known collectors and art lovers were approached without any marked success. The task seemed more and more hopeless as the weeks passed by." As Brown says, "That was a lot of money and obviously beyond the means of a small group of artists. A good deal of soul-and pocket-searching must have gone on, and one can imagine that the outlook was not very encouraging. But Davies had sources he could go to. He never said who they were, but he made the necessary arrangements and underwrote the venture."

Walt Kuhn resumes:

At this time began my friendship with Arthur B. Davies [this should read "close friendship"; as has been said, they met in April 1910, and Walt continued to see him more and more frequently thereafter], which close association remained over a period of sixteen years until the end of his life. During the spring of 1912 he and I had many conversations debating some sort of program for the projected exhibition. The general opinion expressed by knowing people in New York, showed scant hope of securing any important works from European sources. However all this only helped to provoke in me the desire to go and see for myself. So with a growing familiarity of the subject, due to my talks with Davies (who was thoroughly informed) the picture gradually shaped itself. Later in the midst of a painting trip in Nova Scotia I received from him by mail the catalogue of the "Sonderbund" Exhibition then current in

Cologne, Germany, together with a brief note stating, "I wish we could have a show like this."

In a flash I was decided. I wired him to secure steamer reservations for me; there was just time to catch the boat which would make it possible to reach Cologne before close of the show. Davies saw me off at the dock. His parting words were, "Go ahead, you can do it!"

Considering its epochal results, Arthur B. Davies' note, dated 2 September 1912, is worth quoting for the first time in full: "Dear Kuhn, Everything has been going in the usual skip-and-fetch-it fashion — a long siege over the $10,000 bond has gone through successfully, the leases properly sealed by Assn'n stamps are to be endorsed by Gen'l Dyer today at headquarters. Col. Conley said some of us had better call on the Gen'l and talk of the greatness of art and of our fitness for the work of Atlas! I wish we could have as good a show as the Cologne Sonderbund — I think you would do well to see it before the close on Sept. 30th and talk with that man August Deusser who seems to be the main pipe. You could get a heap out of him for many purposes."

Brown says of Kuhn's first weeks in Europe: "They must have been truly hectic and exciting. . . . It is a pity that we have no personal letters of those days, only the official correspondence with dealers in Holland, Germany and Paris outlining the Armory Show plans, asking for cooperation, arranging for loans, shipping and insurance."

Kuhn's first pertinent personal comment is a postcard of 30 September 1912 to Vera: "Sonderbund great show. Van Gogh and Gauguin great! Cezanne didn't hit me so hard. Am going back again in half "an hour." Another postcard on 2 October tells of his meeting Edvard Munch: . . . about 50, a tall nervous sort of fellow with a handsome head. He paints big wild figure things, very crude but extremely powerful. He and I made friends. . . ."

But concerning the Sonderbund Show itself: it was officially the Internationale Kunstausstellung des Sonderbundes Westdeutsher Kunstfreunde und Künstler, or the "International Art Exhibition of the Federation of West German Art-lovers and Artists," almost as cumbersome a title as the full designation of the Armory Show. In his pamphlet Kuhn says of it, "The Cologne Exhibition, housed in a temporary building had been well conceived and executed, in fact, it became in a measure the model of what we finally did in New York. It contained a grand display of Cézannes and Van Goghs, including also a good representation of the leading living modernists of France. The show had languished through half the summer, much maligned by the citizens, but towards the end burst forth as a great success,with big attendance and many sales."America was not the only country slow to catch on.

"I arrived in the town on the last day of the exhibition. In the midst of all the travail of the closing of the show's business, i could get but scant attention from the management. However through the courtesy of one of its directors I was permitted to browse at will during the time of its slow dismantling. Needless to say, I crammed myself with all the information possible. Van Gogh's work enthralled me as much as any. I met the sculptor Lehmbruck and secured some of his sculpture, also works by Munch, the Norwegian . . . " Brown writes, "But the Munchs in the New York Exhibition were prints which arrived at the last minute."

Brown continues: "The show was a stunner. One can imagine that Kuhn was shaken and excited by the experience. It included an overwhelming collection of 125 works by Van Gogh as the *pièce de résistance*, 26 paintings by Cézanne, 25 by Gauguin, 17 by the Pointillist Cross and 18 by his colleague Signac, 16 by the new artistic meteor Picasso, and 32 by Munch. He also saw some of the leading Fauves and most of the German Expressionists as well as one painting which he probably did not notice by Piet Mondrian. . . . However the conception of the Armory Show was set." Another postcard to Vera says, "It was most important that I saw this show. It has given me a key regarding collecting."

And on 2 October Kuhn wrote in a long letter:

Van Gogh and Gauguin are perfectly clear to me. Cezanne only in part, although they say his exhibit is not evenly good, two or three are perfectly beautiful, a couple of portraits and one or two still lifes, his landscapes are still Greek to me, but wait, I'll understand before I get home. One thing I have discovered, and it will please you — I've been on the right track ever since the second time at Blandford. If I live long enough I will be in the class with the best and it will be me [underscored] personally not a swipe and a copy like the rest of the younger set. After seeing the show I felt like throwing my hat in the air I was so happy. I feel that this trip will act as a purgative and clarify things which would otherwise require years.

It sounds much like the young Correggio making a day's journey to see a famous Rafael and exclaiming, "I too am a great painter!"

2

Kuhn had again arrived in a new country — new to him in the arts — with little money, no credentials, and colossal nerve. He was in almost daily touch with Davies, who would eventually send adequate credentials, and who wrote on 5 October, "Don't forget we want a roomful of Futurists and another of Cubists." The futurists had exhibited in Paris for the first time in February 1912. Brown says: "The Association must have had some original commitment from the Futurists, for they continued to announce their participation. It was later said that the Futurists would not show because they insisted on exhibiting as a group. Since the AAPS had announced that they would be presented in that way, that could hardly have been the reason for their defection. The Futurists may have been committed to a European exhibition during that time. At any rate it was a distinct loss that they were not finally included in the show."

Later in October, Davies wrote: "I am gently milking a millionaire friend and must say I have big hopes for his help with our show — he still insists I am a bigger man than old Cézanne, and I shrink at such possibilities — that being the same old provincial loyalty which has hurt us so long." Mistaken loyalties or not, this still nameless millionaire may have been the show's most important angel, though there were many others equally anonymous.

Milton Brown writes: "The problem was now to collect the works, if not to reproduce the Sonderbund, to duplicate, emulate or rival it. Kuhn visited in rapid succession The Hague, Munich and Berlin. At The Hague he saw for the first time a collection of paintings and pastels by Odilon Redon, who was still little known and not widely appreciated." Kuhn wrote to Vera from Berlin on 8 October that at The Hague he had secured "6 Redons, a big Frenchman, hardly known at home, but he is a wonder, already 72 years old and somewhat like Davies, perhaps a trifle more eccentric. He will make a hit in the show." And Brown continues: "With great enthusiasm he began negotiations with the firm of Artz & deBois to bring a large representation of Redon's art to America. He also arranged with them for a group of Van Goghs. In Berlin he made contact with the dealer Hans Goltz and in Munich with Heinrich Thannhauser, and to a large extent the German contingent eventually exhibited at the Armory Show was limited to the men handled by these dealers. He had printed a circular in German, announcing the exhibition and the conditions of participation, which was distributed to German artists."

From Munich Kuhn wrote to Vera of his confidence in the next five years: "The more I get about the more I feel that New York is the coming place for art and everything else. It's a fine thing that we were in at the start." On 23 October he added: "My forced stay in Germany has had one advantage, I am getting more information regarding all those freak cubists etc. . . . So far as I've gone everything has been O.K. and if I get the promised Van G's and Cezannes from The Hague and Berlin I think I can say that I have had more than a success — I am so very [both words underscored] glad that you have awakened to the tremendous importance of our coming show."

Walt Kuhn's pamphlet tells of his reaching Paris at last:

There I looked up that old-timer Alfred Maurer, who introduced me to the formidable Monsieur Vollard, who although willing to listen remained somewhat noncommittal. My mission abroad had already been noised about and I could detect a slightly rising interest all around me. I next looked up Walter Pach, then resident in Paris, who later furnished inestimable service to our undertaking. To his wide acquaintanceship among French artists and dealers, the advantage of his linguistic abilities and general knowledge of art, should be credited a large measure of our success. He later acted as the European agent for the association and during the exhibition in America, took charge of the sales staff, wrote several of the pamphlets, lectured and otherwise lent great and enthusiastic support to it all.

In a 14 December 1912 letter to Vera from New York, Kuhn writes, "Pach deserves a lot of credit, and I shall see that he gets it." He was true to his word. Brown adds: "Davies and Kuhn, shepherded by Pach, spent a frantic ten days trying to round up the best and most advanced art they could find. Without Pach they certainly could not have accomplished what they did."

To backtrack a little, Brown writes of Kuhn in Paris: "He visited dealers, spread the word about a mammoth American showing of the new art, told each dealer that the others had promised to cooperate, painted a picture of an American market ready to accept the latest word, and must have convinced them all that the AAPS was as solid as the Federal Reserve System. The whole affair began to mushroom beyond his expectations . . . ." Kuhn confirms this: "One night in my hotel the magnitude and importance of the whole thing came over me. I suddenly realized that to attempt to handle it alone, without Davies, would be unfair to the project. I cabled him begging him to join me. He responded and in less than a week he arrived. The first night in the hotel we spent without sleep, going over the newly opened vistas of what we could do for the folks at home. It was very exciting. Then came several weeks of the most intensive canvassing. We practically lived in taxicabs." Davies's speedy arrival would have been a physical impossibility then; actually he sailed on the S.S. *Minnehaha* on 26 October, reaching Paris on 6 November.

Brown picks up the tale of how Pach introduced them to the avantgarde collection of the Steins . . . He took them also to the studio of the Duchamp-Villons where Davies was greatly moved by the work of all three brothers, but especially by that of Marcel Duchamp. "That's the strongest expression I've seen yet!" was his comment.

Their visit to Brancusi was memorable. Davies' admiration for Brancusi was immediate and profound. His statement to Pach — "That's the kind of man I'm giving the show for!" — reveals not only the character of his taste but something of his proprietary relationship to the Armory Show. Before they left he bought the marble *Torse* which was later in the Armory Show . . .

It was also largely through Pach that they added to the French contingent the sculptors, Bourdelle and Archipenko, and the Americans, Patrick Henry Bruce, Morgan Russell and Eli Nadelman. They arranged to show Delaunay and the Cubists, Gleizes, de la Fresnaye, Picabia and Leger. They got to the Fauves, Matisse (through the Steins) and Dufy, well as to the less radical of the younger Frenchmen like Dufrenoy, Friesz, Laurencin and de Segonzac. . . .

Ambroise Vollard . . . offering an important group of Cézannes and Gauguins while making a deal to sell his books and lithographs by Cézanne, Gauguin, Bonnard, Vuillard, Redon, Denis and Renoir . . . Bernheim-Jeune let them have a variety of works: Signac, Toulouse-Lautrec, Bonnard, Vuillard and Matisse, and from Durand-Ruel they obtained a group of Impressionist paintings by Monet, Renoir, Pissarro and Sisley. The largest loan of all came from the Galerie Émile Druet, well over a hundred works, a good collection of Post-Impressionist French painting in itself, including works by the Pointillists, Seurat, Signac and Cross; the three great Post-Impressionist masters, Cézanne, Van Gogh and Gauguin; Toulouse-Lautrec, Valloton and Denis; the Fauves, Matisse, Marquet and Rouault; and a selection of the less radical contemporary young French painters, as well as sculpture and drawings by Maillol . . .

What Davies, Kuhn Pach had accomplished was amazing by any standards, but when we consider the time in which it was done, it seems an unbelievable feat. Davies was in Paris for only a little more than a week, so most of the preliminaries must have been handled by the other two.

Kuhn had written to Vera on 28 October: "He [Davies] just sent me a check for $1000 and seems to be delighted with my work. I have made tremendous progress in my sense of good things and will probably be jumped on for bringing over things which they will at first consider too wild but I have been inspired by the possibilities and am going to be a sport. We will show NY something they never dreamed of. It's great that Davies agrees with me."

All this was important to Walt Kuhn the young compeller of events, but it was far more important to Kuhn the nascent artist. One of his most intimate revelations comes in a letter of 6 November from Paris on the eve of the master's arrival. It is as if he needed to sort out in his own mind the jostling tumult of sensations and put them in order before the maelstrom sucked him in again. It begins with the usual form of address, "Dear Chick," and continues:

We have not been able to judge at home what this thing over here really means. The few imitators we knew could not do justice to it. I will try to sum it up for you in a few words. I have had the germ ever since that second summer in NS — it's nothing else but a development of what I was doing right along "The extraction out of nature [last three words underscored] of the most simple and expressive force" — Specifically varied according to temperament, in other words, no more picture [word underscored] painting which you know had been my watchword long before we heard of this. Today it simply means "absolutely no concession to any public other than the will of the artist."

All this is the watchword of this new movement which is as great an event in art history as the renaissance and it's glorious to be in on it.

As for the cubists: "I sum them up as intensely interesting now that I have had a chance to study them — mostly literary, and lacking in that passion or sex evidence which is absolutely necessary for me. However they have helped me understand Cezanne. He's growing every day with me...but just think what it is for us, and how it has paved the way to properly [word underscored] enjoy a trip to Paris in the comparatively near future, for I think it absolutely necessary to come here at least once every 3 years from now on..."Intellectual" or "cerebral" might be better words than "literary" to define Walt Kuhn's opinion of cubism."

On 11 November he wrote again from Paris, and it is hard to see where he found the time and energy: "Davies is not in the best of health and is going to some famous doctor there [London] beside that there are a few English things to pick up in that town. He also has to see a couple of wealthy people who will come up with the cash for our show . . . Our show is going to be fully as good as the one at Cologne, and that's going some. We already have a better Cezanne and Gauguin collection than Cologne, only in Van G's they beat us. Our run of other material is much better . . . The American annex of course will be a sad affair. Instead of being in any way depressed by seeing such great stuff, I feel great, and have mental material to last several years."

The pamphlet carries on the story: "Then with Davies to London to see Roger Fry's Grafton Gallery show. I could see in the glint of Davies' eye that we had nothing to fear by comparison. Here it might be well to say that Davies' thorough understanding of all the new manifestations was due to one thing only — his complete knowledge of the art of the past. Dikran Kelekian speaks of him as one of the great antiquarians of our time."

Milton Brown describes the Grafton Gallery shows:

The Second Grafton Show, officially the "Second Post-Impressionist Exhibition,"was organized by Roger Fry, the English critic and esthetician [and painter], former curator of painting at the Metropolitan Museum of Art and one of the early proselytizers for modern art. This exhibition, which had opened on October 25 and was due to run until the end of the year, was a sequel to an earlier exhibition also arranged by Fry and shown at the Grafton Galleries from November 8, 1910, to January 15, 1911. The First Grafton Show was officially called "Manet and the Post-Impressionists," a designation formulated by Fry which was used for the first time to describe the French painters who had followed and broke from Impressionism. Fry, a perceptive and knowledgeable connoisseur of art and its contemporary manifestations, had in the first show already grouped together the major figures of the movement two years before the Armory Show. Both Grafton shows were small but well selected. The first was limited to French painting, though not French painters, and covered the sequence from Manet to Cubism. The second did not include any of the older men except Cézanne and added English and Russian sections. Matisse was the major figure of this exhibition with 41 works in paintings, sculpture, watercolor and drawing, plus a group of unlisted lithographs. Second only to Matisse was Picasso, represented by 16 examples . . .

In spite of their reservations about the show they were impressed by some of the works they saw. Vollard's two Cézannes, which they had expected would come to New York, they thought the best things in the show, "head and shoulders over everything else." Matisse made so strong an impression that they ordered Pach to get anything he could. They advised him to ask the Steins to intercede with Matisse to let them have his Grafton exhibits and they urged him to visit Matisse's studio to see whether he would lend others. The Steins were cooperative and so was Matisse. As a result the Armory Show had a really brilliant collection of his work, including the plaster bas-relief of a female nude, *Le Dos,* which Davies and Kuhn had wanted more than anything else. . . .

Among the other requests were that Pach work on Kahnweiler; they were anxious to have strong representations of Braque, Derain and, especially, Picasso. They also gave him instructions about a number of artists, Zak, Chabaud, Girieud, Archipenko and Sousa-Cardoza, and they warned him to get plasters rather than bronzes since it might endanger the insurance agreement they had with Lloyds.

Kuhn wrote to Vera from London on 17 November: "ABD is calling on a wealthy lady. I was to go with him but got out of it for today. . . . Our plans were entirely changed owing to a fine deal we made with the Insurance Co., allowing us to double the quantity of pictures." The earlier ones had already been insured for a total valuation of $200,000.

Brown ends this first phase of the story: "When Davies and Kuhn boarded the *s.s. Celtic* at Liverpool on the 21st they were in a jubilant mood."

The major part of the dream had been accomplished. It was not only the success of their negotiations, but the excitement of the art itself and the expectations of its effect on New York which kept Kuhn, at least, spinning in high. He dashed off a last long letter to Pach, mailed when they put in at Queenstown [Cobh], which was full of elation and instructions. They were sure of success, couldn't wait to get home and get things rolling and, he added, "We vote you a brick of the best cubist make." But a sea voyage cannot be hurried and there was plenty of time to discuss, to plan and to dream. Kuhn's mind teemed with ideas for publicity and publication. They found time to plan a series of pamphlets for the Show and Kuhn translated Gauguin's *Noa-Noa* [excerpts from it], which was published, and a series of Van Gogh letters that he dictated to Davies, which were not. [These were probably the first English translations of the famous letters from Vincent to his brother Theo.] The first phase of the

51

project had been accomplished, but they were already thinking and planning ahead. One can only wonder at the optimism and energy of these men.

3

They landed in New York on 30 November and immediately plunged into the infinite but more prosaic details of readying the exhibition for its 17 February opening. The "orgy of art," as Kuhn described it to Prendergast, was over; but if the European accomplishment is unbelievable, what came next, before and during the run of the show through 15 March 1913, with the diminuendo in Chicago and Boston, is unimaginable for anyone acquainted with the complexities of presenting and promoting a large exhibition, and there have been few as large.

Walt Kuhn wrote to Walter Pach on 12 December:

I should have written you before this but Davies and myself have been on the jump every minute since we landed. Today I gave the papers the list of European stuff which we know of definitely. It will be like a bombshell, the first news since our arrival. You have no idea how eager everybody is about this thing and the tremendous success it's going to be. Everybody is electrified when we quote the names, etc. The outlook is great, and after having figured up the likely income we stand to come out ahead as far as money goes. The articles appearing from now on will increase the desire to help by the moneyed "claasses." We owe you a tremendous lot for your indispensable help and advice, but you know that we are all in the same boat for this great chance to make the American think. I feel as though I had crowded an entire art education into those few weeks. Chicago has officially asked for the show, and of course we accepted. . . . I have planned a press campaign to run from right now through the show and then some. . . .

John Quinn, our lawyer and biggest booster, is strong for plenty of publicity. He says the New Yorkers are worse than rubes and must be told. All this is not to my personal taste, I'd rather stay home and work at my pictures, shoving in some of the things I have learned, but we are still in deep water and have got to paddle . . . our show must be talked about all over the U.S. before the doors open. . . . The ball is on now and there will be lots doing. We have a great opportunity in this show, and must try to make it truly wonderful and get all the people there, which owing to the extremely short duration of the show is very hard, and can only be done through the press. So don't ignore my plea for minor information; it may be undignified but it brings the desired result.

But at the end of the New York showing Kuhn told a reporter, "All the advertising in the world and all the press-agenting will do no good if there is nothing for the public to see when it comes."

On 14 December Kuhn wrote to Vera in Washington:

We have adopted an emblem — Taken from the old pine tree flag of the revolution — I got the idea one morning in bed — Davies made the drawing and we'll have it on stationary, catalogues, posters and everywhere. We are also going to have campaign buttons — here is the design. . . . We are going to get them by the thousands — give them to everybody — from bums to preachers — art students — bartenders — conductors etc. — ought to make an immense hit — and get everybody asking questions. . . . Going to send buttons & posters to Prendergast — Boston, Lamb — Washington, Schamberg — Philadelphia, etc. I have convinced Davies that owing to the short time of the show, one month, we must advertise, may also advertise in the street cars. He's right with me and tickled to death. I'm absolute boss in the office. Will not touch comics unless they're a cinch. Davies keeps me supplied with petty cash, and we can easily stick it over the show. Have only been home one day since you left, except at night. . . . Davies and I will be the only two men known as

From *The Story of the Armory Show*, by Milton W. Brown.

Plate 25. The Armory Show

authorities in America on modern art when the show is over. They all say that D. and I were the lucky combination — pardon my immodesty but you've already said that yourself.

These two letters give a slight taste of Kuhn's manifold activities. There has been some tendency, evident even in Milton Brown, to diminish Walt Kuhn's role in the Armory Show. Kuhn himself was scrupulously fair in giving others credit, and Arthur B. Davies' part cannot be overemphasized; but it is not necessary to underplay Kuhn's performance. Davies was certainly the master strategist, but Kuhn was the field commander, in the thick of every action, overseeing and often directing, the least details. He was even capable of modesty; the last sentence of his pamphlet reads, "Perhaps I was after all, as old Mr. Montross used to call me, just a 'war secretary.'"

Almost on disembarking, Davies and Kuhn rented a small office in the Camera Building, 122 East Twenty-fifth Street, near the Armory, later renting larger quarters in the same building and installing a telephone. Milton Brown outlines some of the preliminary problems:

"As expenses began to mount, Davies again came to the fore with a check for $2500, source unspecified. For the next few months the active members had very little time for anything but the Exhibition. They gave their time, their energy and enthusiasm without remuneration. Only MacRae, who had to handle so many of the financial details and, perhaps because he needed the money, was later paid $500 and Prendergast $40 for expenses in coming to New York to help select the American works and hang the exhibition. Walter Pach, who was hired to act as European representative and later as sales manager, and Frederick James Gregg, a newspaper man who served as public relations representative, both were paid $1200."

A letter from MacRae gives the tone at the time: "Davies, Kuhn, Gregg and myself gave up a whole year — Taylor and Tucker part of this time — A great deal of this was office work, most of us poorly fitted for it — With all this hard work, we had the time of our lives — so many thrills, so much excitement. It was a great privilege for me to work side by side, day by day, with such men. There were anxious moments before the Show opened; we had bitten off a lot financially for artists."

The membership of the association met in the office on 17 December to hear Davies report on the "unqualified success" of the European mission. He then proceeded to appoint an ingeniously planned group of committees that involved all of the twenty-five members. Jerome Myers was made nominal chairman of the General Executive Committee, which included the officers, ex officio, and was obviously in control. William J. Glackens was named chairman of the Committee on Domestic Exhibits, which, as it turned out, would have the meanest diplomatic problems. The purely titular Committee on Foreign Exhibits was chaired by Elmer MacRae. Their work had already been done for them, but protocol was observed. Gutzon Borglum was chairman of the Reception and Publicity Committee, and Walt Kuhn was chairman of the Catalogue and General Printing Committee, though actually he was executive director without portfolio.

Brown goes on: "All sorts of things had to be considered — transformation of the armory into an exhibition gallery; times of opening; admission charge; policing the Show; reception of guests; method of hanging since time was so short; hiring of help for the handling of works as well as people; printing the catalogue, posters, booklets and postcards; advertising; handling the press; and invitations to the opening." It is easy to guess who effectively did, or oversaw, all these things.

Walt Kuhn's pamphlet expands on the theme:

Arrangements were made with contractors to fit out the armory with walls, coverings, booths, tables and seats for the weary. We had nothing but an empty drill floor to start with. Owing to the varied distribution of daylight through the skylights of the armory, we had considerable difficulty in planning the sections or rooms. After lengthy discussion it was George Bellows who hit upon a solution. [His father had been a successful building contractor back in Columbus, Ohio.] Mrs. Whitney donated a thousand dollars for greenery and other decorations. . . . Printing had to be done. The catalogue, in spite of the heartbreaking work of such an efficient man as Allen Tucker, was impossible. Exhibits were admitted even after the opening of the show, all due to the zeal of our president whose one desire was to make a fine exhibition and spare no one. It was a bedlam — but we liked it. The catalogue problem was finally overcome with the aid of a large group of art students wearing badges with the word "information." These young men had to memorize the location of all the works shown and act as guides to the visitors.

A supplement to the catalogue, "containing Additions, Errata and Exhibits catalogued but not received," and an index, was published to solve some of these problems, stating, "The catalogue had to be made while the temporary rooms were going up, and before the pictures were hung." There was no time for illustrations to be made, though the Chicago and Boston catalogues did have a few, and how it got done at all is a cause for wonder. The dummy was given to the printers on Thursday, 13 February, and all fifty thousand catalogues were ready for the opening on Tuesday, 17 February (perhaps not fifty thousand, but enough to open the show). As Milton Brown says, "Printing conditions must have been somewhat different in those days." An order for fifty thousand catalogues sounds like dangerous euphoria; but this was no ordinary exhibition, and they were practically sold out. They are unobtainable today, and Mr. Karpel and the Arno Press must be thanked for republishing them in facsimile.

While Walter Pach in Europe was efficiently handling the myriad details of packing, shipping and insurance (with notice to the lenders that insurance had been placed), nature asserted herself: the S.S. *Mexico*, carrying the first consignment, was due on 6 January, but storms delayed her until 13 January. The S.S. *Chicago* with the balance of the works was also delayed but docked on 13 January. A large stable at 28 East Thirty-second Street was rented to store the arrivals. Several promised things were never sent; and as is the case with all large exhibitions, glaring gaps in the roster began to show up. American collectors were called on, and they reacted generously with few exceptions, notably the "terrible-tempered" Dr. Barnes of Philadelphia, whose first modern paintings had been selected by Glackens; three Manets from Boston were also withheld.

The number of private collectors is surprisingly large though, including John Quinn, who, "along with a mass of English and Irish art, featuring Augustus John, lent works by Cézanne, Van Gogh, Gauguin and a large group by Puvis de Chavannes." Two Cézannes came from Boston; Manet, Redon, and Gauguin from Chicago; Toulouse-Lautrec from Canada. Several dealers, including Durand-Ruel, lent; and others like Stieglitz and Stephan Bourgeois lent as collectors, their works marked not-for-sale. The progenitors of modernism, Goya, Delacroix, Courbet, Corot, Monticelli, and Daumier, came from American owners.

None of the works of living European artists could come in duty-free, so bond had to be posted; and when they were sold, customs fees were duly paid. John Quinn would fight this regulation up to Congress, at his own expense, for years with ultimate success.

American ancestors of modernism were also shown. Brown says of the earlier American section: "It was much smaller and revealed a limited understanding of the American tradition. But since they were looking for equivalents of the modern European developments, it is not strange that they should overlook painters like Homer and Eakins and discover as sources such artists as Whistler, Ryder and the two American Impressionists, Robinson and Twachtman. Albert Pinkham Ryder, long ignored by the public, was an important 'discovery' of the Armory Show and very well represented in it. . . . American collectors had, naturally enough, not provided the core of the exhibition which was intended to revolutionize American taste, but some did provide the stuffing to fill the chinks."

Murmurs of dissent were being heard from living American artists, many of whom felt that the exhibition was being deliberately weighted against them, a most unpatriotic act. Invitations to selected "progressive" artists and notices to aspiring unknowns with instructions as to how to submit their work, with no more than two to be exhibited, had been broadcast in the preceding spring; and the Committee on Domestic Exhibits was laboring manfully, finding at last that it had to act as a jury of selection, and a rather hard-nosed one at that, for all of Glackens's fairness and tact. Naturally, the twenty-five members of the association were well represented — it was their show — and Davies was even criticized for not showing enough of his own work. Brown says: "As a matter of fact, the judgments they made are very close to those of history. Out of the mass of works, they accepted examples by Oscar Bluemner, Maurice Becker, Glenn O. Coleman, Stuart Davis, Andrew Dasburg, Edward Hopper, Bernard Karfiol, Joseph Stella and Margaret [*sic*] and William Zorach. Charles Sheeler submitted five paintings [there are six in the Catalogue], but this seems to have been through error. He was apparently invited to exhibit along with his friend Morton L. Schamberg, and a pencilled comment in the Domestic Committee record book notes, 'taken care of by Kuhn.'"

Subsequently, according to Kuhn's pamphlet, "a special meeting was held on January 22, 1913 with all resident members present, when the following resolution was passed unanimously: 'That the policy expressed by Mr. Davies in the selection of the paintings and sculpture be approved by the members. That improved plan of arrangements as submitted on this date, as well as Mr. Davies' policy regarding the distribution of works be approved.'"

The terseness of the minutes of this meeting suggests that there had been some heated discussion, but everyone was in too deep now to change things.

4

The whole exhibition, all eleven hundred or thirteen hundred works, depending on whose figures are accepted, was hung in five days and ready for the press preview on 16 February. The official debut on the evening of 17 February was as glittering as a Metropolitan Opera "first night." Society was there as well as "the art public." It became the fashionable thing to be seen at the Armory Show or to talk about it as if one had, especially in the mornings when the admission was a dollar instead of the twenty-five cent afternoon fee. Mrs. Astor came every morning right after breakfast. Soon two box offices were in operation.

The press went wild with praise or scorn — mostly scorn; there seemed to be no middle ground. And every newspaper writer became an instant critic or humorist. This was exactly as planned; in the American scheme of things all publicity, whether pro or con, is good, or as Marsden Hartley, one of the pioneer modernists of the Stieglitz commune put it: "Art in America is like a patent medicine, or a vacuum cleaner. It can hope for no success until ninety million people know what it is." Perhaps he should have said not "know what is it" but "have heard about it."

Kuhn's pamphlet records the inevitable let down:

Now came a surprise. The press was friendly and willing. Sides were taken for or against, which was good, but in spite of this the public did not arrive. For two weeks there was a dribbling attendance. Expenses went on, a big staff of guards, salesgirls, etc., had to be supported. The deficit grew steadily, when suddenly on the second Saturday the storm broke. From then on the attendance mounted and controversy raged. Old friends argued and separated, never to speak again. Indignation meetings were going on in all the clubs. Academic painters came every day and left regularly, spitting fire and brimstone — but they came — everybody came. . . . Henry McBride was in his glory and valiantly held high the torch of free speech in the plastic arts. . . . Enrico Caruso came, he did not sing, but had his fun making caricatures . . . Students, teachers, brain specialists — the exquisite, the vulgar, from all walks of life they came. "Overnight" experts expounded on the theories of the "abstract versus the concrete." Cézanne was explained in nine different ways or more. The then cryptic words, "significant form," were in the air. Brancusi both baffled and delighted. Matisse shocked, made enemies on one day, developed ardent fans the next. People came in limousines, some in wheelchairs, to be refreshed by the excitement. Even a blind man was discovered, who limited to the sculptures, nevertheless "saw" by the touch of his fingers. Actors, musicians, butlers and shopgirls, all joined in the pandemonium. . . .

On March fourth, the day of Wilson's inauguration, I had the pleasure of escorting the former president, Theodore Roosevelt, through the rooms of the exhibition. Perhaps the Ex-president felt that the Armory Show would be the right kind of counter-irritant to what was just then going on in Washington. If he did, he never showed it, for he was most gracious, though noncommittal. Later in the "Outlook" he discussed the show more freely.

Roosevelt was baffled by most of what he saw, angered by some, but came out strongly in favor of freedom of expression, trusting that the basic sanity of the American people would save them in the end.

Years later Kuhn described Albert Pinkham Ryder's visit, on the arm of Arthur B. Davies. He was long-haired and long-bearded, wearing copper-toed shoes and a Prince Albert coat green with age and with a louse on its collar. His hands were folded gently in front of him, and he beamed beatifically at his own paintings (there were ten of them), some of which he had not seen in years, and left.

The box office receipts indicate that well over seventy

thousand people came, but this does not reckon the thousands of free passes liberally scattered, especially to art students. Estimates of the total vary, but the exact figure cannot be determined. It was less important in some ways than the sales. Not only were the European loans predicated on them, but conviction expressed in hard cash speaks far more loudly than words. Walt Kuhn writes: "One day I lunched with John Quinn at the old Hoffman house. He had begun to enjoy the fight, but he would not buy. I urged and urged, finally I won him over. His purchase of between five and six thousand dollars [actually $5,808.75] reached the ears of Arthur Jerome Eddy, famous in Chicago I was told, for having been the first Chicagoan to ride a bicycle and later the first man there to own an automobile. Eddy bought some of the most radical works in our show." Curiously, several of Quinn's purchases were made in Chicago, where he had followed the show, and Eddy bought chiefly in New York, very little in Chicago. "Others followed suit. Rivalry between the collectors grew. Bryson Burroughs made history — through his efforts the Metropolitan bought a Cézanne, the first ever to be owned by an American Museum."

Kuhn ends the New York chapter of the story: "On the show's last night we paraded with regimental fife and drum, led by the giant, Putnam Brinley, wearing a bear-skin hat and twirling a drum major's baton. Through each of the rooms of the exhibition we marched and saluted our confreres past and present. The work of dismantling began at once and lasted until morning. I spent the night with the workmen. At ten o'clock on St. Patrick's Day the regimental band marched on to the empty floor and saluted our closing with the tune of 'Garry Owen'."

The Art Institute in Chicago wanted only the European section and the works of the association's twenty-five members. In only eight days they moved from wall to wall, another near-miracle. As Kuhn says, "Aided by a thoroughly trained staff we were able to hang the entire show in one day!" Gregg had gone ahead to set up the publicity campaign, and Arthur B. Davies did not go to Chicago; so Walt Kuhn and Walter Pach were in charge. It is said that Davies had planned the hanging down to the last detail of watercolor sketches of the paintings on the walls.

There was a different atmosphere in Chicago, possibly the result of a midwestern attitude of "you've got to show me" regardless of what had happened in New York. The Art Institute's administration was cordial if somewhat apprehensive, and the institute's art school almost delicately hostile. The story persists of how the students, with the urging of their conservative teachers, planned to burn Matisse and Brancusi in effigy. Actually, Elmer MacRae was able to prevent it; and Walt Kuhn managed to keep the teachers from bringing their classes into the galleries to denounce the decadent, anarchistic new styles. There is another story told of the Illinois farmer who demanded his admission money back beacause he could not find the nude in Marcel

Duchamp's *Nude Descending a Staircase*. There were quite a few local champions, however, such as Harriet Monroe, founder of the magazine *Poetry* and a central figure in the Chicago literary renaissance.

Brown concludes: "In some ways the Chicago Exhibition was a disappointment to the Association financially and in terms of artistic impact, but there was no denying the public excitement it had aroused. It had been a publicity success, perhaps for the wrong reasons, but attendance figures of close to 200,000 were some solace for a failure to communicate the message of modern art."

The Boston showing, sponsored by the Copley Society in Copley Hall, was an anticlimax. There was little furor in the press or among the public and fewer sales. As Milton Brown writes: "Kuhn's zeal could do nothing to counteract the obvious inertia which was beginning to stall the caravan. And in the end even he was willing to bow to the inevitable. There were many requests for the Exhibition, in whole or in part, from St. Louis, Milwaukee, Kansas City, Baltimore, Washington, and even Toronto, but the decision was made not to dissipate the impact of the Exhibition by dribbles. As Kuhn announced in a letter to Gregg, 'Nothing doing! We'll chop it off with Boston,' and so they did. The Show ended rather too quietly considering the excitement at its birth."

5

After such a triumph, unprecedented and unequaled since, it may seem petty to point out the Armory Show's few weaknesses. Through no fault of the association the futurists were absent, though Marcel Duchamp's "dynamism," a favorite catchword of the futurists, might qualify him as one of them. It did distinguish him from the more static classic cubists. The German expressionists were sparsely represented by Kandinsky and Kirchner and the mildly post-impressionist Max Slevogt.

Also, there has been a revisionist attitude toward the show in the last few years. Edgar P. Richardson speaks for it:

The Armory Show has become something of a Sacred Cow in the public mind, which is under the impression that it created modern painting in America. On the contrary, it is important to emphasize that the artists who were to emerge as the strong, original figures of this movement in America were on their way before the Armory Show.

What the Armory Show created was an enormous interest in the Post-Impressionist artists of France. It gave a new direction and fresh impetus to the enthusiastic collecting of French painting. The ferment aroused may have been stimulating also to the general public interest in painting. It produced a certain amount of Neo-Fauve, Neo-Cubist, and Neo-Primitive painting, which, being wholly derivative, is already forgotten.

But the important American painters of the movement had to wait another decade for recognition. In the years between the close of the 1914 war and the great depression, reinforced by some able recruits from a still younger generation, they won recognition and gave a new shape to the imaginative life in the United States.

From the vantage of *Twenty-Five Years After*, at the end of Walt Kuhn's pamphlet, he reflects:

In the course of years, since that wild time in 1913, my feelings have turned first hot, and then cold, as to what the whole thing has really meant to us Americans. How did we benefit, if at all?

The late President Coolidge once said, "America's business is business." Therein lies the answer. We naive artists, we wanted to see what was going on in the world of art, and we wanted to open up the mind of the public to the need of art. Did we do it? We did more than that. The Armory Show affected the entire culture of America. Business caught on immediately, even if the artists did not at once do so. The outer appearance of industry absorbed the lesson like a sponge. Drabness, awkwardness began to disappear from American life, and color and grace stepped in. Industry certainly took notice. The decorative elements of Matisse and the Cubists were immediately taken on as models for the creation of a brighter, more lively America. The decorative side of Brancusi went into everything from milliners' dummies to streamline trains. The exhibition affected every phase of American life — the apparel of men and women, the stage, automobiles, advertising and printing in its various departments, plumbing, hardware — everything from the modernistic designs of gas pumps and added color of beach umbrellas and bathing suits, down to the merchandise of the dime store.

In spite of the admittedly first class pieces of "fine art" in the Armory Show, the thing that "took" was the element of decoration. American business, perhaps unconsciously, absorbed this needed quality and reached with it, into every home and industry and pastime.

In the late thirties and early forties Kuhn did not trade on his tremendous accomplishment. He felt that his own painting was more important, and having committed his story to print in 1938, he did not think much more needed to be said. Reminiscences had to be urged out of him, and often took the form of comments on his changed opinions of the great figures. He thought less and less of Gauguin, found that Van Gogh lacked plastic organization, though he did not use the phrase; instead he said that Van Gogh was too often "not in tone," with a few notable exceptions like *L'Arlesiénne*, "slashed on in an hour, background pale citron," according to Van Gogh. Lehmbruck seemed feebler and feebler, just erotic reverie. He told how he and Davies expected Marcel Duchamp's *King and Queen Surrounded by Swift Nudes* to be the big public sensation instead of the *Nude Descending a Staircase*. He had little use for any of the English artists; perhaps he never had. Once he commented on committee members who shirked their jobs and then showed up at the opening "in yellow gloves — the Committee!" One thing he always said of the Armory Show to museum people, dealers, and critics, with complete justice: "And the artists did it all themselves!"

NOTES TO CHAPTER THREE

All of the direct quotations from Milton Brown concerning the DAVIES-KUHN EXPEDITION come from the second chapter of *Armory Show*, 1963, with the exception of the FUTURISTS' OMISSION, which comes from Chapter Three. Although quotations are liberally and gratefully lifted from the first three chapters, only Chapter Twelve out of the remaining eleven chapters is called on.

Kuhn's remark about John Quinn's having then "SHOWN NO INTEREST IN THE NEW MANIFESTATIONS" should be interpreted to mean the living modern innovators. Quinn already owned works by Cézanne, Van Gogh, and Gauguin.

Milton Brown understandably deplores the absence of PERSONAL COMMENTS ON THE ASSEMBLING OF THE ARMORY SHOW. In 1963, the very year his book was published, Brenda Kuhn deposited all her father's personal papers, including many letters from 1912 and 1913, as well as several from Arthur B. Davies, in the Archives of American art. Brown would have made skillful use of them.

ARTHUR B. DAVIES'S 2 SEPTEMBER 1912 LETTER is in the Kuhn personal files in the Archives.

DAVIES'S REMARK ABOUT THE FUTURISTS AND CUBISTS comes from Walt Kuhn's personal papers in the Archives, as does his letter about the MILLIONAIRE FRIEND.

KUHN'S LETTER TO PACH of 2 December is in the Archives of the Armory Show, Brown, *Armory Show*, 1963, pp.55-56.

THE QUOTATION FROM ELMER MACRAE comes from Brown, *Armory Show*, 1963, p. 59.

THE QUOTATION FROM MARSDEN HARTLEY can be found in his *Adventures in the Arts* (New York: Boni and Liveright, 1921), p. 60.

The METROPOLITAN CÉZANNE was the *Colline des Pauvres* or *The Porhouse on the Hill*, price at $8,000 and bought on 16 March 1913 for $6,700.

Richardson's SACRED COW remark comes from his *Painting in America* (New York: Thomas Y. Crowell, 1956), p. 307.

Van Gogh's L'ARLÉSIENNE is number 488 in the 1970 edition of De La Faille, Reynal & Company, New York.

The METROPOLITAN CÉZANNE was the *Colline des Pauvres* or *The Porhouse on the Hill*, price at $8,000 and bought on 16 March 1913 for $6,700.

Richardson's SACRED COW remark comes from his *Painting in America* (New York: Thomas Y. Crowell, 1956), p. 307.

Van Gogh's L'ARLÉSIENNE is number 488 in the 1970 edition of De La Faille, Reynal & Company, New York.

Since their names are not readily available, there might be merit in listing the names of the "300 EXHIBITORS" with whom Walt ends his pamphlet (see Appendix, page 278). It could be an amusing parlor game for a group of museum people or art historians, especially those concerned with American art, to see how many of the three hundred can be identified with a specific painting or sculpture, or, if honesty is strictly enforced, to see how many can even be recognized. The writer refuses to divulge his own score.

Aftermath Years

It took about a year to wrap up the details of the Armory Show. While Arthur B. Davies stayed on in New York in the summer of 1913 tying up many of the loose ends, and getting to an occasional baseball game, Walt Kuhn went to Ogunquit in July for a desperately needed interlude of rest and reflection. On 17 July he wrote to Vera, who had gone to Washington again to be with her family in Chevy Chase: "I am gradually gathering the torn ends of my disorganized brain. Am very curious to see what results I get from my first attempts at work. Isn't it all intensely interesting? If I could only make you more ·contented all would be well. However that too will be remedied."

Again, on 20 July, he wrote: "You are perfectly right when you said that you were the only pal — now don't get cocky about it — but how did you guess it? . . . As I have already hinted to you I think, I have hit upon a new and entirely fresh way of working. It's just a matter of stick to it — and ought to be a big success."

He was too restless or remote from the creative storm center to stay away very long and was back in Fort Lee by 25 July, when he wrote to Vera: "Had another fine visit to the Museum [Metropolitan]. Am just beginning to get at the real value and beauty of the Egyptians. Just to think that such was created thousands of years ago. They certainly have a fine collection — I am getting so that I can discriminate between the really fine things and the more or less indifferent. It's remarkable, but after all the right thing that I should just begin to appreciate the old boys." The next day he wrote: ". . . I went up to the Museum of Natural History (not the art museum). Had a perfectly glorious time with the Indian (Alaskan and otherwise) carvings. The carvings of the aborigines seem to be related pretty much the world over. There were any quantity of things which might have been the models for Gauguin's designing.

. . . Heard from Quinn today, will see him Monday. He was tickled to hear from me again. He's a good sport all right."

After his total immersion in the most-advanced contemporary styles, and perhaps on account of it, it is a healthy sign that Kuhn, partly under Davies' tutelage, was looking freshly at the Egyptians and the newly discovered but misnamed "primitive" arts. One of the most striking and fruitful artistic phenomena of his time was the sudden awakening to the aesthetic importance of African, Polynesian, and American Indian art. It happened simultaneously in both Paris and Dresden about 1908 when revolutionary young moderns stumbled on a whole new language of form and design and promptly put it to use, as members of *Die Brücke,* "The Bridge" group, in Dresden, or as fauves and cubists in Paris.

The anthropologists were completely baffled at first, and are still somewhat bewildered at seeing their ethnological artifacts turn into works of fine art. It was a last-minute rescue at the very moment when political and economic empire was pushing these brilliantly creative cultures to the brink of extinction. In fact, it may have been too late. But it also opened eyes on Pre-Columbian, Archaic Greek, early Christian, early Near and Far Eastern art, vastly enriching the twentieth century, this time to the bewilderment of the classical establishment.

On 31 July 1913 Kuhn wrote to Vera again about his own personal and artistic problems: "Quinn, I think, understands that I want to be left alone for a while, although he calls me up about every two or three days, just to have a chat. The right kind of independence is not offensive to any man who thinks." A telephone had been installed at the Fort Lee house, which kept Vera from feeling too isolated when she was there. During the whole of the Armory Show Kuhn could not have gotten home very often. He goes on: "In about a week I expect to have Gregg out here to pose for me. I have come to the conclusion that I must have a lot of things underway just like the comics. They must overlap so that there is always something to work on without having to face a barren studio. Have made up my mind not to rush things, one really good thing is worth any number of indifferent. I feel very confident as to the future. . . . Glad to hear that Brenda is progressing so well, it will make it easier for both of us." Then he took off with John Quinn to Wawbeek, near Saranac.

The Association of American Painters and Sculptors was a little longer in passing away. A directors' meeting was held on 12 November 1913 with an incomplete treasurer's report; the Boston returns were not in yet. There was general, and probably exhausted, agreement that there should not be another exhibition in the coming season. The directors did not meet again till 29 April 1914, followed by a last complete membership meeting on 18 May. It seemed then that the Armory Show might have made a profit of about $3,000, but the final accounting after a payment of $2,894.35 to the U.S. Customs Office in August 1916, showed income of $93,025.59 and expenses of $93,086.19.

63

The $60.60 deficit was presumably taken care of by Davies. The show was a sizeable operation, and the fact that the association came out almost unscathed was the last but not the least in the long series of miracles.

A real schism had begun to split the association. Henri, Bellows, Mahonri Young, and Jerome Myers were on the side of those who felt that American art had been sold down the river. And it cannot be denied, even without written evidence, that Davies and Kuhn had both foreseen this result. The Henri faction charged that the American artist had been turned back into a "colonial." Davies, Glackens, and Kuhn felt, very much the contrary, that the American artist had been pushed into the world stream, and that it was up to him to sink or swim. In any case Davies wanted no further responsibility; he had never been a joiner, and the younger Kuhn, who remained a member of various somewhat formless organizations for a few years, finally saw the light. When it was quoted to him much later, he heartily endorsed Georges Bernanos's statement in *Lettre aux Anglais* that "the principle of your resistance lies, not in your stomach or your muscles, but in your nerves, as with wild animals, women and artists." Hence none of the three should organize.

In February 1914 Walt Kuhn had a show of paintings and drawings at the Montross Gallery, one of the few that before 1913 had shown a live interest in "progressive" American art. Little is known of what was exhibited or sold, though John Quinn paid $1,925 to Montross that month for paintings by Kuhn, Davies, Prendergast, and the curiously named George F. Of. Probably several of Kuhn's 1912 works were there and possibly a few experiments from the fall of 1913. He spent the summer of 1914 in Grand Manan, New Brunswick, and the fall in Ogunquit with Vera and Brenda. On 30 August from Ogunquit Kuhn wired Quinn a "War Bulletin": "It is reported the Germans have taken Peruna, — Lydia Pinkham."

Only two paintings can be confidently assigned to 1914, and one of them, *Polo Game* (number 21), is his first fully postimpressionist arrival. The first record of its exhibition in New York, though it might well have hung along with works by Davies and Jules Pascin at the Macbeth Gallery in the spring of 1916, is the Maynard Walker Gallery showing of "Early Works by Walt Kuhn" in April and May of 1966. John Canaday, in the *New York Times*, called the exhibition "a careful selection of early works by this American painter who died in 1949, drawn from his estate. Kuhn often had trouble deciding just which of several artists he most admired, and his various decisions en route are reflected in some of these pictures. But he was always a strong painter never afraid to declare his loyalties. Filled with collector's items, this exhibition is also something of a document in American painting during its transition from provincialism to internationalism under the impact of the Armory Show." John Gruen, in the *Herald Tribune*, mentioned *Polo*

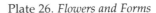

Plate 26. *Flowers and Forms*

Game specifically: "There are fascinating stylistic struggles to be observed in such works as 'Tea' (1923) in which the artist's wife with a lady friend [Brenda] are painted in a mixture of cubism and German Expressionism, or the 1914 'Polo Game' which combines pure impressionism with post-impressionism."

There is very little impressionism or cubism in *Polo Game* and quite a bit of Raoul Dufy. There were two oils by Dufy in the Armory Show, both dating from his best fauve period of 1909, and Kuhn may have seen many more in Paris. With its horizontal bands and a frieze of fluttering flags instead of sunrise in the background, it is a logical successor to *Morning* of 1912. The horses and riders are boldly, clearly drawn, the audience a Prendergast tapestry of color with a few sharply contoured parasols as accents. It is both animated and decorative, the decorative quality being one that Kuhn came increasingly to distrust in himself and not approve of in others.

65

In July 1914, Quinn bought *The Cyclist* and *White Tights* for two hundred and fifty dollars. Neither of them was in the Quinn sale, and there is no record of them other than Reid's statement taken from the Quinn letters. Possibly they were watercolors; the price would be right. Reid goes on to say, "Quinn was pretty willing to take anything Kuhn offered him, out of friendship as well as confidence in his art. But his eyes were really turned abroad." Nor has the rest of 1914 and early 1915 left any records; it must have been a period of bread-earning cartoons and comic strips together with serious painting experiments, Serious enough in 1915 to produce the largest year's output to date. Eight survivors and one victim can reasonably be assigned to that year.

In April 1915 Quinn bought from Montross paintings by Walt Kuhn, Davies, Charles Prendergast (Maurice's devoted, frame-making younger brother), Morton Schamberg, and Charles Sheeler of Philadelphia, all of them except Charles Prendergast veterans of the Armory Show. He paid $2,805 for the package; and again in June, Quinn paid Montross $3,500 for two paintings by Maurice Prendergast, one by Davies, and one by Kuhn. These were fair prices at that time, and probably financed another summer in Ogunquit with Vera and Brenda.

One of the 1915 paintings was not only Kuhn's largest, seven feet high by ten feet wide, but part of an unusual collaboration. Arthur B. Davies had felt that something should be done about the sorry state of mural painting in America, and asked Maurice Prendergast and Walt Kuhn to contribute to a mural series for the Daniel Gallery, founded in 1913 by an eccentric former cafe proprietor whose chief monument is the Ferdinand Howald Collection in the Columbus Gallery of Fine Arts. Howald would buy from no one but Charles Daniel from 1916 on, and even Stieglitz, to his great mortification, was forced to send the twenty-eight John Marins, twenty-eight Charles Demuths, seventeen Marsden Hartleys, and two Arthur G. Doves, among others, to Daniel for sale to Howald. Kuhn's canvas was *Man and Sea Beach* (number 26). It may have been one of those bought from Montross by Quinn, who lent it to the Panama-Pacific International Exposition of 1915 in San Francisco. A small tempera on gesso panel version known as *Beach* (number 27), in the Quinn Sale Catalogue, is possibly a sketch for it. Like *Polo Game*, it too has strong recollections of Dufy with its bold simply drawn figures against an almost uniformly pale background.

Bathers on Beach (number 22) is another matter, a distinct stride forward from *Polo Game*. Kuhn may have made cut-out colored paper silhouettes for the flat figures, beach umbrellas, sails, and flags, moving them around until he found a satisfactory composition. It was a device he used in *The Battle of New Orleans* of 1921 (number 89) and wrote about in detail. For the flat horizontal bands of dark blue sea and light almost blue-green sky, all with no evident brushmarks, he might have followed a method he had learned in Paris that Henri Rousseau used, of blotting the area with damp newspaper to achieve a mat effect. Dufy may still linger in *Bathers on Beach*, but only in the subject and pattern; Dufy rarely made as positive a plastic statement.

In a smaller canvas of 1915, *Flowers and Forms* (number 23), Walt Kuhn finally came to grips with cubism. It has suggestions of Gleizes and rather more of Braque. All of this was experimenting in depth. After ingestion comes digestion, and three years had passed since Kuhn had first seen the "freak" cubists in Germany, and had come to respect them in Paris, if only as stepping-stones back to Cézanne. As he had said in his letter to Vera from Paris, cubism was definitely not for him, but he had had to find out at first hand.

Youth (number 30) is in many ways the most arresting painting of 1915, with its predictions of Kuhn's mature style. It is his first life-size standing figure, a show girl in white tights and slashed trunks with bent knee, one hand on her thigh, the other touching a shoulder strap, head slightly turned to her right, posed against a vertically fluted curtain. Some see Derain's influence in it; others find echoes of German expressionism. Whatever its sources, it forecasts Kuhn's future, his and his alone.

In 1919 *Babe* (number 72), later destroyed by the artist, would follow more purposefully in the same direction, which makes its destruction hard to understand. And again in 1919 *The City* (number 74) would set the markers for the parade. Calliope or band music could be heard far off, and LaSalle Spier came up with an apt subtitle, "Symphony for full orchestra."

Most of the 1915 crop must have been exhibited at the Macbeth Gallery from 22 March to 4 April 1916, though only one, named *Hunt* (number 24), can be so identified. It was in a three-man show with Arthur B. Davies and Jules Pascin. Pascin, who had shown thirteen watercolors and drawings in the Armory Show, was the most international figure in the international School of Paris. He was born Julius Pincas in Vidn, Bulgaria, in 1885, of mixed Jewish, Greek, and Serbian parentage, studied art in Vienna and Munich, moved to Paris in 1905, rearranging his name into something more French-sounding, spent the war years in New York, also painting in Charleston, South Carolina, New Orleans, and Havana, and became an American citizen. He went back to Paris as soon as possible and committed suicide there in 1930. The story goes that he had mistaken the opening date of one of his exhibitions, came a day early to find no one there, and went home to kill himself.

Walt Kuhn knew him well, and had introduced him to the periphery of John Quinn's circle. He said that he could have talked Pascin out of the suicide if he had been there, having seen him through several emotional crises in New York. Kuhn admired him as a born draughtsman who drew constantly, even on a sketch pad in his coat pocket at cafe tables. Whether or not he continued to draw in the erotic settings of his favorite subject matter is anyone's guess. Murdock Pem-

Plate 27. *Nude.* Wood Carving

Courtesy of Kennedy Galleries, Inc.—Kuhn Estate

berton remarked in the *New Yorker* that Pascin's models seemed to get younger each year and that he wished the artist would learn the age of consent. Pascin's sensitive, nervous drawings considerably influenced Walt Kuhn's much stronger style.

Only one extant painting comes from 1916, and that a major one. *Tragic Comedians* (number 31) is now in the Hirshhorn Museum and Sculpture Garden in Washington. Joseph Hirshhorn bought it in 1958 or thereabouts from the Maynard Walker Gallery in his characteristic fashion. Aline Saarinen quotes a friend of Hirshhorn's: "Joe rushed in and bought five Walt Kuhn's, he says, 'In half an hour that dealer's life had changed: he was developing a tic.'" *Tragic Comedians* shows two life-size figures, both in stage costume. The woman looks off to her right, and the man stares straight ahead with his whitened face and skull cap. The drawing is perhaps self-consciously stylized, but the woman's bare left arm is as massively, solidly painted as anything in his later work. The fauve Derain has often been suggested as the inspiration, and there are some resemblances to German expressionism, but not to any single artist; echoes possibly of Kirchner or Max Beckman, whom Kuhn may have seen in Berlin, where he was one of the most rebellious of the Berlin Secessionists. In essence it is pure Walt Kuhn. It was shown at the Montross Gallery in February 1917 in a "Special Exhibition: Arthur B. Davies, Walt Kuhn, Jules Pascin, Charles Sheeler, Max Weber."

Max Weber was one of the first Americans to come in close contact with the new developments in Paris. He studied under Matisse in 1908–9, the one year of Matisse's formal teaching, and came back a thorough convert, alternating between the fauves and the cubists in his own painting. He withdrew his canvases from the Armory Show in a pique because he thought that lesser and undeserving artists, most of them members of the association, had been given more space. But apparently he did not mind the present company in 1917.

Frederick James Gregg reviewed the exhibition in the April 1917 issue of *Vanity Fair*; and in the "little magazine" *Rainbow*, in December 1920, he ended his article, titled "A Spiritual Adventure with Walt Kuhn," with these words:

> His self-expression is as sincere as his critical judgment. Both are based on his profound understanding of art. He has intelligence and intellectuality. Not many are endowed with both.
>
> He belongs to the company of the tragic comedians. There are few of them in our country, where contentment with God's world and satisfaction with God's heaven — which of course we shall all enjoy in time — is not only instinctive but a duty.
>
> If, however, he wears a mask as an artist; if behind the mask is a face that is not a smiling one, he is not likely to spoil the party by taking off the disguise at the wrong time, or in the wrong company.

Horace Brodzky was one of the editors of *Rainbow*, and Gregg's article had appeared in Volume 1, Number 3, with "Sixteen reproductions from the work of Walt Kuhn [including *The City, Youth, Babe,* and *Tragic Comedians.*] Page decorations by the same Artist."

Kuhn's page decorations are less art nouveau than art deco, the unfortunate but serviceable name for the style that came on stage in the Paris Exposition of Decorative Arts in 1925. Its architectural ornament was applied all over the Western world and examples are now being preserved as historic monuments.

2

There are no paintings from 1917. Kuhn wrote to Vera in 1916: "The way it looks now I will paint no more oils but keep on sculpting and then make a bunch of watercolors. . . . Have decided not to show any etchings till next fall." And again: "This is the first of five etchings made this week. It is so good." He had begun to make prints in 1915, etchings and lithographs, and turned them out steadily till 1927, when he seems to have dropped them completely. There are about a hundred of them known today, and they absorbed thousands of his drawings. John Quinn bought nineteen etchings for $125 in January 1917. In 1935 Kuhn noted that he had made "a gift of prints to the New York Public Library — 32 etchings and lithographs executed during the period 1915 to 1925." In many ways they are more advanced than his paintings of the same years, fully as vital, but more mature, with greater ease and distinction. It is one of the mysteries that after 1935 he never spoke of his prints, almost as if he wanted them forgotten. This may have been because he thought they had been scattered too widely, as his early paintings had been, and he could not regain control of them, possibly to destroy some of them.

Another event of 1916 was of no great artistic consequence but one of his greatest personal pleasures, the founding of the Penguin Club. Kuhn had quarreled with members of the Kit Kat Club, a conservative if not stuffy lot for the most part, and gathered a group of young artists to rent rooms on one floor of an old brownstone at 8 East Fifteenth Street. Reid writes of "the rather drab quarters . . . a newly established rendezvous of the group of artists centering around Kuhn." Louis Bouché was one of them. Now a victim of temporary neglect, he had wit and grace as artist and person both. His unpublished memoirs say: "Walt Kuhn organized and ran the Penguin Club, and it could not have existed without him. He was probably the most secretive man I have ever known and told us Penguins nothing. But everything ran smoothly. There were no dues, and we had a lot of fun. Our locale in East 15th Street was very modest, only a parlor floor in a house that had once been a private brownstone. The large front room was used for exhibitions, and the back one for our weekly sketch class. The yearly rent, light, etc. was provided by an annual Penguin Ball sponsored by ourselves."

Louis Bouché adds a thumbnail portrait: "As a matter of fact, Kuhn had enemies and was not liked by many in the art world. Jealousy may have been the reason. He was also very secretive and insisted on being the lone wolf. He was 'pally' with those he trusted and many of the younger artists. He had devoted followers like myself. I did not pry into his secrets and lapped up what he taught me. No one ever taught me more about art. I always felt he was a greater critic than an artist. Kuhn was a fascinating man. It is small wonder that he charmed so many women. . . ."

It was in that large front room that John Quinn, who had helped furnish it, found a home for the "Vorticist" exhibition Ezra Pound had arranged in London and sent to New York. Kuhn had helped unpack it and was "unimpressed." Montross had refused to show it, thereby alienating one of his more profitable clients, so the Penguins took it in.

Alexander Brook, Edward Hopper, and Guy Pène du Bois, the painter-critic, were members of the club, and Max Weber and Joseph Stella collaborated on a twenty-by-forty-foot patriotic poster display the Penguins set up on lower Fifth Avenue. A young women's auxiliary called "Penguinettes" was formed to help with the annual balls, for which Kuhn was sole producer, designer, director, and author of vaudeville turns. Nothing delighted him more, and he reminisced about them much oftener than about any other activities or serious enterprises of those years.

In 1916 Walt Kuhn moved his family to an apartment on West 129th Street, not far from the ferry to Fort Lee, where he kept his studio. And that summer he spent several weekends at John Quinn's summer place, the old home of the Westchester Hunt Club, which he ironically renamed "Purchase Street." Kuhn and Quinn labored one whole Sunday laying out a rock garden, "a la Cézanne" as Kuhn called it.

The summer of 1917 Kuhn spent with his family at Indian Lake in the Adirondacks, and late that fall moved again to an apartment on West Twenty-second Street. 1918 was a good painting year with ten recorded canvases. Four of them stand out, a good percentage for any artist. *Caucus* (number 63) is a large painting, over five feet high and over six feet wide, showing two women seated at a table and one woman standing by it. They have their hair down and are generally dishabille. The table top is tilted artificially toward the observer to make a larger plane, and the sharply linear women's features are typical of his early works, as is the dark opaque color. *Caucus* seems as good a title as any. It was one of John Quinn's two purchases in 1919; he paid $1,125 for it and the same amount for *Harlequin* (number 68). As far as can be judged from photographs of the whole figure, *Harlequin* seems to be a complete success, a landmark as important as *The City* (number 74). But something about it dissatisfied the artist; in 1944 he marked where he had decided to cut it off, and about 1950 Vera and Brenda did so, reducing it from eight feet high by three feet wide to three feet, three inches high by two feet, two inches wide. Originally the full-length figure with beret, ruff collar and domino mask, the belted leotard "all checky" with lozenges, as the heralds would say, leaned slightly against a drapery-covered bench or ledge, his hands clasped between his legs. It could almost be a self-portrait both in face and figure; perhaps it was.

    Man with Ship Model (number 69) was one of the artist's favorite early paintings, reproduced as often as he could manage. It unmistakably recalls Manet's *Portrait of Zola* of 1868, with the sails of the ship model substituting for Japanese prints and a photograph of *Olympia* in the background. Kuhn may have thought it his private proof not that he had mastered the master but that he had penetrated his world. Not everyone would agree, but it is a rich composition. On the other

Plate 28. *Man with Ship Model*

71

hand, *Flower Still Life* (number 66) "is as charmingly sophisticated as any Fauve painting on either side of the Atlantic." There is nothing hesitant, tentative, or derivative about it; and his later essays on the same subject, though bolder and with any hint of charm deliberately shut out, will not surpass it.

Plate 29 (opposite). *John Butler Yeats*

3

Thirteen paintings were produced in 1919, three of them later destroyed. Two are of special interest: *The City* (number 74) and the portrait of *John B. Yeats* (number 83). *The City* waited till 1927 for its formal New York debut, but it had been shown before then at the Pennsylvania Academy of the Fine Arts in Philadelphia and by the Arts Club in the Art Institute of Chicago, and must have been fairly well known in New York since it caused an immediate flurry of attack and defense. Gregg spent most of his *Rainbow* article defending it, while others, denouncing it as downright ugly, said that it was in questionable taste to symbolize the city as an overblown backstage floozy, which is exactly what she is, and by intention. There is a baroque opulence in the décolleté show girl with bent knee, leaning against a dressing room table, a swag of curtain behind her. The metaphor, as Walt liked to describe all his paintings, is easy to read. She is vulgar, tawdry, sensual, but intensely alive; so much for the subject. Her too too solid flesh is drawn with sweeping Rubenesque curves repeated in the curtain and the cluttered floor. White arms, breast, and head are a large flat area played against the lushly modeled torso and legs. The artist controls his large crowded canvas with an authority not always to be found in his early works. Frederick James Gregg wrote:

> The first time I saw Walt Kuhn's painting, "The City," I hated it; the second time I was curious; the third I tolerated; on the fourth it was an interesting acquaintance, and finally I came to regard it as one of the most important works of art made in America in our time.
>
> Now for this evolutionary process, from dislike to admiration, I am no more responsible than for having a useful thumb on my fist, or a useless vermiform appendix concealed about my person. As for the lady herself, as subject, she is no more "appealing" than she ever was.

Gregg was a professional critic, and this is not a bad description of the process of gradually entering into a work of art.

John Butler Yeats, on the other hand, is one of only two formal portraits Kuhn ever painted; although the other one, *Bert Lahr* (number 511) of 1947, may be more than the likeness of a ranking star. It is rather an apotheosis of the clown. Irish-born John Butler Yeats, father of William Butler Yeats and the painter Jack Butler Yeats, began as a barrister, but after his marriage, and study in the School of the Royal Academy in London under Poynter, he became a painter. He painted almost all the distinguished men of his day in Dublin, and emigrated to New York in 1908.

Reid says:

> He had now found his spiritual home in America, the boarding house at 317 West 29th Street run by three Breton women, the sisters Petitpas. He was to live out

his days there [he died in 1922], illuminating that place and making it locally celebrated by his animated and gaily serious presence, his witty, nourishing talk flowing in a rich stream. When weather allowed, the boarders and their guests would dine in a sort of pavilion, an open, roofed shed in the back garden. It is in this setting that John Sloan painted him in 1910 in *Yeats at Petitpas'* [now in the Corcoran Gallery, Washington], with a group of friends about the table, the white-bearded old man in an attitude reminiscent of his son's poem, "his beautiful head thrown back" ("Beautiful Lofty Things"), his teeth clamped on a long black cheroot, his eyes focussed on a sketch pad on which he is drawing. Van Wyck Brooks, one of the young men at the table, memorialized such occasions in a moving essay the title of which he borrowed from Sloan's picture."

Like many Irishmen his real gift was for words, not only "witty, nourishing talk" but letters his poet son might gladly have claimed. One of them to John Quinn carries the memorable statement, "This sense of failure is the melancholy of artists. It is their appointed agony." Yeats was at the center of Quinn's circle, and Kuhn must have known him well. The portrait was bought from the Quinn sale in 1927 by Cornelius O'Sullian, who presented it that same year to the Hugh Lane Municipal Gallery of Modern Art in Dublin. It is a straightforward portrait, strongly drawn and flatly painted, based on some of the principles developed in *Man with Ship Model*. Kuhn painted another less-known version, still in the Kuhn Estate. Kuhn was not an unquestioning believer in the Yeats cult; in a letter of 23 March 1945 to Henry L. Mencken incidentally recalling the John Quinn years he added, "I also found out that Willie Yeats always ate bananas before he gave one of his lectures and that the father of Willie was just about the world's biggest bore."

Petitpas' was not part of the Bohemia sickly flourishing around Washington Square and Greenwich Village, which John Quinn honestly hated. When he learned that one of his law partners was getting too involved with it, he wrote in disgust to Ezra Pound on 12 January 1917, "A self-respecting artist like Arthur B. Davies or Walt Kuhn wouldn't be caught dead within gunshot of that damned place." Artists have always been allowed a certain license in their life-styles; it was the camp-followers who angered Quinn.

By 1919 there was a subtle change in Kuhn's relations with John Quinn. As Reid says: "He still loyally admired Kuhn's art, but some of the warmth had gone out of their old personal friendship. Quinn had begun to feel that Kuhn occasionally 'used' him as Augustus John had done, both as friend and patron. Now when he felt like inviting a masculine companion to Ogunquit or the Adirondacks it was still likely to be Kuhn, but leavened by F.J. Gregg. . . . "It is a common predicament, as old as patronage itself, and often reciprocated in kind by artists, with interest.

All through 1918 and 1919 Walt Kuhn worked on a series of small paintings, none larger than twenty-four by twenty inches, and most of them smaller. A number of drawings and watercolors preceded and accompanied them. He thought of them as a unified group, finally adding one painted in 1923 to complete *An Imaginary History of the West.*

Plate 30. *Indians and Cavalry.*
From *An Imaginary History
of the West*

Courtesy of the Colorado Springs Fine Arts Center, Gift of Vera and Brenda Kuhn

In his files Kuhn specifically stated on the folder of each painting, "Painted from memory from material gathered out of books about the pioneer west."

Many of them were exhibited in his one-man show at Marius de Zayas's Gallery from 22 March to 3 April 1920, at 549 Fifth Avenue. John Quinn bought *Longhorn Saloon* (number 53) and *Entirely Surrounded by Indians* from the 1920 show for $625 each, and *Pow-Wow* (number 40) from a second showing at the Montross Gallery, 1 to 28 January 1922. Miss Lizzie Bliss also bought *Medicine* (number 49), at Arthur B. Davies' suggestion, from the Montross show. *Entirely Surrounded by Indians* disappeared after the Quinn sale in 1927. In 1936 Kuhn assembled most of the group, having bought some of them back, and kept adding a few rediscovered ones to make a total of twenty-nine. He had intimated that they should go to a "Western museum," and in 1950 Vera and Brenda presented them to the Colorado Springs Fine Arts Center. The whole group was shown for the first time in the Memorial Exhibition of 1960, and again in 1964 at the Amon Carter Museum of Western Art in Fort Worth, with an excellent catalogue by Fred S. Bartlett, the Colorado Springs director.

Bartlett gives the literary sources: "A list of the titles in Kuhn's library dealing with the Western subject matter is revealing. In all there are fifty-nine titles representing most of the leading writers on Western subject matter. A few of the titles show the range and kind of his source material: *Fighting Indians of the West*, Schmitt and Brown; *Spy of the Rebellion*, Pinkerton; *I Rode with Stonewall*, Douglas; *Across the Wide Mis-*

75

Plate 31. *Indian Lore.* From
*An Imaginary History of the
West*

souri, DeVoto; *Billy the Kid*, Garrett; *Rise and Fall of Jesse James*, Love; *Wife
of Sitting Bull*, Johnson; *Saga of Billy the Kid*, Burns; *Indian Wars of the
U.S.*, Frost; *Story of the Wild West*, Cody; and many others."

Plate 32. *The Young Chief.* From *An Imaginary History of the West*

Courtesy of the Colorado Springs Fine Arts Center, Gift of Vera and Brenda Kuhn

Kuhn tried a variety of pictorial approaches in the series, abandoning some and developing others. Some of the drawing is almost pure calligraphy; some recalls paleolithic cave painting; some are barely outlined color areas; all the paintings are animated and colorful. A good many are complex figure compositions of the kind the French call a *machine*, referring especially to large salon paintings. The problem of the *machine* haunted Cézanne's career, as can be seen in his series of life-sized *Bathers*. In the *Imaginary History* Kuhn attempted the *machine* several times, successfully, and finally got it out of his system, to the benefit of his later, classic single figures.

In the mid-thirties the painter Yasuo Kuniyoshi asked Kuhn what had happened to the western paintings that had been "greatly admired by artists." Kuhn's reply was typical: "A lot of good that does me! You fellows don't buy pictures." At the time of both the 1920 and 1922 showings the critics too were impressed. To borrow from Fred Bartlett again:

S. J. Kauffman in his famous column *Round the Town*: "For three years he has not shown his work. For ten years he has not had a 'one-man show.' Walt Kuhn. At the deZayas Gallery. An unusual exhibition. By an unusual artist. At an unusual gallery. A gallery where one feels that the commercial aspect is non-existent. Certainly an 'art for art's sake' gallery. Hence the fine shows that have been held there since its inception. Hence the Walt Kuhn exhibition of paintings. An important artist. Who has something new to say in a new way. Kuhn is a real colorist. His paintings are not like color charts. He understands the subtleties. We remember that great Frenchman who said that without subtleties there can be no art. Kuhn's paintings demonstrate that. Perhaps he will not show his work for another ten years. Therefore go see this show. And if you don't like it blame yourself. We were thrilled with it."

Horace Brodzky joined the chorus. He was a young writer and painter of the London Group who in 1915 announced in the Café Royal,

77

that celebrated social center of the English arts, that he meant to be "accepted in New York as a genius or a madman." He had been introduced to John Quinn by an earlier disclaiming letter from Ezra Pound calling him "an amiable bore with some talent." Ezra Pound may have been a sound judge of minor talent, except when his friends the vorticists were concerned, but most people in New York found Brodzky more amiable than boring. Kuhn exchanged letters with him as late as 1943. Brodzky wrote of the exhibition:

. . . As he has not shown his work for some considerable time, I was curious to see how he has developed.

I was surprised, and agreeably so, Kuhn in these few pictures of small dimensions, showed an extraordinary color sense. He is not a colorist in the usual and erroneous conception of the word. A colorist to most is one who plasters his (or her) canvas with brightly hued pigments, much in the manner of a sign painter's color and his pictures were to me a source of infinite joy, rich and harmonious in color. To him black is the most valuable color on his palette. A color that to most is dangerous, has been exploited to a remarkable degree of beauty, and his nuances of color are exquisite.

Certainly Kuhn is a fine designer. He has an elusive quality in his work and his method might be called neo-impressionism. But label him as you will, Kuhn has proved himself remarkably alive and confoundly individual.

To me his show was the most important of the season so far, and one that will linger long in my memory.

Plate 33. *Wild West #1.* From *An Imaginary History of the West*

Courtesy of the Colorado Springs Fine Arts Center, Gift of Vera and Brenda Kuhn

78

On 19 April 1920 John Quinn sent a note of appreciation to Brodzky for his review of the Kuhn show:" . . . I think he is one of the most interesting artists living, and I admire his courage and disinterestedness and fidelity to his own high and austere ideals more than I can say."

On 31 March John Quinn dictated his sole foray into printed art criticism to one of the three secretaries he kept busy with non-legal correspondence on Sundays in his large Central Park West apartment. It was a five-hundred-word letter to the editor of the *Sun and New York Herald*, with a covering note to Gregg: " . . . When I see how the great, sincere art of Kuhn has been pecked at, I feel that what I said about him, every word of which gives my deepest convictions, should be published. "It was, on 4 April, and deserves extensive quoting:

The works that I should like to praise, however inadequately to their merits, reveal one phase of the work of a sincere creative artist who has done fine things, and who is, I believe without any doubt, in the way to do great things. They give us, in subtly contrived flashes and passages, the vanished romance of the West. They are ironical and amusing, amusing in the sense of Rossetti's phrase that poetry should be amusing. These Indians and soldiers and rough men are "what suns and winds and waters made" them. They reveal, as Poe said the true poet should, "a wild effort to reach the beauty above." They have the strangeness without which there is no exquisite beauty. They show what Meredith, that supreme master of the comic spirit, once called a grisly "humor." It is not a "fat humor" or a "sentimental humor." They give us the "humor of the mind," a lean humor. They have the true comic touch and comedy, as Meredith said, "watches over sentimentalism with a birch rod." They give us back a vision of a vanished life that was not all comedy or all tragedy, "but something strangely mixed."

"The Young Chief" is the ideal Indian as he might be imagined by a woman; "Powwow", grotesque dignity; "The Fight in the Canyon", absolutely impossible and unreal, an attempt at the scientific diagnosis of the essence of romance; "Warrior", sculptural design, the real savage, nothing but hunting and fighting and loving; "War Song" bitter sweet color and design, no acid, intrinsically ugly colors that are so perfectly harmonized that they are beautiful; "Commissioners," acid and ink; "The General," a character study of three types of American soldiers; "Mining Camp," a jumble of nature and junk at the temporary hangout of nondescripts; "Entirely Surrounded by Indians," the impossible tragic stupidity of an impending catastrophe; "The Messenger," a satire on order; "The Long Horn Saloon," an affectionate satire of the picturesque, and the great "Aborigine," the most elusive of the lot — the only one executed in practically pure painting—and appreciation of the dignity of the old time Indian that we, all of us, boys and men, have read and dreamed about.

There they are, the fellows of Boone and Crockett and Houston and of Deadwood Dick and Calamity Jane and Wild Bill, and the young Buffalo Bill and the young Custer and the soldiers of his day, and all of the adventurous and brave men of those days in the West. They give us a glimpse of the vanished life of the West and of that life's vanished romance.

The historic accuracy of uniforms and accoutrements was meticulous. Kuhn had spent hours in the Smithsonian, on family visits to Washington, digging into contemporary details and specifications, and in the process rediscovering the western paintings of George Catlin. They were more than illustrations; he said that there was even a touch of Constantin Guys in them. Guys had covered the Crimean War for the *Illustrated London News*, which demanded accurate reporting. In

Plate 34. *The City*

Private Collection

later years Kuhn would often send Brenda to the Smithsonian to continue his research.

Walt Kuhn had traveled a long way from Munich. He had weathered and digested the Armory Show. He had made some mark on American painting. But he was not getting any younger, and he knew that the next ten years would make or break him.

NOTES TO CHAPTER FOUR

THE QUOTATION FROM BERNANOS comes from the preface to *Lettre aux anglais, l'Arbre* (Rio de Janeiro: Atlantica Editoria,1942), and is addressed to the Brazilians, among whom he spent his post-Munich exile.

Details on THE END OF THE ASSOCIATION come from Brown, *The Armory Show*, chap. 13.

QUINNS' 1914 PURCHASES FROM MONTROSS can be found in Reid, *The Man from New York*, 1968, p.192, as can the WAR BULLETIN, p.172.

POLO GAME was exhibited in the Memorial Exhibition, Cincinnati, 1960, and the University of Arizona, 1966.

QUINN'S 1915 PURCHASES FROM MONTROSS are mentioned in Reid, *The Man from New York*, p. 207.

THE MURALS FOR THE DANIEL GALLERY are spoken of in Milton W. Brown, *American Painting from the Armory Show to the Depression* (Princeton, N.J.: Princeton University Press, 1955), pp. 141–42.

Information on the DANIEL GALLERY AND FERDINAND HOWALD comes from Edgar P. Richardson, *American Paintings in the Ferdinand Howald Collection* (Columbus, Ohio: Columbus Gallery of Fine Arts, 1969), p.3.

Reid speaks of YOUTH on pp. 264 and 294, and of TRAGIC COMEDIANS on p. 294.

The text of the University of Arizona Catalogue, 1966, says, on p.23: "*Flowers and Forms* wrestles with Cubism and loses."

JOSEPH HIRSHHORN'S PURCHASE OF "TRAGIC COMEDIANS" comes from Aline Saarinen, *The Proud Possessors*,1958,p.274.

QUINN'S PURCHASE OF ETCHINGS comes from Reid, *The Man from New York*, p. 294, as does information on the PENGUIN CLUB, pp. 253, 292.

LOUIS BOUCHÉ'S AUTOBIOGRAPHICAL SKETCH is in the Archives.THE ROCK GARDEN is from Reid, *The Man from New York*, p. 270.

QUINN'S PURCHASE OF "CAUCUS" AND "HARLEQUIN" is mentioned in ibid., p. 393.

The Memorial Exhibition Catalogue 1960 describes FLOWER STILL LIFE on p.8.

BIOGRAPHICAL DATA ON JOHN B. YEATS can be found in the Catalogue of *Aspects of Irish Art,* an exhibition shown in America in 1974, p. 113.

PETITPAS' is described in Reid, *The Man from New York*, p. 89. YEATS' LETTER comes from ibid., p. 364.

A copy of THE LETTER TO H. L. MENCKEN, dated 23 March 1945, was sent to the writer on the same day.

QUINN'S FEELINGS TOWARD BOHEMIA are quoted from Reid, *The Man from New York*, p. 285.

Quinn's cooling relations with Kuhn comes from ibid., p. 393, and his PURCHASE OF "LONG HORN SALOON"AND "ENTIRELY SURROUNDED BY INDIANS" from p. 467.

LITERARY SOURCES FOR "AN IMAGINARY HISTORY OF THE WEST"are quoted from Fred S. Bartlett in the Catalogue for the Amon Carter Museum of Western Art, Fort Worth, Texas, 1964, p. 9. The quotation from S. JAY KAUFFMAN can be found on pp. 7–8. BRODZKY'S REVIEW is quoted on pp. 5–6. This Catalogue is also the source for JOHN QUINN'S LETTER TO THE "SUN," pp. 6–7.

DATA ON HORACE BRODZKY can be found in Reid, *The Man from New York*, p.248.

"THE GENERAL"AND "WAR SONG" AS WELL AS "THE FIGHT IN THE CANYON" mentioned in John Quinn's letter to the *Sun* have almost certainly undergone a change of title, and are not listed in *An Imaginary History*; hence they are not entered in the catalogue raisonné.

Show Business and
"A Quarter to Twelve"

After the critical and financial success of his show at the de Zayas Gallery, Walt Kuhn bought a cottage at 18 Stearns Road in Ogunquit. It was to be a fixed summer base for his family and his summer painting until 1948. There is a hint of "American Gothic" in the white frame house with its two side porches flanking the projecting parlor, its flower beds and vegetable garden. He was not pinned down to it, however, and often went instead to the Berkshires or the West for fresh landscape ideas, or to Europe, twice with his family.

Not many paintings but several prints came out of 1920. A big one-man show like that of March and April burns up a lot of energy, in preparation of the paintings, carefully plotted publicity, constant brooding over its run, and the aftermath of clinching half-promised purchases. Kuhn never entirely relied on dealers for this vital follow-up, and usually he was his own salesman, for better or worse. Miss Lizzie Bliss bought one of the 1920 yield. (Her name was solemnized into Miss Lillie Bliss by her beneficiary, the Museum of Modern Art in 1934, after a "Memorial Exhibition, the Collection of the Late Miss Lizzie Bliss, Vice-President of the Museum" in 1931.) John Quinn bought two, the better-known of them *Girl with Shawl* (number 87). Collector and artist both may have been attracted by the model, who later posed for *Victoria* (number 120) and *Study of a Girl* (number 82).

Most of the records of Kuhn's activities in the fall of 1920 have to do with John Quinn. Personal relationships may have cooled slightly, but Kuhn was still an invaluable companion and confidant, even in literary matters. In June 1919, for example, Quinn had discussed with him a dramatization he planned to make of Joseph Conrad's *Arrow of Gold*, which the novelist had proposed to dedicate to John Quinn. On reading the first draft, Kuhn called the scenario "melodramatic." When the verdict was relayed to Conrad, his spirited rebuttal came on 31 July: "A melodrama is a play where the motives lack verisimilitude, or else are not strong enough to justify a certain violence of action, which thus becomes a mere fatuous display of false emotions. Violent action in itself does not make melodrama."

Also confided to Kuhn in several letters and presumably many conversations were John Quinn's troubles with the publication of *Ulysses*, at times as convoluted and frustrated as the *Odyssey* itself. On 4 October 1920 he wrote: "If he [James Joyce] really wanted the martyrdom of suppression, he would get it damn quickly." In essence the problem was that Joyce would understandably accept no editing or revisions, and that as he neared the end of his seven years' labor he insisted on its serial publication, in spite of various "mutilations," as he called them, in the *Little Review,* subsidized in part by Quinn. Its lady editors, Jane Heap and Margaret Anderson, almost joyfully invited the stake. Although they accepted John Quinn's financial support, they would listen to none of his warnings. He was a lawyer, and knew that American law, s he hotly pointed out to the intermediary, Ezra Pound, was no more uncivilized regarding the publication of "obscenities" and "indecencies" than English law, on which in fact it was based. It was even more lenient than French or Belgian law, often more honored in the breach than in the observance.

American law simply could not be bent enough to permit the magazine's publication of *Ulysses*. Two issues of the *Little Review* had already been banned from the mails on account of Joyce's novel, but all the would-be martyrs were too stubborn to learn. What Quinn had told the editors of the *Little Review* he also wrote to Kuhn on 4 October: "that Pound and Joyce were in Europe and they were in New York; Europe was civilized and N.Y. was not, and that it was all right for an artist such as Joyce to ask that, but the editor of a magazine ought to have knowledge of the conditions in the place where the magazine is published and exercise independent judgment. . . ." General sale in book form was equally out of the question. Quinn's proposal was to publish a limited edition for private distribution.

Being in the center of a field of such magnetic force must have had a profound effect on Walt Kuhn, but later he rarely spoke of it. His daughter says that he met very few of the celebrated literary figures he knew so intimately at second hand. He may not have, but their invisible presence was a most tangible part of his daily life in those days. Once he did charge Joyce with deliberate obscurantism, though he did not use that phrase. He meant that the writer had refused to build an accessible bridge of communication with the common reader. And that, Walt believed, was inexcusable. He was explicit about it many times, once, fortunately, in print.

He had been asked to write an article in the April 1947 issue of *Art News*. It was titled "Cézanne: Delayed Finale," and reviewed a major exhibition at the Wildenstein Galleries. he wrote:

Every intelligent artist paints subject matter solely to get rid of it. Cézanne, too, must have felt the urge eventually to produce the quality known as universal.

Only by removing any ambiguity of the subject could he induce the average observer to delve deeper and enjoy the inner and vital qualities of painting.

To prepare his final work for just such universal quality Cézanne went through years of struggle. Not until the subject matter of a picture is completely clear can the artist expect a full return of appreciation. Without this almost moronic clarity how can he hope to reach that enormous, elementary strata [*sic*] of would-be art lovers who never in all their lives will see beyond subject matter, who really enjoy just that and nothing more? This is why the works of Cézanne did much to puzzle the public and influence a horde of painters to produce things of precious self-indulgence and to comment upon the bone structure and viscera of art rather than on its entire body.

Separation of artist and general audience is one of the penalties paid by an over-specialized culture, where specialists speak only to other specialists, poets write for other poets, painters paint for painters in a language known only to the initiates. There is often a time gap between specialized artist and general audience; there usually has been, except perhaps in fifth-century Athens or fifteenth-century Florence. But it has grown now to fifty or seventy-five years, and continues to widen. Walt Kuhn saw it widening steadily throughout his mature career, and his opposition to it grew stronger as the years passed. If he felt so in 1947, there can be no doubt as to how he would feel today. Even before his death he was accused of turning his back on the progressive trends he had helped present to an American audience. Kuhn never turned his back on anything. He doggedly followed the path he had seen the older masters follow in their way, in their time.

The difference between the subject and the theme of a work of art is well known. In painting the subject is recognizable and describable in words; if the far more important theme, or true meaning, of a painting could be verbally explained, it would be poetry, not painting. Dante Gabriel Rossetti was not sure of the distinction, and once showed Whistler a sonnet and a picture, both on the subject of the Annunciation. The painter bluntly said, "Now frame the sonnet." Whistler was not unskilled with words, but he knew the difference.

"This almost moronic clarity of subject" that Kuhn wrote of used to be called by psychologists the "level of recognition and recall," normal for a three-year-old who can identify "tree", "bunny," or "mama" from a picture. On this level an adult can take off horizontally into a world of free association with the subject matter, and usually does, instead of probing vertically into the deeper and true meaning of the painting. Possibly this is the essential difference between a picture of some "thing" and a painting, which is a "thing" in itself.

In 1947 Walt Kuhn, the aging Prospero whose magic wand was soon to be broken, was speaking for himself as well as for Cézanne, or Rembrandt, or Vermeer, or Chardin, or any other artist whose recognizable and understandable subjects are introductions to profound truths. Rembrandt was concerning himself with more than butchers and their customers when he painted the small but monumental dressed ox in the Louvre. The mystery of Vermeer is not to be found in his lucid Dutch interiors only; instead it may be the celebration of a "sac-

Plate 35. *Battle of New Orleans*

Courtesy of Kennedy Galleries, Inc.—Kuhn Estate

rament of daily life." Nor was Chardin merely obsessed with kitchen paraphernalia any more than Walt Kuhn was with apples and show girls. They all had serious, sometimes tragic, hurtful or ennobling things to say, but first had to reach their audience.

Kuhn illuminated the problem for at least one listener when he showed a modest watercolor by one of his protégés. The competent artist was an eccentric older man of privileged background who had chosen to live alone in a shack at the base of the New Jersey palisades. He had appeared unannounced at Kuhn's studio one day with some of his work, asking for instruction. The subject was a jumble of fallen rock painted in light and dark ochers. With a gesture of his expressive fingers Kuhn said, "what anguish!"

As has been seen, Kuhn's reading covered a considerable range, from Ibsen to western history. In September 1942 he wrote to Brenda recommending that she read " 'Clarence'—a much better book, it's by far the only good B.H. [Brett Hart]. I suggest you read H. Finn again it's really not a child's book, but disguised like all good art. I read part of Wuthering Heights, there you really have something—although awfully [mixed] up by the style of the period and much too long." Poetry interested him not at all. He once said that the only thing that really impressed him was two lines of Wordsworth,

> One impulse from a vernal wood
> May teach you more of man,

and the next two lines

> Of moral evil and of good
> Than all the sages can.

were so alien to him that he did not even bother to remember them.

85

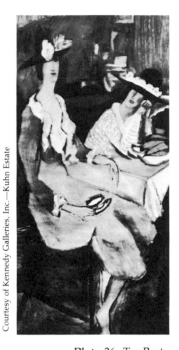

Plate 36. *Tea Party*

Plate 37 (opposite). *Girl in White Chemise*

And it is not as if he had not known of William Butler Yeats, Ezra Pound, and witnessed the publication travails of *The Waste Land*.

In the fall of 1920 Walt Kuhn was a more specific literary adviser. Walter Pach had proposed a memorial volume on Raymond Duchamp-Villon, and Kuhn wrote to John Quinn on 6 September: "I hope you will find it possible to do something for the memory of Raymond Duchamp-Villon. He was the real stuff, and personally a fine chap. I liked him best of the three brothers. Let us hope that Pach, if he does the writing, gets some of Raymond's hardiness and not too much of his own 'slippery elm.'" Raymond Duchamp-Villon was the middle and sculptor brother who was gassed in the trenches and died on 7 October 1918. The brothers had divided the family name for professional purposes; the oldest was Jacques Villon, maker of fine color prints of contemporary paintings and a painter in his own right; the youngest was Marcel Duchamp. There was also a painting sister, Suzanne, who married the artist Jean Crotti. Duchamp-Villon had five pieces in the Armory Show, two purchased by John Quinn and one by Arthur B. Davies. Of course Quinn financed the publication.

There are eleven paintings known from 1921, one of them destroyed in 1942. Most of them were flower still lifes, a subject Kuhn had evidently set himself to master, and six of these were shown in his one-man exhibition at the Montross Gallery from 1 to 28 January in 1922. He withheld one of the most interesting paintings of 1921 for his big turning-point show at the Grand Central Art Galleries in 1927. It was the already-mentioned *Battle of New Orleans* (number 87), which even though it is a fairly large canvas, thirty-four inches high by fifty-five inches wide, belongs in spirit to *An Imaginary History of the West*. There is a Gallic dash about it, with reminiscenses of Raoul Dufy and ·Constantin Guys, as well as an expected attention to the details of military uniform.

Girl in White Chemise (number 100) is a better painting, and of greater promise. It is a half-length simply posed figure, and for almost the first time does not recall other painters; it is simply a good early Walt Kuhn. It was purchased immediately by John Quinn. Many experiments were still to come, but *Girl in White Chemise* is on the main track Kuhn was to follow, with variations, straight through to the end. A dark-haired young woman, décolleté, stands in front of a mantelpiece and a drapery of straight diagonal folds; she turns slightly to her left from the observer. The drawing of the gently inclined head is still linear but used to make a clear boundary between light and dark masses. Her bare right arm and full breast are simply but richly modulated, and a narrow white line serves to define her left arm and hand resting on the back of a chair. The mantel and drapery are a middle value. These are the three basic tones that Kuhn insisted were all a painting should have without risking confusion. Over all there is an air of calm, perhaps wistful, repose, which does not break through the thin ice into sentimentality. It is one of his most satisfying paintings to date.

2

In the summer of 1922 Walt Kuhn began his second gainful career, in the theater. He always contended that it was dangerous for most artists to try to support themselves and their dependents by sale of their serious work. This brought too many temptations to compromise, to repeat popular subjects or styles, to yield to too much influence from dealers and critics. He recommended instead, since that had been his own experience, bread-earning of a nature as far apart as possible from the artist's creative life. He felt that commercial art was too close, and hence possibly corrupting, and dropped his own comic strips, posters, and cartoons as soon as he was adequately established in show business.

His first professional essay in that world was the designing and directing of various acts for Michio Ito's *Pinwheel Revue,* which played the Earl Carrol Theatre in the season of 1922. Then in the winter of 1922–23 he designed and directed numbers for a pantomime, *Lilies of the Field,* that played the Strand Theater and three theaters in Chicago. The acts he designed and directed for Raymond Hitchcock's *Hitchy-Koo* gave him the greatest pleasure. He liked Hitchcock as a person and respected him as a first-rate comedian. He traveled through the Midwest with *Hitchy-Koo,* helping to whip it into shape for Broadway. He would join it later on the road after its New York success, for the necessary sharpening up. In fact he was called on several times as a kind of revue-doctor for other productions.

In a *Newsweek* interview on 8 December 1941 he said, "I probably would never make a good clown, but I can tell a clown what to do."

Plate 38. *Landscape with Cows*

Plate 39. *Sleeping Girl*

Courtesy of Mr. Henry Strater

He described one act he was especially fond of; it had a cast of four hoboes dressed in rags, but with a faintly surrealist touch the rags were not dirty, they were pristine white. The actor Sidney Toler, possibly remembered by some as the first Charlie Chan, referred to this act when he wrote to John Ringling North on 3 February 1941: " . . . I can truthfully say, that everything I have seen of his was of the highest order, extremely unique, and most amusing. His 'Tramp Clown Act' was a classic. I am positive that he is a man of great ideas." In the fall of 1923 Kuhn designed and directed more numbers for the *Forty-niners' Revue*, and one act from it played the Strand during Christmas week

89

that year. His diversions with the Kit Kat Club and the Penguins had not been wasted time. Costume sketches, action outlines, even some dialogue and music are preserved in the Archives. But just as it takes a musician to hear the printed score, it takes a stage director to see the live performance in these shorthand notes.

Evidently the acts were successful, since Kuhn and his family lived in reasonable comfort and could put aside money for travel and the lean painting months. His account books show that royalties kept coming in for several years. How good the acts were is hard to tell at this distance. Such things have butterfly lives, but there is expert testimony. As late as January 1940, Marc Connelly, of *Green Pastures* and many other successes, was enthusiastic about the "clown sketches," and called them to George S. Kaufman's attention. Kaufman, and there could be no better judge, wrote to Kuhn urging him to show them to the Ringling Brothers-Barnum and Bailey Circus, saying, "I certainly hope so because they're great. Idea, costuming, complete execution of the whole thing—no one can touch you at it. From what I've seen of both your acts and the circus acts, they can certainly use you." One of his prized possessions was a press pass to the Ringling Brothers-Barnum and Bailey Circus when it played Madison Square Garden every season from 1941 to 1948.

Walt Kuhn felt completely at home in this setting, and fascinated though he was by the surface glitter and seamy underside, he was as self-critical as ever, in spite of the fleeting nature of what he did. For in his dual role Kuhn was a perfectionist, with a cautionary word for anyone who thought he could get away with less than the best in either the theater or the arts: "There is always someone who knows."

These profitable and exciting excursions consumed a lot of Kuhn's time, but he could return to the solitude of his studio alive with ideas. Then began the lonely, often painful labor of distilling them into paintings. And he turned out quite a few in 1922, thirteen in all, with one destroyed. Not many of them reflect his extracurricular experiences. As well as flower pieces there are two small still lifes, which are something of a departure, one of apples and the other of pears. *Landscape with Cows* (number 116) is a study in straight horizontal lines with blocky cows in the foreground and blocky white houses in the distance. *Victoria* (number 120) is one of his more romantic half-length portraits, which he traded to the eminent antiquarian and collector of modern painting, Dikran Kelekian, for a head of a woman by Derain. *Girl with Cocked Hat* (number 114) and *Sleeping Girl* (number 119) stand out. *Girl with Cocked Hat* is not, as its title might suggest, a show girl with Napoleonic headdress, but a young lady with her then-modish hat set at a slightly rakish angle.

Sleeping Girl is the one painting that hung for years in Kuhn's studio at 112 East Eighteenth Street. He never spoke of it or gestured toward it, it was simply there, and must have meant something special

Plate 40 (opposite). *Mask*

91

Plate 41. *Colt*

to him. Certainly it is one of his best early paintings, almost a mono-chrome, with little local color and little modeling of form. A life-size weary ballerina lays her short-haired head on the crook of her right arm resting on the back of a chair. The strong diagonal of her straight white-clad legs plays from lower left to middle right against the left-curving torso, neck and head. A zebra-striped reverse "C," possibly part of her half-shed bodice, marks the transition. There is less stage setting and fewer accessories than in previous works of a similar kind, though a suggestion of drapery can still be seen at the upper right and the dancer's slippers lie on the floor at lower right. Not unlike *Girl in White Chemise* the effect is of youthful grace and vitality caught in an instant of rest. *Sleeping Girl, Girl with Cocked Hat,* and *Country Road* (number 92) of 1921 were shown in Paris in an exhibition organized by the New York dealer Marie Sterner in 1924 with the title "Exhibition of American Art under the Auspices of Art Patrons of America." It hung in June at the Musée du Jeu de Paume, which then housed the foreign section of the Musée du Luxembourg and was available for occasional special exhibitions. Hopes were high, but, as Kuhn might have pre-

Plate 42. *Chris*

Courtesy of the Cincinnati Art Museum, The Albert P. Strietmann Collection

dicted, it did not cause so much as a ripple in Paris. There were a few polite reviews with thinly disguised condescension. Americans were not expected to paint well unless, perhaps, they lived in France and merged with the French, as Mary Cassatt had, at least in French eyes. Otherwise, cowboys, Indians, prizefighters, and collecting French paintings were proper American concerns.

Before that, both of the *Girls* were shown in "Selected Works by Walt Kuhn" at the Montross Gallery from 5 to 26 January 1924. The show included *Apples* (number 123), *Green and Russet Pears* (number 115), *Landscape with Cows* (number 116), *Portrait* (number 117), *Blanche* (number 110), and two paintings from 1923, the small *Green Plums* (number 122) and *Small Landscape* (number 125).

There was another try at attracting European attention in 1925 with an "Exposition Trinationale" of French, English, and American painters. This time Kuhn took a hand in organizing the American section, arguing correctly that a choice smaller collection with French and English flankers would stand a better chance. It showed at the Durand-Ruel Galleries in Paris in June to the same condescension as in 1924. Even the English reacted the same way, with less reason, when it was shown in London in October. It was seen in New York at Wildenstein's from 25 January to 15 February 1926. There the Americans had at least the comfort of playing on their home field.

C.J. Bulliet mentions the exhibition in his book of 1930, *Apples and Madonnas.* This somewhat random explanation of modern art by a

93

routine journalist enjoyed some success in its day, since there were few popular books on the subject to be had. Bulliet says: "Walt Kuhn, most able and most resourceful of fighters for the recognition of American art abroad, is himself one of the best painters in the group upon whom he relies to back up his promises of merit worthy of international attention. Kuhn, however, is too wide awake to all that is transpiring, too eager to try everything, for his own good. At times he has done studies of young girls, drastically simplified, that have gone a long way toward demonstrating a real leadership. But, of late, he has muddled the effect

Plate 43. *Head of Woman*

Courtesy of Mr. and Mrs. Donald V. Reed, Jr., Princeton, New Jersey

Courtesy of Mrs. John Ogg Ross

Plate 45. *Beryl*

Courtesy of Kennedy Galleries, Inc.—Kuhn Estate

Plate 44. *Study for Sheba*

by creating a series of huge semi-nude females from the theater dressing-rooms, symbolizing various things—but signifying much less than did his quiet little girls combing their hair." Mr. Bulliet seems to have missed the point, as was his custom, and his facts are vague. It would be difficult to locate a series of huge semi-nude females from the theater dressing-room" in Walt Kuhn's painting either before or after 1930. His entry in the Trinationale was, however, *Woman Combing Her Hair* (number 146). It has a certain Gallic flair, though Kuhn would have winced at the mention of Marie Laurencin's name. They both happened to paint young women, but there is no mistaking each artist's gender or nationality.

Bulliet continues:

Kuhn's associates in the American section of the Exposition Trinationale as staged in the Durand-Ruel Galleries, Paris, in 1925, were Paul Bartlett, Paul Burlin,

Robert W. Chanler, Paul Daugherty, Arthur B. Davies, Jo Davidson, William G. Glackens, Herbert Haseltine, "Pop" Hart, Charles W. Hawthorne, Cecil Howard, E.W. Redfield, Charles Sheeler, Allan Tucker, Max Weber, and Gertrude Whitney.

The roster is a curious one. Hawthorne never did cause the Academies to lose sleep, and Arthur B. Davies long has ceased to do so. Glackens, like Davies, was responsible some years ago for many anxious moments, but he appears now as a late Impressionist with no more harm in him than Sargent. Paul Burlin spends a great part of his time in Paris, and his work is nothing more than a rather feeble echo of the Derain School of Cézanne. Walt Kuhn, "Pop" Hart and Max Weber supply what of "guts" there is in the exhibition, with the gentle Charles Sheeler doing his part with lovely things in exquisite taste.

Chanler was known for his carved and lacquered art nouveau screens; Bartlett, Davidson, Haseltine, Howard, and Gertrude Whitney were harmless sculptors; and Sheeler did rather more than lovely and exquisite things. Nor did Walt Kuhn think of himself as a fighter "for the recognition of American art abroad." He fought much harder for the recognition of American art, or any kind of art, at home. However, he did resent the growing domination of Parisian style among the leading New York dealers, even though he had helped substantially to bring it about. One of his bitter observations was to the effect that not until the dealers and critics had run through the whole list of French painters from Picasso and Matisse down to Marie Laurencin was an American artist even considered.

But time brought perspective and a mellower mood. On 7 March 1936 he wrote to his painter friend Otis Oldfield in San Francisco, with whom he kept up a lengthy correspondence, "Not until the coming of foreign dealers and the work of the painters they represent, did New York develop any general art consciousness and get to the point where a sale could be made without asking what might almost be called charity. A market, a world market has been created in New York at last. Excitement and controversy have appeared. This last show at the Harriman Gallery of which I sent you a catalog, has broken the all-time attendance record of the gallery. The Modern Museum packs them in and the Metropolitan has had enormous crowds at the present Goya show." The Harriman Gallery show was paintings by "Cézanne, Derain, Kuhn, Matisse, Picasso, Renoir and Van Gogh." Kuhn was understandably buoyant, and kindly to his European colleagues.

Eighteen paintings, none of them intentionally destroyed later, came from 1924. *Americana* (number 129) was accidentally burned up, but was repainted from the original oil sketch. It is a large horizontal oil, four feet high by five feet, four inches wide, of a dancer from the Beaux Arts Cafe. *Woman Combing Her Hair* and its international adventures have already been mentioned. The portrait of *Angna Enters* (number 131) is a half-length profile figure of the famous "Dance Mime" who turns her head jauntily toward the observer. It is less a formal portrait then the painting of a dancer in costume, possibly one she wore in the dancer Michio Ito's *Pinwheel Revue* where Kuhn met her. Louis Bouché's sister-in-law was married to Michio Ito, and

Bouché's introduction may have been Kuhn's professional entrance to the entertainment world; Louis Bouché was always a loyal friend. Kuhn also painted a tiny six-by-five-inch version of *Angna Enters* (number 132). *Beryl* (number 136), the polar opposite of *Sleeping Girl*, is a life-sized show girl with crossed legs who lounges almost insolently in an armchair and looks out provocatively, as the tawdry side of show business begins to assert itself. In the absence of either a photograph or a

Plate 46. *Still Life, Ducks*

reproduction of *Nude* (number 139), its description in the Quinn Sale Catalogue will have to serve: "Studio interior; in the foreground rises the three-quarter length figure of a disrobed dark-haired young woman. Her left hand is resting on the back of a chair while the right arm hangs loosely by her side." It was the last painting John Quinn was to buy from Walt Kuhn.

John Quinn died on the morning of 28 July 1924. He had undergone surgery for cancer in 1919 and made a gallant recovery, but

Plate 47. *Dressing Room*

Courtesy of the Brooklyn Museum, Gift of Friends of the Museum

was living on borrowed time. Some half-conscious knowledge of it drove him at a pace unusual even for him those last five years. Kuhn's relations with him may not have been as close as before, but the feeling of personal loss was real and deep. It was the ending of an era, an important formative era in Walt Kuhn's life. Quinn's loyalty and professional respect would be missed, but growing income from the theater would make up for the loss of financial support.

John Quinn left what was unquestionably the finest and most inclusive collection of advanced contemporary art in the world. But he did not have the capital to ensure its intact preservation, even if he had not specified that he wanted it dispersed so that others could share some of the pleasure he had taken from assembling it, much of it with Kuhn's advice. No museum in America was ready for it, and probably none in Europe, had Quinn felt so inclined. He did bequeath *Le Cirque* to the Louvre, giving the national museum of France its first and most

Plate 48. *Hare and Hunting Boots*

Plate 49. *Nude on Knee*

Plate 50. *Reclining Nude on Striped Blanket*

important work by Georges Seurat. The cream of the collection, in fact the larger part of it, was sold privately over the next year and a half, and then the balance, including all of Kuhn's work, went on the auction block of the American Art Association for a three-day sale beginning 9 February 1927. Some of the auction prices were ridiculously low and hard on the living artists involved, who were unable to run up the bidding or to buy their works back.

3

The auspices for 1925 were good, beginning with the January exhibition at the Montross Gallery. Then, suddenly, in the early spring it was "a quarter to twelve." A duodenal ulcer almost killed Walt Kuhn. Although he gave the outward appearance of untiring energy, he had obviously been pushing himself beyond his strength, and his health had always worried his close family. There is some reason to believe that "just about every known children's disease" had had a permanent effect; the first trip West may have been therapeutically advised.

The ulcer was medicinally treated, but Kuhn woke from the shock to realize that even though, as he wrote to Horace Brodzky in 1943, he was "constant about trying to do at least one fine piece of art," he had not yet done it. As he put it more extremely at the time, he had not even "done anything the cleaning woman wouldn't sweep out of a deserted studio." This was a gross exaggeration, but it defines the standards he had set for himself.

A family council was called, and all agreed that their savings could see them through the next two years, with one last theater venture in the winter of 1925–26 to design and direct acts for the Deitz and

Ryskind *Merry-go-Round Review.* Otherwise, all time and energy were to go into painting. The visual restorative of another European trip was possible too, so all three Kuhns went to France, Germany, Austria, Holland, and England in the summer. Two maxims of John Constable, which he later copied from Leslie's *Memoirs of the Life of John Constable,* apply here. One, from page 169, reads, " . . . Yet he well understood how important it is that the student should be directed to nature by the assistance of previous art ['how important . . . previous art' under-scored]." The other, from page 229, says that "Constable was of opinion that the best school of art will always be in that country where there are the best living artists, and not merely where there are the greatest number of works of the old masters." If Rubens at the height of his career could copy Titians in Madrid and Rembrandt copy Mughal mini-atures, Walt Kuhn was not above learning from the masters. For all of his American patriotism, amounting at times to chauvinism, Kuhn had no doubts as to where the best living artists were to be found, as well as the greatest number of works of the old masters.

Another distraction of time and energy that Kuhn decided to forgo was his sculpting, as he called it. His sculptures are widely scat-tered now, and very few are to be seen; nor do many photographs survive. But from the beginning up to 1925 he took his sculpture seri-ously. John Quinn owned nineteen examples; five were carved wood panels, and two were bronze reliefs. There were eight other bronzes, all of them small. The rest were wood carvings in the round. Kuhn had a good eye for sculpture; he admired Brancusi at the time of the Armory Show and later came to know him as a personal friend. Brancusi gave him a plaster cast of his marble *Muse* in thanks for Kuhn's work on the famous show, just as Picasso had given him a large charcoal drawing from his 1910 cubist period. Kuhn realized that his sculptures were not up to his paintings and prints, but they undoubtedly had taught him something of the nature of form.

There is good precedent for this, from Daumier to Degas and Renoir. Two major sculptors of recent times even began as painters, Constantin Meunier, the Belgian master of simply modeled large bronze figures of laborers, and the better-known Aristide Maillol. Amadeo Modigliani may have been a better sculptor than painter. Picasso, Matisse, Joan Miró, all have produced serious sculpture, and the sculptors Alberto Giacometti and Alexander Calder have performed with distinction in painting and prints. The modeled sculptures of Thomas Eakins, many of them exercises in human and animal anatomy, are beginning to attract attention, and many more names could be added. For the rest of his life Kuhn went on whittling, in a folk-art manner, for his own and his friends' amusement, and carved several large handsome eagles inspired by his anonymous American predeces-sors. He had early learned the difference between American and Euro-pean eagles; the American eagle is a lean, tautly carved fighting bird, not a heraldic symbol from an imperial past.

101

The new discipline began to show immediate results. There are fifteen paintings from the balance of 1925, two of them destroyed. A large *Study for Sheba* (number 143) of 1924 does not explain why he destroyed the larger version of 1925, five feet, eight inches high by two feet, four inches wide. *Sheba* (number 156) was a standing show girl who leaned on her right hand resting on a table, her right knee bent on a chair, her left hand on her hip. She looked straight ahead, and few accessories were suggested. Also there are two flower studies both titled *Plant Forms* (numbers 151, 152) and three still lifes including his most authoritative one yet, *Still Life, Ducks* (number 158). In it a male and a female mallard hang by their feet against a plain, slightly modulated wall. The limpness of the dead birds, their solidly realized masses and exactly felt textures, induced Miss Lizzie Bliss to buy it and bequeath it to the Addison Gallery of American Art in Andover Massachusetts. She also bought *Hare* (number 150) from the 1927 Grand Central Art Galleries show and Dikran Kelekian bought *Portrait of a Dog* (number 153).

The second of the years budgeted for painting, 1926, produced a striking number of first-rate canvases. Many of them were pointed toward the big exhibition at the Grand Central Art Galleries in January of 1927, which Walt Kuhn felt would in a way be his baccalaureate celebration. There were twenty-three in all, one of them never exhibited anywhere and one of them destroyed. Three of them were withheld from the Grand Central show for reasons that require at least conjectural explanation.

In 1939 Kuhn felt secure enough for a kind of published retrospective. He had always recognized a significant difference between a poet's *collected* works, often sadly in need of an editor, and his *selected* works. His preferred exhibition format, except for the fairly inclusive 1927 showing, inclined toward the selected rather than the collected, so he limited the number to fifty paintings, none from before 1926. He asked Paul Bird, assistant editor of *Art Digest* who had graduated with honors in art and archaeology from Princeton, to work with him on the text. After a one-page introduction the text consists only of an extended caption under the reproduction of each painting. It was published in 1940 as *50 Paintings by Walt Kuhn* with Comments by Paul Bird. The "comments" are Paul Bird's, but their content is original Walt Kuhn. The series begins with the three paintings from 1926: *Bareback Rider* (number 164), *Hare and Hunting Boots* (number 169), and *Mallards* (number 171). It is possible that even in 1927 Kuhn realized that they belonged on the other side of the divide, to a second, mature phase, after the long years of study and experiment. Investigating and observing would continue to the end, but trial and error lay behind.

Amalgam (number 163) leads off for 1926. It is a three-quarter-length life-size chorus girl with a straggly, plumed headdress, one long lock of hair hanging to her right, hands on swaying hips. The large areas are still hard-edged and the attack almost bluntly direct. A hori-

Plate 51. Top. *Sleeping Girl in Coat.* Bottom. *Ena*

Collection of the Museum of Modern Art, New York, Gift of Abby Aldrich Rockefeller

Courtesy of Kennedy Galleries, Inc.—Kuhn Estate

zontal watercolor of the head and headdress called *Arbitra* survives. LaSalle Spier composed a score for *Amalgam* in the 1927 catalogue, marked "Fast and brilliantly."

Pine Tree or *Maine Pine* (number 174) is one of the first successful later landscapes, but *Singing Tree* (number 176) was destroyed. It is an interesting title. *Girl with Blossoms* (number 168) exists only in a *Chicago Evening Post* reproduction of 9 February 1926. It is still linear, a little more complexly composed, with a possibly dangerous gentleness. *Superba* (number 80 is also three-quarter length, and challenges *Beryl* with a dignified forthrightness that saw her through several exhibitions, a "Radical Independents' Exhibition" at the Philadelphia Museum of Art, or the Pennsylvania Museum of Art as it was then in 1929, and a 1927 "Decorative Exhibition" at the New York Wanamaker's art department directed by Louis Bouché that year.

One of the most remarkable paintings of 1926, *Dressing Room* (number 167), summarizes the past rather than predicting the future, as does *Still Life, Ducks.* In 1936 John I.H. Baur, then of the Brooklyn Museum staff, discussed it in his article "Modern American Paintings" in the *Brooklyn Museum Quarterly:*

> But there is one outstanding artist represented in the Museum's collection who belongs in this group and who has had ample contact with Europe during his years of study in France, Germany, Italy, Holland and Spain. This is Walt Kuhn, whose long series of clowns, bareback riders, and other circus performers rank high in the field of romantic portraiture. One of these, the Museum's *Dressing Room* (1926) is typical. There are first the savage colors, the sickly green of the tights with the clashing red of her hair ribbon, and the blue of the background. Still more significant is the powerful emotional treatment of the eyes, extraordinarily large and dark, which stare from the painted mask of the face. It is these which carry the romantic stress, but the colors are almost as important, for they suggest the colors of decay, of tawdriness, and tinsel without its shine. There is no mistaking the artist's intent, his interest in the tragic and human side of his character rather than its traditional glamour, and one is led to the conclusion that Kuhn's art today springs from the same general current which produced the pallid harlots and dance hall queens of Toulouse-Lautrec over a quarter of a century ago.

Baur might be describing something from Berlin of the Weimar Republic days, and parallels to German expressionism in Walt Kuhn's early style have been pointed out by several critics. A few of his early paintings have lately been bought by private collectors in Germany.

Walt Kuhn, speaking through Paul Bird's comment, says of *Bareback Rider:* "We begin with a prophetic picture. Not until years afterward did the artist understand this painting's relation to his own career. In these limbs and torso is the same vibrant tension that so completely characterizes a later Walt Kuhn figure. Here it first appeared, at the time unexpected and unexplained." *Bareback Rider* was in the sale of the Edith Gregor Halpert Collection in March 1973 at Sotheby Parke Bernet, successor to the American Art Association. It brought a good price, and there are rumors that it went to Japan.

And of *Hare and Hunting Boots,* now in the National Gallery as a "Gift of the W. Averell Harriman Foundation in Memory of Marie N.

Plate 52. *Nude with Raised Slip*

Courtesy of Kennedy Galleries, Inc.—Kuhn Estate

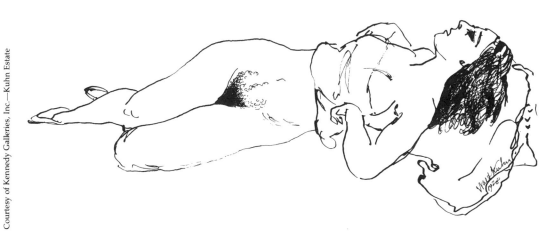

Harriman,"Paul Bird writes: "Out of Dutch painting, Chardin, and the woods of America comes this quiet masculine still life. No theatrics— just a limp rabbit and muddy boots thrown in the corner. But the painting of the soft fur is whipped into convincing simulation of the actual subject. The picture has that strange loneliness of men without women."

The Detroit Institute of Arts acquired *Mallards* in 1944. The comment reads:"The line of the design is constantly yielding, for the painting is really a caress to the soft plumage of these wild fowl. Thousands are killed annually by greedy hunters, yet each new season brings more mallards, equally soft in plumage and identically marked. The Creator's handicraft continues eternally." Related in spirit to *Still Life, Ducks*, the composition varies. The drake lies diagonally toward the observer, his head turned to the left. The female hangs over him by one leg, her left wing stretched lifelessly toward the upper left. Both paintings are truly *nature morte*.

"Exhibition of Paintings by Walt Kuhn" opened at the Grand Central Art Galleries on 20 January 1927 and ran through 9 February. The press was favorable and the sales good. Had the Quinn auction, which began the very night of the closing, come before, the financial results could have been disastrous. Kuhn may have had some foreknowledge of the date and planned accordingly. All that is known is that there was some tension with the administration. He accused the manager, Erwin S. Barrie, of publicly criticizing his paintings. Barrie wrote that it was all a big misunderstanding, that he could not have criticized the paintings because he admired them so much. Whether he did or not, he was too good a salesman to jeopardize the Galleries' commission. And it must be admitted that in 1927 Walt Kuhn's paintings were a little exotic compared with the Grand Central's usual bill of fare.

There were thirty-seven paintings in the exhibition, and LaSalle Spier had written an eight-page text for the catalogue titled "One Approach to the Art of Walt Kuhn." It was, of course, a musical approach. Among other things Spier says:

> It is almost certain that the most casual layman will immediately take an entirely different point of view and derive instant pleasure from Mr. Kuhn's pictures if he will apply to them the same analysis which he employs when listening to the rendition of a musical composition.
> . . . One does not have to search far to discover astonishing examples of rhythm, harmony and counterpoint. Polytonal and atonal chords, even, are frequently to be found. His scale of dynamics is most unusual and ranges from the subdued velvet tones of muted strings to the powerful volume of full orchestra. His color schemes include everything from the wooden clack of the xylophone to the blatant brass blasts of trumpet or trombone.
> In the case of Walt Kuhn we are dealing not only with a composer but also with an orchestral director who assembles his instruments, then plays his score on them. He seems to have every technical and interpretative resource of both composer and conductor at his command.

As Gregg had done before in *Rainbow*, LaSalle Spier concentrates on *The City*, ending his analysis: "In regard to instrumentation,

Plate 53. Top. *Reclining Figure*. Bottom. *Reclining Nude With Knee Raised*

Courtesy of Kennedy Galleries, Inc.—Kuhn Estate

Courtesy of Kennedy Galleries, Inc.—Kuhn Estate

one can detect the tone qualities of many instruments. In the eyes and lips one finds the limpid tones of the flute. The oboe plays an important part, together with the strings, in the slow movement, represented by the bodice with its embroidered design. The English horn, bassoon, French horn, double base and the clarinet in its lower register produce effects similar to the dismal lower right hand corner of the background. In the rose one finds the brilliant, penetrating tones of the piccolo and the trumpet, and of strings, pizzicato. The head and the upper part of the body represent the full orchestra, with the eloquent tones of the French horn and 'cello predominating; the lower part of the figure suggests brass and percussion effects. And so on, indefinitely."

Spier wrote musical scores for *Amalgam* and *Green Plums*; he listed "Musical Titles suggested by Some of the Pictures: The City—Symphony for full orchestra; The Rider—Male chorus, with suppressed power; Amalgam—Atonality in brass; Green plums—polytonality; The dressing room—Orchestra music for a ballet, A major, Allegretto; Exotic Flowers—Violins divided; Singing tree—Folksong for contralto

Plate 54. Top. *Reclining Nude*. Bottom. *Reclining Nude on Elbow*

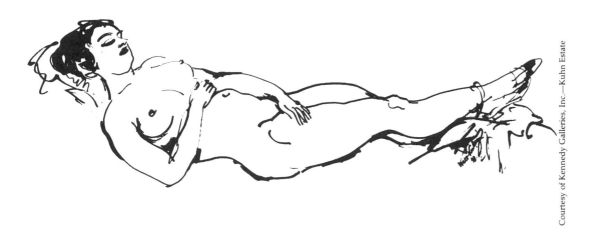

Courtesy of Kennedy Galleries, Inc.—Kuhn Estate

voice, unaccompanied; Man with ship model—Sonata in stark mood for piano; Pine-tree—Gong and bells; Sheba—Barcarolle; Portrait of Miss Enters—Andante for flute and strings; Superba—Organ prelude, full organ." A great deal of study and effort had gone into the essay; it was a more than gracious gesture from a brother-in-law.

The *New York Times* solemnly endorsed the musical interpretation: "For once the two arts are given an intelligible relation, and Mr. Spier's interpretation definitely aids the observer to find his way through the painter's composition with increased interest and recognition of the organic character of the work." And in a burst of parochial or somewhat belated loyalty the *Sunday Star* in Washington on 27 March reprinted the Spier text almost *in toto*. The young *New Yorker*, however, did not take to the musical approach. Its anonymous reviewer said in the 5 February issue:

Walt Kuhn having advertised that he was giving a show in the Grand Central Galleries, and having prepared brochures to the effect that his new pictures would not be like other little pictures, but would sing songs and play symphonies, we

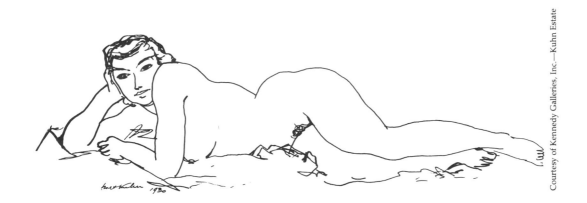

Courtesy of Kennedy Galleries, Inc.—Kuhn Estate

Plate 55. *Sleeping Girl*

rushed over to see what the Vitaphone idea had done to graphic art. The place was plastered with wild Kuhns, the rooms were filled, and there was music. Aghast, we stood before the painting known as "Amalgam," looking at the score provided in the catalog. As we read music but slowly, we had gone no further than "fast and brilliantly," so we couldn't check up with the particular movement that "Amalgam" was playing. But music it was, we could not deny. Singing pictures there are, but they never require a score or book of the play. So please be kind and forget that Mr. Kuhn sponsors this bunk about "melodic curves" and "horizontal counterpoint" and go up to the galleries and see some excellent painting.

Under the sponsorship of the Arts Club the exhibition moved intact to Chicago for the month of March and was hung in the Art Institute. A new catalogue without the Spier text was printed, and Blanche C. Mathias, of the *Chicago Evening Post,* led the cheering. The year before, the *Post* had run a long interview with Kuhn in his New York Studio, and one paragraph bears repeating:

"Sincere painting? That means staying within your own limits. Abstraction must begin with a physical fact, and most sincere painters admit this to be true. Art is based on story. Perhaps the story gets started by the sight of a potato, or a woman's knee, but sure as sure the beginning impulse comes from a physical fact. After that it depends upon what the artist does with the fact. How he places the furniture in the room, what he knows about rhythm, how he orchestrates. How much he imagines, how much he feels, what sense he possesses of dramatics. What his ancestry has bequeathed to him, and on and on, until the picture which started from a physical and tangible fact becomes perhaps an individualized abstraction, until the artist has succeeded in making every violin sound like a violin, every drum beat a pulsing and unmistakable accent."

Musical parallels were in the air before 1927.

4

The balance of 1927 produced twenty-one paintings. Kuhn's opinion of them is implicit in the fact that he later destroyed five and never exhibited two. *Acrobat in Green* (number 188),however, had a New England season, showing in Boston's Museum of Fine Arts, the

Lyman Allyn Museum of New London, Connecticut, the Wadsworth Atheneum in Hartford, and ending up in the permanent collection of the Addison Gallery of American Art in Andover, Massachusetts. The small *Portrait of Brenda* (number 201) is a directly painted head of a sixteen-year-old girl, not untouched with paternal affection, but strictly unsentimental. *Mary with Red Bandana* (number 199) was admitted to the anthology of *50 Paintings*, whose comment is: "Not really a likeness, but an abstract presentation of womanly beauty. She has serenity with alertness, assurance with reticence, nobility and graciousness. She is, of course, above any sordid responsibilities. All this is carried in the finely poised design which lacks yet expresses perfect symmetry. A young goddess of today."

In the winter of 1927—28 Walt Kuhn taught at the Art Students' League, liking it no more than he had before at the New York School of Art. The Art Students' League was even more loosely organized, the students selecting their own instructors or sometimes going the rounds of the whole faculty. Kuhn felt the same lack of discipline in the students, serious though most of them were, and did

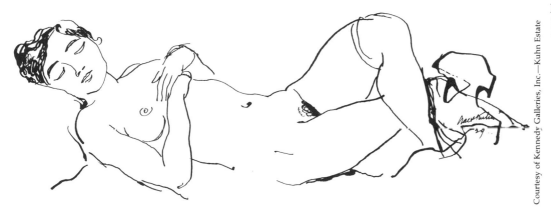

Plate 56. Top. *Sleeping Nude.* Bottom. *Nude with Legs Turned*

Courtesy of Kennedy Galleries, Inc.—Kuhn Estate

Courtesy of Kennedy Galleries, Inc.—Kuhn Estate

Plate 57. *Amalgam*

Plate 58 (opposite). *Portrait of Brenda*

not like the popularity-contest atmosphere; there was too much competing for student favor. He never taught formally again.

Also in 1927 he had stopped making prints, concentrating instead on his drawings. By December 1928 he felt ready for a drastically selected show at Knoedler's, the M. Knoedler and Company, one of the great art-dealer firms, with its own building at 14 East Fifty-seventh Street. Alan Burroughs wrote a perceptive foreword for the catalogue:

> This is dangerous art, with its seeming simplicity and worn subject matter; but do not be misled by the apparent ease. Walt Kuhn is not misled. He dislikes style and admires economy—so that, drawing a torso in three tenuous lines, he keeps color, weight and texture, or glamour, frivolity and sleekness, or as many other qualities as you can find in him to question or approve.
>
> When you first knew him, you saw in his painting the legitimate result of modernism; or perhaps you wondered about the legitimacy. Now you feel, in spite of the dim influence of oriental sculpture upon his work, that he is frankly national. In the American way, he is specific, insistent and canny. He plans things. Behind his gallery of girls is a self-discipline that would do credit to a savage Puritan. He knows that a pretty girl presents the most difficult material he can use, men being less subtle on every count, and that the over-tones of gallantry or morality are dangerous. But the difficult subject drives him hardest; and he tears into it, denying prettiness, using a difficult medium—black ink on plain paper. His pen moves like a flexible razor, marking what it barely touches.
>
> . . . What I am trying to suggest is that Walt Kuhn is capacious. Even when confronted by generic similarities he does not repeat himself. He does not make studies, but grasps total effects. However drab the model, it reaches you through a refined emotion, yet without loss of essential drabness. Perhaps that is the reaction Walt Kuhn desires most, and what he means when he demands "buck-eyes" from himself. He wants his drawing to be perfectly ordinary, with the emphasis on the perfecting, and he insists on combining the obvious and the subtle in what the Greeks called a higher reality. His "buck-eyes" in short, is the sublimation of the commonplace.

"Buck-eyes" are something like what the Germans call *kitsch*; a Viennese sculptor once defined it as "*Kitsch* is what somebody else does." In France they are called *pompiers*. The word comes from the Parisian firemen with their brass helmets, and was first insultingly applied to the bronze-helmeted classical or Napoleonic heroes and auxiliaries of pretentious salon paintings. Once after a pleasant afternoon in Paris with Derain in 1933, Walt Kuhn said, "Now show me some pompiers." Derain answered, "Ah, but *pompiers* are hard to paint."

In 1928 Kuhn also exhibited by invitation in American Annuals in Chicago, Detroit, Cincinnati, and Cleveland. His Cleveland entry, *Rocks, Arizona* (number 226), was burned up with many others in a railroad wreck on its return trip. Insurance was promptly paid, and for years the story was told of how well for a few weeks the artists lived, in their little Bohemia north of Columbus Circle where the Lincoln Center now stands. It was more profitable than selling the paintings, with dealers' commissions and bargaining purchasers.

Rocks, Arizona was one of seven paintings Kuhn kept from an expedition with his family to Prescott, Arizona, in the summer of 1928, followed by a stay in San Francisco. There were eighteen paintings

from 1928, two of them intentionally destroyed. Of the survivors *Girl with Hair Down* (number 216) still shows the linear stress and frontal pose, but *Girl with Mirror* (number 217) is almost a baroque composition, much more broadly painted. It was purchased by Duncan Phillips for his distinguished collection—none more distinguished—in Washington. *Jeannette* (number 219) was Kuhn's favorite child of 1928. Miss Bliss bought it and bequeathed it to the Museum of Modern Art. According to the comment in *50 Paintings, Jeannette* is "One of the first in a series of paintings devoted to the artist's personal conception of feminine beauty. Emphasis upon the lithe, adolescent body, ivory flesh, ruby lips and raven hair. Done with a spontaneity of statement which, at that time, had encouraging effect upon the artist's career."

Francis Kuhn's final illness brought Walt back from San Francisco in the fall. He wrote to a friend there on 5 January 1929: "This is to explain my sudden departure from San Francisco. I received a hurry call to come East on account of my father's condition, and got back in time to care for him in his last weeks of life. He died a few weeks ago. Peace be with him." Another chapter in Kuhn's life had ended.

NOTES TO CHAPTER FIVE

CONRAD ON MELODRAMA is quoted from B.L.Reid, *The Man from New York*, 1968, p. 382. KUHN'S AWARENESS OF THE ULYSSES PROBLEM is mentioned by Reid, ibid., pp. 442,445.

KUHN'S CEZANNE ARTICLE is quoted from *Art News*, April 1947, pp. 16,55.

The QUOTATION FROM WORDSWORTH is mentioned in the Catalogue of the Memorial Exhibition, 1960, p.4. The lines are from the sixth stanza of "The Tables Turned." Wordsworth had little gift for titles.

The DUCHAMP-VILLON MEMORIAL BOOK comes from Reid, *The Man from New York*, p. 468.

On John Quinn's death in 1924 Walt Kuhn did not sever all CONNECTIONS WITH THE LITERARY WORLD, though he was no longer involved with the titans. He had a lively correspondence with H.L. Mencken and Frank Crownishield, knew Edna St. Vincent Millay, whose husband bought *Mario* for her, and corresponded with Genevieve Taggard for years; she wrote the text for the catalogue of his "Landscape Drawing" show at the Marie Harriman Gallery in 1931. In 1935 he said to the author: "You're interested in poetry. Let's see what I can arrange." The next evening Max Weber came in from Long Island for a dinner for three at one of the modest white-table restaurants Kuhn patronized; the group then moved on to a small party with e.e. cummings and his glamorous wife. On 20 December 1946 he proposed to Mencken that he get George Jean Nathan to do an "Ibsen versus Cézanne" article. Probably neither Mencken nor Nathan knew enough about Cézanne to bring it off, though Kuhn knew Ibsen well enough and could have furnished the Cézanne material.

The BULLIET REMARKS are quoted from his *Apples and Madonnas* (New York: Convici-Friede 1930), pp. 223—24.

The circumstances of JOHN QUINN'S ILLNESS AND DEATH as well as the DISTRIBUTION OF HIS COLLECTION are scattered through the last seven chapters of Reid, *The Man from New York*.

The MEDICAL DIAGNOSIS OF 1925 comes from the death certificate of 14 July 1949, on the evidence of an autopsy, which described the earlier ulcers as about twenty-five years old.

The LETTER TO HORACE BRODZKY is dated 5 October 1943.

Kuhn's REMARK ABOUT THE CLEANING WOMAN was published in the Memorial Exhibition Catalogue, 1960, p.9.

Charles Robert Leslie, R.A., published the MEMOIRS OF JOHN CONSTABLE in 1845. He had stayed in America with his parents from 1799 to 1811 and, interestingly enough, returned in 1833 for a brief term as instructor of drawing at West Point. Constable died in 1837.

The difference between SELECTED AND COLLECTED WORKS was published in the University of Arizona Catalogue, 1966, p. 13.

The COMMENT ON "DRESSING ROOM" is from John I.H. Baur's article in the January 1936 issue of the *Brooklyn museum quarterly*, p. 14. The painting is illustrated on p.15, with a detail of the head on the cover. Baur later moved to the Whitney Museum and became its director.

DERAIN'S REMARK ABOUT POMPIERS was published in the Memorial Exhibition Catalogue, 960, p. 9.

The White Clown

The next four years were crowded with major events, major paintings, major exhibitions, major recognition as a leading American artist — but above all, major paintings. However, one event of immediate interest to Walt Kuhn had far more general importance, and that was the birth of the Museum of Modern Art. Ever since 1913, scattered groups of enthusiasts had been talking of the need for such a museum. At the time it was often referred to as an "American Luxembourg," which in those days showed the French state collections of living artists, since the Louvre's regulations required that an artist be safely dead before he could be enshrined in its galleries.

The dispersal of John Quinn's collection spurred on the plans. Had there been such a museum in 1924, he just might have changed his complicated will and advanced the cause of modern style by several years. As in the case of many American art museums, it was an informal committee of women who nursed the idea into robust life by the fall of 1929. Miss Lizzie Bliss was to be the first vice-president, Mrs. John D. Rockefeller, Jr., the first treasurer, and Mrs. W. Murray Crane, Mrs. Rainey Rogers, and Mrs. Cornelius J. Sullivan served on the small, original fourteen-member board of trustees. Mrs. Rockefeller and Miss Bliss owned paintings by Walt Kuhn, and his 1913 reputation was still lustrous. He sat in on many luncheon and tea-time conferences, and claimed to have been the first to suggest Mr. A. Conger Goodyear as president. Legend has it that Conger Goodyear, a noted collector of Cézanne, Gauguin, and others, was edged off the board of the Albright Art Gallery in Buffalo for his part in buying one of Picasso's finest "blue period" canvases for the gallery, and he subsequently removed himself to the friendlier climate of New York.

The Museum of Modern Art opened in November of 1929 at the Heckscher Building on Fifth Avenue, not far from its present site and conveniently near the art dealers' world of Fifty-seventh Street. Its first exhibition was a thunderous salvo of "Cézanne, Gauguin, Seurat, Van Gogh." Kuhn felt that it had used up too much ammunition in that first broadside, but much more was to come. In fact, the Museum of Modern Art put public understanding of the whole modern movement on a solid educational footing with its carefully planned exhibitions and their brilliant catalogues, largely the work of the first and long-time director, Mr. Alfred H. Barr, Jr. Corot and Daumier were shown in the fall of 1930 as founding fathers of modern painting; not the middle-period Corot of the idyllic landscapes, but his abstractly engineered early Italian landscapes and his superb late paintings, which he rarely bothered to exhibit in his time. And it was not the Daumier of *Charivari's* unrivaled lithographs, but his little-known paintings. He burned his eyes out drawing the lithographs at night to save the day-light hours for his paintings, many of them unfinished or, unfortunately, finished by his friends after his death. In February and March 1931 Toulouse-Lautrec, with whom Kuhn was often compared, and Odilon Redon, Kuhn's 1912 discovery and the spiritual father of surrealism, confronted each other in another two-man ancestral show. November of that year brought a large well-explained retrospective of Matisse.

The exhibition program and the growing permanent collection, with Miss Bliss's paintings as its foundation, were for the first ten years a chapter-by-chapter development of the Armory Show, for a much better prepared audience. A film library was created; photographic, architectural, and circulating exhibition departments were added; exhibitions of well-designed useful objects available on the market had a widespread influence on manufacturers as well as consumers.

But the Museum of Modern Art wanted to be more than a port of entry for European artists—there were already enough dealers playing that role—and its second exhibition, from 13 December 1929 to 12 January 1930, was "Paintings by Nineteen Living Americans." The board felt that the selection of the nineteen was its responsibility, and there were lively infighting and jockeying for favorites. Once the nineteen were chosen most of the artists were consulted as to what works they would like to represent them. No one was to have less than five or more than seven.

Alfred Barr said in his foreword:"It seemed best to include less than twenty painters in order that a half dozen paintings by each might be shown rather than two paintings each by fifty painters or one each by a hundred. The nineteen were chosen in the following manner. Ballots containing over a hundred names were distributed among the trustees who were asked to check the fifteen painters who each thought should be shown in the museum's first exhibition of American painting. The results were tabulated and carefully studied by a committee who drew up the list of nineteen."

Plate 59. *Pine on a Knoll*

Courtesy of Mr. W. Averell Harriman

Barr then held out an olive branch:"Possibly several other painters might have been substituted or added, had space permitted, without affecting the standard of the exhibition. The committee wishes to emphasize the fact that future exhibitions will include many painters omitted at present."

The definition of an "American" painter had to be discussed:

It is interesting to observe that of the nineteen Americans five were born abroad: Karfiol, Kuniyoshi, Pascin, Feininger, Sterne and Weber. A similar proportion of foreign-born artists might be found in Paris or in Germany. Three of the nineteen, Pascin, Feininger and Sterne, have lived most of their mature lives abroad, yet the United States can well afford to accept these three of her citizens who are more honored in Europe than any other American painters. America has not hesitated in the past to claim such expatriates as Whistler or Sargent or Mary Cassatt. Some of the other painters in the exhibition are perhaps more obviously and essentially American than Sterne or Weber or Pascin but it is questionable whether any are better painters. Those who chose the exhibition were concerned principally with the quality of these men as artists.

Although most of the nineteen are still fairly well known, some are with the snows of yesteryear. The list begins alphabetically with Charles Burchfield (five watercolors), followed by Charles Demuth (four watercolors and three oils); Preston Dickinson (four oils and one pastel); Lyonel Feininger (five watercolors and two oils); George Overbury "Pop" Hart, a protégé of Walt Kuhn and Mrs. Rockefeller (five watercolors); Bernard Karfiol (five oils); Rockwell Kent (five oils);

Walt Kuhn (five oils); Yasuo Kuniyoshi (five oils); Ernest Lawson (five oils); John Marin (six watercolors); Kenneth Hayes Miller, one of the most influential teachers at the Art Students' League and before that at the New York School of Art (five oils); Georgia O'Keeffe (five oils); Jules Pascin (five oils and watercolors); John Sloan (five oils); Maurice Sterne (six oils); and Max Weber (seven oils). Each artist had two reproductions in the catalogue. Stieglitz, Charles Daniel, the Downtown Gallery and Frank K.M. Rehn were the chief dealers. The cries of the uninvited wounded could be heard for months.

Walt Kuhn chose *Bareback Rider* (number 64) of 1926, *Athene* (number 190) of 1927, *Jeannette* (number 19) of 1928, *Electra* (number 239) of 1929, and, for its first showing, easily the most important painting in the whole exhibition, *The White Clown* (number 248) of 1929. It quickly became one of the better-known modern American masterpieces, reproduced many times in publications as various as the College Art Association's *Parnassus*, in 1929, on the cover; *Theatre Guild Magazine,* as a frontispiece in 1930; Samuel Kootz's *Modern American Painters* in 1930; a textbook called *Art Appreciation* in 1931; an updated edition of Sheldon Cheney's *A Primer of Modern Art* in 1932; and so on.

Kuhn exhibited it only a few times: at the newly founded Marie Harriman Gallery in November 1930, in a 1933 one-man show at the City Art Museum in Saint Louis, and a similar show in Columbus and Dayton, Ohio, in 1935. He repeatedly refused to sell it, even to Averell and Marie Harriman, with whom he was soon to have the most cordial and mutually beneficial association. The Harrimans eventually bought it from Vera Kuhn in 1957; Sanka Knox reported in the *New York Times* on 22 August, "Art Masterpiece Goes to Harriman," for a rumored $25,000. It was a symbol intensely personal to Kuhn. Many important paintings were to follow, but this was somehow his passport to immortality, the "one fine painting" he was content to leave. And it is now, fittingly, in the collection of the National Gallery, given in 1972 by W. Averell Harriman in memory of Marie N. Harriman. *The White Clown* is primarily black and white, simple on the surface but with the subtlest tonal variations. The massive white is the white of Zurbarán's monks, and the deliberately limited palette is another Spanish trait. A pale yellow appears on the skull cap and the hands are a tawny ocher; the red signature and date below them are the only notes of bright color in the painting. Kuhn's own comment, through Paul Bird is: "Peak performance in bulk, weight and substance. Like an animal crouched for the kill, he might instantly charge into his routine. Action strains at the bit. With the simplest colors—virtually black and white—the figure is modeled into a throbbing arabesque, fitted exactly to the canvas. Monumentality in a 30" x 40" area."

Writing in 1967, Frank Getlein, the Washington critic and art historian, came as close as anyone is likely to come to finding words for the inner meaning of *The White Clown:*

He [Walt Kuhn] said later that he was forty years old before he painted a picture really worthwhile. In point of fact he was just over fifty when everything fell into place with the *White Clown*, when Kuhn as he is known in art museums and art histories really came into existence.

. . . The "arabesque" is composed of both the over-all lines of the figure and the indication of the muscle system within those lines. There is the genuine Cézanne sense of form reduced to its most economical statement. And the painter is right about the form being "fitted exactly" to the size and shape of the picture. The enclosing rectangle contributes to the sense of inner pressure generated by the picture. The hunched over figure also adds to that sense, as if the clown drew in a bit to allow for the constricting pressures around him.

All of this was the "abstraction" that was so important to Walt Kuhn. It is geometry. The coloring of the picture, also, can hardly be called emotional. It is austere, almost black and white. But "Euclid alone has looked on Beauty bare," and it is from this austere geometry that the haunting beauty of Kuhn's art arises. The face of the *White Clown* is not particularly tragic. It is sad, somewhat, tired no doubt. Mostly, it is simply there: no longer crinkled into professional smiles, but now at ease in normal introspective concern. The effect comes from the powerful, constricted geometry built up and around to that face. The hulking figure more than the expressive eyes carries the emotional burden of the painting.

The White Clown was not in the exhibition Getlein was discussing, but it had to be cited as the announcement of the artist's maturity.

Kuhn had developed a studio procedure that helped him achieve that exact fitting of figure to canvas. After prolonged thought, preliminary drawings, watercolor sketches, and sometimes trial runs in small oil sketches, he would tack his canvas, often the scraped-off surface of a painting he had decided to destroy in this way, on a sheet of masonite or other hard board. Then he blocked in the large areas, carefully adjusting their main tonal relationships, which he said never came easily to him; all this before the model took his pose. He never worked without a model in the final stages, needing the challenge of the physical fact in front of him. Toward the end he would accent features, figures, or accessories with a few telling, definitive brushed lines. Then, since the canvas was larger than the finished framed painting was intended to be, and not yet on a stretcher, he would adjust the final size with chalk lines, sometimes moving a frame of the proper dimensions around till he found the right placement of the figure on the canvas. Even then he would not stretch and frame the painting; he would put it aside, still tacked to its board, or roll it up after it had dried enough, until once or twice a season his wife and daughter would join him in the review and verdict. If it passed this severe objective trial, he would then sign and date it, finding the exact place where the calligraphy of signature and date would be an integral part of the painting.

But the vital principle of this geometry is more than the exact fitness of figure to containing boundaries. Several photographs of Archaic Greek sculptures always hung on his studio wall. He would gesture to the tense thighs of the "Apollos" or "kouroi" and say that they existed at the precise point where inner and outer pressure met in counterforce. A thrust more of inner pressure would explode them, the least build-up of outer pressure would turn them slack and flabby. It was not the physics of an inflated toy balloon but that of a steel cylinder barely holding the deadly power of compressed oxygen. And there can be found the driving force of his painted abstractions, perhaps their "haunting beauty" as well. To continue the quotation from Edna St. Vincent Millay's sonnet,

> . . . Euclid alone
> Has looked on Beauty bare. Fortunate they
> Who, though once only and then but far away,
> Have heard her massive sandal set on stone.

Three other paintings stand out among the twenty Walt Kuhn produced in 1929. The same model posed for both *The White Clown* and

Plate 60. *The Man from Eden*

119

Plate 61. *Clown with Black Wig*

the smaller *Athlete* (number 234). Nothing could better show Kuhn's indifference to the particularities of portraiture; he needed the model's physical presence, possibly something of his professional background, but not the intrusion of personality. Paul Bird's comment on *Athlete* reads: "Cut clean at the shoulders, this design recalls an inverted cup of glass, except that it is solid. One could almost grasp this figure by the sturdy neck, lift out of the picture, place it right on the mantelpiece and call it Bust of a Man in bronze. It is that weighty. Being that weighty it

Plate 62. *Clown with Red Wig*

Private Collection

represents classicism in art. Real classicism does not mean a diaphonous nude goddess; it means solidity."

High School Rider (number 242) was one of the artist's personal favorites; he says of it: "Super-horsemanship gets so precise as to be almost inhuman. This coldly poised performer has submerged emotion under the terrific discipline of the equestrian art. Its effect is carried mainly by the hard, quick lines of the design itself. A sister of the typical hard-boiled New York career woman." To emphasize this theme, the lines are indeed hard and quick, the large areas quite flat. In some ways it could have been painted five years earlier, but not with the same hardness and sureness.

It is revealing that Kuhn included only two landscapes in his 1940 review of *50 paintings*, while reproducing and commenting on twelve still lifes. That is about their numerical ratio in his last nineteen years. *Pine on a Knoll* (number 246) of 1929, still in the Harriman collection, is one of his distinguished performances. Just as he had arrived at that central theme of all western art, the single human figure simply posed, so are his landscapes usually single trees. In a horizontal format the lone pine stands bristling with life on a rocky hillock with two feathery hardwood trees in the middle left distance. Unlike the increasingly flat and featureless backgrounds of his figures, and of many later landscapes, the clouds and sky are a present and essential part of the whole.

121

2

The long and happy relationship with Marie and Averell Harriman began early in 1930. Marie Harriman's name comes first, since the idea of starting a gallery was hers. Born Marie Norton, she was a rare combination of beauty, charm, and alert intelligence; and her second husband, W. Averell Harriman, enthusiastically went along with the gallery idea, occasionally even taking time from the administration of his economic empire to check the gallery's books. As Walt Kuhn told it, he was approached by Averell's mother, Mrs. Edward Henry Harriman, one of the pillars of society whom Kuhn consistently and success-

Plate 63. *The Guide*

Plate 64 (opposite). *The White Clown*

Courtesy of the F. M. Hall Collection, University of Nebraska Art Galleries, Lincoln

122

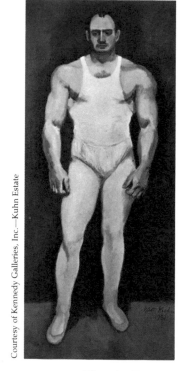

Plate 65. *Top Man*

Plate 66. *The Blue Clown*

fully cultivated, with no climbing pretensions but with a keen eye for profitable patronage. As has been said, Kuhn was always his own dealer. He also had an unflagging curiosity about the whole world around him, and this was a window on one small but important, and ordinarily inaccessible, part of it. At an especially inconvenient time in the late thirties, Mrs. August Belmont telephoned to ask him to design the program cover for some Metropolitan Opera benefit. He promptly dropped other pressing concerns, because he "could certainly afford to do a favor for Mrs. Belmont."

Mrs. Harriman owned the small 1923 still life *Green Plums*, and asked Kuhn if he would "keep an eye on the young people so that they wouldn't make too many mistakes." It was a project ideally suited to

Plate 67. *Hydrangeas*

Kuhn's inclinations and needs. He immediately foresaw a small distinguished gallery, under the most auspicious patronage, where he would have a strong advisory, if not governing, voice, and could show his own work under his own conditions. This last consideration was the most important; all his earlier galleries, including the Grand Central, which was too large and unselective, and the Downtown Gallery, where Edith Halpert was inescapable, had been constricting in one way or another. He wanted no one to tell him how, what, or when to show things. Being in on the ground floor of a new gallery, he believed, correctly, that he could mold things to his own specifications, at least when his own work was involved. Not that Marie Harriman was yieldingly docile or had no mind of her own, but she was eager to learn, and recognized authority as well as experience and showmanship when she saw it.

In its 8 February 1933 issue the *Commonweal* wrote: "They have distinctly amusing shows at this gallery (Marie Harriman), the character of which is perhaps indicated by the fact that Walt Kuhn is their

125

Plate 68 *Trio*

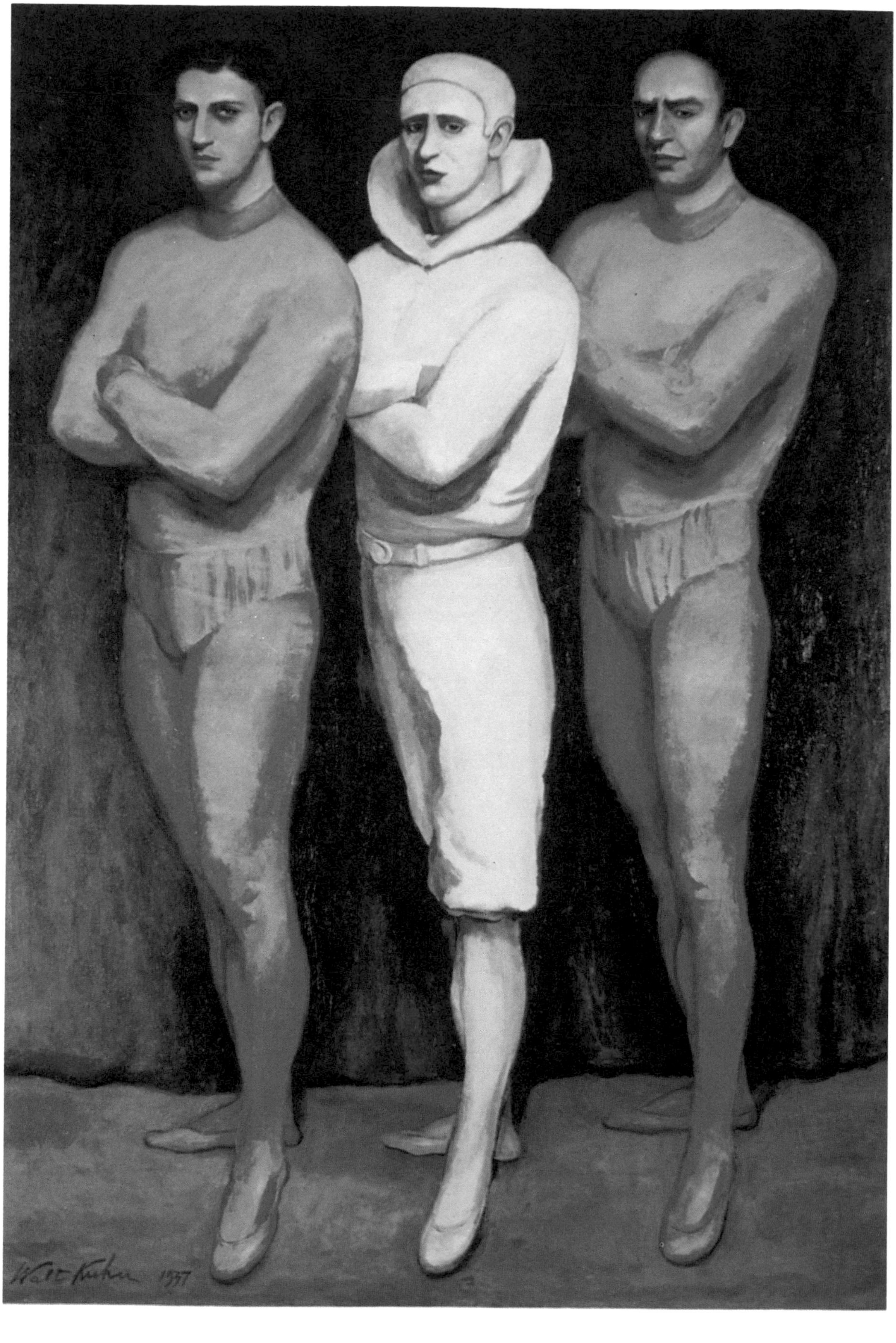

Courtesy of the Colorado Springs Fine Arts Center, Gift of the El Pomar Foundation golden-haired boy. For verve, good paintings and an unmalicious feeling for life and art, he is of course one of the best we have." No one ever accused Kuhn of milking the Harrimans, as they earlier had in the case of John Quinn. For one thing, the Harrimans were not easily imposed on; and more significantly, Kuhn paid his way in full measure. Anyone could tell where such shrewed counseling for both the gallery's and the Harrimans' private collecting came from, as well as the animated exhibition program on whose source the *Commonweal* had put its finger.

One of the gallery's first shows was an "Exhibition of Paintings by Walt Kuhn" from 1 to 26 November 1930, at 61—63 East Fifty-

Plate 69. *Show Girl with Plumes*

127

seventh Street. There were twenty-four paintings, a large number for Kuhn's taste, but this was an inaugural show. *Hare and Hunting Boots* and *Mallards* of 1926 were included, along with *Mountain Rabbits* (number 222) and *Tulip* (number 232), not a flower piece but an upward-blossoming show girl, from 1928. From 1929 came *Black Pine* (number 235), *Cleft Rocks* (number 237), *Electra, Helen* (number 240), *Oak in September* (number 244), *Young Pines among Rocks* (number 253), *Pine on a Knoll, High School Rider* and *The White Clown. Dry River Bed* (number 261) of 1930 completed the group of six landscapes compared to only three still lifes, not a typical ratio.

Alan Burroughs again wrote the foreword to the catalogue, as he had for the 1928 Knoedler drawing show. He was a consistent admirer with a clear understanding of both Kuhn's intention and accomplishment, which were not necessarily always the same. As late as 4 January 1938 he wrote to Kuhn:"This opportunity I seize also to say that the painting you gave me continues to furnish spiritual refreshment—and that is my only test of art." It is not certain what painting Burroughs was referring to, but Walt Kuhn believed in returning favors.

Among other things the foreword says:

What kind of person makes these pictures? He has, of course, a sophisticated taste. And he seems to be aware of some raucous strain in existence. At the same time he apparently has a simple ideal. He wants to paint strongly the things he feels are subtle and general at the same time. He intends to make you feel the full value of a plainly recorded contact with something. Let us be specific. He wants you to see in "Helen" a magnificent set of shoulders, formally posed to show off their massive grace. He wants you to believe in his admiration for these shapes and his restraint in presenting them as objects of admiration. But in "Show Girl" he calls upon you to relish cheap color and a garish model who typifies reds which all but screech and a pose that is almost a case for the professional reformer. "Show Girl" is delicately painted, nevertheless. And if Walt Kuhn is stimulated by the necessity of combining lavender and veridian, one should not object—provided he concocts enough of each to make a stunning combination and keeps them simple. . . . The whole question of subject is up to him. If he chooses a shiny, new tin can to paint, one can only demand that the picture be as tinny and as can-like as possible.

But there is a question in your mind. Walt Kuhn, I said, wants to paint subtle things . . . like tin cans? Exactly, if you accept the tin metaphorically, as a symbol of the definite and unusual in art. A friend of the artist calls it *The Great American Tin Can*, emphasizing in that way the flamboyant, hard and exceedingly commonplace facts which clutter and characterize a phase of American life. All Walt's subjects can be tagged by that symbol, even when not hard or not garish. Cheap finery, he believes, is stimulating to paint, because it is universal and yet so difficult a vehicle for subtle effects. He extracts glamor from even a tawdry subject.

Walt Kuhn would have denied profanely any paternity for the pop art of thirty years later. He could not conceivably have condoned their inferior, sometimes nonexistent, quality as paintings; but he might well have been amused by their purpose, and certainly would have understood it.

The White Clown was the undisputed star of the show. Two smaller paintings, however, played more than supporting roles. One was *The Man from Eden* (number 265), now in the Albright-Knox Art

Gallery in Buffalo by way of Conger Goodyear's collection. The other was *Acrobat with Cigarette* (number 254), a frankly psychological, sociological portrait. *The Man from Eden* is remarkably monumental in scale if not in size. Kuhn's comment in 1940 was: "Not from the Garden of Eden, but Eden, Wisconsin where he grew up as a farm boy. He drifted with the show business to New York, and eventually to the artist's studio. He is a loyal admirer of art and artists and enjoys posing for such reflective pictures. We will meet this Lincolnian figure in a later painting." Actually he appears in two later paintings, *The Camp Cook* (number 270) of 1931 and *Wisconsin* (number 350) of 1936; the model was George Fitzgerald, an actor with Lillies, a producing and booking agency. He had an intuitive sense of Kuhn's requirements and sent him many useful models over the years.

The Paul Bird-Walt Kuhn caption for *Acrobat with Cigarette* reads: "You've seen him in the subway, along Main Street, or at the corner pool parlor. He has no sense of responsibility. He is a sullen incorrigible who made his own decision to run out on his opportunities. It's too bad. Sorry. But don't blame the artist. Painters are not reformers. This one, particularly, takes life as he finds it." But not always in a particular model; Albert Driscoll, who posed for *Acrobat with Cigarette,* also posed for the very different, in theme as well as subject, *Clown with Black Wig* (number 257). Kuhn added it to the exhibition after the catalogue had gone to press, perhaps as a pendant to *The White Clown,* or as an encore for those who wondered what would come next. It has its partisans, including the Metropolitan Museum, which got around to buying it in 1956. It is more colorful, more theatrical, and more relaxed, as the artist and writer comment: "Built on a linear theme of bow-knot designs. Constant repetition and variation of the theme done in a lazy, swinging tempo, yet with precision. Clowning is an ancient, legitimate profession with relatively as many master performers, apprentices, and pretenders as any other profession. Here it is symbolized in cross section." Evidently, subject and theme are not identical if the same model could serve for pool parlor incorrigible and disciplined professional, though Kuhn may be using "theme" in the musical sense of the word. In painting the word should better be construed as the inner meaning, in contrast to the illustrator's subject, though both can and sometimes do coincide.

Of the other paintings, *Show Girl* (number 267) does not seem to be quite so abandoned a type as she did to Alan Burroughs; she is simply a tired, probably cynical, costumed show girl, slumped in an unlady-like cross-legged pose. *Dreaming Girl* (number 258) is fatally sentimental. Kuhn may have suspected this, and commented, a shade defensively, in 1940: "A model often determines the picture. The artist made several unsuccessful paintings of this girl until one day, fatigued, she fell into her natural self—a pensive madonna-like woman. There the artist had his cue. Her metallic blue costume and blue-black hair contribute to the brooding wistful effect." *Elise* (number 262), on the

129

Plate 70. *The Camp Cook*

Courtesy of the Munson-Williams-Proctor Institute, Utica, New York

other hand, though gentle enough, is a much more direct painting. She too is dark-haired, dressed in a pink bodice and white-lined orange wrapper with the accent of one azure shoulder strap. These potentially discordant hues are tastefully controlled. She was the color cover of the 1 January 1931 *Town and Country*, and it is puzzling that she was destroyed. Kuhn distrusted his native taste, and possibly she did not meet some goal set for her in the artist's mind. The exhibition and the new gallery were a success; the *Herald Tribune, Social Calendar, Evening Post,* and the *Times* illustrated various paintings, but most of the sales came later.

Top Man (number 277) brought in the new year of 1931, and Kuhn considered it one of his best, at least while he was still close to it. He did not include it in the *50 Paintings* of 1940, but referred to it often in his letters to Vera from Paris in 1931, calling it his "best to date." In one of the letters he wrote: "The whole story is in his right arm and hand. Of course you know it is not just a picture of a man. My idea was to have that gorilla grow out of the comparatively delicate and perhaps effeminate lower part, which is of course to me very important, more or less signifying the alleged grace of the circus." These are suggestive qualifications, "more or less," and "the alleged grace." The painting could mean much more or something quite different.

Kuhn also wrote to Vera from Paris: "Have seen nothing to touch my best black and white landscapes. I must make them still more loose and free, in fact that also applies to the oils." "Landscape Drawings by Walt Kuhn" was his second, change-of-pace exhibition at the Marie Harriman Gallery in February 1931. They are unquestionably among his finest works, and among the finest works of his time anywhere. He did very few of them, and they are widely scattered. Only a few showings of them are on record, two at the Marie Harriman Gallery, in 1931 and again in 1932, with a preliminary run of the same group in the Milwaukee Art Institute; and in March 1933 the gallery lent a group of thirteen to the Arts Club of Chicago, five of them owned by members of the Harriman family.

The Memorial Exhibition Catalogue says of the eight shown in 1960: "His landscape drawings—much more than drawings, they are actually black and white paintings—closely parallel the Chinese. Not that they derive in any way from the oriental, but they show a striking similarity to a Chinese poet-painter's feeling for rocks, trees, cool-breathing streams. A lesser man would have been content to build a career on such technical mastery." Like the Chinese paintings they do not rely on hue or tint for the sensation of color; black and white in their infinite and subtle tonal adjustments supply the whole spectrum.

Kuhn respected Chinese painting, but found it a different world, telling how he once went into an exhibition of scroll paintings, looked around a single time and left, saying, "Too much perfection." So he did not follow the Chinese in these modest masterpieces, but he traveled a similar road in the same direction. Although Kuhn was capable of the most demanding self-discipline, the Chinese scholar-painter's lifelong practice toward a single end was not in his temperament, and probably not in the temperament of any Western artist. Perhaps it is closer to the daily practicing of the performing musical virtuoso than to the painter's. Kuhn could see it in the acrobats' unending muscular and nervous exercise, but theirs is a transient, limited statement.

Plate 71. *Trude*

131

It was appropriate for a poet to write the brief interpretative text of the one-fold catalogue for the 1931 exhibition, with its two illustrations and no list of the drawings. Genevieve Taggard says:

> This is trigger-timed stuff built on essentials. Walt Kuhn follows the impulse familiar to the poet, the composer, and his fellow-painter; with mastery behind him he comes back to A.B.C.—discards the wealthy possibilities of color and big canvas, to see what can be done in black and white, on paper, size 19 inches by 24 inches. To see, that is, how much can be done with how little. Poverty of means under these circumstances becomes the zest of the work; the artist at such a time grows bold; if he is capable of retaining his mastery he pushes the inquiry to the limit; *can almost anything be done with almost nothing?* If he gets a Yes to that, no one can stop him.
>
> . . . These pictures have been put down at top speed. No need, here to slow up, to paint, rub and scrub for days. This is instantaneous, sharp, quick,—not nervous—quick. As if the eye were allowing the duration of a drowning-wink to the performing hand. But the composition, the putting-together, on which this adept hand has waited, shows years of composing. . . . I see years of clarity, years of intuitive meditation, years of metaphysical study and feeling, not in any one of these true lines, but, by implication, in the picture they draw. If this timeless knowledge had not been behind this agile line it would all be "who died yesterday" by the time the things were hung. But the marks are made on paper, and now that the pictures are before you this sanity is nowhere and everywhere — you cannot isolate it or put your finger on one complicated simplicity that permitted this perfection and speed. It looks wonderfully ordinary. Plain. It looks from one angle as if the picture were pure object, emptied of painter. From another angle it is all painter. Technical mastery could take down the thing in that moment of energy-plus when the ink ran. Only mastery of another sort, call it what you like, could make it.

This was Kuhn's "buck-eye" ambition, to look "wonderfully ordinary."

3

After the close of the exhibition Walt Kuhn went to Europe in March. He was to meet the Harrimans later in Paris, but some nostalgia of the blood drew him first to Spain, "to my mother's country." Also he wanted to see more of Goya. From Córdoba in March he wrote home with his customary greeting, "Dear Girls," telling them how fascinated he was by the colors of the country and the people, "spotless clean," "absolutely no gypping," and no tourists. He had seen and heard authentic flamenco dancing and singing in Seville. A few days later he wrote: "Yesterday morning in Madrid I spent about 3 hours in the Prado Museum. The Goyas looked a bit dusty to me as painting goes, but his characterization still hits me hard. It was on account of this museum that I came this way. I have an idea that this trip will have been well spent."

Then on to Paris and the Harrimans; he always stayed in their suite, and there were many long late discussions of the day's findings. Among Kuhn's first recommendations were two paintings by Henri Rousseau, still not widely known or collected in America.

He wrote that the Cézannes were the best of the collection bought on this trip: "Should hold a long time till time is ripe — and keep many for themselves." Some of them can now be seen in the

National Gallery. "H. . . . cools easily but if M. wants it it usually goes over." "H's went to see Picasso yesterday. I refused to go. A.H. agrees with me that P. has never done himself completely in one picture. "I avoid meeting other artists, refused to go see Braque yesterday, and will also not see Leger if they go there. . . . Much better to keep under cover until I have at least six more first class pictures. Which will not be long." "It looks to me like more seclusion but self-protection and economy of energy for us." What a difference there was between the Walt Kuhn of 1912, the young man eager to meet everyone, to learn everything new, and the mature, accomplished artist of 1931.

Kuhn may have refused to see some of the painters, but he renewed his friendship with Brancusi: ". . . The other night Brancusi and myself said exactly the same thing at the same moment, 'Have every possible experience and after that just do work. The judging may come later — but never try to figure out how you are to apply the formes [sic] to the latter.'" "I looked at Ingres the other day in the Louvre, and have begun to absolutely hate his work. Tin plate without a soul or sensibility."

In May, Kuhn sent home an epigram: "There are two kinds of art experts—one looks and the other looks it up." He also wrote of many conversations with Bela Hein, antiquarian, connoisseur, and dealer in modern as well as older arts. His gallery was on the Left Bank, and he was a close associate of his fellow Hungarian dealer in New York, Joseph Brummer. Kuhn found him a broadly informed and experienced man from whom much could be learned. "Hein agrees with me that a peculiar balance of culture and brutality is necessary to produce a really fine painting." "I said to Hein once when he mentioned Goya — 'and where did he get his stuff?' Whereupon Hein says, 'Why, Velasquez of course.' I said, 'But I see nothing of Velasquez in Goya.' Hein says, 'Ah yes, if you did Goya would be no good.'" Kuhn wrote from Berlin of the Harriman party's royal reception at the Adlon Hotel, and summed up the whole expedition: "This trip most important since the Armory."

Walt Kuhn came back to paint, and very well by his own hypercritical estimate. There was only a half-year remaining, but of the recorded twelve canvases from 1931 none were later destroyed, one was never exhibited, and no less than five were admitted to the 1940 anthology. There were no still lifes and only one landscape among the twelve.

The Blue Clown (number 269) very soon became one of his best-known paintings. It was bought by the Whitney Museum before 1934 and generously lent by it during the artist's lifetime. On different occasions it was seen in Baltimore; Portland, Oregon; San Francisco; Pittsfield, Massachusetts; Washington, D.C., Saginaw, Michigan; and Pittsburgh—a varied coverage. It also went to the "Nineteenth Biennale" in Venice in 1934 and to an "American Exhibition" at the Tate Gallery in London in 1946. The latter exhibition was supervised by John

Plate 72. *Apples in the Hay*

Collection of the Museum of Modern Art, New York, Given Anonymously (by Exchange)

Plate 73 (left). *Sibyl*

Plate 74 (right). *Kansas (Portrait of the Artist as a Clown)*

Private Collection

On display at the Broadmoor Hotel, Colorado Springs, Colorado

Plate 75. *Apples from Maine*

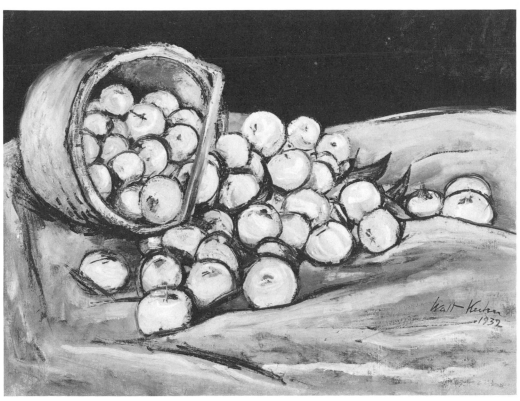

Courtesy of the Metropolitan Museum of Art, George A. Hearn Fund, 1950

Walker, then curator and later director of the National Gallery in Washington, and the noted London critic, R.H. Wilenski said of it in an *Art News* article, "A London Look at U.S. Painting," in August 1946: "I have known of this artist as a fearless fighter for the modern movements. *Blue Clown* is the first of his work I have seen. It leads me to record him as an American equivalent of Toulouse-Lautrec. He himself, I fancy, will know just what I mean." The fancy was well-founded; on 6 August 1946 Kuhn wrote to Vera from Ogunquit, "The more I look at Wilenski the more I feel he is a real critic."

The *Blue Clown* was the color cover of the 1 January 1933 issue of *Vanity Fair*, and figured many times in books and magazines over the years. Oddly enough, there was practically no critical mention of it in the reviews of its first exhibition in January 1932. Its description in *50 Paintings* is one of the more penetrating comments: "A revival of the sheer glory of pigment, and a bouncing revel in impasto, supported soundly by a design suggested in the falcon eye of the sitter. This theme is picked up by a rhythmic series of interlocking, tendril-like hooks that repeat, expand and finally enfold the entire figure giving him a self-embracing aspect." The absence of reference here to an inner meaning derived from the subject is both eloquent and revealing. It is impossible to recognize the sitter, Vittorio Falconi, as the model for the "gorilla" rising from the delicate legs of *Top Man*. And the difference is more than one of costume, pose, and make-up.

Walt Kuhn once said that nudes and flowers were the most difficult subjects to paint, not only because of their banality but because

135

Private Collection

Private Collection

their evanescence made it hard to find a fulcrum to lever the subject onto the canvas. Perhaps the precision of the pen line made nudes easier to draw than to paint, and the vase or other container in flower pieces may have given that stability. *Miss A* (number 268) is one of his few painted nudes or semi-nudes. The model was an interesting personality as well as a pictorial challenge. She was Ailes Gilmore, a Martha Graham dancer and sister of the sculptor Isamu Noguchi, whose mother was Irish and her father a Japanese who collaborated with the widow of Lafcadio Hearn on his biography. The comment in *50 Paintings* reads rather more like the writer than the painter: "The picture is an appreciation of the sheer beauty of this model's skin—its color and delicate texture. Out of that, as material, the artist has produced a picture which gives itself over completely to the ivory richness of flesh. A man's affectionate but non-possessive attitude toward women." Kuhn was always reticent about his intimate relations with women, which by all indications were plentiful and successful, but this reticence may have blocked his painting of nudes. After all, there are only two great nudes in Spanish painting, and they are great exceptions.

The Camp Cook (number 270) comes near to being a straight portrait of George Fitzgerald, as the 1940 comment admits: "The Man from Eden returns, this time as the camp cook. This is one of the few pictures in this book where subject matter is preeminent, largely because of the familiarity of the model with the artist's studio. [He even wears the same apron Walt used for painting.] Despite the prominence of subject matter, a strong armature of design is ever-present." *Clown with Red Wig* (number 272) is a horizontal variation in pose. The white-faced clown crooks his right arm over a draped chair top; muscular tawny hands grip to complete an ellipse of the massive white arms from which the head rises on a column-like neck, glancing downward and inward instead of looking straight ahead. The model for *Fox Farmer* (number 273) was officially said to be Henry Borton, a Maine farmer with grizzled beard, drooping gray mustache, spectacles, necktie, and high-crowned felt halt. Mr. Borton may have suggested the idea; but he was not at hand, so the actual model was the artist, in make-up.

So he was in *The Guide* (number 274), which swept the critic Henry McBride off his feet. The idea of the painting came from Jim Ames, a bona fide Maine guide; but since the Maine woods were far away from the New York studio, Kuhn donned flaring mustaches, a corncob pipe, galluses, and the familiar wide-brimmed hat in front of a mirror. The 1940 comment says: "Besides the artist's contentment at discoursing on this man of the woods and his characteristics, humorous or otherwise [is there a hint of verbal self-portraiture here?], the painting has a delight of linear rhythm. A metallic grill of swerving lines and curves put together in the manner of well-attached and complimentary cables — as in a cat's cradle." Fresh from Goya and the stimulus of Paris conversation, Kuhn was working at high speed.

Plumes (number 276), now in the Phillips Collection, is the first of one of Walt Kuhn's most successful subjects and themes that he returned to often; a routine, underpaid show girl wearily crowned by a fantasy of theatrical finery. The caption says: "Think of a vase or bulb with a large graceful flowering. Or think of a fountain with arching sprays of beautiful color. But this does not have the charming setting of the Fountains of Versailles. These plumes spring from 'show business.' Fragile feathers on solid shoulders. Beauty supported by the commonplace." *Trude* (number 278), as were the *White Clown* and *Blue Clown*, is a complete arrival. She was among the first and one of the best full-length show girls, and Kuhn seemed to know it. Its 1940 caption briefly reads: "'The show must go on.' Blond, clean, and striking a

Plate 78. *Elm*

Private Collection

137

powerful stance, proud Trude remains, as either principal or chorine, ever victorious."

4

Walt Kuhn's exhibition in January 1932 was headline news on the art pages; the critics at last began to hear a bandwagon. Kuhn never respected American critics, with the exception of Henry McBride. He had been really shocked to learn in the early twenties that the leading art critics and writers of France could be, and in fact expected to be, paid to do a favorable article or review; it was normal to the exhibition process. Kuhn never accused American critics of being mercenary, in spite of their meager salaries. He acknowledged them as a necessary part of the publicity apparatus, but simply thought them unequipped for their jobs. Some of them had moved over from the sports desk, and none of them had the wide acquaintance with the other arts characteristic of J.G. Huneker's generation. Henry McBride's review in the *New York Sun*, Saturday 9 January 1932, gives a summary of Kuhn's previous experiences with the critics: "Walt Kuhn, in his time, has received a flattering amount of attention from the critics," much of it unfavorable or at best baffled, but flattering because they would not have written so much, even "continual howls," if they had not dimly sensed a force, an as yet not fully realized quality in his work. McBride continues: " . . . Now that Kuhn has painted several excellent pictures, and one, at least, of the very first class, there is the temptation, to say: 'I told you so,' though for the life of me I cannot recollect the critic who did tell me so, unless you include the late Miss Lizzie Bliss among critics, for she was always staunch in insisting that Kuhn would finally 'come through.'" He then singles out *The Guide*:

> It is Kuhn's best picture to date, and one of the finest paintings produced in America within the recent years. It has uncontestably that quality that all the watchers on the tower, during the recent wave of patriotism that has swept the country, have been searching for ardently—the quality of being one hundred percent. . . .
> This guide achieves picturesqueness by disdaining it, much as Mr. Kuhn achieves style in the painting by forgetting it in his excitement. No doubt everything is there for use. The soft felt hat is pulled down to the eye-rim so that it won't blow off in the wind; the shirt has been purchased at the nearest village store and washed in the waters of the creek; and the corn-cob pipe has been whittled out by hand. . . .
> Mr. Kuhn tells all this with unhesitating strokes and much technical grace. The spacing is admirable. The cob pipe comes to exactly the right place in the composition and the blacks of the background are nicely balanced and the soft felt hat is really a marvel of painting. Altogether Mr. Kuhn does himself and his guide proud.

McBride was sure that the Whitney Museum of American Art, the Duncan Phillips Memorial, and the "Modern Museum" would all "desire" it.

They managed to restrain themselves, but *The Guide* is well housed in the University of Nebraska's excellent collection of American painting at Lincoln; *Athlete* at Wellesley College; *Trude* was given to the Santa Barbara, California, Museum of Art by Vera Kuhn as a memorial

Plate 79. *Trout Stream*

Courtesy of the Howard S. Wilson Memorial Collection, University of Nebraska—Lincoln Art Galleries

to her husband; *Miss A* is with Colby College, Waterville, Maine; and the Munson-Williams-Proctor Institute of Utica, New York, bought the *Camp Cook* in 1957.

"The recent wave of patriotism that has swept the country," directing Mr. McBride's applause to the "one hundred per cent" *Guide*, was the "American Scene" school that had emerged from the agrarian heartland in the depths of the Great Depression. Grant Wood of Iowa, John Steuart Curry of Kansas, and Thomas Hart Benton of Missouri were its evangels. The older Benton had undergone an artistic evolution not unlike Walt Kuhn's, and both Wood and Curry had studied in Europe before developing their self-consciously indigenous styles. The art world of New York was shaken to its foundations by a movement it had not fostered and could not for a while control. Converts swarmed to the altar, and the American Scene was briefly as despotic in the visual arts as the proletarian novel was in letters. "If it isn't about coal miners it isn't art." was the edict. Walt Kuhn was merely amused. It was nothing but subject matter after all; and if there was any quality in the painting, the movement could survive its admirers. It did not; but it is instructive that even so astute a critic as Henry McBride focused on *The Guide* to the neglect of *Top Man* and *The Blue Clown*.

Beginning with the January 1932 catalogue Kuhn dispensed with forewords, saying, ". . . This exhibition offers you another opportunity to go with Walt Kuhn on a number of new and specific adven-

Private Collection

Plate 80. *Fallen Birch*

From the Collection of Mr. and Mrs. G. Gordon Hertslet

Plate 81. *Falls in Catskills*

tures in design, color and human psychology." There were only twelve
paintings, all of them illustrated, eight from 1931 and four earlier ones
borrowed from the the Addison Gallery, the Phillips Memorial Gallery,
and Miss Betty Bliss, to show that it was respectable to own a Kuhn.
The show was a hit with sophisticated artists too. Charles Demuth of
Lancaster, Pennsylvania, one of the modernist forerunners, exquisite
watercolorist, and Paris protégé of the Steins as well as an economic
mainstay of the Steiglitz group, wrote on 25 January, "Your show looks
grand — I'd like to see the models — this too meant [*sic*] as a comid-
ment [*sic*]. Demuth."

Walt Kuhn was also getting to be fashionable. In the 24 September 1932 issue of *The New Yorker* Alexander Woollcott, on his page
Shouts and Murmurs, toyed with the idea of a rental system for paintings: "I know I want to spend a few weeks with a Hopper. Has anyone
got a good Monet he would like to rent out? I must talk to Marie
Harriman about a Walt Kuhn. I even find myself wondering if Jules
Bache has any winter plans for the little Vermeer." Kuhn could certainly
not have objected to the company of Monet and Vermeer, and he always respected Hopper, who had gone his own stubborn lone way. But
Kuhn said Hopper was not for him, "hard as nails."

5

The critical success of the January exhibition was followed up
with a second showing of landscape drawings — black-and-white wash

drawings they should correctly be called — in April. Then with a certain amount of daring, for it might seem to have been pushing his luck, came another major exhibition, this time only "Seven Paintings by Walt Kuhn," in November. It was a good year, noteworthy for the appearance of two major still lifes. There were thirteen paintings in all, three of them destroyed—*Boy with Straw Hat* (number 283) as late as 1944; another and large one, *Clown with Drum* (number 284), was destroyed in 1938. But of the remaining ten paintings, six figured in the November show. *Apples in the Hay* (number 281) was traded for the earlier *Dorothy* in Mrs. Rockefeller's collection, and soon was given to the Museum of Modern Art. *Apples from Maine* (number 282) was a surprise to most of the critics, and entered Kuhn's canon with the lyrical comment: "They could come only from one section of the country — 'down East,' where the rolling waves and the spume of the sea invigorate the people and the land. There is a crisp tang in the color of the apples as characteristic as the salty twang of Yankee speech. The fruit topples out of the weathered old basket and tosses about on the wavy light-blue cloth like part of a jettisoned cargo." The Metropolitan Museum bought it in 1950.

Plate 82. *Island, Golden Gate Park*

Kansas (number 286) hangs in the Broadmoor Hotel in Colorado Springs. The model was ostensibly a professional clown, Ralph (Kansas) Osgood, but the artist stipulated that after his death it be retitled *Portrait of the Artist as a Clown*. The comment in *50 Paintings* starts with a sociological footnote: "Most of the nation's circus clowns come from Kansas and neighboring states. Why, nobody knows. This is one of the artist's most severe paintings. It has a hard, granite quality of form, with every non-essential trimmed away. Fearless individualism. Splendid isolation." It was indeed a self-portrait. *Tiger Trainer* (number 291) was a personal favorite, and Kuhn comments in *50 Paintings*: "No artist is 'ahead of his time.' Art is time itself. But understanding takes additional time, or a keen perception based on faith, the well-spring of culture. Here is calligraphy in flowing arbitrary colors. Vivid red, sky blue against violent green. A valid new American taste." Kuhn several times used "faith" as if it were an end in itself, never specifying faith in what.

Young Clown (number 292), now in the Denver Art Museum, is commented on: "Despite the dashing technique of brush, the artist has retained his characteristic rich paint quality. Design here is composed of slashes which converge climactically in the facial expression. Somewhat uncertain of his role in life, this model enquires with the disarming honesty of a perplexed young man: 'Whither.'" *Studio Corner* (number 290) is one of Walt's last complex compositions. A décolleté show girl in a bicorne hat sits at the corner of a table piled with books, a pair of high-heeled slippers, a fan, and even a loaf of bread. Edward Alden Jewell said of it in the *New York Times*, " . . . 'Studio Corner' in which the circus girl becomes merely one adjunct of a still-life arrangement and indeed appears of less intrinsic importance than the pitcher of bright flowers." Kuhn later had his own doubts about the painting. *Miss X* (number 287) is another half-length nude. The artist-writer's

141

Plate 83. *Trees at Noon*

comment is: "Compact and firm, apprehensive of her prematurely developed adolescence, she is nevertheless savagely prepared to face the future. Bland in color and without heavy modeling, this figure has an alabaster texture, with tonal nuances playing over classic bulk. The nude, done in a modern, technically economic version."

Rose Clown (number 288) is described as a "Daring color composition in rose, black and white, each carefully balanced. Out of the center projects the sinister, stolid expression of a man who forced himself up from razor-back to entertainer. At first glance a simple poster, but on closer inspection those hard edges turn into live form." *Sibyl* (number 289) is a show girl Edward Alden Jewell found "faintly terrifying — full-length, big as life, wearing ever so little and looking, from the shoulders up, just as sternly intellectual as such entertainers ought to look." But Jewell recovered in the last paragraph of his review in the 4 November *Times*: "Green 'Apples from Maine' tumble out of a basket onto a blue cloth with the apparent fortuitiousness that Cézanne could sometimes achieve (did achieve, for example, in the splendid 'Corbeille de pommes' in the Birch-Bartlett collection at the Chicago Art Institute). But Kuhn's debouching apples, like Cézanne's are composed with scrupulous care. Try tampering with them — try making the arrangement actually instead of apparently impromptu — and see what happens to the design."

All the leading critics reviewed the exhibition favorably. Carylyle Burrows wrote, in the *Herald Tribune* on 13 November: "Not every artist can make a well rounded show with seven paintings as Walt Kuhn does in his exhibition at the Marie Harriman Gallery. . . . Mr. Kuhn uses a simple pallette, with grays predominating, builds his images with broad, generalizing brush strokes and with direct illumination invests both color and form with heightened intensity. Especially striking in this way is the portrait of a clown, 'Kansas.' At the same time this artist strikes a new note of richness and vigorous expression of form in the tumbled profusion of 'Apples from Maine.' The latter makes a powerful impression in the exhibition."

Margaret Breuning, in the 5 November *Evening Post*, said: "If anything, he has pared down his statements, already laconic and terse, to even more conciseness. Yet the thing he is interested in he compels you to see, whether the scowling assurance of 'Kansas,' the alertness and resilience of mind and body of 'Tiger Trainer' or the tawdry splendor of 'Sibyl.' A canvas of 'Apples from Maine' appears an astounding interlude, not at all Cezannesque on their blue cloth, yet, probably owing much unconsciously or consciously to all the hard, green apples of Cezanne in their conception of form and spatial relations." Ralph Flint, in the 5 November issue of the *Art News*, found a literary analogy, "Mr. Kuhn, hitherto noted for his rigorous Hemingway-like statement of fact, has taken on a new potency by certain added graces of tone and color. . . . Harking back to his last season's show of portraits and figure pieces — not the wholly delightful monochromatic landscape studies

Plate 84 (left). *Trees–Vermont*

Plate 85 (right). *Grenadier*

that Mrs. Harriman also showed here on two occasions. . . . But it is 'The Camp Cook' that I shall always recall in summing up Mr. Kuhn's abilities, and I strongly recommend it to any collector desiring a perfect example of this painter's work."

Henry McBride, who began the chorus in January, also found a literary parallel. His review in the *Sun* of 5 November says in part: "These pictures are all the sort of pictures that might be painted by an artist who answers to the name of Walt. That is to say, there is a good deal of that other Walt in them — Walt Whitman. All these people who stare at you from his canvases are downright 100 per cent. They are unconcerned about your opinion and unworried about the depression or anything else. They are, like the original Walt, nonchalant." The identity of first names and common energetic Americanism induced many people to find such similarities. On the other hand, nothing could be farther from Walt Whitman's loose declamatory style than Walt Kuhn's terse concision. In one instance there may be a legitimate comparison, some community of feeling, when Walt Whitman muted his lyre in 1860 to write:

I saw in Louisiana a live-oak growing,
All alone it stood, and the moss hung down from the branches;
Without any companion it grew there, uttering joyous
 leaves of dark green.

The last enterprise of 1932 was arranging Kuhn's first important out-of-town show since the Chicago Arts Club's presentation of the Grand Central Galleries 1927 exhibition. This time Walt Kuhn chose the City Art Museum of Saint Louis for a careful selection of paintings, and went out to oversee it. On 1 January 1933 he wrote to Vera: "I was

143

Plate 86 (right). *Lavender Plumes*

Plate 87 (opposite). *Veteran Acrobat*

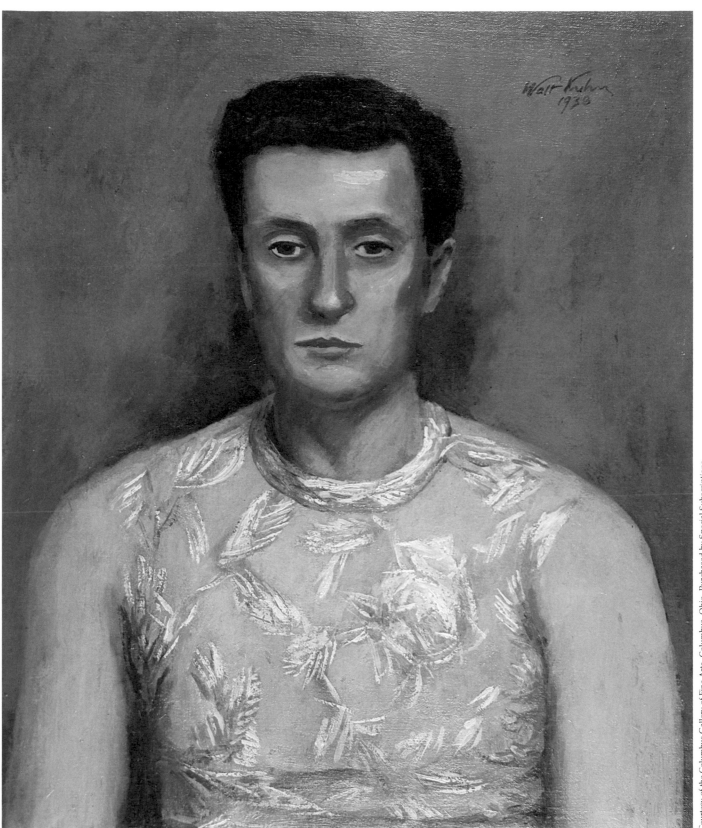

Plate 88. *Green Apples with Scoop*

pleased to see that almost all the pictures held up. The Clown with Black Wig is about the only one which doesn't please me and the Studio Corner as we know lacks class. The others just shine. Acrobat with Cigarette makes good and White Clown is still a wow, the show could have stood a full length or two. . . . " Dejection followed on exhilaration, however, and on 3 January Kuhn wrote again: "At our present pace and method it would take us fifty years at least to get any concrete recognition. People have got to be dragged out of this lethargy." Nothing in particular had gone wrong, and there had not been time for sales; it was just a predictable let-down after the conspicuous, the resounding, success of 1932.

146

NOTES TO CHAPTER SIX

Aline Saarinen remarks, on p. 234 of *The Proud Possessors:* "Lawyers are famous for writing IMPOSSIBLE WILLS for themselves. Quinn was no exception."

The quotations from ALFRED BARR'S FOREWORD to the Catalogue of *Paintings by Nineteen Living Americans,* 1929, are taken from pp. 9—10.

FRANK GETLEIN has written for the *Milwaukee Journal, Washington Star, New Republic, Commonweal,* and other journals. He published *The Bite of the Print* in 1963 (New York: Clarkson N. Potter). His remarks on *The White Clown* come from the admirable text he wrote for the Kennedy Galleries' exhibition, "Walt Kuhn," 1967, pp. 8—9.

EDNA ST. VINCENT MILLAY'S FAMOUS SONNET was number twenty-two in *The Harp-Weaver and Other Poems,* first published in 1923 (New York: Harper & Bros.).

In a letter of 14 November 1975, AVERELL HARRIMAN wrote to the author: "I have no knowledge of the conversation [between his mother and Kuhn] but it sounds reasonable and could well have taken place. Walt Kuhn had a great influence on me in developing my knowledge and understanding of painting but he did not have any influence that I can recall on any major purchases which we made on special trips to Europe. Walt did go with us on some visits and I remember the joy of going through a number of European galleries with him and getting his vivid and penetrating reactions. He had very great integrity. He only let pictures which he believed were first class out of his studio. He destroyed the others. This was not the custom of the time. He had a very definite opinion of painting and especially admired the painters who had strength and vitality. He called some of the popular colorful paintings 'millinery.' . . . He was a student of paintings throughout history and had his definite judgments in every period. He saw value and strength in many of the less accepted painters of the period. As I have said, I value greatly our trips to Europe together and the museums we visited. I was very fond of Walt. He was great company, always lively in his opinions."

THE COMMONWEAL QUOTATION can be found on page 397 of the February 1933 issue.

ALAN BURROUGHS was the son of Bryson Burroughs, painter and curator of the Metropolitan Museum. He was one of the founders of the Technical Research Department of the Fogg Museum, Harvard University, and published *Limners and Likenesses: Three Centuries of American Painting* (Cambridge, Mass.: Harvard University Press, 1936), as well as *Art Criticism from a Laboratory* (Boston, 1938).

THE TEXT OF THE CHICAGO ARTS CLUB'S EXHIBITION OF LANDSCAPE DRAWINGS catalogue consists of quotations from Elizabeth Luther Cary in the *New York Times* of 15 February 1931, a review in the *New York Sun* of 23 April 1932, and one by Edward Alden Jewell in the *New York Times* of 20 April 1932. The *Sun* remarks: "All the drawings, in fact, have an aristocratic air, due to the simplicity that has been so strongly insisted on." It is refreshing to hear any of Kuhn's works called "aristocratic," since he was so generally criticized for the vulgarity of his subjects if not his manner of painting them. Edward Alden Jewell says: "In all of this work the artist has made his observations with the aid of a technique equipped at every point to communicate facts that lie deeper far than the play of light on bark and leaf."

GENEVIEVE TAGGARD was born in 1894 and taught at Bennington College and Sarah Lawrence College. Her foreword of 1931 comes between two books of verse, *Travelling Standing Still* (1928) and *Not Mine to Finish* (1934). Her best-known work is *Collected Poems: 1918–1938.*

HENRY McBRIDE was the chief art critic of the *New York Sun* for thirty-seven years and editor of *Creative Art.* He was an important contributor to the *Dial* as well as to other journals. He was the author of *Matisse* and *Some French Moderns.* His letters have been recently compiled and edited by the late Daniel Catton Rich, former director of the Art Institute of Chicago and the Worcester, Massachusetts, Art Museum.

One of WALT KUHN'S MAXIMS, jotted down later in his own hand, says, "Some of the most famous art writers have been successful dealers under cover [sentence underscored]. Something like a policeman selling burglar tools on the side."

To those who went through it, this may seem to be a cursory dismissal of the AMERICAN SCENE, but it is an exact description of Walt Kuhn's reaction.

CHARLES DEMUTH'S SPELLING may have been a deliberate play with words, as can be seen in his little-known verse. Kuhn was amused at his interest in the male models. Demuth died prematurely in 1935 after a lifetime of illness.

"A Strong Siege of Experimenting"

By this time Walt Kuhn had almost stopped showing in museum annuals of American painting around the country, primarily because too many of them were beginning to have juries of award. Naturally, he never submitted his work to a jury of selection, and he stated his opinion of prize-giving in a letter of 13 July 1943, to John O'Connor, Jr. of the Carnegie Institute in Pittsburgh, refusing an invitation to the Carnegie International with its much-publicized imported jury: "I thought it was pretty well known by this time that I never lend pictures to shows where prizes are given. . . . Why doesn't some Museum correct this evil of prize-giving by simply announcing that so and so much money will be devoted to purchases and thus eliminate the very doubtful method of grading work by artists which is the legitimate office of professional art critics and not of biased art juries."

He liked O'Connor, and an invitation to the Carnegie International was generally considered to be an honor; but there is a rasping tone to the letter, as there was in most of Kuhn's pronouncements. It startled and annoyed many of his listeners. Nonconformists are rarely popular, and their chosen exile from the majority does not induce a conciliatory manner, nor invite one. It is often taken as a personal affront and begets resentment that sometimes leads to outright enmity. On his part the nonconformist has paid in many ways for his independence, necessarily rugged, and his hackles tend to rise at any overture, no matter how innocent or well-meant.

Kuhn's position, however, though logical as well as outspoken, was not a practical one. Most museums were not organized to act as he suggested; they were burdened by trustee committees of accession who were wary of advance commitments, and prizes were often endowed for only that purpose, as well as being eagerly sought by the majority of artists. They were also excellent publicity for both the winners and the donors. As usual Kuhn was ahead of his time; juries of both selection and award have by now almost ceased to exist, and many museums have become, if anything, overzealous in acquiring contemporary works.

The one museum Kuhn was consistently loyal to, as were most artists, was the Whitney. They felt that it was their museum, concerned for their welfare and their interests, which was precisely what Mrs. Gertrude Vanderbilt Whitney had meant it to be. She was a serious, if uninspired, sculptor who had begun to show young American artists in her Greenwich Village studio as early as 1908. Out of this a gallery grew in 1941, later called the Whitney Studio Club, and with the capable and magnetic Mrs. Juliana Force as its first director became the Whitney Museum of American Art in 1930. Mrs. Whitney's own collection of about six hundred American works was the nucleus of its permanent holdings, in two adjoining houses on Eighth Street. Needing larger quarters and doubtless wanting to be nearer the center of things, in 1954 the Whitney raised a new building forming an "L" at the western end of the Museum of Modern Art on Fifty-third Street. Before that, the Metropolitan Museum's brilliant director Francis Taylor had carried on a brief but ardent courtship, proposing that the Whitney bring the dowry of its endowment and collection to add its own wing to the Metropolitan and take over the department of American art with its troublesome Hearn Fund, an endowment for the purchase of American works. After a mutual and noisy rejection the Whitney physically if not corporately married the Museum of Modern Art and sold off all its pre-twentieth-century paintings. Now in its handsome Marcel Breuer structure of 1966 on Madison Avenue near Seventy-fifth Street, it is painfully trying to replace them.

Part of the early Whitney's attraction to artists was that there were no juries and no prizes, but a fair amount of buying. Nor were specific works of art invited for exhibition; the artists were invited to select their own. Artists may not always be the best judges of their offspring, but they think they are, and this led to a congenial atmosphere as well as to some occasionally erratic exhibitions. Hermon More, a painter of the Woodstock colony, succeeded Juliana Force as director, and Lloyd Goodrich was the scholarly curator, later director. Lloyd Goodrich too began as a painter at the Art Students' league, but started to write for *Arts* under its editor Forbes Watson. They ably carried on Mrs. Whitney's and Mrs. Force's tradition, as shown in a letter Walt Kuhn wrote on 24 April 1946: "Incidentally I forgot to mention that Goodrich and More did a first class job at the Whitney. Never have I seen such justice and exact discrimination as there expressed. My hat's off to them." Considering Kuhn's low opinion of Museums and their staffs in general, this was praise from Caesar. In November 1932 the Whitney began its series of "Biennials," alternating exhibitions of oil paintings with sculpture, watercolor, and print combinations. The

149

first was "Contemporary American Paintings," and Kuhn sent *Top Man* to it.

The Saint Louis venture, however, was the beginning of Walt Kuhn's new independent out-of-town exhibition formula. Periodically he would select a new city, if it had shown any interest, assemble a small show for it, and then spend about a week there, feeling the local artistic pulse, looking for promising unknowns, and locating potential buyers. In the spring of 1935, for example, he sent *The White Clown* and *The Camp Cook,* with a supporting cast, to Columbus and Dayton, Ohio, going along for his own explorations and promotion. This kind of scouting was useful to the Marie Harriman Gallery too, and at his instance it sent a young woman, with counsel from Kuhn, to explore the whole country, not neglecting Canada. Her confidential notes on the state of museums, private collections, and prospective clients are a delightful and accurate survey of the art scene in America outside New York in the mid-thirties. Needless to say, an introduction from the Harrimans opened all doors.

In the spring of 1933 Kuhn felt that his creative batteries needed recharging and took Vera and Brenda to Portugal and France. He stayed on alone for a while in Paris and, not being this time so identified with the Harrimans' buying program, was more free to visit fellow artists, including Picasso. He wrote home, ". . . I saw Picasso — I may see him several more times. Am getting a perfect line on him. His way is just the opposite for me to go." There is no doubt of his grudging respect for Picasso; one time he wrote that he was "watching Picasso like a hawk." But he thought that Derain was the most intelligent and clear-sighted, as well as sympathetic, of all his contemporaries. If any outside influence can be seen in Walt Kuhn's painting of the 1930s, it is that of Derain — an affinity of attitude, not style. But Kuhn thought that Derain's informed, fastidious taste diluted the force of his painting. As evidence he cited Derain's studio, decorated in the olive greens and earth browns of his canvases, with the muted bronze accent of old band instruments on the walls; the paintings grew too easily, without enough visual conflict, from such a setting. Also Derain's luxurious style of living drove him to turn out too many pot-boilers when funds ran low.

Kuhn wrote to Vera from Paris: "I spent a delightful hour with Derain. I first showed him the [John Singleton] Copley photos which excited him very much, and then about eight of my best reproductions cut from the three catalogues, and they went over big. He picked Kansas, Electra and Trudy [*sic*] as the best, and this all brought about an entirely different attitude in him, almost like magic."

On this trip Kuhn spent a considerable amount of time with Dikran Kelekian. The great antiquarian owned three houses on the Place Vendôme, with his gallery at Number Two. Mary Cassatt, a close friend, had introduced Kelekian to modern French painting about 1906; and in 1900 he had had the singular distinction, for a dealer in an-

Plate 89. *Apples and Pineapple*

tiquities, of serving on the jury for the Beaux Arts section of Paris's Exposition Universelle. He was a regal figure, with a tiger's beard and little patience for the pretentious ignorant. He had galleries in Cairo and New York and race horses at Auteuil. His taste was catholic, embracing all periods and styles from Egypt to China to Medieval France to the most advanced modern movements. His specialties were the arts of his native Near East, ancient and Islamic, where he was unrivaled. On a momentous day in 1911 Dikran Kelekian noticed two artist types studying a Persian miniature in his gallery window. He sent an attendant to invite them in; they were Picasso and Matisse.

Matisse had made a special trip the year before to see the famous Near Eastern exhibition in Munich, which opened Western eyes for the first time to the greatness of earlier periods, not the familiar rugs, tiles, and miniatures of the sixteenth and following centuries, decoratively attractive though they are. But here at Number Two Place

151

Plate 90. *Zinnias*

Vendôme was Matisse's first chance to get close to, to touch and really weigh in his own hands, a treasure of new artistic ideas, to the profit of the whole Western world. Probably no artist has ever refashioned the color and design sense of his time to the extent that Matisse remolded the twentieth century's outward appearance to his own taste. Matisse traded drawings with Kelekian for Coptic textiles from Christian Egypt, until the prima donnas shortly parted company. In much the same way, in both Paris and New York, Walt Kuhn could commune with and absorb, by a kind of osmosis, masterworks of the centuries in the presence of a man with immense knowledge and instinctive judgment. Both men prized the quality of force, that intense vitality that distinguishes the work of art from the artifact, no matter how historically and stylistically informative the latter may be.

2

Kuhn's last letter to Vera from Paris said, ". . . I'm not complaining, in fact we did just the right things the last ten years, but I have full grown wings now, and a fine equipment, and I'm going to get what I want ["I'm . . . want" underscored]." At the moment he wanted to paint still lifes. *Apples from Maine* had in its own way been as significant an arrival as *The White Clown*. Of the eighteen paintings from 1933, two of them destroyed, twelve were still lifes. What was this compulsion?

Plate 91. *Three Apples*

Collection of Mr. and Mrs. Gregory H. Doherty

For the general public that Kuhn so earnestly wanted to reach and teach, still lifes as subject matter have never been as popular as figures or landscapes, and the term itself is a catchall for any kind of painting that is not strictly portrait, figure, landscape, animal, or, today, nonobjective painting.

In quality still life can range from the microscopic cataloguings of minor Dutchmen to the symphonic majesties of Cézanne. It is at least as old as the Roman mosaic masters, who bent their laborious technique to the picturing of fruit and flowers, sometimes even the scraps from banquet tables, but its more modern history begins along with landscape painting as a stage setting for the human event. Landscape and still life grew together in importance, gradually taking on independence, and finally almost crowding the human actors off the scene. This was part of a specializing trend that first showed itself in seventeenth-century Holland; but since figure painting of all kinds, especially portrait painting, declined in direct ratio to the rise of the landscape and the still life, there must be explanations, having something to do perhaps with man's relation to the rest of the cosmos.

Renaissance man had no doubt of his leading role in the scheme of things: he bestrode the world like a colossus. The Leonardos and Francis Bacons of the age would admit of no limit to their intellectual powers. The following century, however, invented both the microscope and the telescope, and man's stature began to shrink visibly

153

while the universe grew. Such changes do not happen neatly or all at once, but by the middle of the nineteenth century, painting, whose business is to record and express ideas, had registered two major reactions. One of them was landscape painting's turning away from man toward nature — nature seen and interpreted by man to be sure, but with a shift in emphasis. The other and opposite reaction was still life painting's turning inward to man, dismissing him as its ostensible subject yet finding its springs deep in him, becoming at last a distillation of man himself.

In his admirable book, *Still Life from Antiquity to our Times,* Charles Sterling of the Louvre quotes Henri Focillon's remark that the "capacity for astonishment" is the base of all true creation, and goes on to say that the purpose of still life painting is simply to witness man's "astonishment before the beauty of things." But it is significant that the modest "things" of still life have all been made or processed by man. Perhaps that is the implied meaning of *nature morte,* not nature dead in the course of nature but nature affected by man, bearing his imprint, which is so often, but not necessarily, deadly. In this sense still life does not deny the human being as the central theme of Western art, it celebrates him — not only his poetic astonishment with the beauty of things but also man the artisan, man the husbandman. And so the objects of man's use or making are glorified, their abstract shapes and colors are ultimately refined into a statement of mathematical thought. If Dostoevsky could "see the universe in a square foot" certainly Chardin could find truth on a kitchen table.

But the Spanish with their *bodegones* ("kitchen subjects") and *floreros* ("flower paintings"), as they call their still lifes, are different from the French. "Solemn and magic" Sterling calls them, saying of a painting by Sanchez Cotan, "Has he not hung a quince and a cabbage to make them turn and gleam like planets in a limitless night?" Poetry and geometry blend in the unmistakable Spanish temper revealed by its *bodegones,* somber and sumptuous at the same time. Whatever this Spanish quality may be, it is timeless, common to both Picasso and Zurbarán. It gives weight to a Luis Melendez, who could not escape, even if he would, the lightness of his eighteenth-century touch. It saves Juan Gris from the scientific impersonality of his beloved cubism, and finds its final definition in the few extraordinary still lifes that Goya painted.

As for the French, from Chardin on, many major painters including Delacroix and Courbet have painted still lifes, and the 1870s gave them a new importance. It became the private laboratory where painters, much like early anatomists and with the same need, could dissect nature, analyzing its constituent forms. Impressionism produced this new need by successfully imitating the look of nature, thereby proving that appearance is a secondary and often deceiving attribute, that true painting of all styles or periods is a creative language of form and the arrangement of form. But woe to the painter who took public liberties with the accepted canons of figure painting or even tampered with the agreed-on color of trees. Still life with its "unimportant" subject matter was the solution. So pots and pans, guitars and wine bottles — or, in the case of Walt Kuhn, apples and pears—became the new iconography. Somehow these unlikely vessels managed to contain not only a new style but the concentrated philosophies of their creators. Where can the grandeur of Cézanne's rationale be better seen than in his still lifes, or the radiant materialism of Renoir, or the humanitarian fervor of Van Gogh? But that has always been still life's

Plate 92. *Roses*

155

Plate 93. *American Beauty*

function; it is the painter's private but most explicit language, understandable to anyone who will listen.

Kuhn may not have reasoned in such classroom terms, but then again, possibly he did; the teachings of Arthur B. Davies and John Quinn's literary salon cannot be discounted. When similar interpretations were later proposed, he listened attentively and nodded agreement. He made only one recorded comment on the still lifes of 1933; otherwise none was necessary. Of *Apples and Pineapple* (number 296) he said in *50 Paintings:* "If any one quality most characterizes Walt Kuhn it is dynamism. It is also the salient quality in this simple still life. A tense pressure and threat of explosion are imprisoned in this humble fruit. Derived from the pressure-filled arms and thighs of early Greek sculpture, developed in his earlier painting, The White Clown, the artist puts that tension into inanimate objects. A plate of bombs and a hand grenade!" Obviously he was not using the word *dynamism* as the futurists did, meaning motion, and he confirms the earlier analysis of *The White Clown's* vital force. The painting is still in the collection of Averell Harriman, who gave *Zinnias* (number 312) to the National Gallery. Five others are in private collections. *Apple Basket* (number 295) is a quieter version of *Apples and Pineapple,* without pineapple and with apples filling the basket and scattering on the table top; a large swirl of apples to the right contrasts with the compact group in the basket and one isolated on a rumpled cloth.

Kuhn often asked someone else, usually Vera or Brenda, to arrange his still life objects so that the unintended grouping could surprise him with a new idea. Then he might make a few adjustments, while avoiding the danger of unconsciously repeating himself. Collectively the fruit or flower still lifes are not unlike a musical fugue, or variations on a musical theme, partly planned, partly improvised while the score is written. *Apples and Red Watering Can* (number 297) is a larger, more populated canvas, with a cluster of light-toned apples and watering can in the foreground against a stack of logs and a suggestion of open field at the extreme top. Its calculatedly rustic look is a foil for the velvety elegance of the equally large *White Peonies* (number 308). *Pears in the Barn* (number 303) returns to the farm, the pears on a white cloth supported by a stoneware cider jug and a pile of logs cut for the fireplace. *Yellow Apples* (number 311) replaces the jug with a florally decorated white pitcher and the cloth with a basket. *Bouquet* (number 298) is one of two vertical compositions in the group, a casual clutch of zinnias and feverfew rising against a dark background from a pitcher on a light-toned table. *Roses* (number 305), also vertical, is the smallest of the series; boldly brushed and though completely finished, it manages to keep the direct feeling of a sketch. Judging from their subjects and appurtenances, these still lifes must have been painted in Ogunquit in a single creative burst.

Back in New York in the fall Kuhn painted figure pieces, only one of them a show girl, later destroyed. *Woodsman* (number 309) is a distant cousin to *The Guide,* and Kuhn thought well of it; in *50 Paintings* he says: "A painting of ruggedness. The color is dark and austere. . . . It has the beauty of carved hard wood." *Wrestler* (number 310) is a study in male vanity; Kuhn told of how the model used to comb his shaggy forearms, and called it, "Rhythm in bulges. . . . An actual portrait of a well known wrestler whose role is the 'heavy', or villain, who is always thrown by his more glamorous partner. Yet there is humor and sentiment in those eyes." *Acrobat in White* (number 293) is a half-length figure with broadly painted arms and trunk; one sharp curved line draws the whole left hand tucked under the right arm, and other sharp lines define the scowling features.

Fourteen paintings were shown at the Marie Harriman Gallery in February 1934, two of them from 1932. There was no text in the catalogue, but every painting was illustrated. Press reviews were routine; Kuhn's sudden departure into still life may have baffled the critics, and still lifes are difficult to write about. Henry McBride in the 3 February issue of *The New York Sun* renewed his praise of *The Guide* and gradually got around to *The Wrestler* by way of commending Walt Kuhn as "the most masculine of American painters since George Bellows. . . . The cult of the he-man, so sedulously nursed by Ernest Hemingway, William Faulkner and others among present-day novelists, has its disciples in the painting world too." Finally, and in conclusion, he nodded to the still lifes, "Also, Mr. Kuhn has been doing some flower pieces. This seems to be an item of news. At any rate, somebody ought to tell Ernest Hemingway and William Faulkner. They have not done flower pieces. The flowers have been touched in with the same brushes that

Plate 94 (opposite). *Juggler*

did the wrestler's massive hands. They seem equally packed with dynamite. They are unlike the flowers in eighteenth century pictures. They are unmistakably of this strenuous Rooseveltian era. That's as it should be, you'll agree." It is evident that the formal critics could not be relied on to see either the surfaces of Walt Kuhn's canvases or under them. Hence his own comments in *50 Paintings* are so often quoted.

Fifteen paintings came from 1934, none destroyed and one of them never exhibited. Nine of them were still lifes; the drive was still strong. Even before Kuhn's 1936 Hollywood trip the producer Sam Goldwyn had bought *Hydrangeas* (number 322) as well he might have. It is one of Kuhn's finest flower paintings, and some think it one of the best of all modern flower paintings. Kuhn was frank to acknowledge absolute accomplishment by contemporaries or predecessors, preferably his predecessors, and said that no one could paint a rose as well as Henri Fantin-Latour. But there is legitimate pride in *50 Painting's* caption: "Fragrance need not always be sweet. Here it is richly pungent like musk. The painting is composed of acid, yellowish-white blossoms that generously fill the canvas [H. 30″ W. 40″], and with austere green leaves against a tobacco background. The colors are not graceful nor charming, but they have an illusive flavor which appeals to sophisticated tastes. . . ." It is an accurate description.

Waiting for the Robert E. Lee (number 328) poses two costumed show girls seated with legs crossed; one wears a feathered headdress, the other a bicorne, and both look off to the left. Not until *Trio* (number 364) of 1937 would Kuhn successfully solve a large composition with more than one figure, and then feel free to leave the problem. But *Juggler* (number 322) is one of his outstanding paintings. He says in *50 Paintings*: "After considerable experimentation, including instructive if not very successful juggling, the artist discovered that impending action is more exciting than the action itself. Explaining to the artist the basic principles of juggling, the model sagaciously advised: 'The catching is easy enough. You've got to know how to throw them.'" Kuhn left unstated the inner meaning of the painting, later calling it a portrait of "self-pity." It is now in the William Rockhill Nelson Gallery of Art in Kansas City, Missouri. The noted publisher's family executed his wishes by building and endowing the museum in the early 1930s, even including his stipulation that no work be acquired until thirty years after the artist's death. Accordingly, in 1936 the Nelson Gallery promptly bought a late Cézanne landscape of the Montagne Sainte-Victoire; it would be impolitic to ask if it waited for the exact deadline of 22 October. In order to stay in touch with its times, however, the gallery quickly formed a society of Friends of Art, unshackled by the provision of the founder's endowment, and one of its first purchases was the *Juggler*. Among the 1934 still lifes was a frontal attack on the ultimate banality, *Pink Roses in Blue Pitcher* (number 324). Kuhn brought it off with a few decisive brushed lines that give living substance to the otherwise cloying hot-house blooms. Here indeed is a buck-eye, and a successful one.

Plate 95. *Dryad*

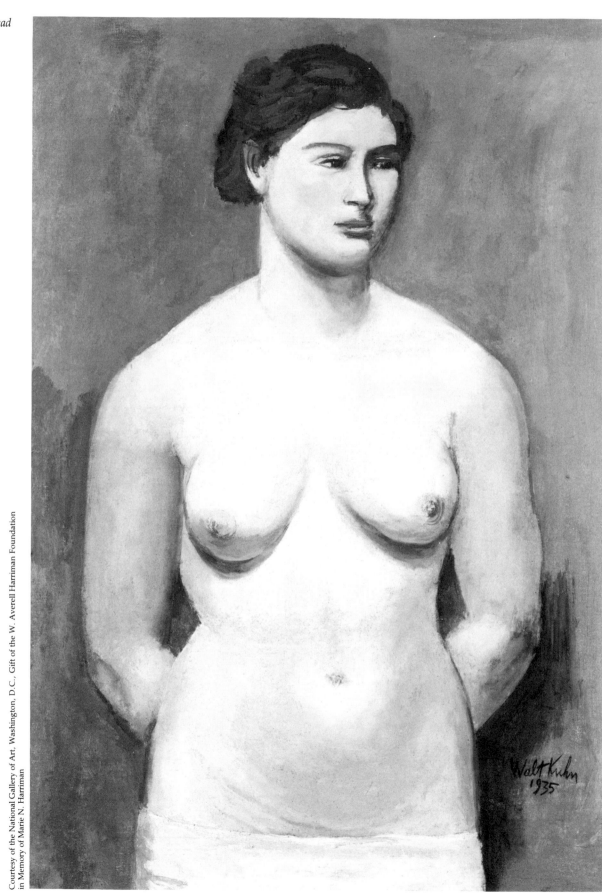

On 13 February 1935, Kuhn wrote to Otis Oldfield in San Francisco: "As money isn't too plentiful here, I am getting my recreation out of a strong siege of experimenting. For the past two months I have stopped all notions of turning out my accustomed sort of thing and instead have sought new ways of putting things down. It's lots of fun." The experimenting was with what Kuhn called "arbitrary color." He defined it as a deliberate combination of normally discordant and clashing colors, guaranteed, if mastered, to counteract any tendency to over-dulcet harmony, to give a vibrating sense of actual life in all its frequent vulgarity. He often went to burlesque theaters, not only for the obvious reasons or because anything on stage interested him, but to find such unintentional brassy combinations, the negation of "taste." The Irving Place Theatre, where the young Gypsy Rose Lee and Georgia Sothern costarred, was handy to Kuhn's Eighteenth Street studio. It was a last citadel of this art form before Fiorello LaGuardia cleansed New York of the abomination, little foreseeing what was to come.

    Kuhn was also fascinated to discover that none other than Renoir, who was at times downright sugary in the prettiness of his palette, had experimented in the same way on his Italian journey in

Plate 96. Top. *Reclining Nude*. Bottom. *Reclining Figure, Undraped*

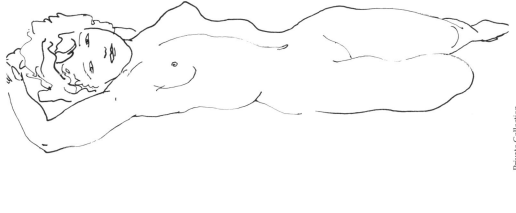

Private Collection

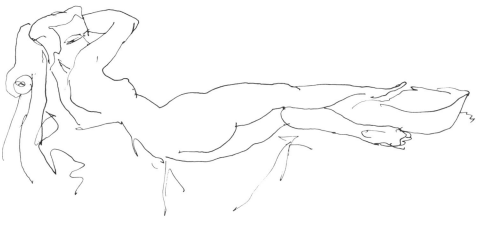

Courtesy of Kennedy Galleries, Inc.—Kuhn Estate

161

Plate 97. Top. *Nude on Sofa.*
Bottom. *Reclining Figure*

Private Collection

Courtesy of Mr. and Mrs. Philip R. Adams, Cincinnati, Ohio

Courtesy of Kennedy Galleries, Inc.—Kuhn Estate

Plate 98. *Half-raised Figure*

1882. Kuhn thought that the stripes of a Roman sash may have given him the idea, which he soon abandoned, writing to Durand-Ruel: "I am still suffering from experimenting. I'm not content and I am scraping off, still scraping off. I hope this craze will have an end. . . . I am like children in school. The white page must always be nicely written and bang—a blot. I am still at the blotting stage — and I'm forty." Walt Kuhn was fifty-seven and enthusiastically blotting. After his Italian experiments Renoir did, however, restore black to his impressionist palette, from which it had been sternly banished in the early 1870s, exclaiming, "Why, black is the queen of colors." And by 1900, as a complete postimpressionist, Renoir had adopted an earth red, almost an Egyptian red, as his basic color, perhaps thereby acquiring something of the Egyptians' sense of monumental form. Kuhn was not a special admirer of Renoir; once when Courbet was criticized for the vulgarity of some of his subjects, Kuhn said, "If you want a vulgarian look at Renoir!" It is a matter of definition. Kuhn did not keep many of his experiments with arbitrary color; *American Beauty* (number 313) is one of them, a reclining show girl with a plumed fan, in a pose familiar from many of his drawings. But he had learned further control over the whole range of painted color.

162

Also in this year of experiment Kuhn felt that his drawing needed to be strengthened and set himself to weeks of straight pen-line figure exercises. In a review of all his drawings two periods stand out — that of 1928–29, when he had stopped making prints, and that of 1934–36, bracketing 1935. The catalogue for "Drawings and Watercolors by Walt Kuhn," an exhibition presented by the Kennedy Galleries from 3 to 31 December 1968, says: "All uncertainty of approach has ended by 1928. Scant draperies, shoes, stockings, pillows, tumbled sheets are accessories to the artist's frankly sensual intent. They also lend texture and play a kind of counterpoint to the increasing authority of the contour. An American Empire couch was not only a studio property but also a useful linear frame for some of the figures. . . . Two reclining nudes . . . predict the classic style of 1934–36." Earlier the same text remarks: "In these drawings his style developed a singular purity of line, best seen in the 1934–1936 group where mass, volume and component details are vividly, elegantly stated by a simple contour that Ingres in his probity might have called 'noble.'"

The American correspondent for the *Connoisseur*, Marie Louise d'Otrange Mastai, delivered a conclusive verdict on Walt Kuhn's drawing and handed down a trenchant opinion on his style in general in the London magazine's issue of August 1966. Mrs. Mastai was reviewing Kuhn's large retrospective exhibition presented by the University of Arizona in the spring of 1966, entitled "Painter of Vision," together

Plate 99. *Clown with Mandolin*

Courtesy of Mrs. John Converse

163

Plate 100 (left). *Carnival Girl*

Plate 101 (right). *Wisconsin*

with a much smaller concurrent exhibition, "Early Work — 1904–1929," at the Maynard Walker Gallery in New York. She wrote:

> The stature of Kuhn, and the true strength of his famous jabbing, stabbing, brutally faceted, ponderously monumental style, is not, as one might reasonably expect, the display of muscular strength — as that of the circus performers who were his favourite models. Instead, to continue the comparison, it is instead the hidden kill and delicacy. I am not an unreserved admirer of all of Kuhn's works indiscriminately, but I do rank him as a great artist on the merits of a dozen or so of his major works alone, and, unhesitatingly, of each and every one of his admirable drawings. That, after all, was, is, and always will be, 'the acid test'. The names of Constantin Guys and of Pascin have been brought up in connection with Kuhn's draughtsmanship. But the filiation, it seems to me, goes back further—and much higher.

As a result of this self-imposed discipline, there are only eight paintings from 1935; one of them, *Flower Piece* (number 334), bought by a law partner of John Quinn, was never exhibited. Two are mentioned in *50 Paintings*, where *Red Roses* (number 335) is identified as a buck-eye, along with the artist's definition of the word and the dangers of painting them. *Dryad* (number 333), now in the National Gallery, is probably the finest of Walt Kuhn's nudes, certainly the least sensuous and most sculptural. He called it: "A devotional essay on the eternal stability of womankind. The Amazonian model [three-quarter length] stands like a Doric column with gentle entasis of design. Surface detail is subordinated but not sacrificed to the central idea. The strong side of the

Plate 102. *Miss R*

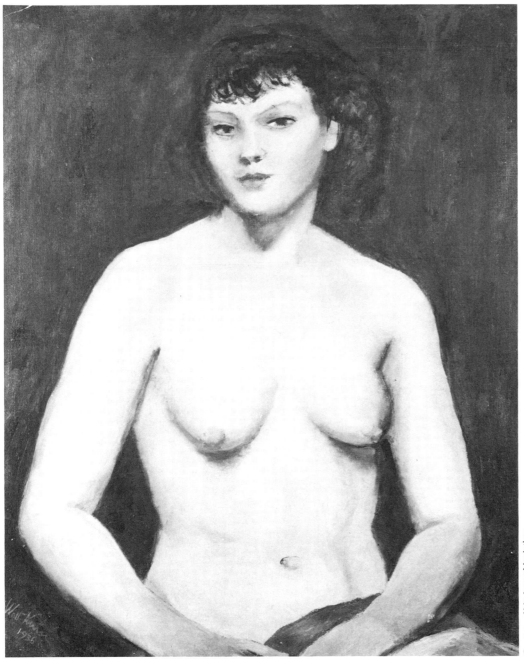

Courtesy of Mr. James MacArthur

weaker sex." Kuhn once remarked that there are a few absolutes in the visual arts, forms or designs that having reached their final state after a long evolution are immutable. One is a Doric column, another the shape of a violin, and a third the Scotch plaid. All of the innumerable efforts to alter or modify them have been proven historic failures.

Clown with Mandolin (number 331) is almost a monochrome contrast of light and dark, somewhat in the manner of Daumier; Gary Cooper bought it in 1936 when actor and painter got to know and respect each other in Hollywood.

Apples with Salmon Cloth (number 330) is the principal still life of 1935. Kuhn entered it in the Marie Harriman Gallery show of Febru-

165

Plate 103. *Fruit Platter*

Courtesy of Kennedy Galleries, Inc.—Kuhn Estate

ary 1936, together with *Miss R.* (number 348), fresh from the easel in January 1936. As mentioned before, the exhibition was a distinguished gathering of Cézanne, Derain, Matisse, Picasso, Renoir, and Van Gogh, with Walt Kuhn the only American present. There was some derision among Kuhn's enemies, but he, Marie Harriman, and the majority of the audience were not disturbed. Edward Alden Jewell had no objection, ending his review in the *New York Times* of 19 February on a climactic note: "Walt Kuhn's 'Apples with Salmon Cloth' (they are red apples and the ground is also red) contrives startling color harmony and carries the design through with gusto. But very much more consequential is his puissantly and subtly painted nude [*Miss R.*], in which he argues that naturalism need not be academic; also, by having naught to do with such traits, that mere slickness and cleverness can never pave the way to vision that is either high or deep." Helen Hayes found the show a well-balanced one and proceeded to buy *Miss R.* Kuhn was to enjoy a long and amiable relationship with Helen Hayes MacArthur and Charles MacArthur.

Kuhn was also an active correspondent in 1935, with two revealing letters on 14 February. That date he wrote to a friend: "I don't get very much in the way of recreation, money is too scarce. Instead I have put a nice little kitchen in my studio, and occasionally give a dinner party to a few selected friends—simple food, off a plain wooden

Plate 104. *Red and Yellow Roses*

Courtesy of Kennedy Galleries, Inc.—Kuhn Estate

table with a gallon of red California wine. My work goes on. . . . I agree with you that there isn't any marked movement in art which amounts to anything. I suppose all the potential talent was lost in the war. But it will come again. Maybe we will not know it when it does." He would have recognized a marked movement in the 1950s, but it is doubtful that he would have thought that amounted to anything. In fact, he said as much in his last interview, with Alexander Eliot in *Time*, 22 November 1948, on the eve of his nervous breakdown: 'It's gotta stop!'" Eliot supplied the dialect: "These young fellows don't know where the Sam Hill they're at."

The Peggy Guggenheim–sponsored gallery, Art of This Century, between 1943 and 1946 had already given one-man shows to Jackson Pollock, Hans Hofmann (hardly a "young fellow" even then, since he was only three years younger than Kuhn), Robert Motherwell, Mark Rothko, Clyfford Still, and William Baziotes. The vaguely named "abstract expressionists" were well launched. But at the time of Kuhn's 1935 letter the Section of Painting and Sculpture of the U.S. Treasury Department was in being — successor to the Public Works of Art Project started in December 1933, soon to be followed by the Federal Art Project of the Works Progress Administration — and had kept several of the soon-to-be abstract expressionists alive in the depths of the depression. It was the embodiment of all that Kuhn distrusted in government patronage. He was a firm believer in free enterprise, even in the arts —

especially in the arts—and violently opposed to what he considered government charity and control. He would almost shout, "If they produce one good artist, just one, I'll be satisfied." He did not find reason to be in his lifetime.

It is difficult to tell how much Kuhn actually saw of this "marked movement." He alienated many of his contemporary artists by refusing to see their exhibitions, saying, "Why should I look at their work? We're all in the same box trying to look out." It was a case of *déjà vu* for him anyway; he had seen dadaism, surrealism, many forms of expressionism, and nonobjective painting of all kinds come and go and come again. From all of them he had taken what was necessary to him, and could not be bothered any more. He had found his own path through this jungle of styles, and it was hard enough to follow his unswerving course without such distractions.

The other 14 February letter throws some light on his personal position. It was in answer to a proposal from Marius de Zayas in Paris that he promote certain sales to his collecting friends: "There is one thing you must know before going further into the matter. I have never taken a profit on the sale of a piece of work, other than my own, in fact no one can vouch for this better than you. If I had been so inclined during the John Quinn days, I could have cleared considerable cash, or at least a first class modern painting collection for myself. I don't feel for an instant that it is illegitimate to take a profit, but not doing so has been a great asset to me in advancing my modest talent and keeping my prices relatively high, considering the general unpopularity of my output. I regret that I don't sell more than I do, but anyway I don't have to supply an ignorant dealer with any lesser work at lower prices."

On 5 April Kuhn wrote an endorsement of Edward Weston's application for a federal government assignment to photograph erosion problems. Kuhn and Weston shared a respect for each other's arts and styles, as well as an intermittent correspondence beginning in 1928 when they had spent some time together in San Francisco. Weston took one of Kuhn's best photographic portraits that year, and Kuhn admired his still life photographs and nudes. He was both flattered and amused by Weston's writing to him that he was the only artist to be asked for an endorsement, the others were "a museum director, an art collector, a photographer, an insurance broker."

Kuhn also wrote his "Recipe for Antique Finish of Frames" in 1935, three single-spaced pages of Vera's typing. He believed that a proper frame was as important to a painting as personally styled make-up was for a woman and, with the lesson well learned from dealers, rarely showed anyone a painting in undress. Following the current Parisian fashion that Picasso had helped to start when he was too poor to buy even secondhand frames and hunted in junkyards for weather-beaten moldings, Kuhn fancied the *décapé* look of carved rococo frames with all but a few glisters of gold leaf worn off, leaving the bone-white gesso and traces of the gilder's red earth showing through. He would buy new unfinished frames, usually from J. J. Augustin, and then elaborately antique them, matching the tone and the scattering of gold to the needs of the individual painting. In the case of the 1938 *Grenadier* (number 371) he was careful to find the type of plain Empire molding that David or Ingres might have used, to suit the show girl's period uniform. Working on frames was a relaxation from the wearing labors of creation.

Sometime in 1935 Kuhn wrote down a few notes on his own style for Lily Cushing, possibly to help her explain to her society friends the eccentric character she was studying with: "One would hardly call Kuhn a nice painter. Survived the temptation of making things merely to decorate people and their environment [a temptation Lily was prone to but also survived in her feminine way]. No American has to our mind achieved such simplicity. Kuhn's paintings are intended for men and for virile women." What he meant by "virile women" might be explained by a line from a popular song of the late nineteen-fifties: "I'm glad I'm a she-male female."

3

In 1936 Walt Kuhn was appointed consulting architect for the Union Pacific Railroad's new streamline trains, with a monthly retainer. He redesigned an American eagle for the engine of the first one, the

Plate 105. *Water Butt*

Plate 106. *Mario*

City of Denver, and ruled on the color of the stockings the stewardesses wore. They were unhappy with the color the couturier had ordered and appealed the problem to Kuhn, who voted with the girls. He was consulted on the color and lettering of station signs, insisting that there should be plenty of them because passengers wanted to know where the train was stopping or for what town it was slowing up. His chief project, though, was to design the interior of the lounge car. He decided on the "Frontier Shack" motif in deliberate contrast to the train's sleek exterior, and put his western lore to work with playbills, sheriffs' notices, and "Fair ladies" plastered on the walls. In 1937 he designed the "Little Nugget" club car for the *City of Los Angeles*, and in 1941 planned the decorative panels of a "Hollywood" club car for a second *City of Los Angeles*." The *City of Los Angeles* had to have a theatrical theme, and the "Little Nugget" raised diplomatic problems; obviously no living actors or actresses could be featured in this recollection of a Gay Nineties gin-palace, so he called on his show business lore to find photographs of the safely removed great and near-great. There was a "History of the Corset" in the ladies' room and a cock-fighting frame around the men's room mirror. In April 1938 he noted down the list of actors for whom he had found photographs. The "Little Nugget" survives the demise of the railroads in the Griffith Park Railroad Museum, "Traveltown," in Los Angeles.

As a preparation for these Union Pacific ventures, Kuhn traveled West with the Harrimans in their private car in the summer of 1936. It was rather different from the first western trip in 1899. He spent several weeks in Hollywood and its environs, seeing a great deal of Gary Cooper, who was working on a Wild Bill Hickok movie that Kuhn thought was later called *The Plainsman*. At Kuhn's suggestion, the actor was willing, in fact wanted, to wear a Wild Bill mustache, but the unbreakable laws of the star system ruled against it; Gary Cooper with a flowing mustache was not Gary Cooper to his public, and that was that. Kuhn was amazed and impressed by the technical skills of movie-making, and pleased that the bit-part players and extras came to him for advice on details of costume and manner. The year before Kuhn was born, Wild Bill Hickok was shot in the back at a poker game, holding his "dead man's hand" of two pairs, aces and eights, but the West of 1899 that Kuhn knew well and had so keenly observed was much the same as in 1876. Gary Cooper was under contract to Sam Goldwyn, who, in spite of his reputation as a rough-diamond Mr. Malaprop, was a discriminating, gifted producer and civilized host. Kuhn was invited to more than one of his small Saturday dinners and saw his *Hydrangeas* over the Goldwyn mantel; he thought it "handsome."

All this, with great detail, was poured out in a series of daily letters to Vera, together with daily not-too-good reports on his health; Hollywood has exhausted more rugged constitutions. Vera's reaction was unexpected; she wrote on 25 July: "A great schmatz to you for that highly interesting letter about Cooper and the movies. . . . You sound like olden times. The life of the stage is yours and always has been. The last few years have taken you too far away from it — Perhaps it would be well for us to take stock, whether we haven't become too 'precious' in our insistence on 'fine art'." It must have been a strong temptation, coming from such a source, but Kuhn held to his charted course.

On top of this crowded and demanding schedule Kuhn turned out fourteen paintings in 1936, one destroyed. It was *Spanish Plate* (number 349), which closely resembled, and was not in the artist's eyes as successful as, *Fruit Platter* (number 342). Kuhn had found *Fruit Platter* set up for him on a drugstore counter; he said the curves of the bananas were the angry resistance of a twisting steel cable imprisoning the oranges and recumbent pineapple. Three others are in the upper category: *Carnival Girl* (number 338), *Fancy Dress* (number 341), and *Wisconsin* (number 350). *Miss R.* has already been mentioned. Seven of the fourteen were in his 16 February to 13 March 1937 show at the Marie Harriman Gallery, where Kuhn identified them in the catalogue by small outline sketches instead of the usual black and white cuts. They were reinforced by *Theatre* (number 306) from 1933, *Juggler*, *Red Roses*, and *Dryad* from 1935.

They were all painted in the fifth-floor studio at 112 East Eighteenth Street, where he had moved in 1933 from the fourth floor of the same now-vanished building. It was a long, low-ceilinged narrow room with a species of living quarters at the south end where the stair door opened, containing a small lavatory, a hot plate, a few chairs, and the American Empire couch. At his own expense Kuhn put a skylight in the north end of this room; the light in the studio on the floor below had been so inadequate that he had spread newspapers all over the floor to get enough reflected light to paint *The White Clown*. A labyrinthine passageway lined with racks of costumes, boxes of all kinds of properties, and stacked or rolled paintings connected the two lighted areas. Not many visitors saw the north working end of the room, and the five steep flights of stairs were an effective barrier to casual passersby. Kuhn must have had friends among the local fire inspectors. He recognized the hazards himself and kept most of his finished paintings in a warehouse; he said that it was a distraction to have them around anyway. Smoking was not encouraged except for his own cigars, and it was as different as possible from a movie set or stage designer's idea of a painter's studio. William Merritt Chase or John Singer Sargent would not have felt at home. But it was a setting conducive to long conversations when Kuhn needed an interruption or when he wanted to pump out-of-town visitors who had been going the rounds of dealers and museums.

The model for *Carnival Girl* was Ruth Johnston, a modest, unassuming person who did not look at all like the cabaret acrobatic dancer she was. Like George Fitzgerald she had a sympathetic understanding of Kuhn's needs in a model and posed for many of his paintings, among them *Miss R.* early in the year and *Fancy Dress* (number 341), another show girl with a large two-horned ruffle-edged paper headdress. Kuhn called *Carnival Girl* "a young man's painting," and it happens to be the only one from 1936 included in the anthology, where its caption reads: "It glows with color — greens, yellows, reds, flesh and a background of quiet rose. A dancing girl from a summer carnival where Broadway's unemployed get between-engagement jobs. The costume is authentic though seemingly improvised. A song to the loyalty, independence and sheer bravery of these people." The glowing local colors are all there, but the total effect is of one light, muted, almost dry tone.

Alfred M. Frankfurter, editor of *Art News*, wrote an article on the exhibition titled "Kuhn: Master of the Painting Language," in his 27 February 1937 issue. Alfred Frankfurter was a close friend, and in a certain sense a disciple of Walt Kuhn, leaning heavily on the older man's experience and perception. Himself a well-trained art historian and one-time pupil of Bernard Berenson, Frankfurter had a scholarly perspective rare in American art journalism. In the nature of things his primary concern had to be with contemporary developments, but he tried to see them "under the aspect of eternity," much to Kuhn's approval. This association gave Kuhn a useful publicity tool that he used with the greatest discretion. Frankfurter focused his article on *Carnival Girl, Fancy Dress, Wisconsin,* and *Fruit Platter,* reproducing the last two. He found a new element in these paintings, contrasting avorably with the "static" character of earlier works:

Plate 107. *Moist Forest*

Courtesy of Kennedy Galleries, Inc.—Kuhn Estate

173

Plate 108 (left). *Musical Clown*

Plate 109 (right). *Lancer*

The result is a group of figures precisely and yet widely fixed in space, at once candid in self-characterization and remote from connection with artist or spectator. It is amusing to note that, though technically and compositionally there is not one whit of indebtedness, the development in Kuhn's art parallels that of Velasquez, that, under the function and restrictions of contemporary painting, there is in this recent painting of an American a good deal of the temperate, even cool observation of heat and heated temperament which was the particular greatness of the greatest Spanish master. Alongside *Las Meninas* and the icily observed passions of Aragonese court dwarfs, Kuhn's acrobats and jugglers and vaudeville girls take on a new and special kind of credibility.

But, curiously, quiet as Velasquez pierced to the core only when he caught his still subjects off the tense guard which motion always implies, Kuhn does far better with the deliberate quality of his still figures than with the prestidigitation of his *Long Nosed Clown* or *Theatre*, the latter a view of a circus drummer in action. In the serene records of the Wisconsin countryman, of the unaffected model called *Dryad* or of the girl troupers, there is far deeper characterization and a much more sweeping rhythm. It is difficult to decide whether one must seek the answer from artist or subject, though the example of Velasquez is classic evidence on behalf of the former.

Frankfurter also read deeper social meanings into them:

Colors which have absolute virtues in themselves are here at each other's throats exactly as there are any number of, in themselves, positive elements in modern society. The still-lifes currently shown are the best guides to this astonishing translation into truly pictorial terms of a problem which has been a root impulse in modern art, but the same principle has also been applied by Walt Kuhn to the lower world of the theatre — of the craftsmen who support the artists at the top of the profession — which he delights to paint. The wild combinations of rose and green satins, the vivid hues of make-up and lipstick, the green-grey pallor of wan skin are all commentaries perhaps even more profound, akin to the natural discords of the soda-fountain fruit. This is vital observation in terms of paint and canvas.

Alfred Frankfurter was at least trying to get at the inner meanings, hampered though he was by the social and economic determinism of the times and the final impossibility of stating such meanings in words.

4

Andrew Mellon, "the greatest Secretary of the Treasury since Alexander Hamilton" and master of an immeasurable fortune in aluminum and oil, in December 1936 offered to build, endow, and give to the nation a National Gallery of Art at Washington. He also donated his small but magnificent collection of painting and sculpture, which he hoped, "would attract gifts from other citizens to contribute works of art . . . to form a great national collection." Several of the key paintings had been acquired from the Soviet government in the late twenties and early thirties when the Russians were desperate for foreign capital. Knoedler's had made the first successful negotiations, but the ineffable Joseph Duveen had contrived to take over. Some cynics and political leftists called the gesture a plea-bargaining deal for tax purposes, but it was an act truly generous in motive, munificent and modest; he did not want his name attached to the institution, although for years it was popularly called "the Mellon Gallery."

On 24 March 1937 Congress accepted the gift, pledging the "faith and honor" of the United States government to the maintenance and operation of the gallery. It was the first time such a phrase had been used in an act of Congress. A farsighted provision of the gift was that the endowment income was not to be under direct government administration, but was to provide for accessions and the professional staff. This was a consummation that Walt Kuhn had devoutly wished, but he foresaw dangers, and on 11 January 1937 he wrote to Mrs. Thomas Hitchcock, Jr., who owned one of his paintings:

> I have been made conscious from the newspapers as well as other sources, that many schemes for commercial exploitation are already under way. I am so jealous of this one clean start at a national museum, that I cannot resist this opportunity to voice my fears to you, who I know have ready access to the ear of Mr. Mellon.
> There is only one way to safeguard against the inclusion of contemporary interests of the destructive sort. Neither by purchase nor gift should any work of art be eligible for the museum until thirty years after the death of the artist concerned. This would give the best critic of all, a chance to judge, and that critic is Time.

It was the sort of stipulation that the William Rockhill Nelson Gallery had nimbly sidestepped in acquiring the *Juggler,* and Averell Harriman's gift of five of Walt Kuhn's paintings to the National Gallery in 1972 beat the Kuhn-proposed time limit by seven years.

175

Kuhn kept fourteen paintings from 1937, two of them never exhibited, and three of the first rank: one a landscape, one a still life and one the largest figure composition he had painted since 1915. *Trees — Vermont* (number 363) is the most elaborately composed of his landscapes. Two large tawny maple trees in the foreground form a kind of proscenium for a meadow with post-fence, a field in the middle distance, and a backdrop of forested hillside. In *50 Paintings* the observer is invited to "take a walk among these trees. This is nature's temple, a corridor through the fields and down the hill where the dignity of natural growth is presented in its severe and classic fullness. Call it Arcadian if you will, but there is no impressionistic dressing up; there are no color 'effects' nor any romping nudes. Vermont maple sugar comes from the trees, but there is not a grain of it in this painting." It is probably his closest approach to Constable, whom he suspected of occasional sentimentality, and also a dismissal of Corot's popular middle period. The color of the proscenium tree trunks is more like the color of sycamores than maples, but Kuhn said many times, as countless other artists have, "painting is not copying."

Water Butt (number 365) is unlike any of his other subjects; a half-barrel held in place by heavy wooden stakes against a post-and-rail fence catches the jet from a nozzle for "the barnyard overlords." The dominant colors are green and a dark, almost black brown. Edna St. Vincent Millay was enchanted by it; she had one like it in her own barnyard and on an early morning had seen a yearling deer drinking from it. She dashed off a verse on the theme, never published, and sent it with a covering note to Kuhn on 10 October 1941. Only the note survives. Painting may not be copying alone, but Kuhn caught the sound as well as the look of the white froth from "a mountain stream." Subject does seem to be the important element here, and Kuhn called it "a poem to 'the old oaken bucket.'" It was his choice for the 1937 Whitney Annual, by no means a crowd-catcher and difficult for the critics to pigeonhole.

Trio (number 364) "is the artist's most ambitious undertaking to date. It summarizes years of experimentation in both form and color and rigorous training in exactitude." So says the artist. Alexander Eliot, quoting from his *Time* interview, quotes Kuhn in turn:

"Why, if I do one good picture a year I'm tickled to death." Kuhn's art was as specific as his words were general. His paintings were frankly narrow in intent, but a plow also has a narrow blade, and Kuhn could cut a marvellously straight furrow.

Trio is one of Kuhn's "good" pictures, and it stands among the major achievements of modern American art. The one-two-three, red-white-red composition is as buoyantly symmetrical as a triple somersault performed in mid-air — and has much the same mystifying air of inevitability and ease. As an old showman himself, Kuhn naturally chose entertainers for his subjects, and by seizing them from the spangled entertainment world into a silent, neutral zone, he made them seem more colorful than ever. By posing them in stiff immobility, he underscored their capacity for action; even though grounded, the trapeze artists seem to soar as a team. Beyond their sharply individual personalities, they share an impersonal dignity, the courage of indomitable transients posing for the audience of eternity.

Plate 110. *Hat with Blue Ribbon*

Private Collection

Kuhn himself climbed a high, twisting ladder to reach such moments of greatness as his *Trio* represents. . . .

A detailed watercolor study for *Trio* shows something of its evolution. The pose is already set, the figures complete except for their feet. The two flanking figures are light brown with red ornament on the borders of collars and trunks, the center figure has red accents on the cheek and forehead of his white face; he wears a green and gold bolero and green knee-pants with gold spangles down the side seam. None of these colors and accents are in the final red-white-red painting. As Whistler said, in all fine art there is a "tact of omission." When the three models, who were not a working act but were all veteran acrobats, appeared for the start of the project their physical presence was a bit overpowering. Kuhn admitted that he was disconcerted and unsure of how to begin. Then he asked them what they proposed. Mario Venendi, the center figure, said, "Hup!" and they instantly took the inevitable pose.

177

Alexander Eliot's comment is just and adequate, and his literary image of the straight furrow was anticipated by Horace Brodzky in a letter of 23 August 1943, from England: ". . . I hope you have 'arrived' as far as the public is concerned. I know you always carved a lonely and difficult furrow, and I know that things are slow, but I should have imagined that you have educated the public by now. Anyhow I hope so." Kuhn answered on 5 October: "My lonely and difficult furrow (as you put it) is still as difficult, and if anything, more lonely. I haven't made it any easier for myself. . . . Naturally having been around as long as I have, the law of averages has made it possible for me to do enough business to get along. But no miracles have happened, and nobody is exactly breaking down my doors to come and buy a picture away from me. . . . Outside of a few artists of thirty or less, I see few people of the profession. Beginning next year I hope to spend more time in the country and do less worrying."

Trio was first shown at the Marie Harriman Gallery in 1940, the Whitney Annual that same year, and as a one-painting exhibition in Columbus, Ohio, and Kansas City. In 1947 it was the star of a traveling exhibition organized by the Colorado Springs Fine Arts Center and circulated to San Francisco, Santa Barbara, Los Angeles, Omaha, and Cranbrook, Michigan. Kuhn had great hopes for this show, and in June 1948 the El Pomar Foundation of Colorado Springs bought *Trio* and gave it to the Art Center.

Kuhn was not yet ready to sound the valedictory note of his 1943 letter to Horace Brodzky, but a sixtieth birthday can bring reminiscence, as can twenty-fifth reunions; and in the fall he began to assemble notes for *The Story of the Armory Show,* his own and unique contribution to its twenty-fifth anniversary. On 28 February 1938 he sent copies of the pamphlet to Derain and Matisse, not necessarily in the spirit of Thomas Hardy's "An Ancient to Ancients," unless he thought of the word "ancient" in its French sense. After all, they were fellow alumni, and many vintage years lay ahead.

NOTES TO CHAPTER SEVEN

The JURY SYSTEM whether of selection or award was at best a chancy undertaking. Even at its height many dealers would not let their artists risk such a gamble. Rejection or failure to win an important prize could be denigrating, and even prize-winning had little real value in enhancing an artist's reputation. Eugene Speicher told of having the same painting rejected by six juries in one season, only to win the first prize at the Corcoran Biennial.

WALT'S PRAISE OF THE WHITNEY MUSEUM comes from a letter to the author.

Information about DIKRAN KELEKIAN, whom the author was privileged to know well, came from his son and successor, Charles Kelekian, in preparation for an unpublished article.

THE DISCUSSION OF STILL LIFE PAINTING is adapted from the catalogue of "Still Life Painting since 1470," organized by the Milwaukee Art Institute and the Cincinnati Art Museum in the fall of 1956, pages 2 to 4, by the present writer.

CHARLES STERLING'S BOOK, *Still Life from Antiquity to our Times,* was originally published in French in 1952, with a revised edition in English (Paris: Pierre Tisné, 1959). The quotations come from the French edition and are not included in the later English version.

RENOIR'S LETTER TO DURAND-RUEL is quoted from John Rewald, *The History of Impressionism* (New York: Museum of Modern Art, 1946), p. 359.

WALT'S NEED TO STRENGTHEN HIS DRAWING was told to Robert M. Coffin, the artist-educator, who records it in the manuscript of his yet unpublished book on drawing.

The quotations from the text of the KENNEDY GALLERIES' "DRAWING AND WATERCOLOR" CATALOGUE, by the present writer, come from pp. 3, 4, and 5.

THE 14 FEBRUARY LETTER was addressed "Dear Margy," who has not yet been identified.

THE "SHE-MALE FEMALE"LINE comes from the Rodgers and Hammerstein *Flower Drum Song* which opened in New York in December 1958.

THE PRESENT WHEREABOUTS OF THE "LITTLE NUGGET" comes from Fred Bartlett's catalogue *An Imaginary History of the West*, 1964, p. 9.

DATA ON WILD BILL HICKOK comes from *The New Century Cyclopedia of Names*, (New York: Appleton Century-Crofts,1954). James Butler Hickok was killed at Deadwood in the then Dakota Territory.

"THE PLAINSMAN," co-starring Gary Cooper and Jean Arthur, was directed by Cecil B. DeMille, produced by Sam Goldwyn, and released in 1936.

"WALTER BUTT'S" NATURALISM worked against its sale one time. A prospective lady purchaser had taken it home to try it out, usually a successful semifinal to the closing of the deal, but returned it because her "husband couldn't stand the sound of running water."

THE QUOTATION ABOUT "TRIO" comes from Alexander Eliot, *Three Centuries of American Painting* (New York: Time Inc.1957), pp. 284, 286. The painting is reproduced full-page in color on page 285. Eliot grouped Kuhn with Andrew Wyeth, George Bellows, and Edward Hopper in his last chapter, "The Realist Tradition."

THE WATERCOLOR STUDY FOR "TRIO" is reproduced in color on page 72 of the Memorial Exhibition catalogue, 1960.

"My Brushes Carry Out My Instructions"

Still in a reminiscent mood, Walt Kuhn wrote to Charles Sheeler on 29 January 1938: "I have often wondered how you were doing and how things fare with you — one never sees you. On a recent Western trip I spent a most delightful evening with the Arensbergs. We talked much of you and the old days." The Arensbergs were part of the old days; originally from Pittsburgh, the young Walter Arensberg had come down from Boston to see the Armory Show, and from it bought a Vuillard lithograph that was turned in for a small Jacques Villon oil when the show came to Boston.

It was a tentative but significant beginning of an important collection. By 1916 Arensberg was living in New York, supporting "little magazines" and small galleries of modern art, among them that of Marius de Zayas, and seeing Kuhn fairly often. Aline Saarinen wrote of Arensberg: "Walter Arensberg's mind was as intricate as the inside of a calculating machine. It led him to two dedications: one was with the deciphering of symbols and supposedly cabalistic signs in Shakespeare's plays in order to prove the authorship of Francis Bacon, and the other was the sensitive purchase of cubist and surrealist modern art — by such men as Duchamp, Klee, Brancusi, Picasso — in which intellectuality was the touchstone. He had discriminating and cerebral taste." There were skeptics who thought it fitting for a Baconian to buy *Nude Descending a Staircase*. In 1915 the Arensbergs began collecting Pre-Columbian sculptures as well. They later moved to southern California, and finally, after considerable courting by other museums, bequeathed their collection to the Philadelphia Museum of Art.

As he later wrote Brodzky, Kuhn was no longer seeing any of his contemporaries except for an occasional, often accidental, meeting. It is a well-known phenomenon of the artist's growing process; first the gathering of young painters, writers, musicians to talk long into the night about the arts of their devotion. Often such groups had centered around an unofficial leader like Courbet at his Brasserie, or Manet at the Café Guerbois on the Grande rue des Batignolles. Monet recalled them in a letter of 1900: "Nothing could be more interesting than these *causeries* with the perpetual clash of opinions. They kept our wits sharpened, they encouraged us with stores of enthusiasm that for weeks and weeks kept us up, until the final shaping of the idea was accomplished. From them we emerged tempered more highly, with a firmer will, our thoughts clearer and more distinct." For a later generation there would be the Café du Dome, the Coupole, Rotonde, the Deux Magots. A history of modern French art could be written about the theme of the cafés of Paris; some may have been. They were the true academy.

As a faint echo, the Penguin Club was such a group for Walt Kuhn. Then as the members began to reach their late thirties or early forties, as their individual styles began to crystallize, the groups slowly dissolved, sometimes never to meet again or only by chance. Once-warm friendships tended to cool, or latent enmities came to the surface. But those spring days were always fondly remembered, growing brighter with distance.

Kuhn was long past this stage when, on 28 March 1938, he answered a letter from Henri-Pierre Roché in Paris. Since 1915 Roché had been John Quinn's most trusted agent in France, and had kept up an intermittent acquaintance with Kuhn. This time Roché had written to propose an American Armory Show for Paris, first asking how things were with Kuhn who replied: "Considering that I am insistent as always in painting exactly what I want, I suppose you might say that things are going well with me too [as well as with Brancusi]. I have more or less arrived at the point where I can make my brushes carry out my instructions. The subject matter is just about the same — show people, along with still lifes and landscapes." As for an American Armory Show, Kuhn thought it impossible: "I haven't the slightest idea with what you would fill it. . . . You know I have come to the conclusion that people abroad object to the use of the classics by us Americans. They seem to feel that they have a copyright. From America they want Mickey Mouse and night club entertainment — even Picasso told me how much he liked Laurel and Hardy, the film comedians." This seems to have been the only compliment Picasso could pay to American art, and Walt Kuhn ends, "Art isn't national anyway, and I know you agree."

There is a quiet voice of authority in this letter, and the paintings of 1938 confirm it. As he often said of himself, Kuhn was a late bloomer, but to a large degree this is typical of most painters. There are a few great exceptions, very great — Masaccio, Giorgione, Watteau, Seurat — but they are still exceptions. Lyric poets and theoretical physicists may flower early, some of the lucky poets even die young:

Wordsworth's reputation would have benefited from his death at thirty-seven, after his first collected poems were published. But if Goya or Rembrandt had died at forty, they would be little more than footnotes for art historians. Renoir at seventy said, "Now that my brushes are strapped to my hands I am beginning to learn to paint." At sixty-one, with nine years of mature accomplishment behind him, Walt Kuhn could say, "I have more or less arrived at the point where I can make my brushes carry out my instructions."

The instructions he gave were by now more specific. *Grenadier* (number 371) was to be "today's illogic, uncomprehending elements marshalled into an ingenious philosophy of tradition. The girl, not understanding, costumed by the wardrobe mistress in a Czarist Grenadier's uniform. . . . Present fact and past grandeur fused. . . ." This sounds like verbalizing after the fact, but the fact was present in the costume Kuhn had already designed, that his wife had run up on a portable Singer sewing machine and hung on the loaded rack from which the model herself picked it out. Once it was put on, the artist was in full control. Rigid frontal pose, expressionless wooden face, green tunic with white-frogged scarlet facing, white epaulets and gloves, with the white spurt of an aigret from the brass helmet emphatic as an exclamation point or a parade ground command — all add up to one of Walt Kuhn's literally classic statements.

At the opposite extreme, *Mario* (number 375) is deliberately one of Kuhn's most romantic paintings. Intention and result are one. The artist wrote: "A rare type of professional aristocrat who could have been Greek or Elizabethan but is a New Yorker. Costumed in gold brocade [with arms crossed and a white felt conical hat over his skull-cap], he poses with insistent dignity as a star among the clowns. His valid pride is expressed in the directness of technique — like easy, distinct handwriting." Small wonder that Edna St. Vincent Millay fell in love with it; her devoted Dutch husband, Eugene Boissevain, bought it to hang over her desk. When his importing business was wiped out by the Japanese invasion of the East Indies, Kuhn bought the painting back. The model was Mario Venendi, who had posed for the center figure in *Trio* and was to be the *Veteran Acrobat* (number 384); he was another who grasped the painter's various purposes and resented what he felt was Kuhn's neglect or misunderstanding by the critics and public.

It was as if with these two paintings Kuhn had set the outer boundaries of his style, just as after *Trio* he had concentrated on single figures. They baffled many otherwise discerning people with their bare simplicity. A generation conditioned by James Joyce and T.S. Eliot, as Kuhn himself could have been, or by the sophistries of Picasso and Matisse, was not prepared for it. After years of the most rigorous discipline Kuhn was utterly convinced that he was hewing to the right line. Had he known it, he might have cited the Greek Anthology's definition of an epigram: "Two lines of epigram exhaust their topic. With one line

Plate 111. *Girl in Pierrot's Hat*

more the thing becomes an epic." Walt Kuhn often called his paintings metaphors, but he could also have called on the dictionary meaning of an epigram: "any terse, witty, or pointed statement, often antithetical." Wit may be a matter of personal taste, but it is undoubtedly antithetical to speak of courage, pride, dignity, and faith in terms of buffoons and "pallid harlots." As for terseness and pointedness there are few parallels in any of the modern arts to the stripped spareness of Walt Kuhn's statement. A.E. Housman and Robert Frost come to mind; but Hous-

183

Plate 112. *Dancing Clown*

Private Collection

man, the classical scholar, was often waved aside for his adolescent pessimism, and Frost was sometimes accused of rustic affectation.

Six other paintings stand out from the carefully screened seventeen of 1938. From this time on, no paintings listed in exhibitions or recorded in the artist's files were destroyed, though many may have died in coming to birth. *Lavender Plumes* (number 372) is a variation on *Plumes* of 1931 with a gentler touch, a romantic grace that might have

Plate 113. *Clown Dressing*

come from the model, Ruth Johnston. Kuhn said of it: "Sheathed in cerulean feathers, crowned with soaring plumes, she is a fairy queen for the moment — and carries it off. Yet she is a hard-working American girl whose day includes four shows, then home to house-work for her mother. . . ." *Apples in Wooden Boat* (number 367) belongs in the company of *Apples from Maine* of 1932 and *Green Apples and Scoop* (number 387) of 1939, and it too is in a museum collection.

Of the two landscapes, only *Sunlit Pine* (number 383) is included in *50 Paintings* with a rapturous caption: "A tree brought to maximum. The right season; the right day; the right tree; and, perhaps, the right artist. Under a blazing sun this old pine warrior brandishes his might with a reverberating clang that shakes the surrounding landscape. In color this is a crescendo of brasses." Dazzling white clouds and a line of intense blue sky are the background for this portrait of a single tree. Kuhn had written Vera that summer from Ogunquit: "Pines are about all they have here, that and elms. Elms don't suit me much for painting, not husky enough although I like them well enough for B and Whites." In the same way that he wanted to keep Goya's inspiration out of sight in his figures, Kuhn made every effort to conceal Constable's influence in his landscapes. If it can be seen at all, it is probably Constable's sense of the anatomy of trees. There is this feeling in *Moist Forest* (number 376), where a grove of very damp white pines could illustrate a forestry text.

Another of *Trio's* models posed for *Musical Clown* (number 377), technically known as raggedy-pants comedian, with frock coat, battered top hat, white gloves, and a large tarnished baritone horn. "This drab clown," as Kuhn called him, has no hint of the drama, pathetic or otherwise, that he sometimes allowed to creep into paint-

Plate 114. Top. *Rehearsal.*
Bottom. *Clowns Waiting.*

ings of other clowns, and yet the *Musical Clown's* stolid resignation is moving. The low-keyed colors are a subdued accompaniment to the sonorous climax of the horn. Like all painters up until the twentieth century, when every object, natural or man-made, was subject to arbitrary distortion, Kuhn painted musical instruments with an affectionate accuracy, possibly out of respect for the craft skill of their makers, or even in unconscious acknowledgement of Plato's observation that any instrument capable of voicing a perfect sound is in itself beautiful. Kuhn sent the painting to the Whitney Annual of 1943, where it was later bought. *Veteran Acrobat* (number 384) is one of his masterpieces, a tribute to the "fine craftsmanship" of this "top-flight performer and a veteran of both European and American stages." Mario Venendi was also an Italian veteran of World War I, and Kuhn found poignant overtones in his taut, terra cotta features. Whether or not it is a "dirge on war," the whole painting, subject included, has a patrician bearing. Against a cool darker green background the warm light green, almost chartreuse jersey flashes with silver embroidery. This metallic illusion fashioned from the simplest opaque pigments is a tour de force.

2

Kuhn was still beguiled by Hollywood, apart from Vera's nudge in that direction. There was talk about his designing the set for another Gary Cooper western. It would not have been a gamble; in the *Merry-go-Round* revue of 1928 Kuhn had helped to launch Libby Holman's career by designing the set and costumes for a number called "Hogan's Alley"; it was a success, though the revue was not. Also in 1939 his pedagogic impulses were still strong; combining the two urges, he spent several weeks on a documentary film, *Walt Kuhn's Adventures in Art*, which was finished on 17 September. He was quite pleased with it and convinced that a single showing would persuade the blindest Philistine. It did not, but as late as the fall of 1948 he was still promoting it as part of a lecture program.

On 5 January 1939 Kuhn got in touch with Elmer MacRae in Cos Cob, Connecticut, asking him to come into town for a visit. He wrote to him on 10 January, "What memories we both have of times together!" MacRae was one of the last insiders of the great days of 1913, and the reunion must have reached a nostalgic peak. Kuhn got up to Ogunquit while the documentary was being processed, "hunting pictures, the trees couldn't be better anywhere," he wrote to Vera. "Also strange to relate, at long last I seem to have acquired a certain popularity — here in Ogunquit." This is to his credit; nineteen years is a fairly short probationary period for summer people in New England.

Although only two minor landscapes came from Ogunquit that summer, two first-rank still lifes did. One was *Green Apples with Scoop* (number 387), now in the National Gallery. Its first New York appearance was in the great 1946 show at Durand-Ruel. The show was extensively reviewed, but only two critics, both somewhat unexpected, spotted *Green Apples with Scoop*. Marion Summers, in the 14 November 1946 issue of the *Daily Worker*, wrote: "For solid and magnificent painting I recommend his large still lifes, *Peaches* and *Green Apples with Scoop*. The latter especially is built with simple grandeur and its color fairly sings with joy." Charles Z. Offin, in his own small magazine *Pictures on Exhibition* said: "Walt Kuhn paints the most structurally vital still life pictures of any artist living today, and these canvases stand out predominantly in his one-man show at the Durand-Ruel Galleries although he has included a clown which is likewise powerfully painted. But the human interest and dramatic overtones in Kuhn's clown subjects help to build up the emotional impact, whereas in the studies of green apples and other still life, the structural organization and the bold handling of pigment are so electrifying in their effect that no other dramatic associations are needed. The still life canvases date back to 1939 and 1940, and are really significant paintings, which cannot be said of more recently painted tree subjects." It seems that Kuhn was at last fulfilling Horace Brodzky's hope that he would educate the public, or at least the critics, and almost single-handedly where still lifes were concerned. The wooden scoop lies at a slight diagonal across the light orange-tinged ocher tabletop and rumpled light blue cloth, in front of a bushel basket; the green apples are scattered over the cloth and table and fill the basket. The background is a featureless dark brown.

The other important still life of 1939 is hardly second to *Green Apples and Scoop*. It is *Still Life with Apples* (number 392) and has no recorded exhibition history until it entered Joseph Hirshhorn's collection in 1962; it is now in the Hirshhorn Museum and Sculpture Garden in Washington. It is closer to Cézanne than any other of Kuhn's still lifes, perhaps because of its light French tonality. A cream-glazed compotier and pitcher stand on a tobacco-colored cloth against a French gray background; the red and green apples gather close to the two vessels and five of them fill the compotier. There is a mystique about Walt Kuhn's apples that cannot be easily defined, if at all. He was once quoted as saying that he painted apples because they reminded him of women's backsides, but that was a bawdy brush-off of a difficult question. In October 1948 he wrote to the publicity agent for his traveling exhibition in Colorado Springs:

> My picture, "Red Apples" was painted in 1944 at my camp in Maine. The job covered at least four years of investigating apples in general.
> Contrary to the mass production methods of today, both here and abroad, I have always clung to the somewhat outmoded theory that a painter should leave at least a few examples of epic quality, viz to pry into the subject and emerge, aided by luck and perhaps a little talent, with something lasting, if not a final comment on the subject.
> I have tried "Greenings", "MacIntosh", "Delicious", and many other types, but finally decided that the "Winesap" was the very apple which Eve offered Adam, and which every school boy polished for his teacher. That was good enough for me.
> Whether this effort has been successful or not, I promise you I shall never look another bowl of red apples in the face.

Plate 115. Left. *Frightened Horses.* Below. *Clown Walking Tight Rope – Arms Extended*

This quasi-serious comment is about as close as possible to an explanation, though there is still Cézanne's famous dictum that the sphere is one of the three basic forms in nature, an axiom that the cubists took to heart.

Four quite individual paintings of young women complete the 1939 roster. *Lancer* (number 389) is a more active companion to *Grenadier.* As the artist says: "The chief interest in this picture is its definite and acute design made up of upward-lunging scimitar strokes. In color not one of the arbitraries, but an outgrowth of that interesting experiment." It is taller and narrower than the usual format, to stress this upward lunge, and the aigret does curve like a sabre blade. The Currier Gallery of Art in Manchester, New Hampshire, which acquired it in 1958, reports that it still disquiets some of the more conservative visitors, an indirect compliment to its brassy vitality. In contrast, *Hat with Blue Ribbon* (number 388) is a study in repose; the model is dressed for a Gilbert and Sullivan chorus from *Patience* or *The Pirates of Penzance.* She wears a garden-party hat whose blue ribbon falls in front of her left shoulder, and stands quietly, weary or bored, in a pastel Empire gown that slips from her right shoulder.

Young Girl (number 396) is an almost clinical document. It does not stylistically recall the studies of deranged types that Géricault painted for his friend Dr. Georget, a pioneer psychiatrist of the Salpêtrière Hospital, but is in much the same spirit. The seated nude

Plate 116. **Right.** *Clown with Finger to Nose.* **Below.** *Two Equestriennes*

model, a Martha Graham dancer, may not have seen herself in this light, but the artist raises a thin tortured face with wild staring eyes above the full body and abundant breasts. Kuhn wrote of it: "Tawny in color with almost a black background, it has a stark power and defiance in the face of terror. It immediately recalls the best of Spanish painting." And rightly said; Goya of the "black paintings" would not have disowned it.

Nothing could be more different from it than *Tricorne* (number 394). Kuhn thought it one of his finest paintings, and it is deceptively simple, deceptive because a world lies between the richness of simplicity and the poverty of plainness. He called it: "A lump of weighted form, the one, the universal substance of art. Trying to get it makes art history. The Greeks had it, lost it; Rubens caught it, then it slipped through Van Dyck's fingers. Cézanne chopped it up to see how it is made; his followers fooled with the pieces. Here it is whole again." Only a master is permitted self-praise, and Walt Kuhn had earned the privilege. He admitted his failures; he knew when he was good. After the blazing uniforms of *Grenadier* and *Lancer* the color is calm, the tones closely tuned. The gold braid edging of the tricorne repeats the warm flesh of the ample arms and oval face; the white collar and jabot match the turquoise dress and hat, all against a dark slate background. The red make-up of cheeks and lips is echoed in one short brush stroke at the armpit and in the signature. The Cincinnati Art Museum bought it in 1957 through a generous and graciously phrased endowment for the purchase of paintings, "preferably American."

3

There are no records of outside activities in 1940; it must have been a quiet year, with only twelve rather minor paintings and three important till lifes. At this point Kuhn was spending considerable time coaching and guiding one of his New England discoveries, Patsy Santo of Vermont. He was an American-born Italian housepainter whom the Germans would call an *autodidakt* and the French a *naif* — in other words, not that much misused term a "primitive," but simply self-taught. Kuhn thought that Patsy Santo had a "natural" talent, and, not wanting to see his disarmingly unsophisticated style spoiled, guarded him from too much self-improvement or well-meant outside influences, while arranging New York exhibitions for him.

Kuhn stayed that summer on Lake Buel in the Berkshires near Great Barrington, Massachusetts. There he had decided to concentrate on small paintings, a species of exercise something like his life-drawing program of 1935, and wrote to Vera: "Spent the second day on another 10 × 12 oil, they are getting constantly better. I think this small picture scheme will work out." He was also working on small watercolors and drawings of circus subjects, pointed toward a late 1941 show, writing Vera again that he had to "start a couple of man-sized pictures. If I did nothing but these little circus things my morale would go all to pieces."

191

One of the man-sized pictures was *Stumps* (number 406). It could be thought of as either a still life or a landscape; his own description was: "Ordinary stumps from the field have been pulled together here to inspire this powerful and beautifully interlocked composition which is predominantly ashen in color. One need not be interested in design as such each time but here its reality of expression cannot be escaped." He went on to preach a short sermon on "Man's crime against nature. This world of mutilated forms. Devastation." He also thought highly of *Chair with Apples* (number 398), frequently exhibiting it, saying that "the vivid, clashing colors close in to create a new taste." It was first shown in New York in 1946, and Aline Saarinen, then Aline Louchheim, was impressed. She wrote in the November 1946 issue of *Art News*, where she was assistant editor: "You are struck by the rightness which controls daring color dissonance (the almost vulgar orange of the chair, the forest-green walls, and the pale, cool green of the apples in *Chair with Apples)* and transforms it into an affirmation of chromatic strength. You are arrested by the justice of tonal progressions, which move like the stirring chords of a Bach chorale. And you are aware at once of the coherence and logic with which the compositions [of all the paintings in the show] are built. . . ."

Potatoes (number 404) needs no defensive rhetoric, the artist saying: "There could be no humbler subject for an artist than the lowly potato, the staple of every kitchen in the land. . . .In this still life the artist has permitted his emotion to project primarily through the color. Mould and rust set against a background of shimmering, irridescent green. The tuber enthroned." The potatoes and iron pot are there, with the presence, the inevitability, of the wooden clogs in Van Eyck's *Jan Arnolfini*, the Hispano-Moresque albarello in Van der Goes' *Portinari Altarpiece,* Balthasar's red boot in Brueghel's *Adoration of the Kings*, the gold-framed painting on the wall of Vermeer's *Girl with Guitar*, or Cézanne's oranges, or Chardin's rabbits.

Only seven canvases came from 1941. Decorative panels for the "Hollywood" club car of a new *City of Los Angeles* took Kuhn to Chicago, where the new trains were built, and to Hollywood in the early months of 1941, and for a while he simply felt painted-out. He knew that active preparation for the watercolor and drawing show in December would use up most of November, so he left for the Berkshires earlier than usual in June and started in again on small still lifes. At Lake Buel he found a lot of tinkering to do on the cottage, with its screened porch fronting on the lake, and amused himself by building toy steamboats powered by tiny steam engines, about which he wrote home oftener than about his painting. He was not feeling well physically, and the best medication seemed to be his own simply cooked stews and vegetable soups made from good local produce.

As late as September he wrote to Vera: "After six weeks [of painting] I usually fizzle out." A bit later he wrote: "A painter who likes to swing his arm as I do, finds it hard to stay at these little pictures for

Plate 117. *Five Clown Heads*

Courtesy of Kennedy Galleries, Inc.–Kuhn Estate

too long. So today I blew up and got a 25 × 30 still life underway—at present it looks like it might come off. . . . I was really getting to feel ashamed of myself, painting those little pot boilers." He had gotten a second wind by 27 October, writing: "I'm just bursting to do figures. The freedom produced by the summer's work should have a fine effect on the figure stuff. . . . Anyway the two pumpkin paintings have got my swing back. The swing I had 20 or 30 years ago and which I had perforce to give up for the time being to arrive at quality, precision and class. We are at the threshold of my 'big period!' Am I not right?" He definitely was, if he could recapture the youthful verve, the swing, and bring its animation to the quality, precision, and class he was fully justified in claiming. But the test would have to wait until the new year.

There was a more personally revealing letter in midsummer: "If you hadn't handled 'the office' so well I would never have been able to keep working steadily as I have — the best thing for our outfit is for me to be ever producing — nothing spent on production can ever be wasted." This is a comment on one aspect of Walt Kuhn's private life that mystified many of his friends and that his enemies used against him, though it was not a matter of appropriate concern for either — the complete exclusion of his family from the rest of his social activities. As

Plate 118 (opposite).
Tricorne

has been seen, his wife and daughter were a vital part of his professional life. Kuhn valued their judgment above all others except his own, and Vera managed "the office," finances, exhibition details, and correspondence, with unflagging skill and loyalty. They even had a joint checking account, that acid test of mutual trust. Many of Kuhn's associates knew Vera well by telephone and letters without ever meeting her. The Kuhns' small but comfortable apartment was in the Hotel Albert at 65 University Place, the hotel built by Albert Pinkham Ryder's brother and named for him. It had a living room, bedroom, kitchen, and a room for Brenda down the hall, and was a secured retreat from his studio and his outer world, where Vera and Brenda never ventured.

This was a strange character trait, rarely encountered, and may have come from the native secretiveness he had in common with Arthur B. Davies. Some thought that his Spanish pride was deeply wounded by his having only one child, a daughter in poor health, and a wife who did not want to, or could not, mingle easily with the varied assortment of people in his other lives. On the contrary, Kuhn was proud of Brenda; their father-daughter relationship was closer and more affectionate than many families can boast. And if there was anything Spanish in Kuhn's attitude, it can easily be understood in terms of the Spanish tendency, inherited from centuries of close contact with the oriental Moors, to seclude their families, especially their women. In any case, the pattern of separation was set early, as early perhaps as the first year of their marriage, and after their daughter's birth developed naturally from Vera's long visits to her family and Kuhn's long withdrawals to the necessary isolation of painting and travel. Its growth can be traced from the beginning. The daily letters and postcards, mostly from Kuhn during these separations, are enviable evidence of shared sympathy and understanding. Vera seemed content with her role in his artistic life, and that is all that can be asked. As for other possible causes, Kuhn once said in another connection, "Thank God, nobody knows what goes on between a man and a woman." It could be said of every marriage since the institution was founded. And, as Frank Getlein writes, "Kuhn was also given to keeping his friends in somewhat separated compartments, with himself being the only element common to half a dozen different worlds of artists, collectors, cartoonists and Maine villagers."

Six of the seven paintings from 1941 are still lifes; *Bananas* (number 411) is a forthright portrait of the whole yellow bunch hanging against a plain green background. It was included in the Durand-Ruel show of 1946. *Pumpkins* (number 413) has an atypical degree of detailed surface rendering almost worthy of a Victorian salon. Possibly as part of a reviving interest in that maligned era, it was reproduced in London by *Apollo* in 1968 and by the *Gazette Des Beaux Arts* in Paris in 1969. *Red Bananas in Iron Dish* (number 414) had a different and curious history. The war had put a stop to federal welfare support of artists, but in 1946 the State Department surprisingly decided to buy two representative

Plate 119. *Still Life with Apples*

groups of American paintings, one for European showing and the other for circulation in the "Other American Republics," as the countries of Central and South America were being diplomatically called. *Red Bananas* was bought for Europe, showing first at the Metropolitan Museum in New York, and then at the Musée d'Art Moderne in Paris, the successor to the Luxembourg. *Pine at 5 O'clock* (number 482) from 1945 toured Latin America. When the government decided in 1948 to unburden itself of this unaccustomed baggage, *Red Bananas* was exhibited in a "War Assets Sale" at the Whitney, and acquired by the Owego, New York, Public School System.

The big December exhibition at the Marie Harriman Gallery was a smash hit. Kuhn's timing was excellent as usual; he had not had a show of oil paintings or even landscape drawings for some time, and the change of pace in subject matter was good showmanship, perfectly suited to the Christmas season. Elizabeth Scaroff, in PM's *Weekly* of 7 December 1941, said: "Walt Kuhn's show at the Marie Harriman Gallery is the next best thing to a circus. In fact, you'll see a lot of the circus — 65 drawings and watercolors complete with clowns and all. You'll even smell the sawdust. It is a delightful interlude — and you don't have to be art minded to enjoy it. Even at the private preview Monday night people were actually looking at the pictures. And that isn't all — they bought 25 of them." On 6 December Emily Genauer, in the *New York World-Telegram*, struck a similar note:

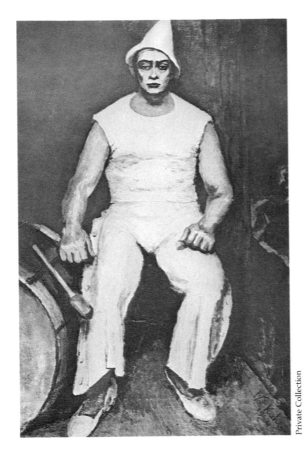

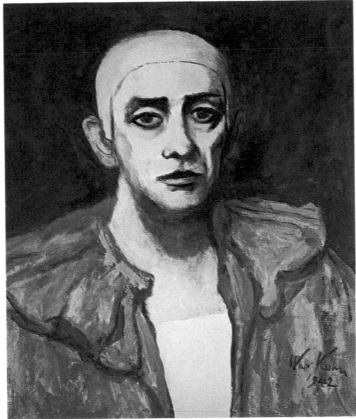

Private Collection

Private Collection

Plate 120 (left). *Clown with Drum*

Plate 121 (right). *Veteran Clown*

The gayest, sprightliest, wittiest show in town is that of drawings and water-colors by Walt Kuhn at the Marie Harriman Gallery. They're drawn from the well-known painter's experiences with circus, burlesque and other show people over a period of almost 20 years. Some of them are portrait studies for his more ambitious paintings, and while they have the strength and starkness of the better of those, they haven't the gusto, the unlabored vitality, the spontaneity which marks his backstage sketches. Most of these are line drawings, or drawings touched with color. They depict clowns shooting dice, or squabbling, or dressing: equestriennes getting dressed, acrobats doing a quick-change act. They have the line quality of Gavarni, the lustiness of Rowlandson, the heart of Daumier. They're beautifully composed as well. Altogether these are warm, human, authentic, unpretentious but thoroughly satisfy-ing things. Of the real watercolors (real in the sense that color is an integral part of the structure), the rich and splashy Jumble of Clowns is best.

Newsweek, on 8 December, began with a short interview and went on to tell how Kuhn had

come to know hundreds of circus, vaudeville, burlesque and night-club performers. They call him by his first name and visit his big barnlike studio in Manhattan to gossip or to pose for pictures. The highest tribute they are apt to pay his work is to declare respectfully: "You sure got the droop on those pants just right."

Unlike Watteau, Degas, and Toulouse-Lautrec, three of the many French artists who have been fascinated by theatrical folk, Kuhn doesn't paint performers at their glamorous best — singing, acting, or dancing in the yellow glare of gas foot-lights, or taking curtain calls. Instead, he prefers to catch them off guard back stage; clowns making up or shooting dice, acrobats resting, chorines gossiping, horses waiting their turn in the big tent. "There isn't a footlight in the show," Kuhn says.

Prices in the Christmas exhibit, much lower than those for the same artist's oils, range from $15 to $200.

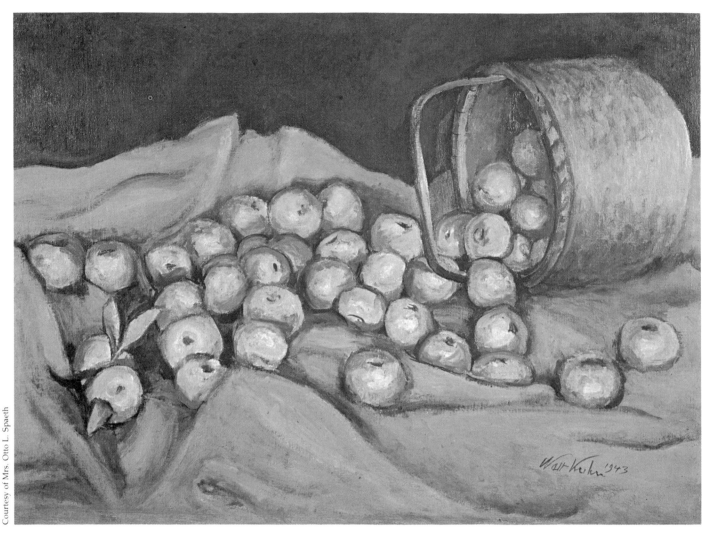

Plate 122. *Green Apples on Blue Cloth*

Henry McBride, in the 5 December *New York Sun*, probed a little deeper: ". . . For the first time he takes us backstage, opens the dressing room doors and shows us the secrets of the trade. He does this in swift watercolor and line drawings that add to the impromptu effect of revelations not originally intended for our inspection. Not that vaudeville artists mind what we see or do not see. They are completely certain of their vocations and wouldn't accept life on any other terms than those of vaudeville." They have

a convention in dressing their "acts" that might be appalling if it were not so pathetically wedded to the conventions of this "art."

All this makes them perfect material for an artist and Walt Kuhn is certainly lucky to have got next to it. He has been painting them for years with a seriousness quite equal to their own. Never a stroke of anything like criticism has he allowed himself in his dealings with these boys and girls who, or so I judge from these drawings, would like to do time at "The Palace" but are not above joining up with the circus in the summer solstice. He puts himself rather on their level than on ours when painting their portraits and includes nothing in the picture that would be above their heads.

It was the wish, possibly, not to throw confusion into the minds of these prospective customers, that led Mr. Kuhn to hold these lighter, gayer, less tangible watercolors so long from public view, for these are evidently better suited to us than to the artist's friends backstage. He is quite as sincere and faithful to the canons of vaudeville as ever, but the swiftness necessary to an impression doesn't give a chance to erase the lines that are not quite right and which are still visible besides the lines that are final. This pleases astute connoisseurs who know how technic is arrived at but it might bother the acrobats who never, themselves, are allowed to give dress-rehearsals but appear only when the "act" has been perfected in all of its details.

Walt Kuhn may have done himself a grave disservice by identifying himself too much with the circus. Even in his own last years the circus had stopped casting the spell it had for generations before. There are still some who can remember it: the seasonal blossoming of the billboards with the big bright posters; the hoarding of pennies and nickels for the great day to come; the almost unbearable excitement of an indulgent father waking the children early to take them down to see the circus unload; the animals prodded into their wagon cages, one with a tank for the hippopotamus; the huge tents rising, the roustabouts driving the stakes with miraculous timing, elephants doing tractor work; and then, glory of glories, the morning parade with bandwagons, shuffling camels, beautiful circus ladies, and bringing up the rear, after the string of elephants each holding the tail of the one in front with his trunk, the steam calliope.

It was interesting to learn later that the German army had sent specialized logistics officers to study the amazing, split-second operation of the American circus. And most of the acts can still be seen, indoors now in a few larger cities; they are as skilled as ever, but a dimension is missing. The big-top does not rise anymore, and the morning parade no longer touches Main Street with magic; so Walt Kuhn is too often shrugged off as a "mere" painter of the clowns and carnival girls of yesterday. Of course that is his best-known subject matter. But so it was for Watteau with his Italian Comedians, his French Comedians and the Louvre's heroic *Gilles*, now in a place of due honor in the Long Gallery. So it was for the younger Tiepolo with his Punchinellos and Pantaloons. Daumier could feel the pulse-beat of all human kind in his strolling mountebanks, and Degas found the "little rats" of the ballet, on stage or in the wings or dressing rooms, the musicians in the orchestra pit, enough subject matter for a lifetime. The cabarets of Montmartre were the home of Toulouse-Lautrec's spirit. And of course this "little world" was a timeless symbol, a metaphor for all of them.

E. B. White may never have seen a painting by Walt Kuhn, nor even heard of him; but he was speaking directly for Kuhn when he wrote "The Ring of Time (A Letter from the South), Fiddler Bayou, March 22, 1956," published in the *New Yorker*. He was fresh from a visit to the winter quarters of the Ringling Brothers-Barnum and Bailey Circus, and said:

> In attempting to recapture this wild spectacle I am merely acting as recording secretary for one of the oldest of societies — the society of those who, at one time or another, have surrendered, without even a show of resistance, to the bedazzlement of

Plate 123. *Clown with Top Hat*

the circus rider. As a writing man, or secretary, I have always felt charged with the safekeeping of all unexpected items of worldly or unworldly enchantment, as though I might be held personally responsible if even a small one were to be lost. But it is not easy to communicate anything of this nature. The circus comes as close to being the world in microcosm as anything I know; in a way it puts all the rest of the show business in the shade. Its magic is universal and complex. Out of its wild disorder comes order; from its rank smell rises the good aroma of courage and daring; out of its preliminary shabbiness comes the final splendor. And buried in the familiar boast of its advance agents lies the modesty of most of its people. For me the circus is at its best before it has been put together. It is at its best at certain moments when it comes to a point, as through a burning glass, in the activity and destiny of a single performer out of so many. One ring is always bigger than three. One rider, one aerialist, is always greater than six. In short, a man has to catch the circus unawares to experience its full impact and share its gaudy dream.

4

On 18 March 1942 Kuhn wrote to Otis Oldfield in San Francisco: "About six weeks ago I made up my mind decidedly that work in the studio would have to go on, and lots of it. I put all my completed pictures aside and picked one I had done ten years ago as a starting point — got me a couple of good models, a man and a girl and worked from them on alternate days. Sort of a grand rejuvenation. I think I'm good for several weeks more of intense campaigning." The male model was Joe Pascucciello, known as Pasco, who was an exhibition bagpuncher and in his own way helped produce three first-class paintings: *Acrobat in Red and Green* (number 418), *Clown with Drum* (number 420), and *Veteran Clown* (number 433). *Acrobat in Red and Green* was bought through the Metropolitan Museum's Hearn Fund in 1950. It is a bustlength, almost frontal portrait in loud but not arbitrary color, and the balding Pasco wears no make-up as he turns his head slightly to his right.

Clown with Drum could be all the *Pagliaccci* who ever broke their hearts in public under their motley, but he is not. He sits in simple dignity, "a workman needing not to be ashamed." White conical hat over the white skullcap, white make-up on the face, white undershirt, long full white trousers, and shoes are the light tone. Muscular arms, bass drum, and reddish floor are the middle tone, against dark greenish background with a suggestion of crumpled red-bordered drapery at the right. His right hand rests on the drum, his left hand on his thigh. Rarely has so theatrical a banality been so understandingly, so nobly treated; it is not presumptious to recall *Gilles* himself. There may be a tragic, perhaps only a sombre, overtone to *Veteran Clown*; but it is subdued, as is the flame color of his ruffle-collared costume, opened to show a white undershirt. White face make-up and fawn skull-cap against a dark bluish slate background complete the apparently easy, unstudied canvas, where art is concealed by art such as only a master can command.

Except for a few small clown subjects in oil, Kuhn could not have painted many more than these three before he undertook a unique venture. "Never again!" was the verdict he wrote to Vera in late April from Columbus, Ohio. He had agreed to teach for three weeks, from 11 April to 1 May 1942, in the Art School of the Columbus Gallery of Fine Arts, as well as to give a lecture to the gallery membership on 10 April. The schedule was grueling, with three afternoon and three night classes each week "open to all art teachers, students and painters, professional or amateur." It was a fully developed, if small-scale, campaign; the terms were travel and living expenses, in a nearby residential hotel, and the purchase of a painting. *Veteran Acrobat* of 1938 had already been approved in principle by the Accessions Committee, and thirteen other paintings accompanied it for a month-long miniature retrospective of a kind that Kuhn had never before permitted himself or his dealers.

Still Life with Ducks of 1925 was lent by the Addison Gallery of American Art as was *Acrobat in Green* of 1927. *Dressing Room* was lent by the Brooklyn Museum to represent 1926, and the Whitney lent *The Blue Clown* of 1931; 1932 was represented by *Young Clown* from the Denver Art Museum. The *Juggler* of 1934 came from the William Rockhill Nelson Gallery, and Kuhn lent *Apples in Bowl* (number 314) of the same year. He also lent *Carnival Girl* of 1936 and *Musical Clown* of 1938, not yet bought by the Whitney. Edna St. Vincent Millay lent *Mario* of 1938, supplemented by *Grenadier* of the same year from the artist, as well as *Lancer* of 1939 and *Red Bananas in Iron Dish* of 1941. The gallery *Bulletin* broke a lance in attempting to explain the meaning of Walt Kuhn's painting: "But what bearing do acrobats and show-girls have on us, on

Plate 124. *Potatoes*

Courtesy of Kennedy Galleries, Inc.-Kuhn Estate

Plate 125. *Zinnias in Black Crock*

the present? Perhaps they are typical of an over-machined, over-urbanised society's almost frantic search for entertainment and escape which has created such strange phenomena as Hollywood, whose neurasthenia is accurately mirrored in the night clubs' tinsel vulgarity. Yet these hired entertainers are at the same time products of an exacting discipline. To be a good acrobat requires years of training, a severely regulated life. They are among the last living inheritors of the craft tradition. They are aristocrats in a world of mass production and mass reaction."

In spite of his regular commitments and crowded social program that could not be avoided, Kuhn kept up his daily letters to Vera, writing on 15 April: "The real success here are the paintings themselves and that's as it should be. Anyway I have got me a good vaudeville act, which may be very important for the future. . . . " On 19 April he wrote: "Luckily the people here are 100 percent on the level, but this would have been some fool break with any other outfit." He sought out the local artists, whose vanity had in some instances been wounded, as he had known it would be, and invited about six of them to a return dinner at what he insisted should be a plain restaurant "with sawdust on the floor, where we can sing." And he found one real talent, writing on 20 April to Sturgis Ingersoll, who was on the committee to commission sculptures for Fairmount Parkway: "I also see you have the Columbus sculptor (Erwin F.) Frey working on two figures for Philadelphia. You couldn't have picked a better man — at his best his work rates with anything being done anywhere in the world today. I endorse your judgment completely." He summed up the exhausting project in a letter to Vera on 30 April: "Of course I had to make a record here, which will probably stay just that — I never expected such treatment and cooperation." It had not been easy for his hosts either, and after thirty-five years they will find it heart-warming to read such a compliment.

Columbus may not have restored his faith in human nature, but he came back to New York eager to paint again. He had no immediate exhibition plans; Marie Harriman had closed her gallery in the spring of 1942, due to Averell's growing involvement with government affairs. This had begun as early as the NRA days of 1934 when Harriman broke with his Republican inheritance and horrified his friends by becoming an inner member of the Roosevelt administration in a variety of capacities. In the early months of 1941 as the war came closer to the United States, he had been a special representative of the president in Great Britain, and in March was chairman of a commission to Russia with the rank of ambassador. Then he stayed on in London representing American shipping interests for the government until he returned to Russia as full ambassador from 1943 to 1946. Naturally Marie joined him in London and Moscow, so the gallery was no more.

Kuhn took his time in planning for a new outlet. At first he thought of Hans Schaeffer, whose gallery, just across the landing from Marie Harriman's, dealt in old masters; there would be no competition with other contemporaries, but preliminary discussions did not materialize. On 27 August Paul Rosenberg wrote to ask for a one-man show in the coming season. It was tempting; Rosenberg was the most distinguished of the war-transplanted Parisian dealers, with a near monopoly on Picasso and a most-favored status with several others of the French stars. But Kuhn stalled; he saw future possibilities with Rosenberg, but had also seen American contemporaries too often used as come-ons for the real European stock-in-trade. Max Weber and others had been shamefully imposed on in this way. There was no rush; he had several carefully cultivated patrons and occasionally sold a painting from his studio. Besides, he had at least four more important paintings in embryo.

Teal (number 432), the only still life of the year, harks back to *Mallards* and *Still Life with Ducks.* In a horizontal canvas the two dead birds lie on a triangular white cloth with their heads at sharp right angles to their bodies. There is no "caress to the soft plumage of these wild fowl"; they are simply dead, which may be the point of the painting. *Girl from Madrid* (number 425) is either one of the best or one of the worst of Kuhn's canvases; he thought it one of his best and kept it near at hand. The hot vermilions and crimsons set off the ivory flesh, which he especially liked, and the fall of coal-black hair. The face is almost crudely sensual, sullen, not inviting. He always consciously fought off the intrusion of "taste," which might seem paradoxical for a painter, and succeeded here, whereas *Girl Reading* (number 426) is one of his few lapses into it.

He never exposed *Girl from Madrid* to the New York critics, but *Girl Reading* was a success in the 1946 show at Durand-Ruel. Emily Genauer, in the 16 November *New York World Telegram*, said: "His portrait of a 'Girl Reading' is another high spot of the show, sensitive in its surface, and much more tender in mood than one expects of Kuhn." Aline Saarinen, in the November *Art News*, commented on "the gleaming white flesh of *Girl Reading.*" It was the same flesh, the same bodice, and the same black hair as *Girl from Madrid*, but Kuhn had again set up polar opposites. The *Times* later asked permission to reproduce *Girl Reading* in its book review section.

Walt Kuhn painted only two self-portraits as such, though he had often made up to pose for other, unavailable, subjects; one is little known, from 1943 (number 445), showing a summer's growth of beard and a somewhat romantic air. The other, of 1942 (number 431), is larger and completely unmannered, not even signed, just dated. It is a penetrating likeness; he wears a light blue shirt buttoned at the collar, the gray-white hair catches a few blue reflections from it, and the eyes are a defiant piercing ice-blue.

Hand Balancer (number 427) is an intellectual among acrobats. He wears a long-sleeved leotard, vertically striped bikini trunks and a light sash tied in a crisp flower-like bow at his left. One lean muscular hand rests on his right hip, the other hangs by his left thigh. Body and head curve slightly to his right and the studious, intelligent face, with no make-up, looks straight at the observer. His whole bearing is one of relaxed professional assurance. There are a few incisive lines at the left armpit, the bow, and the cuff of the left sleeve. They are the period at the end of a sentence, the little flourish with which Kuhn finished his paintings, if he was satisfied with them. Sometimes, to amuse Brenda, he used his little finger instead of a brush for the last one.

After he had thought a problem out, or after a spirited discussion, Kuhn would occasionally jot down a maxim, or deliver it over the dinner table to Vera, who faithfully recorded it. One of them dates from 1939: "You cannot refute laws, if they can only be seen." In his last few years he wrote or dictated many more of them, some quite memorable.

And about this time in 1942, even though for the moment he was painting no landscapes, he copied out for Vera's typing several passages from Leslie's *Memoirs of the Life of John Constable.* Some of them have already been quoted; they echo a great many of Kuhn's own feelings and considered opinions, arrived at after years of experience. From page 74 comes Constable's statement: "I may say all this to you, though you do not want to be told that I know very well what I am about, and that my skies have not been neglected, though they have

Plate 126. *Bananas*

Plate 127. *Pumpkins*

Courtesy of the National Gallery of Art, Washington, D.C., Gift of the W. Averell Harriman Foundation in Memory of Marie N. Harriman

often failed in execution, no doubt, from an over-anxiety about them, which will alone destroy that easy appearance which nature has in all her movements."

On page 112 Constable quotes a rule of the novelist Laurence Sterne. Kuhn had read both *Tristram Shandy* and *A Sentimental Journey*, though his general tastes were more contemporary; "Never mind the dogmas of the schools, but get at the heart as you can." And on page 141 Constable quotes again, from the older painter Northcote: "It should be the aim of an artist to bring something to light out of nature for the first time. Something like that for which mechanics a patent would be granted; an original invention or a decided improvement; patents are not given for making a time-piece or a telescope, as long as it differs not from others."

On page 162 Leslie says: "While finishing the picture of the 'Dell' Constable was one day beset with a great many suggestions from a very shallow source, and after adopting some of them, he felt inclined to make a stand, which he did by saying to his adviser, 'Very true, but don't you see that I might go on, and make this picture so good, that it would be good for nothing ["I might go on . . . good for nothing" underscored by Kuhn].'" On page 240 Constable says: "In such an age as this, painting should be understood [word underscored by Kuhn] not looked on with blind wonder, nor considered only as a poetic aspiration, but as a pursuit legitimate, scientific, and mechanical (last four words underscored by Kuhn)." On page 242 Constable says again: "None of the greatest painters were eccentric in their works. They were too consistent with themselves to merit such an epithet; too sensible of what they were about." And on page 247: "If you had found painting as easy as you once thought it, you would have given it up long ago."

Finally, in the famous quotation from page 182, John Constable and Walt Kuhn speak with the same voice: "My art flatters nobody with imitation, it courts nobody by smoothness, it tickles nobody by *petiteness*, it is without *fal-de la* or *fiddle-de-dee*, how then can I hope to be popular?"

NOTES TO CHAPTER EIGHT

Aline Saarinen's comments on WALTER ARENSBERG come from *The Proud Possessors*, p. 242. Information on his PURCHASES FROM THE ARMORY SHOW comes from Milton W. Brown, *The Story of the Armory Show*, p. 102.

MONET'S LETTER describing the Café Guerbois gatherings is quoted in John Rewald, *The History of Impressionism* (New York: Museum of Modern Art, 1946), p. 169.

The DEFINITION OF AN EPIGRAM in the *Greek Anthology* is by Cyrillus in the Declamatory Poems, and comes from Humbert Wolfe's translation *Others Abide* (London: Ernest Benn Ltd., 1927), p. 87.

The "HOGAN'S ALLEY" act is described by Frank Getlein, Kennedy Galleries, 1967, p. 6.

The APPLES AND WOMEN'S BACKSIDES quotation comes from Frank Getlein, ibid., p. 12. An irreverent secretary in Cincinnati once remarked that she had never seen "anyone get so much mileage out of a peck of apples."

CÉZANNE'S NAME recurs so frequently because, apart from his being Walt Kuhn's chief mentor, every serious artist of the first half of the twentieth century has been influenced by him in one way or another. As dissimilar a painter as Matisse said, "Cézanne is the father of us all."

VAN EYCK'S *Jan Arnolfini and His Wife* is in the National Gallery in London, as is BRUEGHEL'S *Adoration of the Kings*. VERMEER'S *Girl with Guitar* (properly a vihuela) is also in London, in Lord Iveagh's collection, Kenwood. The VAN DER GOES altarpiece is in the Uffizi.

The Frank Getlein quotation concerning the SEPARATED COMPARTMENTS OF KUHN'S LIFE comes from Kennedy Galleries, 1967, p. 5.

Sacheverell Sitwell comments on GILLES in his foreword to *Masters of Painting: Antoine Watteau* (London: "The Studio," 1925), p. 5: "So far, out of all the pictures described, the *Gilles* has been the best, and it is interesting to think of that masterpiece compared with the *Harlequin* or the *Mardi Gras* of Cézanne, or with the innumerable and in no way inferior *Harlequinades* of Picasso." Earlier on the same page he remarks: "We come now to one of Watteau's biggest pictures, *Gilles* (Plate V), of the Louvre, hung badly, as all the pictures there are hung but looking even in that stamp-collecting arrangement as though the oil-painting was longing for sustenance and wanted feeding and cleaning. In some ways it is the most beautiful of all his creations, far excelling — at least in this writer's estimation—the much more famous *L'Embarquement pour Cythère* (Plate XI). The composition and arrangement of the picture seem based on some memory of Callot's actor-etchings, where the comedian, generally of a pseudo-military arrogance, is posed standing straight up in the foreground like the *Gilles* of this picture. This is a painting of the very highest order which, alone, places Watteau as a master. The doltish, round-faced Pierrot stands in a kind of diurnal moonlight reserved for his figure alone, while Columbine, the Doctor and the rest of the company are chattering noisily in the background under the cynical smile of a garden-term beneath the trees. The first sight of this lovely picture is a deep emotional experience."

E. B. WHITE'S "A Ring of Time" was later published with several related short pieces in *Points of my Compass*, (New York: Harper and Row, 1962). The quotation comes from pp. 52-53.

The comment on THE MEANING OF WALT KUHN'S SUBJECTS comes from the *Columbus Gallery of Fine Arts Bulletin*, April 1942, p. 2. Obviously the author was closely involved with the Columbus expedition, since he was at that time director of the Gallery of Fine Arts there.

The PURCHASE OF "VETERAN ACROBAT" was strenuously opposed by a senior member of the Accessions Committee who was a minor collector of minor old masters. He objected to public showing of a "sub-social" type, which genuinely surprised Kuhn when he heard of it. The use of gallery funds was blocked, even though they had been bequeathed by Ferdinand Howald, mentioned in connection with the Daniel Gallery, who certainly knew of Walt Kuhn though he did not buy a painting by him. Howald's active collecting was over well before his death in 1934, and before Kuhn had reached his mature level. Anyway, Howald's taste was rather more delicate and inclined toward Prendergast, Davies, Hartley, Demuth, and Preston Dickinson, but did include Pascin and Marin. Understanding private donors had to be solicited.

Climax and Epilogue

Walt Kuhn liked pithy statements and coined a number of them himself. One he often used when a fellow artist complained of his hard financial lot was, "No one ever told you to paint pictures." He wrote this one on both his studio wall and door, from which Vera copied down several like it, such as, "The artist is the only one who can make a silk purse out of a sow's ear." Others were: "No immaculate conception in art"; "The art of decoration instead of penetration"; "People never fail — they just stop before they reach their objective"; "Why it's hard to paint a simple thing — the more clews the easier the solution"; "A work of art must be national in character, international in appeal." One may have come from Constable, since he added the name with a question mark: "Every man who distinguishes himself stands on a precipice." Or perhaps he meant that Constable was an example. On his studio door he copied from Carl Schurz: "A thing basically wrong can never be right in production."

In February 1945 he wrote to Vera: "Nature note — In New England the trees were made by God, in Florida they were made by Dennison." And he quoted an observant Frenchman who on first visiting this country said, "America must abandon the whole European ornament." It is rather a cryptic statement, but it had meaning for Kuhn who often repeated it. Speaking of another time and country, Walt made the pregnant remark, "You can fake a man, but you can't fake a period." This was remembered by many who heard it in conversation, as they did his injunction to young artists: "No athlete wants to run against anything except the world record; Ruisdael could paint a tree and Corot could paint a figure. If you can't paint a tree as well as Ruisdael or a figure as well as Corot, you're not painting."

Early in 1943 Walt Kuhn had found a suitable setting for his exhibitions, at the Durand-Ruel Galleries on East Fifty-seventh Street.

Although the family firm of Durand-Ruel was preeminent in the French impressionists and postimpressionists, it did not handle the major contemporaries, luring hesitant novice collectors instead with harmless minor Parisians. Kuhn at first seemed too hearty a dish for Durand-Ruel's Continental menu. He had realized this in his overtures to the American manager Herbert Elfers, and wrote to Vera the summer before that he would get "Elfers started with 'Patisserie'. . . . I had told Elfers before leaving, that I had given you full authority to act for me — (Bless you!)". Sometimes Kuhn called these little enticements "millinery"; in this case the patisserie or millinery was an exhibition of small oils of circus subjects, modeled on his last Marie Harriman show but not nearly as large, and timed to coincide with the circus's annual appearance at Madison Square Garden. It did its introductory job adequately, selling quite well. In April 1945 Kuhn could write to an old acquaintance, "The last couple of years I have confined my exhibiting in New York to Durand-Ruel, people most honest and agreeable."

Rosamund Frost reviewed the show in *Art News* under the title "Walt Kuhn Clowns in a Great Tradition," beginning: "Small works prove the big artist; or by their sketches you shall know them. This is the point that is unmistakably made by Walt Kuhn's new show at Durand-Ruel. In these foot-square canvases the visitor immediately senses quality — a quality reminiscent of a great tradition. . . ." *Mandolinist* (number 374) of 1938, a smaller cousin of Gary Cooper's 1935 *Clown with Mandolin,* especially caught the reviewer's eye with its "entirely different overtones" that led her to think of Daumier and Wat-

Plate 128. *Teal*

Private Collection

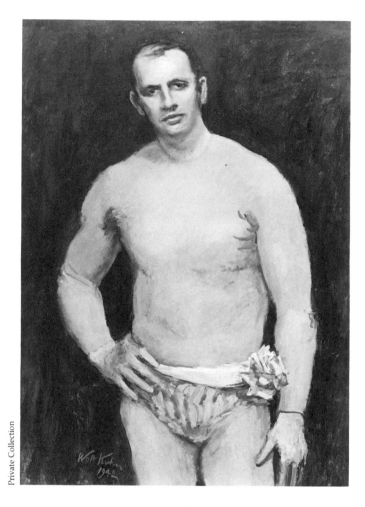

Plate 129 (left). *Girl from Madrid*

Plate 130 (right). *Hand Balancer*

teau. She went on to say: "Gradually you realize that here is our nearest link into the unbroken chain of French figure painting — the tradition sustained in turn by Corot and Manet which has found its last representative in Walt Kuhn, an American." She also praised the "verve, humor and rock-solid composition" of *Clowns Dressing* (number 436). She was too young to remember *An Imaginary History of the West* in 1920, and commented: "From the persistence with which this artist, in his big pictures, has harped on the single figure, his public has up till now never had a chance to find out whether or not he could handle groups. The answer is, he can, and in such a way that it would never occur to you that they had been composed." In a sense this is true, since *Trio* is really a colonade of three figures, not a "composition" as most people use the word, certainly not a *machine*.

The next exhibition at Durand-Ruel, in November 1944, would have "big pictures" including several from 1943, and the biggest was *Clown in his Dressing Room* (number 435). It is as if the *Clown with Drum* had stood up, tossing his skullcap on a chair to the right; the baritone horn from *Musical Clown* stands on the floor at the left, and his top hat hangs on the background wall, next to a Napoleon hat. Accessories do not a painting make. His arms are even more muscular. The Carnegie

Institute in Pittsburgh exhibited it twice, in "Painting in the United States" in 1945 and "Paintings by Walt Kuhn" in 1948, wanting very much to keep it for the permanent collection but finding it too expensive. *Girl in White and Silver* (number 438) is exactly that, with shako, epaulets, and hands crossed on her lap. The Metropolitan Museum bought it through the Hearn Fund in 1950.

Although by its title it might seem to be another in the long series of still lifes with the same subject, *Green Apples on Blue Cloth* (number 439) is an ultimate in the very elegance Kuhn so often denied himself. But it is not a weakening element here; for all their reference to the eighteenth century's *palette fatiguée* with its slightly world-weary muted colors, the apples are tart and crisp as always, the blue cloth exquisitely toned to them, the basket's handle decisively drawn. *Green Apples with Gray Curtain* (number 440) is a close relative, in its pastel colors, with two sprigs of leaves and no basket. The small narrow horizontal *Peaches* (number 444) is also elegant, suggesting a jeweled necklace in its black satin-lined case. Disallowing any such imputation of glamor, Kuhn said the idea of the composition came from "peas in a pod." The French ambience of Durand-Ruel may have gentled Kuhn a little, but more probably he was by this time so sure of his control that he could let his native taste, so long distrusted, add its increment of charm to abstractions as solidly constructed as ever.

From 27 February to 27 March 1944 Walt Kuhn joined Karl Knaths in a two-man show at the Phillips Memorial Gallery in Washington, something he would have done for no one but Duncan Phillips. And he sent some of his best paintings for it: *Green Apples on Blue Cloth, Acrobat in Red and Green, Peaches*. The Whitney lent *The Blue Clown*, and Marie Harriman lent *The Guide*. Three of the Phillips Gallery's four paintings were, naturally, included. Duncan Phillips had written several times about Kuhn, and said in the catalogue:

> The clowns are of many different types and reveal many individual idiosyncracies and even complexities. Kuhn uses the language of design to aid him in suggesting these undercurrents of character beneath the make up and the costume. Far from describing his models, in all their flamboyant or grotesque professional appearances, with the exaggerations of subjective fantasy, he imposes upon himself the challenge of confronting only the facts about some very human personalities, conditioned to specialized jobs in burlesque, vaudeville and circus. . . . Somebody's kid who dreamed of glory in the carnival looks disillusioned and sullen under her plumes. He paints the feathers with consummate skill and the face with startling frankness and just a hint of his understanding and compassion. . . . And when he turns to still life or landscape what a feeling for fruit pulp or flower petal, rock or tree! He is a master of white as a sensuous pigment. His "Bread and Knife" [later to become part of the Phillips Collection] is like a detail from a Zurbaran but with more bulk. . . . Kuhn must wish for his statement a plastic simplification—a decorative epigram. But it is his challenge to himself and to his training to come to terms with the inartistic, even the blatant, even with what is usually called the vulgar. America is full of it and it has a native flavour which the artist can use if he can cope with it, if he can make it live with the application of ancient principles and the exact choice of the expressive colors and contours and the significant details of psychological portrayal.

2

After Washington, Kuhn began to paint and plan for his first showing of big pictures at Durand-Ruel in the fall. He wrote to Vera from Ogunquit on 4 August: "From now on I want to have a ham-and-eggs existence to paint the few more good pictures left for me to deliver." He read a lot that summer, too, rereading Ibsen, and wrote on 27 August: "I don't know what I would do without the library here." He was a Brooklyn Dodgers fan, and Red Barber's play-by-play announcing kept him company, along with Mozart when he could find him on a classical music station, probably in Boston. Music was important to Kuhn all his life, though he rarely spoke about it except in a casual way. Once when the prelude to the third act of *La Traviata* came on the air, he said, "Ah, Wagner without the beer."

Twenty-five paintings came from 1944, five landscapes and four still lifes; there were a few small clown portraits and three small portraits of women. Although there were four or five ranking canvases, it was not one of his most distinguished years, and the November exhibition stirred no great critical excitement. Margaret Bruening chose an appropriate title for her review in *Art News*, "Walt Kuhn's Austere Modern Classics." She reproduced *Clown with Folded Arms* (number 455); and when the Pennsylvania Academy of the Fine Arts in Philadelphia bought it in 1945, Walt's relations with Durand-Ruel were firmly

Plate 131. *Green Apples with Gray Curtain*

Courtesy of the Indianapolis Museum of Art, Gift of Mr. & Mrs. Henry R. Hope

Plate 132. *Peaches* (1943)

cemented. *Acrobat in White and Silver* (number 451) cannot be over-looked, nor can *Clown in Beaver Hat* (number 454); it brought a hand-some price at Parke-Bernet in 1972 when it was featured in a sale of "Important 20th Century American Paintings, Drawings, Watercolors and Sculptures." *Portrait of a Young Man* (number 470) was in the Wash-ington show and later bought for the Phillips Collection. But *Pending Storm* (number 406) is unique; it is Kuhn's one formal painting of the sea, in spite of so many summers in Nova Scotia and Maine. Perhaps he did not want to challenge Winslow Homer, for whom he had only reluctant respect as a gifted illustrator. He had a higher regard for Eakins, though he disliked his "tobacco juice" color. All through the thirties Marie Harriman had teased him to bring back a sea painting, and in 1944 he finally did, when she was in Moscow. Frank Getlein wrote of *Pending Storm:* "Typically of Kuhn, it brings in, even in a seascape, all the compressed tension of his figure paintings. Typically, too, he selects a moment *before* the storm. The elements of violence are all gathered together, but the violence is still withheld." Winslow Homer was more explicit.

Kuhn spent the early winter months of 1945 in Hobe Sound and Stuart, Florida, seeing a great deal of Bertrand and Olive Taylor. Bertrand Taylor was prominent in New York financial circles, and his wife had had some experience in the theater, which made for pleasant gossiping. She also had some talent as a painter, and Kuhn traded lessons for dinners. He wrote to Vera that he hoped to develop the Taylors into valuable patrons. Such plans were not one-sidedly venal; Kuhn gave as much in good company and counseling as he received. But the relationship broke up in the winter of 1947, when many rela-tionships came to an end. By 19 February 1945 Kuhn was homesick for both his family and the stimulus of the masters, proposing to Vera that they meet soon in Washington, where "all three of us will go to the Mellon Gallery, which I need very much." He also said, "With great

213

Plate 133. *Clown in His Dressing Room*

patience I shall be able to control Elfers — Thank God we have that gallery — 'Compelling Pictures Incorporated [underscored].'" "That gallery" was probably not Durand-Ruel, but their own private "outfit," which they had so long, so strenuously fought for. Back home in New York on 10 April, Kuhn wrote to William Bahr: "I think I am having my share of success, and am trying to do less and better pictures. The job of an American artist has always been a difficult one, but I have no gripes or bitterness. It has been a good fight."

And there were fewer pictures in 1945. It was a strangely unproductive year, a lull before the creative storm of 1946 or a natural period of gestation for the major works to come. Several landscapes from Maine, a few show business subjects, and one notable still life make up the list, which includes three small heads of clowns. *Pony* (number 481) was sent to the Whitney Annual in December 1945, and *Star Performer* (number 487) was reproduced in the *Daily Worker. Green Bananas and Oranges* (number 479) repose in the same white compote that will barely contain the explosive *Green Bananas* (number 497) of 1946, now in the Des Moines Art Center.

Kuhn described his 1946 winter activities in a letter of 24 April: "During the past two and a half months I have put in just the most terrific painting campaign that I can remember. So now that I've blown my top, I'm spending most of the time rechecking doubtful pictures of the recent years, and much to my surprise I have found quite a few first

Plate 134. *Pending Storm*

class ones. It takes time to judge correctly. . . . Now that I no longer care a hell of a lot, the breaks are coming my way. The miracle may happen — I may live to see!" The "terrific painting campaign" produced three of his finest figure subjects, two of them masterpieces.

As a result he needed more than ever to get away to Maine,where he was in poor health most of the summer, asking Vera on 6 August to send some proprietary medicines that he could not find in Ogunquit. His spirits were still low on 18 August, when he wrote to Vera,"I'm afraid Europe will be of little use to us anymore." But he was

Plate 135. *Roberto*

Private Collection

215

Plate 136. *Peaches* (1946)

Plate 137. *Black Butterfly*

Plate 138. *Loaf of Bread*

Plate 139. *Apples on Red Cloth*

continuing his diplomatic minuet with Paul Rosenberg by mail, and added, "Elfers will have the show [in November] enjoy its popularity and Rosie will reap later, and get my best pictures to sell at good prices." Things were looking up by 22 August: "My strength has come back completely; that is, the physique side of it. I still get knocked out when I paint intensely. I finished the bread picture — even that left me pretty exhausted. I suppose my nerves have been hit pretty hard (the picture is good); I enjoy working with my hands, and feel better after it." And there were the Dodgers and Red Barber.

Plate 140 (opposite). *Acrobat in White and Blue*

A telephone call redeemed the summer; he wrote to Vera on 26 August:

> Just had Frankfurter on the phone . . . he saw Matisse, Picasso, Rouault and Utrillo. . . . Picasso brought up the subject of my work. He knows it by reproductions (probably doesn't know that I'm the same fellow he met on several occasions). He says I'm the strongest painter in the U.S.A. He doesn't understand why American art is so wishy-washy when by nature it should be the strongest.
> I have a few pictures and they are all good.
> Peaches — large
>   "   with red cloth
> Green Bananas in white bowl
> Large Pine
> 16 × 20 bowl with peaches
> 16 × 20 Bread — not many but all good.

He stayed on in Maine until early October, writing on 12 October: "Back in the old burg and up to my neck preparing my show which opens November 6 and continues through November 30. Elfers has let down the bars a bit, so I shall be able to spread my wings and give a more representative exhibition than the first large oil show, which I didn't think was any too hot in showmanship."

Whether it was Kuhn's showmanship spreading untrammeled wings, or the cumulative impact of over a half-dozen of his best works, it was Walt Kuhn's finest exhibition, and by this time the critics knew it. So did the buying public; *Roberto* (number 506) was bought by a long-distance telephone call for $10,000, believed at the time to be the highest price ever paid for the work of a contemporary living American painter. Mr. Harry Daniel of Bristol, Tennessee, had seen a newspaper reproduction and was a man of swift decision. (The painting was resold in 1969 for almost ten times the original price, according to well-founded rumor.) As Herbert Elfers told it, Kuhn was stunned for a moment when he heard the news, but quickly rallied, saying, "Of course it was bound to happen."

And of course it was a triumph and the chief recognition a commerical society can give to an artist. However, it still was not the kind of popular recognition Kuhn seemed literally to yearn for but for which he would not have altered a single brush-stroke. Perhaps he wanted to be a household name like Maxfield Parrish, or Norman Rockwell, or, in very different terms, Pablo Picasso. Or possibly it was what Augustus St. Gaudens, dean of official American sculpture, described in his *Reminiscences* in telling of his presence at the unveiling of

Plate 141. *Green Bananas and*
Oranges

Private Collection

his memorial to Colonel Shaw in the Boston Commons. The sculptor
had been sitting modestly in a back row but at a certain point in the
official ceremonies was called to the front of the platform for a
twenty-minute ovation. He said it was the first time he realized what a
reward it must be for the performing artist, the actor or musician, to feel
an audience come alive for him. Kuhn had felt this power many times
in the theater, as designer or director, if not as actor; and though he
knew how lonely the lot of the painter is, he still hungered for that kind
of applause. On the evidence of his private letters and many conversations, he never quite reconciled these two sides of his personality, at
what cost only a professional can judge. Playing amateur psychiatrist is
far too popular, and dangerous, a game. Doubtless he said the last

word himself, in his article on Cézanne in the April 1947 issue of *Art News*, which is nearer being his credo than even his *50 Paintings by Walt Kuhn* of 1940: "There are, of course, painters living, who with reverence are doing what they can to incorporate forever into history the great lessons of Cézanne. Of them there is little need to talk here; their work will certainly take care of itself."

Kuhn may not have been carried shoulder-high down Fifty-seventh Street, but the critics for once abandoned their caution. The veteran Henry McBride led off, on 8 November in the *Sun*, with his usual comments on Kuhn's refusal to "emotionalize" his show business subjects, which he felt was to Kuhn's credit, and ended: "It is therefore a pleasure to record that the 'Roberto' in the present collection is one of the most vital and arresting portraits that the artist has ever done. It is not only a live 'Roberto' but a symbol of what these chalk-faced artists mean to us. Walt Kuhn is at last telling us what he really thinks." Speaking for a younger generation, Emily Genauer headed her 16 November review in the *World-Telegram* "Walt Kuhn Growing," and went on to say:

Walt Kuhn has been a figure of consequence in the American art world for more than thirty years. His newest pictures, on view now at Durand-Ruel's, prove beyond a doubt that in his quiet, unsensational, sober way, he continues to grow in strength.

There are, for instance, two of his typical circus portraits, as powerful in form and characterization as ever, and richer in surface. But while it's not too hard, perhaps, to make an acrobat look strong, putting that kind of solidity and substance into a painting of a loaf of bread is something else again. And Kuhn does it brilliantly in a crusty brown loaf that's not just *a* bread, but the whole staff of life.

Carlyle Burrows wrote, on 10 November in the *Herald Tribune:*

One of our top-ranking contemporaries whose exhibition opened last week at the Durand-Ruel Gallery is Walt Kuhn. A fine colorist and robust painter, Kuhn

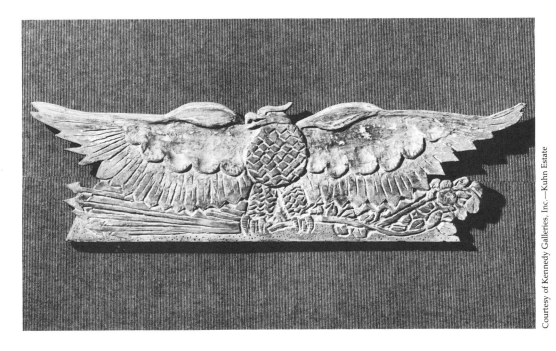

Plate 142. *American Eagle*

Plate 143. *Studies for Roberto*

cannot be easily pinned down as the realist he appears to be. One has always to take into account the strength of his modern view of painting. Through the recent years his subjects have remained much the same, and Kuhn can be seen now still painting apples and chorus girls and acrobats with the stark simplicity, which is yet subtle and poetic, which is inseparable from him. More than half the exhibition is composed, however, of subjects with a 1946 dating. The two or three small still lifes are good, "Peaches and Old Wood" is deep in color and the "Pine" flings its stalwart shapeliness against a blue sky with commanding authority. But perhaps the best of these pictures is "Roberto," the clown.

Even the *Sunday Mirror* unexpectedly added its bit, Harry Hershfield writing on 10 November, "Your loss if you miss Walt Kuhn's exhibit treat at Durand-Ruel Galleries." The *Daily Worker's* praise of *Green Apples and Scoop* has already been cited.

Aline Saarinen, whose *Art News* review in the November issue has already been quoted in connection with *Chair with Apples,* made the final statement:

> Look at the contrasts of form between the knobby, plastic bulges of bread on bland white cloth and the steely blade in the foreground—and sense the tension, presage the moment when the knife will cut.
>
> But look longest at *Roberto,* man of the circus, which is Kuhn's most familiar subject, for it is surely among the few masterpieces of our time. The painting is

Plate 144. *Miss D*

composed with stresses and strains as balanced and inevitable as those of architecture. The virile figure is magnificently painted; the raspberry pinks of the tights shimmering in light, the tensive hands a brilliantly accented foil to the face on which the dead white make-up obscures and reveals.

He never surpassed *Loaf of Bread* (number 499), whose latent power both Emily Genauer and Aline Saarinen had felt. The knobby loaf lies on a white table cloth against a gray-green slightly modulated background. The handle of the horizontal knife is centered below the bread, its blade stabbing to the left. As Kuhn said, "The bread is female,

223

the knife male." Shortly after it was painted, the Otto Spaeths added it to the several Kuhn Paintings they already owned. They had met Kuhn in the early forties when they were living in Dayton, Ohio, and on moving to New York became close friends, relying on his advice when French paintings were considered. *Oak* (number 501) is another of his superior paintings, the portrait of a single majestic tree that he had known for many years in York County, Maine. A long wooded hill lines the low horizon, a mass of white cloud is the background for the tree's vivid green, with a strip of bright blue sky at the top.

3

Two top paintings of 1946 were not included in the November show. Kuhn may have been saving *Sandy* (number 507) for the Whitney Annual, which opened on 10 December. It is now in the Minneapolis Institute of Arts. *Black Butterfly* (number 491) would have been a dramatic pendant to *Roberto*, perhaps too dramatic. It had been painted early in the year and shown at Indiana University in Bloomington in April. She is the last of the life-size show girls, clad in black tights, low-cut strapless black bodice, with panniers of purple and white feathers repeated as a kind of fall from her blond hair. She holds a long white staff and stands in almost regal dignity. The only warm colors are the flesh tones of breast, upper arms and face. The whole figure from there on down to her French heels is reduced to a black silhouette, recalling

Plate 145. *Oak*

Courtesy of Kennedy Galleries, Inc.—Kuhn Estate

Plate 146. *Green Bananas*

Velasquez' treatment of his male subjects. In his portraits of Infantas and other ladies of the court, Velasquez was required to pay much more attention to the lavish costumes with their elaborate metal-thread embroidery, painted with the same ease and actual sketchiness Kuhn had caught in *Veteran Acrobat*. Alfred Frankfurter had invoked Velasquez in trying to define the scientific impersonality of Walt Kuhn's painting, and in his own Cézanne article Kuhn also speaks of him: "The persistent criticism of Cézanne's lack of draftsmanship has become tiresome, for we know today that with a clear completion of the painter's statement, all requirements of drawing have been met. Few 'natural' draftsmen make good painters. Probably two outstanding exceptions are Velasquez and Degas."

Plate 147. *Bert Lahr*

Courtesy of Mr. Richard A. Manoogian

Just before that paragraph, while speaking of Cézanne, Kuhn defined his own superb black and white landscapes, watercolors without color: "After years of discipline brought about by his constant fitting of tone to tone in his oils, Cézanne turned to watercolors. His watercolors are peerless. Truly watercolor is a medium only for the most mature of painters — one like an expert marksman who, after years of practice, arrives at the point where he can shoot from the hip. Cézanne's watercolors are a light and easy rendering of echoes of his past as an artist. When he produced them he certainly knew most of the answers."

There is a quality in *Loaf of Bread, Black Butterfly,* and, above all, *Roberto,* however, that sets them off from Kuhn's previous works and that informs many of the paintings from his last two years. It is unquestionably the Spanish element, which has been mentioned many times, but which still requires some attempt at definition, partly because of the light it throws on Kuhn's personal actions from 1946 on, as well as on his paintings. Truisms have the disconcerting habit of being true; and it is true that the average Spaniard, even today as Spain rushes desperately to catch up with the industrialized world, is "grave," "courteous," and "dignified," and the personal dignity from which the other attributes derive counts most. Certainly the Spanish sense of "honor" comes from it.

Salvador de Madariaga, in his extended essay *Englishmen, Frenchmen, Spaniards,* advances the theory that the foremost gifts to Western culture were the English concept of the Gentleman, French Logic, and the Spanish sense of Honor. It has a long historic sanction; proud of their *fueros,* the rights written into the charter of their mountain monarchy as early as the eighth century, the common men of Aragon were used to say, "We are as noble as the King, but he is richer." Since it took free men with the personal privileges and property rights of free men to fight off Moorish raids and push the Christian Reconquest inexorably south in the manner of the American frontier's westward drive, serfdom never even existed in Castille, whereas it was general for centuries in other parts of Christendom. Hence Spanish

Plate 148. *Sap Bucket and Apples*

Courtesy of Mr. Richard A. Manoogian

227

dignity and honor transcend all social strata, from the field hand to the grandee; in fact, most Spaniards think of themselves as *hidalgos,* Sons of Someone. The institution of the siesta, which kills the best working hours of the day, often when neither climate nor weather justify it, can be interpreted as the Spaniard's gesture of proving that, hardworking and industrious though he has to be, the vulgar necessity of earning a living is somehow beneath him. Spanish honor is the result of an intense individualism that can take extreme forms of pride verging on arrogance, quickness to insult, resistance to imposed discipline, and that ultimate extravagance which only one of the greatest Spaniards could define as "quixotic."

And Spanish humor is often bitter and paradoxical, Cervantes not excepted. Walt Kuhn might have been amused by a revealing Spanish story from World War II that grades the merits of paratroops: best are the English, always sporting and gallant, and the Germans who unquestioningly jump on command. Well down the list are the French, who begin talking about women and forget to jump, then the Italians, who are simply disinclined to jump. But worst are the Spaniards; they start impugning each other's courage and jump without parachutes.

Brooding over all is *The Tragic Sense of Life,* title and substance of Miguel de Unamuno's masterwork. Federico GarcíaLorca, Spain's greatest modern poet, defined some of its particularities: "The chopping knife, the cartwheel, the clasp knife, and the prickly beard of shepherds, and the baldheaded moon, and the fly, and dank cupboards, and rubble, and the images of saints covered in lace, and quicklime, and the stabbing outline of eaves and baywindows, they all have in Spain the minute grasses of death, associations and voices which an alert mind will perceive, which recall to our memory the frozen air of our own departure." Most visual of writers, Lorca might be speaking of Spanish painting instead of Luis de Góngora, the seventeenth-century poet, when he said: "A poet must be a Professor of the five bodily senses. Of the five senses in the following order: sight, touch, hearing, smell, and taste. To command the most perfect images, he must open doors of communication between all of the senses. . . . The metaphor is always ruled by vision, though at times by a sublimated vision; it is the vision too which limits a metaphor and gives it reality. It does not permit a shadow to blur the outlines of an image it has seen clearly drawn. . . . All images are born in the visual field. The metaphor links two antagonistic worlds through an equestrian leap of imagination." Lorca goes on to say of Góngora, as if he were writing of Kuhn: "He combines astronomic sensations with the tiny details of the infinitely small. . . . So an apple and an ocean are the same to him, for he knows that the apple is as infinite as the sea, each within its own world. The life of an apple from the time when it is a delicate flower to the moment when, golden-russet, it drops from the tree into the grass is as mysterious and as great as the perpetual rhythm of the tides."

Plate 149. *Bobby Barry, Comedian*

4

Soon after the Durand-Ruel show closed, Walt Kuhn went south again to Hobe Sound and Stuart, Florida, after making rather unusual arrangements for the sale of his work. Although Durand-Ruel had all the prestige that could possibly be wished for as a setting of major exhibitions, they had too many other irons in the fire, chiefly their own unrivaled inventory of classic impressionists and postimpressionists, to take much interest in the promoting and selling of Kuhn's paintings in the interims. So Kuhn deposited a range of small subjects, both paintings and drawings, as well as a few larger canvases, with Maynard Walker, who in the mid-thirties had been the dealer for the leaders of the American Scene. Walker and Kuhn were physical and temperamental opposites, but Maynard Walker had taste, judgment, and respect for Kuhn's ability. He would continue to represent the Kuhn Estate until 1967, seeing Vera and Brenda through some of their most complicated early problems.

Kuhn's next big exhibition was to be in November 1948, and soon after that Durand-Ruel would close its New York Gallery. He was still savoring his November success and felt confident that the traveling show to be circulated by the Colorado Springs Fine Arts Center would spread the word from California to Nebraska to Michigan. It was a miniature retrospective again with twenty-four paintings in all, including some of his best, beginning with *High School Rider* of 1929, *Trude* of 1931, *Trio* of 1937, *Moist Forest* of 1938, *Lancer* of 1939, *Potatoes* of 1940 and *Clown in His Dressing Room* of 1943.

About the middle of January he wrote to Vera: "There is one way, and only one, to beat the European, viz Picasso racket: do better stuff. This season's success has given me complete confidence. 'You haven't seen nothin' yet!' I have got to build up ["build up" underscored] several magnificent pictures, that's all which is necessary." Yet on 31 January he wrote: "Incidentally something new seems to be cropping up in my career. Everybody seems to be taking pot shots at me.

Plate 150. *Apples in a Wooden Bucket*

Courtesy of Kennedy Galleries, Inc.—Kuhn Estate

. . . You can see now how anyone in any profession has to lock his doors against the wolves as soon as he gets anywhere." This is the first time such a knell is sounded, though there have been many references, one in the previous summer, to increasing loss of physical and nervous energy. And that loss seems to have been directly connected to his mental collapse in November 1948, if not the primary cause of it. The closest approach to a medical definition of that breakdown came in a letter to Vera on 4 August 1949 from James H. Wall, M.D., medical director of the Westchester Division of the New York Hospital. Dr. Wall writes: "As you are aware from your discussions with Dr. Hamilton, Dr. Ellison, and Dr. Bell, Mr. Kuhn was a man of great energy who was particularly proud of his great capacity for energy output. He prided himself on his youthful appearance and had been able to lead the particularly vigorous life of a man of much younger years. Before the development of his mental symptoms he had noted a loss of this vigor, had resented signs of old age, and it had been emotional conflicts over this which apparently precipitated the mental illness." Kuhn had not been a cooperative patient—some psychiatrists would call him a "hostile" patient—so the doctors may not have had all the evidence necessary for a more detailed diagnosis. And there is always the question as to whether or not a highly gifted creative temperament — the overworked and misused word "genius" is deliberately not invoked — reacts to physical and nervous strains as the generality of people do. Nevertheless there the matter stands. On 22 September 1947 Kuhn wrote to Vera from Ogunquit, "Did you ever see me do as little as I did this summer?"

In spite of his optimism in January there was not enough energy for Kuhn "to build up several magnificent pictures," though one at least answers to that definition: *Acrobat in White and Blue* (number 510), now in the Hirshhorn Museum and Sculpture Garden. Whether it is imminent tragedy or the steady emergence of the Spanish quality, there is no mistaking the somber dignity of both subject and theme. And unproductive as the summer in Ogunquit may have seemed at the time, at least three first-class still lifes came from it: *Butternut Squash* (number 513), *Challa* (number 515), the ceremonial Jewish bread, and *Sap Bucket and Apples* (number 522). In New York between Florida and Maine, Walt coaxed Bert Lahr into posing for him (number 511), and possibly about that time *Bobby Barry* (number 512) was painted. Bobby Barry was a popular burlesque comedian and, though not to be mentioned in the same breath with a star of Bert Lahr's magnitude, was, like him, the personification of a clown. So the paintings are sympathetic portraits.

On 12 November 1947 Marius de Zayas wrote from France proposing to buy a Walt Kuhn painting for the museum at Grenoble, the best collection of modern paintings in France outside Paris. Only a year before Kuhn would have considered this another proof of final, and inevitable, recognition, but he delayed answering it until 4 Decem-

231

ber and somewhat listlessly proposed *Fruit Basket,* one of his lesser still lifes that cannot be positively identified. Nothing came of it. Although outwardly appearing to be much the same as always, and keeping up most of his old relationships, his private letters to Vera grew more and more agitated.

Kuhn spent February of 1948 at the winter quarters of the circus at Sarasota, Florida. Out of that, thanks to Mark Hanna, a public relations expert who had done several commissions for the Union Pacific, notably on Sun Valley, and who had voluntarily taken over Kuhn's national publicity, came a two-page spread in the 10 April issue of *Collier's* called "Sketches in Sawdust," with nine color-touched drawings and a short text by Walt Kuhn. In April, Kuhn went out again to California, by way of Colorado. It was probably on this trip that tentative plans were made for a hunting expedition in northern Mexico in January 1949 with Gary Cooper and two archaeologists. Mitchell Wilder, director of the Colorado Springs Fine Arts Center, was an experienced outdoorsman and advised Kuhn about buying a double-barreled Winchester shotgun from Abercrombie and Fitch, who would see that the stock was tailored to his needs. Kuhn reported to Mitchell Wilder on his negotiations in a letter of 23 October.

In June, Kuhn "fulfilled a life-long ambition," according to Brenda, by buying a house on River Road, Cape Neddick, five miles south of Ogunquit. He stayed there through September, planning to close his New York studio the next spring and move its contents to Cape Neddick, where he could paint landscapes from April to October. There he would also stage the

Cape Neddick Follies
August 8, 1949
Big open air stage with sound amplifiers, overlooking the Cape Neddick River with the ocean as a backdrop — modern lighting system — cast of 200 — satirical ballets — burlesque melodramas — many clown acts. 100 beautiful Amazons in a grand drill — many professional guest stars. Grand parade from Portsmouth N.H. through all towns including Portland, Maine under the auspices of the Governor of Maine for the benefit of the York Hospital and the police and fire departments of Ogunquit and York. Indications are that the attendance will run into many thousands. Production will require several months to prepare and will be delivered at the professional pace of a Broadway show.

These details come from his own notes; the project was a near obsession that the attending doctors later forbade Vera and Brenda to discuss with him.

By the fall of 1948 Kuhn's eccentric behavior was becoming more noticeable. He denounced dealers and critics, an age-old privilege of artists; but Walt did it with unusual vehemence, announcing that he would become a critic himself. He openly and violently broke with friends of long standing, and held others helpless on the phone for long ranting hours. Everyone who had any dealings with him that fall used the same word: Kuhn was a "sick" man. But he was also preparing with professional thoroughness for his November exhibition at Durand-Ruel, which, he announced in the *New York Times,* would be his last

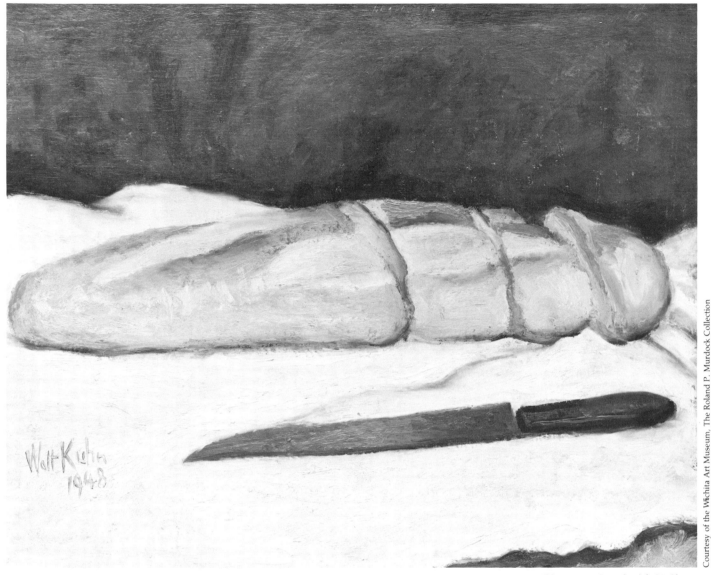

Plate 151. *Bread with Knife*

one-man show, entitled "Fifty Years a Painter." And there were several good paintings ready for it, even though some were not included: *Apples on Red Cloth* (number 525), *Apples in a Wooden Basket* (number 527), *Chico in Silk Hat* (number 530), and *Chico in Top Hat* (number 531). In *Apples on Red Cloth* and the two *Chicos* the Tragic Sense of Life is inescapable. And the end was near. The exhibition opened on 8 November and ran through 4 December. With Kuhn not in active and astute command the press was tepid, and there was not a single sale.

Earlier that fall Kuhn had bought a .22 caliber target pistol at Stoeger's Shop on Fifth Avenue after "an attack by a thug just inside my studio door," and applied for a police permit to carry it. He was enraged by the law's delays, insisting that he was experienced in handling small arms, which he was. It is possible that the police accurately sensed a dangerous instability. Another of his obsessions was the need to expose and destroy the American Medical Association, against whom he claimed to have incontrovertible evidence of criminal activity.

With this "evidence" and his .22 he dashed off to Washington, succeeding only in terrifying his wife's family. Finally he was apprehended, still with his .22 pistol, trying to force his way into the house of the publisher of the *New York Times*, who had not answered several of his letters demanding the exposure of the AMA. His friends realized that immediate action must be taken, so at ten on the morning of Friday, 26 November, Alfred Frankfurter, Lily Cushing, and Mark Hanna met with Otto and Eloise Spaeth in their Park Avenue apartment. They agreed that only Vera had the legal authority to commit Kuhn as a danger to himself and others. At noon they telephoned to ask Vera and Brenda, whom none of them had met, to join them. They had also alerted the Harrimans, who made all arrangements for as humane treatment as possible. Vera and Brenda arrived at two in the afternoon and after an hour came to the agonizing decision. On the morning of Sunday, 28 November, Vera, Brenda, and Charles MacArthur met Kuhn by appointment at his Eighteenth Street studio. A police ambulance was standing by, and Walt Kuhn was delivered to Bellevue Hospital. On 3 December he was transferred to the Westchester Division of the New York Hospital.

On 30 March 1949, Vera reported: "News from the hospital was exceptionally good yesterday. . . . A little later in the spring, they hope to start their 'on visit' system with him. If everything progresses according to expectations, he will be permitted to leave the hospital together with an attendant or relative, for varying lengths of time, winding up by staying away as much as a week or two at a time before being finally discharged. . . . He made lots of drawings of many kinds for fellow patients among whom he has found several artists, a writer, a scientist and a priest." The "on visit" system did not develop, and on 13 July 1949 Walt Kuhn died suddenly from a perforated ulcer of the very kind that had shocked him into creative life in 1925. As Dr. Wall later wrote to Vera: "It is not unusual to find ulcers associated with individuals of Mr. Kuhn's temperament. . . . As you know, since last Fall there had been a gradual lessening of his physical vigor so that his physical resistance was not great enough to overcome the assault of a perforated peptic ulcer."

When Kuhn was properly dressed after the postmortem, Vera and Brenda put his favorite drawing pen into the breast pocket of his coat. On 27 October 1949, his ashes were interred with no formal ceremony in the Kuhn family plot in Woodlawn Cemetery, the Bronx.

EPILOGUE

It is sad to record the ends of lives, more sad, it would seem, when their last months were clouded, as were Walt Kuhn's. But artists have their own way of cheating mortality; as long as a painting physically survives and there are eyes to see it, the artist still lives. And it is good that the end came soon; it is impossible to imagine Walt Kuhn meekly escorted in and out of the hospital precincts by attendants "on visits." There is a Spanish irony too in the fact that wherever there were people he could be interested, so he had found "several artists, a writer, a scientist and a priest." Naturally he "made lots of drawings of many kinds"; he would have done so in a straitjacket. Certainly there were no clouds in the mind that saw those last few paintings, or in the eyes that brought them to life on canvas. His "open intransigence," as one physician called Kuhn's conduct that fall, could have been no more than a logical, if extreme, extension of the qualities with which he had so fiercely defended his independence, his artistic integrity, his honor. It

Plate 152. *Chico in Silk Hat*

235

had been "a good fight," and there are those who believe that "all the trumpets sounded for him on the other side."

Finally, what is Walt Kuhn's position in the honorable, though often provincial, annals of American art? He was no provincial, but he defies other classifications so dear to critics and art historians, possibly suffering for it. He belonged to no group; even in his younger Penguin Club days, his aloofness and secretiveness were marked. In his mature years he almost never took part in group exhibitions, and he refused to join any dealer's "stable" of artists.

He has been called a colorist, which he certainly was — and much more. He has sometimes been ranked with those painters who merely manipulated paint for its own sake. To be sure, he was a skilled executant, as his drawings alone show, but underneath those finely wrought surfaces lies a complete mastery of the abstract foundations on which all true paintings are built. He has been called a romantic, once even a "tormented romanticist." He has been called more often a realist, and his subjects are instantly recognizable, by intention. But a definition of these terms raises many philosophic questions to which there are more answers than questioners. To Walt Kuhn his realistic subjects were metaphors, speaking of things that indeed "do often lie too deep for tears."

From here on words are futile, even Wordsworth's. Walt Kuhn was a classic painter in the great tradition and a poet of the human mystery.

NOTES TO CHAPTER NINE

The FULL AUTHORITY Kuhn gave Vera is one of many confirmations of their mutual trust.

The OLD ACQUAINTANCE Kuhn wrote to in April 1945 was A. William Bahr, the collector-dealer in Far Eastern art. "IT HAS BEEN A GOOD FIGHT" comes from the same letter.

ROSAMUND FROST'S REVIEW appeared in the 1 to 14 May issue of *Art News*, p. 11, reproducing the two paintings mentioned, and *Two Veterans (Two Clowns)*.

FRANK GETLEIN'S COMMENT ON "PENDING STORM" comes from Kennedy Galleries, 1967, p. 51.

THE LETTERS OF 24 APRIL 1946 AND 12 OCTOBER were addressed to the author.

The quotation "THEIR WORK WILL CERTAINLY TAKE CARE OF ITSELF" comes from "Cézanne: Delayed Finale," *Art News*, April 1947, p. 56. THE OTHER QUOTATIONS come from p. 55.

A new edition of Salvador de Madariaga's *Englishmen, Frenchmen, Spaniards* was published by the Oxford University Press in 1931.

Miguel de Unamuno's *Del Sentimiento Tragica de la Vida* was published in 1913.

THE FIRST QUOTATION FROM GARCIA LORCA was part of a lecture he gave in Cuba in 1930, included in Arturo Barea, *Lorca the Poet and his People*, New York: Harcourt, Brace & Co., 1949), p. 85. The following quotations were part of a lecture on Luis de Góngora, the enigmatic seventeenth-century poet, given in Granada in 1927 and are also taken from ibid., pp. 118-19. The tricentennial celebrations of Góngora had an effect on Spanish writers not unlike that which the rediscovery of the metaphysical poets had had in English letters.

VERA KUHN'S 30 MARCH LETTER was sent to the author.

"SKETCHES IN SAWDUST" is to be found on pages 26 and 27 of the 10 April 1948 issue of *Collier's*.

THE QUOTATIONS FROM JOHN BUNYAN'S "THE PILGRIM'S PROGRESS" in the Prologue and Epilogue should be identified for the benefit of the increasing number of unfortunates who are not acquainted with this masterwork. Its images and metaphors began to enrich the English tongue when the "Tinker of Bedford" first published his famous allegory in 1678, after writing it in jail.

The "TORMENTED ROMANTICIST" comes from William E. Steadman's foreword to the University of Arizona's Catalogue, 1966, page 7.

WORDSWORTH'S VISUAL SENSIBILITIES are perhaps unique in English poetry. Crabb Robinson tells in 1826 how William Blake, who had a better right than most to say so, penciled on the margin of the Preface, "perhaps they are the opinions of a landscape painter." It is not impious to compare many of Wordsworth's apparently simple but profound statements to some of Walt Kuhn's best paintings.

Catalogue raisonné of Oil Paintings

1904

1.

Maasluis
H. 15" W. 9"

EXHIBITED: University of Arizona Art Gallery, Tuscon, Arizona, "Painter of Vision: A Retrospective Exhibition of Oils, Watercolors, and Drawings by Walt Kuhn," 6 February through 31 March 1966, catalogue published by the Board of Regents of the Universities and State College of Arizona, 1966, foreword by William E. Steadman, text by Philip R. Adams, catalogue number 17 (hereafter referred to as U of A, 1966); Maynard Walker Gallery, New York, "Walt Kuhn: Early Works, 1904–1929," 18 April through 7 May 1966, number 16 (*Maaslius*) (This gallery hereafter will be referred to as MWG, and this exhibition as MWG, 1966).

1905

2.

Nocturnal Landscape
H. 11⅝" W. 15⅝" Signed and dated lower left.

COLLECTIONS: Walter S. Goodnough, director of art education, Brooklyn Schools, 1905 to 1919; Esther M. Crockett, Keene, New Hampshire; the Currier Gallery of Art, Manchester, New Hampshire, gift of Miss Esther M. Crockett.

EXHIBITED: Annual Sale Exhibition, Salmagundi Club, New York, 1905; bought by Mr. Goodnough, 1905; the first New York exhibition and sale.

1906

3.

Edgewater, N.J.
H. 14" W. 10"

COLLECTIONS: Milch Galleries, New York; Mr. and Mrs. Alfredo Valente.

EXHIBITED: U of A, 1966, number 18.

4.

The Eye-Opener
H.   W.   Signed and dated lower right.

COLLECTIONS: Albig, Fort Lee, New Jersey; Castellane, New York, bought from Albig's daughter.

PUBLISHED: *Art in America*, number 1, 1961, page 121, advertisement.

1908

5.

Albig's Painted in Fort Lee, New Jersey.
H. 20¼" W. 24¼" Signed lower left.

COLLECTIONS: Castellane, New York; Joseph Gonzalez.

PUBLISHED: Sotheby Parke Bernet, "Important 18th, 19th, and 20th Century American Paintings," 23 May 1974, New York, number 78, illustrated.

Mr. and Mrs. Albig operated a restaurant in Fort Lee, New Jersey. It was popular with local artists and visitors from Manhattan. The woman is probably Mrs. Albig, and the man on the left may be Robert Henri.

6.

Houses on Street Painted in Fort Lee, New Jersey.
H. 20" W. 24" Signed lower left.

1910

7.

The Frozen River
H. 22" W. 27" Signed lower right.

COLLECTIONS: John Quinn till 1927, purchased in 1911 for $300.00.

PUBLISHED: "Paintings and Sculptures — The Renowned Collection of Modern and Ultra-Modern Art Formed by the Late John Quinn — Including Many Examples Purchased by Him Directly from the Artists," American Art Association, Inc., New York, 9–11 February 1927, number 102 (dated 1910–11) (hereafter referred to as the John Quinn Sale, 1927); B. L. Reid, *The Man from New York: John Quinn and His Friends* (New York: Oxford University Press, 1968), page 93.

7-A.
Landscape
H. 12" W. 16"   Signed lower left.

COLLECTIONS: Baker-Pisano, New York.

8.
Rowboat at Shore with Houses
H. 16" W. 20"

9.
Salt Mists   Painted in Nova Scotia.
H. 28½" W. 30"   Signed lower left.

COLLECTIONS: John Quinn till 1927, purchased in 1911 for $200.00.

PUBLISHED: John Quinn Sale, 1927, number 245; *Art in America*, August 1963, page 142, advertisement.

10.
Summer Interlude   Painted in Nova Scotia.
H. 30" W. 43"

EXHIBITED: Cincinnati Art Museum, Cincinnati, Ohio, *Walt Kuhn 1877–1949: A Memorial Exhibition*, October 1960, catalogue published by the Cincinnati Art Museum, 1960, text by Philip R. Adams, catalogue number 2, illustrated page 7 (hereafter referred to as CAM, 1960); Nasson College, Learning Center, Springvale, Maine, "Walt Kuhn: Paintings, Drawings, Carvings," 2 May to 10 June 1964; catalogue number 1 (hereafter referred to as Nasson College, 1964.)

11.
Tow Team   Perhaps 1909.
H.   W.

PUBLISHED: Robert Henri, "The Exhibition of Independents," *Craftsman*, May 1910, illustrated page 165.

12.
Under the Parasol
H. 24" W. 20"

EXHIBITED: CAM, 1960, number 1.

13.
Vera Kuhn Sitting on Grass in Blandford, Nova Scotia
H. 33" W. 40"

14.
Walking along the Seashore
H. 20" W. 24"

PUBLISHED: *Art in America*, July 1973, page 94, advertisement.

1912

15.
Four Boats
H. 20" W. 24"   Signed lower right.

COLLECTIONS: Mr. and Mrs. Brenwasser, Wykoff, New Jersey.

EXHIBITED: U of A, 1966, number 19, illustrated page 50; MWG, 1966, number 18 (*Four Boats, Ogunquit*).

16.
Girl with Red Cap
H. 20" W. 24"   Destroyed in 1929.

COLLECTIONS: John Quinn till 1927, purchased from the Armory Show, 26 February 1913, for $350.00.

EXHIBITED: "International Exhibition of Modern Art given under the auspices of the Association of American Painters and Sculptors" at the Armory of the Sixty-ninth Regiment, N.G.N.Y., Lexington Avenue at Twenty-fifth Street, 17 February to 17 March 1913, known as "The Armory Show"; later shown with some modifications in Chicago and Boston; catalogue number 863 (hereafter referred to as the Armory Show, 1913.)

PUBLISHED: *Arts and Decoration*, Special Exhibition Number, Volume 3, Number 5, "The American Section: An Interview with the Chairman of the Domestic Committee, Wm. J. Glackens," illustrated page 162, as *Landscape*; John Quinn Sale, 1927, number 103, illustrated page 45; Milton Brown, *The Story of the Armory Show* (New York: Joseph Hirshhorn Foundation, New York Graphic Society, 1936), p. 258.
The model was the artist's wife, Vera Spier Kuhn.

17.
Morning   Painted in Nova Scotia.
H. 33" W. 40"

COLLECTIONS: John Quinn till 1927, purchased from the Armory Show, 26 February 1913, for $600.00; Norton Gallery and School of Art, West Palm Beach, Florida, gift of Mr. Sam Lustgarten, Chicago, 1946.

EXHIBITED: The Armory Show, 1913, New York, number 862; Art Institute of Chicago, 1913, number 201; Cincinnati Art Museum, "Paintings for Peace," partial reconstruction of the Armory Show, 1945; Amherst College, Amherst, Massachusetts, 1958; Sarasota Art Association, Florida, Fall, 1961; Lowe Art Museum, Miami, Florida, "American Prophets," 2 February–25 March 1973, Number 29, page 18; Munson-Williams-Proctor Institute, Utica, New York, 1973.

PUBLISHED: John Quinn Sale, 1927, number 252; Brown, *The Story of the Armory Show*, page 258; *Art Digest*, 1 April 1944, illustrated page 44; Lloyd Goodrich, "The Decade of the Armory Show," *Art in America*, February 1963, illustrated page 59, identified as "[cat. 862]"; S. Tillim, "Dissent on the Armory Show," *Arts*, May 1963, illustrated page 98.

18.
Vera Kuhn Reading by Seashore Painted in Yarmouth, Nova Scotia.
H. 20″ W. 24″

COLLECTIONS: L. H. Aricson, Philadelphia, Pennsylvania; Mr. and Mrs. Isadore Izzo, Manhasset Hills, New York
The model was the artist's wife.

19.
Work Horses
H. 20″ W. 24″   Signed lower left.

COLLECTIONS: Edith Gregor Halpert, Downtown Gallery, New York.

PUBLISHED: Sotheby Parke Bernet, "20th Century American Paintings and Sculpture, Edith Gregor Halpert, Part II," 16 May 1973, number 38, (hereafter referred to as Edith Gregor Halpert Sale).

1914

20.
Nude
H. 30″ W. 28″   Signed lower left.

PUBLISHED: *Connoisseur*, November 1966, illustrated page LXXXIV, advertisement.

21.
Polo Game
H. 25″ W. 30″

COLLECTIONS: Mrs. Laura P. Taylor, Irvington, New York, purchased 1967.

EXHIBITED: CAM, 1960, number 3, illustrated page 11 (dated ca. 1915); U of A, 1966, number 20, illustrated in color page 11; MWG, 1966, number 2, illustrated in color page 8.

PUBLISHED: *Art Journal*, spring 1963, illustrated page 185; *Connoisseur*, November 1965, illustrated page LXXVIII, advertisement.

1915

22.
Bathers on Beach
H. 30″ W. 40″   Signed lower left.

COLLECTIONS: Hirschl and Adler, New York.

EXHIBITED: U of A, 1966, number 22, illustrated in color page 69 (lent by Maynard Walker Gallery, dated ca. 1915); MWG, 1966, number 1, illustrated in color on cover of catalogue.

PUBLISHED: *Burlington Magazine*, April 1966, illustrated page XXXVI, advertisement.

23.
Flowers and Forms
H. 16″ W. 14″   Signed lower left.

EXHIBITED: U of A, 1966, number 21, illustrated page 51 (dated ca. 1915); MWG, 1966, number 3, illustrated page 4 (dated ca. 1915).

PUBLISHED: *Art Journal*, summer 1966, illustrated page 407.

24.
Hunt
H.   W.

EXHIBITED: Macbeth Galleries, 22 March to 14 April 1916.

25.
Man and Sea Beach
H. 7″ W. 10″
Possibly a sketch for the large painting in the Quinn Collection.

26.
Man and Sea Beach
H. 84″ W. 120″   Signed lower left.

COLLECTIONS: John Quinn till 1927.

EXHIBITED: Montross Gallery, 1915; Panama-Pacific International Exposition, San Francisco, California, 1915.

PUBLISHED: *Vanity Fair*, May 1915, illustrated p. 40; John Quinn Sale, 1927, number 375; Milton W. Brown, *American Painting from the Armory Show to the Depression* (Princeton, N.J.: Princeton University Press, 1955), pages 141-142.
Part of a mural series, with Arthur B. Davies and Maurice Prendergast, for the Daniel Gallery, 1915.

27.
Man and Sea Beach   (*Beach* in John Quinn Sale)
H. 11″ W. 16″   Tempera on gesso panel; signed lower left.

COLLECTIONS: John Quinn till 1927; Elton Hyder, Jr., purchased 27 January 1964.

EXHIBITED: MWG, 1966, number 14, illustrated page 10.

PUBLISHED: John Quinn Sale, 1927, number 195 (H. 10″ W. 14″).

28.
Surf
H. 11″ W. 16″

PUBLISHED: *Art Quarterly*, Summer 1963, illustrated page 274, advertisement.

29.
Woman with White Hat
H. 20″ W. 16″

COLLECTIONS: John Quinn till 1927.

PUBLISHED: John Quinn Sale, 1927, number 95.
The model was the artist's wife.

30.
Youth   Painted in Fort Lee, New Jersey, studio, Hudson Terrace.
H. 78″ W. 59″

COLLECTIONS: John Quinn till 1927, purchased in 1916 for $1,000.00.

EXHIBITED: Macbeth Galleries, winter of 1915–16.

PUBLISHED: Frederick James Gregg, "A Spiritual Adventure with Walt Kuhn," *Rainbow*, December 1920, pages 10–11, illustrated page 12, vignette sketches and page decorations by Walt Kuhn (hereafter referred to as Gregg, *Rainbow*); John Quinn Sale, 1927, number 373; Reid, *The Man from New York*, page 294.

1916

31.

Tragic Comedians   Painted in Fort Lee, New Jersey, studio, Hudson Terrace.

H. 95" W. 45"   Signed lower right.

COLLECTIONS: John Quinn till 1927, purchased in 1917 for $1,250.00; Mrs. Meredith Hare, New York; Mr. Paul Rabout, Westport, Connecticut; Herbert Benevy Gallery, New York; Mrs. Solomon Ethe, New York, 1958; Mr. Joseph Hirshhorn, Greenwich, Connecticut; Hirshhorn Museum and Sculpture Garden, Smithsonian Institution, Washington, D.C.

EXHIBITED: Montross Gallery, "Special Exhibition: Arthur B. Davies, Walt Kuhn, Jules Pascin, Charles Sheeler, Max Weber," 3 to 28 February 1917; Montross Gallery, "Paintings by Walt Kuhn," 3 to 28 January 1922, number 13; CAM, 1960, number 6 (Misdated 1922).

PUBLISHED: Frederick James Gregg, "The Newest Work of Six Painters," *Vanity Fair*, April 1917, illustrated page 57; James B. Townsend, "Modernists at Montross Gallery," *American Art News*, 17 February 1917, page 3; Gregg, *Rainbow*, illustrated page 13; *Catalogue of the John Quinn Collection of Paintings, Watercolors, Drawings, and Sculpture*, with foreword by Forbes Watson (Huntington, N.Y.: Pigeon Hill Press, 1926), page 23; John Quinn Sale, 1927, number 516; "The Sale of the Quinn Collection Is Completed," *Art News*, 19 February 1927, page 11; Reid, *The Man from New York*, page 294; *Catalogue of the Hirshhorn Museum and Sculpture Garden* (New York: Harry H. Abrams, 1974), illustrated in color number 385.

A girl called Casey was the female model, and a professional model named Wilson posed for the male figure.

1918-1923

An Imaginary History of the West

The following paintings are listed as a group in spite of their range in date from 1918 to 1923. The artist considered them a unified series, and as such his wife and daughter gave them to the Colorado Springs Fine Arts Center, Colorado. They are listed in the order of their approximate dates.

32.

Defending the Blockhouse   1918

H. 10" W. 13"   Signed and dated lower right.

EXHIBITED: CAM, 1960, number 2; Amon Carter Museum of Western Art, Fort Worth, Texas, 1964, illustrated on page 27 of the catalogue published by the Amon Carter Museum in 1964, with a foreword by Fred S. Bartlett, director of the Colorado Springs Fine Arts Center (hereafter referred to ACM, 1964.)

33.

Aborigine   1918

H. 9½" W. 5¾"   Signed lower right center, dated lower left.

EXHIBITED: CAM, 1960, number 8; ACM, 1964, illustrated page 20.

34.

Attack on the Stagecoach   1918

H. 14" W. 19"   Dated and titled lower right.

EXHIBITED: CAM, 1960, number 9; ACM, 1964, illustrated page 24.

35.

Combat   1918

H. 11½" W. 17½"   Signed, titled, and dated lower left.

EXHIBITED: CAM, 1960, number 10; ACM, 1964, illustrated page 36.

36.

The Commissioners   1918

H. 9¾" W. 15¾"   Signed and dated lower left.

EXHIBITED: Arts Club, Art Institute of Chicago (hereafter referred to as AI of Chicago), 1923, number 8; CAM, 1960, number 10; ACM, 1964, illustrated in color on cover.

37.

Indian Lore   1918

H. 12½" W. 8½"   Signed and dated lower left.

EXHIBITED: CAM, 1960, number 13; ACM, 1964, illustrated page 35.

38.

Indians and Cavalry   1918

H. 9¾" W. 13"

EXHIBITED: CAM, 1960, number 14; ACM, 1964, illustrated page 15.

39.

Pequod   1918

H. 17" W. 12"   Signed lower right.

EXHIBITED: AI of Chicago, 1923, number 24; CAM, 1960, number 15; ACM, 1964, illustrated page 23.

40.

Pow-Wow number 1   1918

H. 12" W. 17"   Signed and dated lower right.

COLLECTIONS: John Quinn till 1927.

EXHIBITED: CAM, 1960, number 16; ACM, 1964, illustrated page 38.

PUBLISHED: John Quinn Sale, 1927, number 61 (H. 9½" W. 15½").

41.

Pow-Wow number 2   1918

H. 12" W. 16"   Signed and dated lower left.

EXHIBITED: CAM, 1960, number 17; ACM, 1964, illustrated page 30.

42.

The Messenger 1918
H. 12″ W. 16″   Signed lower left.
EXHIBITED: CAM, 1976, number 18; ACM, 1964, illustrated page 18.

43.

The Young Chief 1918
H. 9¾″ W. 14″
EXHIBITED: CAM, 1960, number 19, illustrated page 27 upper; ACM, 1964, illustrated page 21.

44.

Three Indians 1918
H. 14″ W. 8″   Signed lower left.
EXHIBITED: CAM, 1960, number 20; ACM, 1964, illustrated page 29.

45.

Warrior 1918
H.12¾ ″W. 10″   Signed and dated lower right.
EXHIBITED: CAM, 1960, number 21; ACM, 1964, illustrated page 25.

46.

Ambushed Horseman 1918
H. 8″ W. 11″   Dated lower right.
EXHIBITED: CAM, 1960, number 34; ACM, 1964, illustrated page 33.

47.

Cavalry Outpost 1919
H. 10″ W. 15¾″   Signed and dated lower left.
EXHIBITED: CAM, 1960, number 22; ACM, 1964, illustrated page 17.

48.

Imaginary History 1919
H. 15″ W. 12″   Signed lower left, dated lower left center.
EXHIBITED: AI of Chicago, 1923, number 11; CAM, 1960, number 23; ACM, 1964, illustrated page 31.

49.

Medicine 1919
H. 10″ W. 8¼″   Signed lower left, titled lower left "Study *Medicine.*"
EXHIBITED: CAM, 1960, number 24; ACM, 1964, illustrated page 37.

50.

Mining Camp 1919
H. 12″ W. 17″   Signed and dated lower left.
EXHIBITED: AI of Chicago, 1923, number 27; CAM, 1960, number 25; ACM, 1964, illustrated page 22.

51.

Vigilantes 1918
H. 4¾″ W. 6¾″   Signed lower left, dated lower right.
EXHIBITED: CAM, 1960, number 26; ACM, 1964, illustrated page 14.

52.

Wild West 1919
H. 16″ W. 20″
EXHIBITED: AI of Chicago, 1923, number 16; CAM, 1960, number 27; ACM, 1964, illustrated page 26.

53.

The Long Horn Saloon 1919
H. 20″ W. 24″   Signed and dated lower left center.
COLLECTIONS: John Quinn till 1927, purchased in 1920 for $625.00.
EXHIBITED: CAM, 1960, number 28; ACM, 1964, illustrated page 8.
PUBLISHED: Gregg, *Rainbow,* illustrated page 22; John Quinn Sale, 1927, number 229; Reid, *The Man from New York,* page 467.

54.

Western Cafe 1919
H. 20″ W. 24″   Signed and dated lower left.
EXHIBITED: CAM, 1960, number 29; ACM, 1964, illustrated page 9.

55.

Bar Room Fight 1919
H. 9¾″ W. 10¾″   Signed and dated lower left.
EXHIBITED: CAM, 1960, number 30; ACM, 1964, illustrated in color, frontispiece.

56.

Indians Attacking Covered Wagon 1919
H. 12½″ W. 11″
EXHIBITED: CAM, 1960, number 35; ACM, 1964, illustrated page 34.

57.

Wild West number 2 1919
H. l2½″ W. 15″   Signed lower left.
EXHIBITED: CAM, 1960, number 36; ACM, 1964, illustrated page 32.

58.

Indian Raid 1920
H. 10¾″ W. 9″
EXHIBITED: CAM, 1960, number 31; ACM, 1964, illustrated page 28.

59.

The Council Table 1920
H. 16″ W. 20″   Signed and dated lower right.
EXHIBITED: CAM, 1960, number 32, illustrated page 27 lower; ACM, 1964, illustrated page 19.

60.

Indian Fighters 1923
H. 13″ W. 9″   Signed lower left.
EXHIBITED: CAM, 1960, number 33, illustrated page 28; ACM, 1964, illustrated page 16.

1918

61.

Burlesque Show
H. 8¾″ W. 13⅞″   Mounted on composition board, signed lower left.

EXHIBITED: Marius de Zayas Gallery, New York, 2 March to 3 April 1920; U of A, 1966, number 27; MWG, 1966, number 13.

62.
Burlesque
Small.

EXHIBITED: Montross Gallery, 1922; AI of Chicago, 1923, number 14.

63.
Caucus Painted in Fort Lee, New Jersey, studio, Hudson Terrace.
H. 65½" W. 75"   Signed lower right.

COLLECTIONS: John Quinn till 1927, purchased in 1919 for $1,125.00.

EXHIBITED: American Art Galleries, 1927; U of A, 1966, number 27 (ca. 1918); MWG,1966, number 5.

PUBLISHED: Gregg, *Rainbow*, illustrated page 15; John Quinn Sale, 1927, number 129 (dated 1919, with height given as 5 feet 6 inches, width, 6 feet 4 inches); Sheldon Cheney, *A Primer of Modern Art* (New York: Liveright,1932), illustrated page 231; *Index of Twentieth Century Artists* (New York: College Art Association of America, 1933–37), vol. 4 (1936), page 348 (hereafter referred to as *Index*, 1936); Brown, *American Painting from the Armory Show to the Depression*, page 142; Reid, *The Man from New York*, page 393.

64.
Figure at Window
H. 8" W. 10"

EXHIBITED: Marius de Zayas Gallery, 1920; AI of Chicago, 1923, number 28 (*Figure Appearing at Window*).
The model was a small porcelain doll.

65.
Flowers in a Vase
H. 16" W. 10"   Signed lower right.

COLLECTIONS: Goldstone, purchased 25 May 1962.

EXHIBITED: U of A, 1966 (lent by Maynard Walker), number 25.

66.
Flower Still Life
H. 35" W. 20"   Signed lower right.

COLLECTIONS: John Quinn till 1927.

EXHIBITED: CAM, 1960, number 4, illustrated in color page 5; U of A, 1966, number 24, illustrated page 52 (lent by Maynard Walker); Kennedy Galleries, New York, "Walt Kuhn," 10 October to 7 November 1967, text by Frank Getlein, number 15 (misdated 1936) (the Kennedy Galleries hereafter will be referred to as KG, and this exhibition as KG, 1967).

PUBLISHED: John Quinn Sale, 1927, number 508.

67.
Girl in Tights
Full length; destroyed.

68.
Harlequin
H. 39" W. 26"   In 1944 the artist marked at what points he intended to reduce the size. This was done about 1950 by Vera and Brenda Kuhn. Its original dimensions as given in the John Quinn Sale catalogue were H. 96" W. 36". Signed lower left.

COLLECTIONS: John Quinn till 1927, purchased in 1919 for $1,125.00; Mrs. Alexander Liebermann, Philadelphia, Pennsylvania.

EXHIBITED: Metropolitan Museum of Art, New York, 1921; "Architectural League Exhibition," MWG, 1962; Nasson College, 1964, number 3; U of A, 1966, number 26.

PUBLISHED: Gregg, *Rainbow*, illustrated page 19; Catalogue of *the John Quinn Collection of Paintings, Watercolors, Drawings, and Sculpture*, Pidgeon Hill Press, 1926, foreword by Forbes Watson; John Quinn Sale, 1927, number 377, illustrated; Brown, *American Painting from the Armory Show to the Depression*, illustrated page 143; *Art Quarterly*, Summer 1962, illustrated page 181; Parke-Bernet, "Collection of Mrs. Alexander Lieberman," number 116, illustrated; Reid, *The Man from New York,* page 393.

69.
Man with Ship Model
H. 42" W. 32"   Signed lower right.

EXHIBITED: Sally Lewis's First Western Tour, 1922—23; Grand Central Art Galleries, New York, "Exhibition of Paintings by Walt Kuhn," 20 January to 9 February 1927, text by LaSalle Spier, "One Approach to the Art of Walt Kuhn," number 7 (this gallery will hereafter be referred to as GCAG, and this exhibition as GCAG,1927); AI of Chicago, 1927, number 6; Whitney Museum of American Art (hereafter referred to as Whitney), 1946.

PUBLISHED: Gregg, *Rainbow*, illustrated page 16; Alfred M. Frankfurter, "O Pioneers!—The Whitney Examines the Pathfinders of Modern Art in America,"*Art News*, April 1946, illustrated page 36.

70.
Pink Flowers
H. 13" W. 8"   Given as a present.

EXHIBITED: Montross Gallery; AI of Chicago, 1923, number 10.

1919

71.
Aborigine
Narrow vertical, Indian standing with gun.
PUBLISHED: Gregg, *Rainbow*, illustrated page 21.

72.
Babe
Life-size; standing girl in tights and bodice, with hat.
PUBLISHED: Gregg, *Rainbow*, illustrated page 18.

73.
Beach
H. 9½" W. 13½"

EXHIBITED: Montross Gallery, 1922; AI of Chicago, 1923, number 15, GCAG, 1929.

PUBLISHED: Grand Central Art Galleries' Yearbook, 1929, illustrated; *Index*, 1936, page 347; *Antiques*, December 1954, illustrated page 456, advertisement.

74.
The City
H. 89" W. 52"

EXHIBITED: Pennsylvania Academy of the Fine Arts, Philadelphia, 16 April to 15 May 1921; AI of Chicago, 1923, number 13, illustrated page 1; GCAG, 1927, number 14, illustrated page 12; U of A, 1966, number 4, illustrated page 1; MWG, 1966, number 4, illustrated page 1.

PUBLISHED: Gregg, *Rainbow*, illustrated page 17; *Connoisseur*, April 1966, illustrated page LV, advertisement; Fridolf Johnson, "Walt Kuhn: American Master," *American Artist*, December 1967, illustrated page 52 (hereafter referred to as Johnson, *American Artist*).

Spier's suggested musical title: "Symphony for full orchestra."

75.
Study for the City
H. 32" W. 19"

COLLECTIONS: Mrs. S. L. Schlesinger, Metairie, Louisiana, 1967.

EXHIBITED: U of A, 1966, number 29, illustrated page 53.

76.
Entirely Surrounded by Indians
H. 16" W. 23" Signed lower left.

COLLECTIONS: John Quinn till 1927, purchased in 1920 for $625.00.

PUBLISHED: Gregg, *Rainbow*, illustrated page 22; John Quinn Sale, 1927, number 473; Reid, *The Man from New York*, page 467.

77.
Flowers
Vertical; spherical vase.

PUBLISHED: Gregg, *Rainbow*, illustrated page 14.

78.
Hunter's Cabin Painted from a train window.
H. 12" W. 14½" Signed and dated lower right.
COLLECTIONS: Mrs. Otto L. Spaeth, New York.
EXHIBITED: GCAG, 1927, number 21.

79.
Indian
Vertical, almost square; destroyed.

PUBLISHED: Gregg, *Rainbow*, illustrated page 20.

80.
Marionettes
H. 8" W. 10"

EXHIBITED: Marius de Zayas Gallery, 1920; Montross Gallery, 1922; AI of Chicago, 1923, number 13.

81.
The Prop Tent
Horizontal.
PUBLISHED: Gregg, *Rainbow*, illustrated page 14.

82.
Study of a Girl
H. 20" W. 16" Signed lower right.
COLLECTIONS: John Quinn till 1927.
PUBLISHED: Gregg, *Rainbow*, illustrated page 15; John Quinn Sale, 1927, number 331.

The model was Victoria Levant, who also posed for *Victoria* and *Woman in Shawl*.

83.
John Butler Yeats
H. 39¾" W. 29¾"

COLLECTIONS: John Quinn till 1927; Municipal Art Gallery, Dublin, gift of Mr. Cornelius O'Sullivan, 1927.

PUBLISHED: John Quinn Sale, 1927, number 262, illustrated; *Catalogue, Hugh Lane Municipal Art Gallery of Modern Art, Dublin*, 1928, number 128, illustrated plate 38.

John Butler Yeats was a painter himself, and the father of the poet William Butler Yeats and the painter Jack Butler Yeats.

1920

84.
Belle
H. 20" W. 16"
COLLECTIONS: Miss Lizzie P. Bliss, New York.

85.
Head of Woman
H. 12½" W. 17¾"

86.
Girl in Red Tights
H. 26" W. 9¼"

87.
Girl with Shawl
H. 30" W. 24" Signed and dated lower left.

COLLECTIONS: John Quinn till 1927; purchased by N. A. Fish from John Quinn Sale in 1927 for $80.00; Mrs. Emmy Lou Stein, New York.

PUBLISHED: John Quinn Sale, 1927, number 356.

The model was Victoria Levant, who also posed for *Victoria* and *Study of a Girl*.

88.
Glow
H. 16" W. 11" Signed lower left, W. Kuhn.
COLLECTIONS: John Quinn till 1927.
PUBLISHED: John Quinn Sale, 1927, number 467.

1921

89.
Battle of New Orleans
H. 34" W. 55" Signed and dated lower center.

EXHIBITED: GCAG, 1927, number 5; AI of Chicago, 1927, number 4; ACM, 1964, illustrated page 39; U of A, 1966, number 20.

90.
Brunette with Top Knot
H. 25" W. 15"   Destroyed in 1942.
EXHIBITED: Montross Gallery, 1925.

91.
Concert
H. 56" W. 24"   Birds, foliage, and blossoms against salmon background.
COLLECTIONS: C. C. Rumsey Estate

92.
Country Road
H. 11" W. 14"
EXHIBITED: Musée de Jeu de Paume, Paris, "Exhibition of American Art," 1924, organized by Marie Sterner.

93.
Flowers with Black Silhouette
H. 14" W. 22"
EXHIBITED: Montross Gallery, 1922; AI of Chicago, 1923, number 22; AI of Chicago, 1927.

94.
Flowers – Blue and Green
H. 12" W. 10"
COLLECTIONS: Miss Sally Lewis.
EXHIBITED: Montross Gallery, 1922.

95.
Flowers – Blue and Yellow
H. 8" W. 12"   Destroyed in 1936.
EXHIBITED: Montross Gallery, 1922 (*Flowers*).

96.
Flower Piece
H. 20" W. 14"
COLLECTIONS: Miss Lizzie P. Bliss, New York.
EXHIBITED: Montross Gallery, 1922; Museum of Modern Art, New York, "Memorial Exhibition, the Collection of the Late Miss Lizzie P. Bliss, Vice-President of the Museum, 17 May–27 September 1931." (The Museum of Modern Art hereafter will be referred to as MOMA, and this exhibition as the Lizzie P. Bliss Memorial Exhibition.)

97.
Flowers on Red Base
H. 9" W. 14¼"
EXHIBITED: Montross Gallery, 1922; AI of Chicago, 1923, number 19; GCAG, 1927, number 25; AI of Chicago, 1927, number 19.

98.
Flowers – Stars
H. 10" W. 8"
EXHIBITED: Montross Gallery, 1924; GCAG, 1927, number 26.

99.
Girl in White
H. 30" W. 25"
EXHIBITED: Downtown Gallery, 1929. (The Downtown Gallery hereafter will be referred to as DTG.)

100.
Girl in White Chemise
H. 30" W. 25"
COLLECTIONS: John Quinn till 1927; Mrs. John Ogg Ross, New York.
EXHIBITED: CAM, 1960, number 5, illustrated page 25 (ca. 1920); Nasson College, 1964, number 11; U of A, 1966, number 32, illustrated page 7; MWG, 1966, number 11.
PUBLISHED: "Catalogue of the John Quinn Collection of Paintings, Watercolors, Drawings, and Sculpture," Pigeon Hill Press, Huntington, New York, 1926, foreword by Forbes Watson, page 169; Johnson, *American Artist*, December 1967, illustrated page 52; B. L. Reid, *The Man from New York*, illustrated third plate after page 430.

101.
Head of a Young Girl
H. 13" W. 10"
EXHIBITED: "Spring Salon" in cooperation with American Museum of Natural History and Brooklyn Institute of Arts and Sciences, 21 May to 9 June 1923, illustrated; GCAG, 1927, number 33; AI of Chicago, 1927; Paris, "Salons of American Art," May 1933, illustrated.
PUBLISHED: *Index*, 1936, page 348.

102.
Interior (Brenda in Ogunquit)
H. 50" W 30"
EXHIBITED: GCAG, 1927, number 1; AI of Chicago, 1927, number 1; Memorial Art Gallery, Rochester, New York, 1930; Art Institute of Chicago, fall 1930; U of A, 1966, number 31, illustrated page 54.

103.
Intermezzo
Harlequin and Pierrot back to back; destroyed.
EXHIBITED: Montross Gallery, 1922; Sally Lewis' First Western Tour, 1922-23; AI of Chicago, 1923, number 11.

104.
Pom Poms
H. 21" W. 16"

105.
Prospectors
H. 50" W. 33"

106.
Study for Concert
H. 30" W. 25"

107.
Swan
H. 50" W. 30"

108.
Tea Party
H. 72″ W. 34″
EXHIBITED: U of A, 1966, number 34, illustrated page 56; MWG, 1966, number 8, illustrated page 3.
The models were Vera, for the upright figure, and Brenda Kuhn, for the lower figure.

1922

109.
Apples
H. 6¾″ W. 8⅛″   Oil on cardboard.
EXHIBITED: Montross Gallery, 1924.

110.
Blanche
H. 9″ W. 6″ approximately; destroyed.
EXHIBITED: Montross Gallery, 1924; AI of Chicago, 1923 (*Head of Woman*); Salley Lewis's Second Traveling Exhibition, 1924; GCAG, 1927, number 6 (*Young Woman*).

111.
Exotic Blossoms (Flowers – Exotic)
H.   W.
EXHIBITED: GCAG, 1927, number 20; AI of Chicago, 1927, number 20.
Spier's suggested musical title: "Violins divided."

112.
Flower Piece
H. 24″ W. 15″
COLLECTIONS. Dikran Kelekian, New York; Marie Harriman, New York.

113.
The Heroine
Vertical; bust.
PUBLISHED: *Vanity Fair*, November 1923, illustrated page 61, "From a Painting by Walt Kuhn."

114.
Girl with Cocked Hat (Girl in Rose and Black)
H. 20″ W. 15″
EXHIBITED: Montross Gallery, 1924; Chambre Syndicale de la Curiosité et des Beaux Arts, Paris, "Exhibition of American Art under Auspices of Art Patrons of America," July 1924, number 96, illustrated; Art Students' League, 1927; J. B. Neumann, New Art Circle, 1930.
PUBLISHED: *Arts*, August 1924, illustrated page 105; *Index*, 1936, page 348.

115.
Green and Russet Pears
H. 9″ W. 12″
EXHIBITED: Montross Gallery, 1929.

116.
Landscape with Cows
H. 11″ W. 16″   Signed lower right.

EXHIBITED: Montross Gallery, 1924; Sally Lewis's First Western Tour, 1922-23; U of A, 1966, number 23, illustrated page 55; MWG, 1966, number 6.

117.
Portrait
H. 24″ W. 16″
COLLECTIONS: California Palace of the Legion of Honor, San Francisco, California.
EXHIBITED: Montross Gallery, 1924; AI of Chicago, 1923, number 18; J. B. Neumann Gallery, 1925.

118.
Portrait
H. 20″ W. 16″   Signed lower left.
COLLECTIONS: John Quinn till 1927.
PUBLISHED: John Quinn Sale, 1927, number 483.

119.
Sleeping Girl
H. 53″ W. 42″
COLLECTIONS: Mr. Henry Strater.
EXHIBITED: Montross Gallery, 1924; AI of Chicago, 1923, number 9; Musée du Jeu de Paume, Paris, "Exhibition of American Art," 1924, organized by Marie Sterner; GCAG Traveling Exhibition, 1926; GCAG, 1927; CAM, "Annual Exhibition," 1928; CAM, "Painting 1900-1925," 2 February to 4 March 1951, illustrated; CAM, 1960, number 7.
PUBLISHED: *Chicago Herald Examiner*, 25 February 1923, illustrated; *Cincinnati Enquirer*, 1 July 1928, illustrated.

120.
Victoria
H. 30″ W. 17″
COLLECTIONS: Dikran Kelekian, New York, in exchange for *Head of a Woman* by Derain; Raphael Soyer, New York
EXHIBITED: DTG, 1929; Rains Gallery, New York, "Private Collection of Dikran Kelekian," 1935; Dikran Kelekian, Inc., "Artists of the Remote Past and Their Grandchildren," 1942, number 22.
PUBLISHED: Brown, *American Painting from the Armory Show to the Depression*, illustrated page 143.
The model was Victoria Levant, who also posed for *Woman in Shawl* and *Study of a Girl*.

121.
Woman in Black Hat (Girl in Black Hat)
H. 12″ W. 16″
EXHIBITED: GCAG, 1927, number 20.

1923

122.
Green Plums
H. 8″ W. 10″
COLLECTIONS: Mrs. E. H. Harriman, New York.
EXHIBITED: Montross Gallery, 1924; GCAG, 1927, number 27.

Spier's suggested musical title: "Polytonality." Spier, note to score, page 8: "Green Plums, on the contrary is a polytonal composition; conceived in two keys simultaneously. The effect is that of enhanced sonority, in harmony as we know it, traditionally."

123.

Maine

H. 30" W. 33" Destroyed; sketch retained — red barn with black fence in foreground.

124.

Portrait

H. 20" W. 32" Destroyed.

125.

Sma l Landscape

H. 12" W. 15"

EXHIBITED: Montross Gallery, 1924; GCAG, 1927; AI of Chicago, 1927.

126.

Surrounded by Indians

H. 16" W. 24" Signed lower left.

COLLECTIONS: John Quinn till 1927.

PUBLISHED: John Quinn Sale, 1927, number 473.

127.

Willow Tree and Cow

H. 30" W. 25" Signed and dated lower right.

EXHIBITED: U of A, 1966, number 35; MWG, 1966, number 7, illustrated page 4.

1924

128.

Adventure

H. 32" W. 36" Signed and dated lower left.

EXHIBITED: Montross Gallery, 1925; Whitney, "Abstract Painting in America," 1935.

129.

Americana

H. 48" W. 64" Destroyed by fire in 1929; repainted that year from the original oil sketch.

PUBLISHED: *Arts*, February 1925, illustrated page 111.

The model was a dancer from the Beaux Arts Café.

130.

Anemone

H. 24½" W. 13⅝"

131.

Angna Enters

H. 39" W. 24" Signed lower right.

EXHIBITED: GCAG, 1927, number 12; AI of Chicago, 1927, number 11; U of A, 1966, number 37, illustrated page 57.

PUBLISHED: *New York Sunday World*, 30 January 1927, illustrated.

Spier's suggested musical title: "Andante for flute and strings."

The model was the well-known "Dance Mime," artist, and writer.

132.

Angna Enters

H. 6" W. 5"

COLLECTIONS: Dr. B. D. Saklatwalla, Pittsburgh, Pannsylvania.

EXHIBITED: Carnegie Institute, Pittsburgh, Pennsylvania, "Paintings from the Collection of Dr. Saklatwalla," 1934.

PUBLISHED. Parke Bernet, "Modern Paintings from the Collection Formed by the Late Dr. B. D. Saklatwalla," 1 May 1946, number 1.

133.

Apples

H. 9" W. 15" Six red apples against white and blue-gray background.

EXHIBITED: GCAG, 1927, number 29; AI of Chicago, 1927.

134.

Ballet in Red and Yellow

H. 12" W. 15"

EXHIBITED: GCAG, 1927, number 23; AI of Chicago, 1927, number 17.

135.

Beach Scene

H. 12" W. 16"

EXHIBITED: GCAG, 1927, number 30; AI of Chicago, 1927.

136.

Beryl

H. 52" W. 42½" Signed lower right.

COLLECTIONS: Mrs. John Ogg Ross, New York.

EXHIBITED: J. B. Neumann's New Art Club, 1924; GCAG, 28 January to 15 February 1930, number 70, illustrated; U of A, 1966, number 38; MWG, 1966, number 9, illustrated page 6.

PUBLISHED: *Index*, 1936, page 348; *Apollo*, April 1966, illustrated page xliii, advertisement.

137.

Dancing Pears

H. 12" W. 15" Signed and dated lower right.

COLLECTIONS: Norton Gallery and School of Art, West Palm Beach, Florida, gift of the artist, October 1948.

EXHIBITED: Society of the Four Arts, Palm Beach, Florida. "From the Armory Show to the Present," 1950.

138.

Interior with Plant

H. 40" W. 24"

EXHIBITED: GCAG, 1927, number 31; AI of Chicago, 1927, number 23 (*Interior with Green Plant*); U of A, 1966, number 39.

139.

Nude

H. 38" W. 24"   Signed lower left.

COLLECTIONS: John Quinn till 1927

PUBLISHED: John Quinn Sale, 1927, number 121.

140.

The Rider

H. 50¼" W. 33½"   Signed lower left.

EXHIBITED: GCAG, 1927, number 10, illustrated page 11; AI of Chicago, 1927, number 9, illustrated page 10; U of A, 1966, number 9, illustrated page 10.

Spier's suggested musical title: "Male chorus; with suppressed power."

141.

Still Life with Wallpaper

H. 12" W. 8"

142.

Still Life in Wicker Basket

H. 12" W. 10"

EXHIBITED: GCAG, 1927, number 19 *(Still Life)*; AI of Chicago, 1927, number 29; Whitney, "Abstract Painting in America," 1935.

143.

Study for Sheba

H. 36" W. 16"   Oil on paper.

EXHIBITED: U of A, 1966, number 13 (ca. 1924); MWG, 1966, number 19, illustrated page 8 (H. 16" W. 13").

The painting *Sheba*, 1925, for which Spier suggested the musical title "Barcarolle" in the GCAG exhibition of 1927, number 13, was later destroyed. A wash drawing also survives: Kennedy Galleries, "Catalogue of Drawings and Watercolors by Walt Kuhn," 1968, number 3, H. 20" W. 11", signed and dated lower left.

144.

Tulip Buds

H. 10" W. 12"   Sometimes dated "between 1918 and 1925."

COLLECTIONS: Phillips Collection, Washington, D.C.

EXHIBITED: Phillips Memorial Gallery, Washington, D.C., 1944, number 14.

PUBLISHED: Duncan Phillips, *A Collection in the Making,* Phillips Publication no. 5, E. Weyhe, New York, 1926, illustrated plate 120; Duncan Phillips, *The Artist Sees Differently,* Phillips Publication no. 6, 1931, illustrated volume 2, plate 173, lower; *Index,* 1936, page 348; *Phillips Collection Catalogue,* Thames and Hudson, New York and London, 1952, page 59, illustrated page 182b.

145.

Vegetables

H. 12" W. 15"

EXHIBITED: GCAG, 1927, number 22; AI of Chicago, 1927, number 16.

146.

Woman Combing Her Hair   Prior to 1925.

Vertical.

EXHIBITED: Durand-Ruel Galleries, Paris, "Exposition Trinationale," 1925; London, Tri-National Exhibition of Art," October 1925; Wildenstein Galleries, New York, "Exhibition of Tri-National Art, French, British, American," 26 January–15 February 1926.

PUBLISHED: C. J. Bulliet, *Apples and Madonnas* (New York: Covici, Friede, 3d ed., 1933), page 224.

1925

147.

Angel

H. 40" W. 30"

COLLECTIONS: Miss Alice O'Brien

EXHIBITED: Marie Harriman Gallery (hereafter referred to as MHG), 1931.

148.

Girl with Blossoms

H.   W.

PUBLISHED: Blanche C. Mathias, *Chicago Evening Post,* 9 February 1926, illustrated.

149.

Girl with Dark Eyes

H. 12" W. 15"

EXHIBITED: GCAG, 1927, number 37; AI of Chicago, 1927, number 28; DTG, 1928.

PUBLISHED: *Creative Arts,* February 1938, illustrated page XXVI *(Girl with the Dark Eyes)*.

150.

Hare

H. 38½" W. 22"

COLLECTIONS: Miss Lizzie P. Bliss, New York.

EXHIBITED: GCAG, 1927, number 17; MOMA, "Lizzie P. Bliss Memorial Exhibition," 1931, illustrated plate 90.

PUBLISHED: *Index,* 1936, page 348.

151.

Plant Forms

H. 30" W. 30"

EXHIBITED: Montross Gallery, 1925.

152.

Plant Forms

H. 14" W. 11"

EXHIBITED: Whitney, "Abstract Painting in America," 1935.

153.

Portrait of a Dog

H. 8¾" W. 11"

COLLECTIONS: Dikran Kelekian, New York.

EXHIBITED: Rains Gallery, New York, "Private Collection of Dikran Kelekian," 1935.

154.

Reclining Figure

Square

PUBLISHED: *Chicago Evening Post*, "Magazine of the Art World," Blanche C. Mathias, 29 February 1926, illustrated.

155.

Reclining Nude

H. 12" W. 20" Signed lower right "Walt Kuhn," lower center left, "Walt Kuhn, Paris, 1925."

EXHIBITED: KG, "Walt Kuhn," 1–18 March 1972, number 26, illustrated.

156.

Sheba

H. 68" W. 28" Destroyed; at least two studies, one oil on paper and another a wash drawing, survive.

EXHIBITED: GCAG, 1927, number 13.

Spier's suggested musical title: "Barcarolle."

157.

Still Life

H. 12" W. 16" Signed lower right.

PUBLISHED: Sotheby Parke Bernet, "Very Old American and Other Paintings, Drawings, and a Group of Marine Paintings," 30 April 1969, number 319, illustrated.

158

Still Life, Ducks (Ducks)

H. 33" W.24" Signed and dated lower right.

COLLECTIONS: Miss Lizzie P. Bliss, New York, till 1931; Addison Gallery of American Art, Andover, Massachusetts, Bequest of Miss Lizzie P. Bliss.

EXHIBITED: GCAG, 1927, number 2, illustrated page 18 (*Ducks*); Columbus Gallery of Fine Arts, Ohio, "Paintings by Walt Kuhn," 3 April to 4 May 1942, number 1 (the Columbus Gallery of Fine Arts hereafter will be referred to as CGFA).

159.

Study for "Mrs. C."

H. 14" W. 10"

EXHIBITED: U of A, 1966, number 41; MWG, 1966, number 10.

160.

Study for "Mrs. C."

H. 15" W. 18" Oil on paper.

EXHIBITED: U of A, 1966, number 42.

161.

Study for Superba

H. 36½" W. 18"

EXHIBITED: U of A, 1966, number 43; MWG, 1966, number 15.

162.

Young Woman
H. 24" W. 20" Destroyed in 1946

EXHIBITED: GCAG,1927,number 6; AI of Chicago, 1927, number 5; Whitney Studio Gallery, New York, 1927; DTG, 1928; CAM, "Annual Exhibition," 1928; Durand-Ruel, New York, 1944, number 2.

The model was Reland Gray, a dancing teacher.

1926

163.

Amalgam

H. 60" W. 40" Signed lower left.

EXHIBITED: GCAG, 1972, number 11, illustrated page 22; AI of Chicago, 1927, number 10.

The model was Reland Grey. A horizontal watercolor study of the head and headdress survives, titled *Arbitra,* Kennedy Galleries, "Catalogue of Drawings and Watercolors by Walt Kuhn," 1968, number 5, H. 12½," W. 21", signed and dated twice lower left, number 5, illustrated page 7.

Spier's suggested musical title: "Atonality in Brass." Spier also suggests a score for the painting on page 8 of the GCAG catalogue.

164.

Bareback Rider

H. 40" W. 30" Signed lower left.

COLLECTIONS: Dr. B. D. Saklatwalla, Pittsburgh, Pennsylvania, till 1946; Shelburne Museum, Vermont; Edith Gregor Halpert, New York, till 1973.

EXHIBITED: MOMA, "Paintings by Nineteen Living Americans," 13 December 1929 to 12 January 1930, number 47; Carnegie Institute of Technology, Pittsburgh, Pennsylvania, 1934; DTG, "New Acquisitions," 1959–60; Dallas Museum of Fine Arts, Dallas, Texas, "Collector's Choice," November–December 1961, illustrated; DTG, "36th Annual Spring Exhibition, The Figure," 1962; Dallas Museum for Contemporary Arts, Dallas, Texas, "Arts of the Circus," 1962; DTG,"Survey of American Art," 1965; U of A, 1966, number 46, illustrated page 45; DTG, "41st Anniversary Exhibition," 1966; National Collection of Fine Arts, Washington, D.C.,"Opening Exhibition," 1968; DTG, "The Performing Arts," 1969; National Collection of Fine Arts, Washington, D.C.,"Edith Gregor Halpert Memorial Exhibition," 1972, number 11.

PUBLISHED: *Carnegie Magazine*, Pittsburgh, Pennsylvania, April 1934, illustrated page 5; Paul Bird, *50 Paintings by Walt Kuhn* (New York and London: Studio Publications, 1940), number 1, illustrated; Parke Bernet, "Modern Paintings from the Collection Formed by the Late Dr. B.D. Saklatwalla," 1 May 1946, number 70, illustrated; Sotheby Parke Bernet, "20th Century American Paintings and Sculpture, Edith Gregor Halpert," 14–15 March 1973, number 86, illustrated in color.

165.

Blond

H. 9" W. 6" Destroyed.

EXHIBITED: GCAG, 1927, number 32.

166.

Clown

H. 15" W. 12"

COLLECTIONS: Miss Lizzie P. Bliss, New York; Mrs. John Parkinson, Jr.

EXHIBITED: GCAG,1927, number 18; MOMA, "Lizzie P. Bliss Memorial Exhibition," 1931, illustrated plate 88.

PUBLISHED: *Index*, 1936, page 348.

167.

Dressing Room

H. 44½" W. 33¹/₁₆"

COLLECTIONS: Brooklyn Museum, Brooklyn, New York, Gift of Friends of the Museum.

EXHIBITED: GCAG, 1927, number 15; AI of Chicago, 1927, number 14; DTG, 1929; CGFA, "Paintings by Walt Kuhn," 1942, number 2; U of A, 1966, number 15.

PUBLISHED: John I. H. Baur, "Modern American Painting," *Brooklyn Museum Quarterly,* January 1936, illustrated page 15, detail of head on cover; *Index,* 1936, page 348.

Spier's suggested musical title: "Orchestra for a ballet, A major, Allegretto."

168.

Girl with Blossoms

Vertical.

PUBLISHED: *Chicago Evening Post,* "Magazine of the Art World," Blanche C. Mathias, 29 February 1926, illustrated.

169.

Hare and Hunting Boots

H. 29" W. 27"   Signed and dated lower left.

COLLECTIONS: W. Averell Harriman, New York, 1960; National Gallery of Art, Washington, D.C., Gift of the W. Averell Harriman Foundation in Memory of Marie N. Harriman.

EXHIBITED: MHG, New York, "Exhibition of Paintings by Walt Kuhn," 1 to 26 November 1930, illustrated; Albany Institute of History and Art, New York, "Walt Kuhn," 11 June to 6 July 1958, number 1 (hereafter referred to as Albany, 1958); CAM, 1960, number 38, illustrated page 29; National Gallery of Art, Washington, D.C., "Exhibition of the Marie and Averell Harriman Collection," 15 April to 14 May 1961, illustrated page 42 (hereafter referred to as National Gallery, "Harriman Collection," 1961); U of A, 1966, number 49.

PUBLISHED: *Studio News,* December 1930, illustrated page 1; *Index,* 1936, page 348; *50 Paintings by Walt Kuhn,* 1940, number 2, illustrated; *Art Quarterly,* summer 1959, illustrated page 19; National Gallery of Art Annual Report, 1972, number 2601.

170.

Landscape

H.   W.

EXHIBITED: GCAG, 1927, number 9; AI of Chicago, 1927, number 8.

171.

Mallards

H. 32¼" W. 24¼"   Signed and dated lower right.

COLLECTIONS: The Detroit Institute of Arts, accessions number 44.63.

EXHIBITED: MHG, "Exhibition of Paintings by Walt Kuhn," 1930, illustrated; MHG, "Summer Show," 1931; Art Students' League, 1931; Fogg Art Museum, Harvard University, Cambridge, Massachusetts, "Still Life," 1931; CGFA, 1935; Dayton Art Institute, 1935 (hereafter referred to as Dayton AI); City Art Museum, Saint Louis, Missouri (hereafter referred to as CAM, Saint Louis), 1933; Willard Straight Hall, Cornell University, Ithaca, New York, "Ten Paintings by Walt Kuhn," 2 February to 1 March 1942, number 1 (hereafter referred to as Cornell U); CAM, 1960, number 37; U of A, 1966, number 48.

PUBLISHED: *Art Digest,* 15 April 1931, illustrated page 6; *Index,* 1936, page 348; *50 Paintings by Walt Kuhn,* number 3, illustrated.

172.

Maternity

H. 30" W. 40"   Signed lower right, dated lower left. Bitch seated on haunches.

EXHIBITED: GCAG, 1927, number 4, illustrated page 14; AI of Chicago, 1927, number 3; Henry Art Gallery, University of Washington, Seattle, Washington, 1929; California Palace of the Legion of Honor, San Francisco, California, 1930.

173.

Pears in Blue Wicker Basket

H. 8" W. 10"

174.

Pine Tree (Maine Pine)

H.   W.   Signed and dated lower center. Road to Robert Laurent's house, Cape Neddick, Maine.

COLLECTIONS: Miss Lizzie P. Bliss, 1928; exchanged for *Athlete* by Mrs. Elizabeth Bliss Parkinson, New York, 1928.

EXHIBITED: GCAG, 1927, number 36; AI of Chicago, 1927, number 27; Montross Gallery, 1928; MOMA, "Lizzie P. Bliss Memorial Exhibition," 1931; William Rockhill Nelson Gallery of Art and Atkins Museum of Fine Arts, Kansas City, Missouri, 1934 (hereafter referred to as Nelson, Kansas City); CGFA, 1935; Dayton AI, 1935.

PUBLISHED: *Art Journal,* Spring 1967, illustrated page 307.

Spier's suggested musical title "Gongs and bells."

175.

Portrait (Head of Woman)

H. 12½" W. 17¾"

XHIBITED: GCAG, 1927, number 16; AI of Chicago, 1927, number 15.

176.

Singing Tree

H. 30" W. 40"   Destroyed.

EXHIBITED: GCAG, 1927, number 35; AI of Chicago, 1927, number 26.

Spier's suggested musical title: "Folk song for contralto voice, unaccompanied."

177.

Still Life

H.   W.

EXHIBITED: GCAG, 1927, number 19; AI of Chicago, 1927, number 29.

178.

Study for Bareback Rider

H. 36½" W. 25"   Oil on paper.

COLLECTIONS: Senator William Benton, 1966.

EXHIBITED: U of A, 1966, number 45; MWG, 1966, number 12, illustrated page 5.

179.

Study for Flowers

H. 19" W. 31"   Oil on cotton.

COLLECTIONS: John Quinn, not in sale.

Never exhibited.

180.

Superba

H. 39" W. 25"   Signed and dated lower left.

EXHIBITED: GCAG, 1927, number 3, illustrated page 20; AI of Chicago, 1927, number 2, illustrated page 10; Wanamaker's "Decorative Exhibition," directed by Louis Bouché, 1927; The Detroit Institute of Arts, 1928; Philadelphia Museum of Art, "Radical Independents' Exhibition," 1929; U of A, 1966, number 44, illustrated page 58 (dated 1925).

Spier's suggested musical title: "Organ prelude, full organ."

181.

Vase (Woman in Tights)

H. 72" W. 33"   Destroyed.

182.

Woman Combing Her Hair

H.   W.

EXHIBITED: GCAG, 1927, number 8; AI of Chicago, 1927, number 7.

Prior to 1927

183.

Apples

H.   W.

EXHIBITED: GCAG, 1927, number 30; AI of Chicago, number 21.

184.

Beach Scene

H.   W.

EXHIBITED: GCAG, 1927, number 30; AI of Chicago, 1927, number 22.

185.

Head of Young Girl

H.   W.

EXHIBITED: GCAG, 1927, number 33; AI of Chicago, 1927, number 24.

186.

Pears

H.   W.

EXHIBITED: GCAG, 1927, number 34; AI of Chicago, 1927, number 25.

187.

Riders Waiting

H.   W.

EXHIBITED: GCAG, 1927, number 24; AI of Chicago, 1927, number 18.

1927

188.

Acrobat in Green

H. 40" W. 30"   Signed and dated lower right.

COLLECTIONS: Addison Gallery of American Art, Andover, Massachusetts.

EXHIBITED: MHG, "Exhibition of Paintings by Walt Kuhn," 1932, number 3; Museum of Fine Arts, Boston, "Society of Contemporary Art Exhibition," 1932; Lyman Allyn Museum, New London, Connecticut, "American Paintings," 1934; Wadsworth Atheneum, Hartford, Connecticut, "American Painting and Sculpture from the 18th Century to the Present Day," 1934; CGFA, "Paintings by Walt Kuhn," 1942, number 3.

PUBLISHED: Alan Burroughs, *Limners and Likenesses* (Cambridge, Massachusetts: Harvard University Press, 1936), illustrated figure 182, page 182; *Boston Herald*, 30 August 1931, illustrated; *Hartford Times*, Connecticut, 1 March 1934, illustrated; *Index*, 1936, page 347; Brown, *American Painting from the Armory Show to the Depression*, illustrated page 144.

The model was Arthur Chester. A fully developed watercolor of this painting, called *Tumbler*, exists.

189.

Mrs. Edward H. Asherman

H. 15" W. 12"   Destroyed.

"Never finished as model failed to keep appointments."

190.

Athene

H. 12" W. 25"

COLLECTIONS: Private Collection, New York.

EXHIBITED: DTG, 1928; MOMA, "Paintings by Nineteen Living Americans," 1929-30, number 48.

The model was Athene Taylor.

191.

Babe

H.   W.

Never exhibited.

192.

Bedouin

H. 15" W. 12"

COLLECTIONS: Mr. Thomas Hitchcock, Jr.

EXHIBITED: Montross Gallery, 1929.

193.

Elise

H. 14" W. 20"

Never exhibited.

The model was Elise Cavanaugh, actress.

251

194.

Girl with Black Hat

H. 18" W. 12"

EXHIBITED: GCAG, "Exhibition of Paintings and Sculpture by Artist Members of the Galleries," 1927, number 32.

PUBLISHED: GCAG, *Yearbook*, 1927; *Index*, 1936, page 348.

195.

Girl in Gray Furs

H. 16" W. 20"   Signed lower left.

COLLECTIONS: Mrs. Elizabeth Bliss Parkinson, New York.

EXHIBITED: MHG, 1932, number 1, illustrated.

PUBLISHED: *Cincinnati Enquirer*, 17 January 1932, illustrated; *Index*, 1936, page 348.

The model was Virginia Swan, a student.

196.

Girl from Maine

H. 12" W. 15"

EXHIBITED: GCAG, "Founders Exhibition," 1928, number 29, illustrated.

PUBLISHED: GCAG, *Yearbook*, 1928, illustrated page 38; *Index*, 1937, page 348.

The model was a local waitress.

197.

Head of Mary

H. 12" W. 10"   Destroyed in 1942.

198.

Mary

H. 15" W. 12"

199.

Mary with Red Bandana

H. 15" W. 12"   Signed lower right.

COLLECTIONS: Mrs. Edward Jordan, New York; Mrs. William H. Bender, Bronxville, New York.

EXHIBITED: Gallery of Living Art, Washington Square Campus, New York University, 1927-28; Cleveland Museum of Art, Cleveland, Ohio, 1928; DTG, 1928; DTG, April 1929, "Walt Kuhn Retrospective," illustrated.

PUBLISHED: *World*, New York, 28 April 1927; *New York Sun*, 28 April 1927; *50 Paintings by Walt Kuhn*, number 4, illustrated; *Art Digest*, June 1955, illustrated page 29; Sotheby Parke Bernet, "20th Century American Painters," 13 December 1973, number 77, illustrated; Sotheby Parke Bernet, "American 19th & 20th Century Paintings, Drawings, Watercolors & Sculpture," 27 October 1977, number 198, illustrated.

200.

Muriel

H. 24" W. 12"

Never exhibited.

"Unfinished due to model's failure to show up." The model was Muriel King, friend of Louis Bouché.

201.

Portrait of Brenda

H. 15" W. 12"   Signed lower left.

EXHIBITED: Beaux Arts Galerie, San Francisco, California, 1928; CAM, 1960, number 39, illustrated page 30; Nasson College, 1964, number 13; U of A, 1966, number 50, illustrated page 60 *(Brenda)*.

PUBLISHED: *San Francisco Chronicle*, 16 August 1928, illustrated.

202.

Reland (Head of Woman with Fur Collar)

H. 15" W. 12"   Destroyed.

203.

Ruth with Blue and White Headcloth

H. 15" W. 12"

The model was Ruth Lloyd-Jones, local waitress.

204.

Ruth with Green Headcloth

H. 12" W. 15"

EXHIBITED: DTG, 1928.

The model was Ruth Lloyd-Jones.

205.

Ruth with Hanging Hair

H. 12" W. 15"

The model was Ruth Lloyd-Jones.

206.

Ruth in Red Dress

H. 15" W. 12"   Destroyed.

207.

Ruth with Red Bandana

H. 15" W. 12"   Destroyed.

208.

Tan Dress

H. 12" W. 15"   Destroyed in 1942.

EXHIBITED: DTG, 1928.

209.

Head of Virginia

H. 13" W. 11"

The model was Virginia Swan.

1928

210.

Builders   Painted in Prescott, Arizona.

H. 16" W. 20"   Destroyed.

EXHIBITED: DTG, 1929; GCAG, 1929.

211.

Blond in Flowered Kimono

H. 24" W. 20"

212.

Dorothy (Flapper)

H. 30" W. 25"   Destroyed.

COLLECTIONS: John D. Rockefeller, Jr.

EXHIBITED: DTG, 1929; Dwight Art Museum, Mount Holyoke College, Holyoke, Massachusetts, 1933.

PUBLISHED: *Arts*, May 1929, illustrated page 324; Edward Alden Jewell, *Americans* (New York: Alfred M. Knopf, 1930), illustrated plate 50; *Index*, 1936, page 348.

213.
Dry Riverbed
H. 16" W. 20"

214.
Eva
H. 8" W. 11"
EXHIBITED: DTG, 1929.
The model was Eva Ball.

215.
Eva B.
H. 11" W. 8"   Signed and dated lower right.
COLLECTIONS: Harold B. Van Fossen, Abingdon, Pennsylvania.
PUBLISHED: Sotheby Parke Bernet, "20th Century American Paintings," 13 December 1973, number 116, illustrated.

216.
Girl with Hair Down
Vertical
EXHIBITED: CAM, "Annual Exhibition," 1929.

217.
Girl with Mirror
H. 24" W. 20"   Signed and dated lower right.
COLLECTION: Phillips Collection, Washington, D.C.
EXHIBITED: DTG, 1929; MHG, 1932, illustrated; Art Institute of Chicago, "A Century of Progress — Exhibition of Paintings and Sculpture," 1 June to 1 November 1933, number 586; Phillips Memorial Gallery, Washington, D.C., "Walt Kuhn — Karl Knaths," 27 February to 27 March 1944, number 15.
PUBLISHED: *Art and Understanding* (Washington, D.C.: Phillips Memorial Gallery Publication, 1929), vol. 1, no. 1, illustrated; Duncan Phillips, *The Artist Sees Differently* (New York: E. Weyhe, 1931), Phillips Publication, no. 6, illustrated volume 2 plate 184; *New York Times*, 10 January 1932, illustrated; *Fine Arts*, June 1933, illustrated page 44; *Index*, 1936, page 348; *Phillips Collection Catalogue* (New York and London: Thames and Hudson, 1952), page 59.

218.
Janice
H. 8" W. 12"
COLLECTIONS: Arthur Brisbane
EXHIBITED: DTG, 1929.

219.
Jeannette
H. 30" W. 25"   Signed and dated lower right.
COLLECTIONS: Miss Lizzie P. Bliss, New York; Museum of Modern Art, New York, Bequest of Miss Lillie P. Bliss.

EXHIBITED: DTG, 1929; MOMA, 1929-30, "Paintings by Nineteen Living Americans," number 49, illustrated page 44; MOMA, "Lizzie P. Bliss Memorial Exhibition," 1931, number 91, illustrated; MOMA, "The Lillie P. Bliss Collection, 1934," number 42, illustrated; Albany, 1958, number 2; U of A, 1966, number 51, illustrated page 61.

PUBLISHED: *Index*, 1936, page 348; *50 Paintings by Walt Kuhn*, number 5, illustrated.

The model was Jeannette Reichstatter.

220.
Landscape with Mountains and Boulders   Painted in Prescott, Arizona.
H. 12½" W. 17¾"   Signed and dated lower right.

221.
Margaret   Painted in California.
H. 40" W. 30"
EXHIBITED: MHG, 1930, number 11; The Detroit Institute of Arts, "17th Anniversary Exhibition," 1931; CAM, Saint Louis, 1933; Nelson, Kansas City, 1934; CGFA, 1935; Dayton AI, 1935.
The model was Margaret Nichol, dancer.

222.
Mountain Rabbits   Painted in Prescott, Arizona.
H. 16" W. 20"
COLLECTIONS: Amon Carter Museum of Western Art, Fort Worth, Texas, 1966.
EXHIBITED: MHG, 1930, number 18; CAM, Saint Louis, 1933; Nelson, Kansas City, 1934; CGFA, 1935; Dayton AI, 1935.

223.
Pierrette
H. 15" W. 12"
EXHIBITED: Montross Gallery, 1929.

224.
Portrait of Janice
H.   W.
EXHIBITED: DTG, 1928, illustrated.

225.
Rock with Trees   Painted in Prescott, Arizona.
H. 12" W. 15"

226.
Rocks, Arizona
H. 25" W. 30"   Destroyed by fire in railroad wreck, 1929.
EXHIBITED: DTG, 1929; Cleveland Museum of Art, 1929.

227.
Rocks with Trees, Arizona (Trees with Boulders)
H. 12½" W. 16"
EXHIBITED: MWG, "An Exhibition of Landscape Paintings by Walt Kuhn," 18 November to 7 December 1957, number 9.

228.
Rosalie
H. 10" W. 8"

229.
Russian
H. 20" W. 16"   Destroyed

230.
Thumb Butte   Painted in Arizona
H. 25" W. 30"   Destroyed in January 1934.
EXHIBITED: MHG, 1930.

231.
Trees.
H. 25" W. 30"
EXHIBITED: DTG, "Walt Kuhn Loan Exhibition," 1929,

232.
Tulip
H. 20" W. 16"
PUBLISHED: *Social Calendar,* 3 November 1930, illustrated page 8; *Index,* 1936, page 348.
The model was Martha Marsh.

1929

233.
Apples in a White Bowl
H. 15" W. 20"   Signed and dated lower left.
COLLECTIONS: Sloan Galleries of American Painting, Valparaiso University, Valparaiso, Indiana, purchased 7 June 1965.
EXHIBITED: U of A, 1966, number 54.

234.
Athlete
H. 20" W. 24"   Signed and dated center left.
COLLECTIONS: Given to Mrs. John Parkinson, Jr.; Jewett Art Museum, Wellesley College, Wellesley, Massachusetts.
EXHIBITED: MHG, 1932, number 5, illustrated; Phillips Memorial Gallery, Washington, D.C., 1932; CAM, 1933; CAM, Saint Louis, 1960, number 42.
PUBLISHED: *Critic,* December 1934, illustrated; *Parnassus,* January 1932, page 8; *Index,* 1936, page 348; *50 Paintings by Walt Kuhn,* number 6, illustrated.
The model was Herbert (Teddy) Bergman, actor at the Grove Street Theatre, who later took the professional name of Alan Reed for movies and television.

235.
Black Pine
H.   W.   Signed and dated lower left.
COLLECTIONS: Bliss Estate.
EXHIBITED: MHG, 1930, number 24, illustrated.
PUBLISHED: *Index,* 1936, page 438.

236.
Blonde in Flowered Kimono
H. 24" W. 20"

A watercolor study, fully developed, of 1928 survives; H. 20" W. 14½".

237.
Cleft Rocks
H. 16" W. 20"
EXHIBITED: MHG, 1930, number 23, MHG, 1931.

238.
Cuban (Bust Portrait of a Woman)
H. 25" W. 30"   Signed and dated upper right.
EXHIBITED: DTG, 1929; Municipal Art Gallery, Atlantic City, New Jersey, number 36, illustrated; Art Institute of Chicago, "42nd Annual Exhibition of American Painting and Sculpture," 1929.
PUBLISHED: *New York Evening Post,* 27 July 1929, illustrated; *Index,* 1936, page 348.

239.
Electra
H. 40" W. 30"   Signed and dated lower right.
COLLECTIONS: Private collection, New York.
EXHIBITED: MOMA, "Paintings by Neneteen Living Americans," 1929-30, number 51; MHG, 1930, number 5.
PUBLISHED: *Index,* 1936, page 348; *50 Paintings by Walt Kuhn,* number 7, illustrated.

240.
Helen
H. 40" W. 30"
EXHIBITED: MHG, 1930, number 7.
The model was Helen Miller, burlesque girl.

241.
Helen Miller of Boston
H. 30" W. 25"
EXHIBITED: MHG, 1930, number 13.

242.
High School Rider
H. 40" W. 30"   Signed lower left.
EXHIBITED: MHG, 1930, number 15, illustrated; CGFA, 1935; Dayton AI, 1935; Colorado Springs Fine Arts Center (hereafter CSFAC) Traveling Show, 1947, illustrated page 7, shown in CSFAC; San Francisco Museum of Art; Santa Barbara Museum of Art; Los Angeles County Museum of Science, History, and Art; Joslyn Memorial, Omaha, Nebraska; Museum of Cranbrook Academy of Art, Bloomfield Hills, Michigan.
PUBLISHED: *Index,* 1936, page 348; *50 Paintings by Walt Kuhn,* number 9, illustrated.

243.
Nell
H. 20" W. 17"
COLLECTIONS: Hamilton Easter Field Foundation; permanently exhibited at the Barn Gallery, Ogunquit, Maine.
EXHIBITED: DTG, "Hamilton Easter Field Collection Exhibition," sponsored by the College Art Association, 1934, shown at the University of Kentucky,

Lexington, November 1934; Art Institute of Chicago, December 1934 to January 1935; Broadmoor Art Academy, Colorado Springs, Colorado, 1935; Toledo Museum of Art, Ohio, 1935; Richmond, Virginia, 1935; Museum of Fine Arts, Springfield, Massachusetts, 1935; Denver Art Museum, Colorado, 1935; Seattle Art Museum, Washington, December 1935 to January 1936.

PUBLISHED: *New York Times*, 7 October 1934, illustrated; *New York Post*, 6 October 1934, illustrated.

The model was Nellie Gray, actress.

244.
Oak in September
H. 25″ W. 30″

EXHIBITED: MHG, 1930, number 21; Durand-Ruel, New York, 1944, number 10.

245.
Performer Resting
H. 24″ W. 20″   Signed and dated lower right.

COLLECTIONS: Phillips Collection, Washington, D.C.

EXHIBITED: MHG, 1932, number 4, illustrated; Phillips Memorial Gallery, Washington, D.C., 1932; Newhouse Gallery, New York, 1932.

PUBLISHED: *Art and Understanding*, Phillips Memorial Art Gallery Publication, Washington, D.C., November 1929, illustrated page 68; Duncan Phillips, *The Artist Sees Differently*, Phillips Publication no. 6, 1931, illustrated volume 2, plate 185; *Index*, 1936, page 348; E. Weyhe, New York; *Phillips Collection Catalogue*, (New York and London: Thames and Hudson, 1952), page 59.

The model was Herbert (Teddy) Bergman.

246.
Pine on a Knoll
H. 25″ W. 30″   Signed lower left.

COLLECTIONS: W. Averell Harriman, New York.

EXHIBITED: MHG, 1930, number 19; CAM, Saint Louis, 1933; Albany, 1958, number 3; CAM, 1960, number 41, illustrated page 40; national Gallery, "Harriman Collection," 1961, illustrated page 43; U of A, 1966, number 52, illustrated page 109.

247
Rocky Hollow   Painted in Maine.
H. 30″ W. 40″

248
Trees on a Ridge
H. 25″ W. 30″

COLLECTIONS: Mrs. John S. Pratt

EXHIBITED: MHG, 1930; MHG, 1937.

249.
The White Clown
H. 40″ W. 30″   Signed and dated lower center.

COLLECTIONS: W. Averell Harriman, New York, 1957, purchased 11 June; National Gallery of Art, Washington, D.C., Gift of the W. Averell Harriman Foundation in Memory of Marie N. Harriman.

EXHIBITED: MOMA, "Paintings by Nineteen Living Americans," 13 December 1929 to 12 January 1930, number 50, illustrated page 47 (Private Collection, New York); MHG, 1930, number 1, illustrated; MOMA, "Travelling Exhibition of Clowns," 1953 to 1955; Albany, 1958, number 4, illustrated on cover; Solinski Park, Moscow, "American National Exhibition," 25 July to 5 September 1959; CAM, 1960, number 40, illustrated in color page 6; National Gallery, "Harriman Collection," 1961, illustrated page 45; U of A, 1966, number 53, illustrated pages 62 and 108.

PUBLISHED: *Parnassus*, December 1929, illustrated on cover; *Theatre Guild Magazine*, February 1930, illustrated as frontispiece; Samuel Kootz, *Modern American Painters* (New York: Brewer and Warren, 1930), illustrated plate 31; M. Rose Collins and Olive L. Riley, *Art Appreciation* (New York: Harcourt Brace and Co., 1931), illustrated number 150, page 126; Sheldon Cheney, *A Primer of Modern Art* (New York: Liveright, 1932 edition), illustrated page 236; *Index*, 1936, page 348; Forbes Watson, *American Painting Today* (Washington, D.C.: American Federation of Art, 1939), illustrated page 87; *50 Paintings by Walt Kuhn*, number 8, illustrated; *Art Digest*, June 1941, illustrated page 11; *New York Times*, "Art Masterpiece Goes to Harriman," Sanka Knox, 22 August 1957, illustrated; *El Mercado de Arts*, "Un Payaso Muy Costos—el Godernador de Nueva York Paga $25,000 por un Cuadro." illustrated in color, 1958; *Life Magazine*, 3 February 1958, illustrated; *Art in America*, Summer 1959, illustrated page 93; *College Art Journal*, Summer 1959, illustrated page 293; *Christian Science Monitor*, August 1959, illustrated; Fridolf Johnson, *American Artist*, February 1967, illustrated in color page 53; National Gallery of Art, Washington, D.C., Annual Report, 1972, number 2602, illustrated page 35; Eloise Spaeth, *American Art Museum* (New York: Harper and Row, 1975, 3d ed.), page 88, illustrated.

The model was Herbert (Teddy) Bergman.

250.
Woman in Red Cloak
H. 24″ W. 20″   Destroyed in January 1946.
The model was Martha Marsh.

251.
Woman with Black Necklace
H. 30″ W. 25″

PUBLISHED: Samuel Kootz, *Modern American Painters* (New York: Brewer & Warren, 1930), illustrated plate 30; *Index*, 1936, page 348.

252.
Yellow and White Flowers
H. 15″ W. 12″

253.
Young Pines among Rocks
H. 25″ W. 30″

EXHIBITED: MHG, 1930, number 20; Cleveland Museum of Art, 1931; MHG, 1932.

1930

254.

Acrobat with Cigarette

H. 24″ W. 20″   Signed and dated right center.

COLLECTIONS: Fayez Sarofim, New York, purchased 26 May 1967.

EXHIBITED: MHG, 1930, number 12, illustrated; MHG, 1932; CAM, Saint Louis, 1933; CGFA, 1935; Dayton AI, 1935; CAM, 1960, number 45; Nasson College, 1964, number 2.

PUBLISHED: *Creative Arts*, November 1931, illustrated page 393; *Formes*, January 1932, illustrated figure 7, between pages 200-201; Columbus, Ohio, *Citizen*, 24 April 1935, illustrated; *Index*, 1936, page 347; *50 Paintings by Walt Kuhn*, number 13, illustrated.

The model was Albert Driscoll.

255.

Anne

H. 30″ W. 25″   Signed and dated lower left.

COLLECTIONS: Mrs. Percy Uris, New York, 1964.

EXHIBITED: MHG, 1930, number 10, illustrated; CAM, Saint Louis, 1933; CSFAC Traveling Show, 1940, number 2; Cornell U, 1942.

PUBLISHED: *Arts*, November 1930, illustrated in advertisement page 29; *New York Herald Tribune*, 9 November 1930, illustrated.

The model was Anne Stockton.

256.

Blanche with Cocked Hat

H. 24″ W. 20″   Destroyed.

EXHIBITED: MHG, 1932.

257.

Clown with Black Wig

H. 40″ W. 30″   Signed and dated lower left.

COLLECTIONS: Metropolitan Museum of Art, New York, George A. Hearn Fund, 1956.

EXHIBITED: MHG, 1930; Anderson galleries, American Art Association, "Salons of American Art," 1930, illustrated; Phillips Memorial Gallery, Washington, D.C., 1931; Pennsylvania Museum of Art, Philadelphia, 1931; CAM, Saint Louis, 1933; CAM, 1960, number 43, illustrated page 41; U of A, 1966, number 57, illustrated page 63.

PUBLISHED: *Social Calendar*, 8 April 1930, illustrated; *Index*, 1936, page 348; *50 Paintings by Walt Kuhn*, number 11, illustrated; *Metropolitan Museum of Art Bulletin*, October 1956, illustrated page 43; *Arts*, May 1957, illustrated page 13; *Apollo*, December 1957, illustrated page 194; *Metropolitan Museum of Art Bulletin*, N.S. July 1957, illustrated page 24; David W. Scott, *Britannica Encyclopedia of American Art*, (New York: Chanticleer Press, 1973), illustrated figure 3, page 326.

The model was Albert Driscoll. A fully developed watercolor exists.

258.

Dreaming Girl

H. 20″ W. 16″   Signed and dated upper right.

EXHIBITED: MHG, 1930, number 9, illustrated; Studio Club, Phillips Memorial Gallery, Washington, D.C., 1932; CAM, Saint Louis, 1933; CGFA, 1935; Dayton AI, 1935.

PUBLISHED: *Creative Arts*, November 1931, illustrated page Sup. 59, advertisement; *Index*, 1936, page 348. The model was Lil Liandre.

259.

Dreaming Girl

H. 12″ W. 15″

COLLECTIONS: LaSalle Spier, Washington, D.C., 1935.

260.

Dressing Room

H. 10″ W. 12″

COLLECTIONS: Herbert A. Goldstone, purchased 6 September 1968.

EXHIBITED: Phillips Memorial Gallery, Washington, D.C., 1937; U of A, 1966, number 56.

261.

Dry Riverbed

H. 16″ W. 20″

COLLECTIONS: Mrs. Charles C. Rumsey, New York, 1930.

262.

Elise

H. 24″ W. 20″   Signed and dated lower right; destroyed

EXHIBITED: MHG, 1930, number 2, illustrated.

PUBLISHED: *Town and Country*, 1 January 1931, illustrated in color on cover; *Index*, 1936, page 348.

The model was Elise Merer.

263.

Girl in Shako

H. 30″ W. 25″

COLLECTIONS: Mrs. Rafael Navas, Wichita, Kansas, purchased 1952.

EXHIBITED: DTG, 1930: MHG, 1930, number 4, illustrated.

PUBLISHED: *New York Evening Post*, 8 November 1930, illustrated; *Index*, 1936, page 348.

264.

The Grenadier

H. 30″ W. 25″

EXHIBITED: MHG, 1930, number 3.

PUBLISHED: *New York Herald Tribune*, 2 November 1930, illustrated.

265.

The Man from Eden

H. 30″ W. 25″   Signed and dated center right.

COLLECTIONS: Mr. Conger Goodyear, New York; Mrs. Theodore G. Kenefik, Buffalo, New York; Albright-Knox Gallery, Buffalo, New York.

EXHIBITED: MHG, 1930, number 6, illustrated; CAM, Saint Louis, 1933; Musée du Jeu de Paume, Paris, "Exhibition of American Artists," 1938; MOMA,

"20th Century Portraits," 1943; Albany, 1958, number 6; CAM, 1960, number 44, illustrated page 42; U of A, 1966, number 55.

PUBLISHED: *Parnassus*, November 1930, illustrated page 45; *Index*, 1936, page 348; *50 Paintings by Walt Kuhn*, number 10, illustrated; Albright-Knox Gallery Notes, Summer 1958, illustrated page 5.

The model was George Fitzgerald, an actor in Lillies, who sent many models to the artist and posed himself for *The Camp Cook* and *Wisconsin*.

266.
Margaret
H. 40" W. 30"
EXHIBITED: The Detroit Institute of Arts, "17th Annual Exhibition of American Art," 1931.

PUBLISHED: *Theatre Guild Magazine*, November 1930, page 47; *Art Digest*, 1 May 1931, page 13; *Index*, 1936, page 348.

267.
Show Girl
H. 40" W. 30" Signed and dated lower left.
EXHIBITED: MHG, 1930, number 9, illustrated; Nelson, Kansas City, 1934.

PUBLISHED: *New York Times*, 9 November 1930, illustrated; *Creative Arts*, November 1930, illustrated sup. page 72; Fred J. Ringel, ed., *America as Americans See It* (New York: Harcourt Brace & Co., 1932; Literary Guild), facing page 99; *Index*, 1936, page 348.

The model was Blanch Underwood.

1931

268.
Miss A
H. 30" W. 25" Signed and dated lower right.
COLLECTIONS: Colby College, Waterville, Maine.
EXHIBITED: MHG, "Exhibition of Paintings by Walt Kuhn," 1932, number 8, illustrated; CAM, Saint Louis, 1933; Nelson, Kansas City, 1934; CGFA, 1935; Dayton AI, 1935; Grace Horne Gallery, Boston, 1941; Cornell U, 1942, number 4; CSFAC Traveling Show, 1947, number 3, illustrated page 11; U of A, 1966, number 58.

PUBLISHED: *Art Digest*, January 1932, illustrated on cover; *Index*, 1936, page 348; *50 Paintings by Walt Kuhn*, number 14, illustrated.

The model was Ailes Gilmore, a Martha Graham dancer and sister of Isamu Noguchi. Her mother was Irish and her father a Japanese who collaborated with the widow of Lafcadio Hearn on his biography.

269.
The Blue Clown
H. 30" W. 25" Signed and dated lower right.
COLLECTIONS: Whitney Museum of American Art, New York.

EXHIBITED: MHG, 1932, number 10, illustrated; Baltimore Museum of Art, Maryland, 1934, illustrated; Venice, "19th Biennale," 1934; Portland Art Museum, Oregon, 1935; Berkshire Museum, Pittsfield, Massachusetts, 1935; California Palace of the Legion of Honor, San Francisco, 1935; Whitney, "Summer Exhibition," 1936; Whitney, "20th Century Artists," 1939; Carnegie Institute, Pittsburgh, Pennsylvania, "Survey of American Painting," 14 October to 15 December 1940, illustrated; CGFA, 1942, number 4; Phillips Memorial Gallery, Washington, D.C., 1944, number 11; Tate Gallery, London, American Exhibition supervised by John Walker, 1946; Saginaw Museum, Michigan, 1948, illustrated; Albany, 1958, number 7; CAM, 1960, number 51, illustrated page 48.

PUBLISHED: "Kuhn's Psychological Art in New York Show," *Art Digest*, 1 January 1932, illustrated page 9; *Art News*, 2 January 1932, illustrated page 9, advertisement; *Vanity Fair*, 1 January 1933, illustrated on cover; *New York Herald Tribune*, 21 May 1933, illustrated; Holger Cahill and Alfred H. Barr, Jr., *Art in America in Modern Times* (New York: Reynal and Hitchcock, 1934), illustrated in color plate 3; *Index*, 1936, page 348; *Pictures on Exhibit*, October 1939, illustrated on cover; *50 Paintings by Walt Kuhn*, number 16, illustrated; *New York Times Magazine*, 14 February 1943, illustrated; R. H. Wilenski, "London Look at U.S. Painting," *Art News*, August 1946, illustrated page 26; *New York Times Magazine*, 8 April 1951, illustrated; *Art Digest*, December 1951, illustrated page 6; David M. Robb, *Harper History of Painting: The Occidental Tradition* (New York: Harper, 1951), illustrated page 926; *Miami Daily News*, Florida, 6 June 1953, illustrated; *Arts*, April 1956, illustrated page 46; *Knickerbocker News*, Albany, New York, June 1958, illustrated; *Art in America*, September 1966, illustrated in color page 32; Johnson, *American Artist*, December 1967, illustrated page 54.

The model was Vittorio Falconi, who also posed for *Top Man*. A watercolor of the head and shoulders, done after the oil, survives.

270.
The Camp Cook
H. 40" W. 30" Signed lower right.
COLLECTIONS: Munson-Williams-ProctOr Institute, Utica, New York, 1951.

EXHIBITED: MHG, "7 Paintings by Walt Kuhn," November 1932, number 7, illustrated; CGFA, 1935, illustrated on *Bulletin* cover April 1935; Dayton AI, 1935, illustrated on *Bulletin* cover; CAM, Saint Louis, "30th Anniversary Exhibition of Paintings by American Artists," 4 January to 16 February 1936; Cornell U, 1942, number 3; U of A, 1966, number 59, illustrated page 64.

PUBLISHED: *Gotham Life*, 30 October 1932, illustrated; *New York Sun*, 5 November 1932, illustrated; *New York Times*, 6 November 1932, illustrated; "Walt Kuhn's Vigor like Walt Whitman's," *Art Digest*, 1 January 1933, illustrated page 15; *Creative Arts*, October 1933, illustrated page 217; *London Studio*, March 1934, illustrated page 117; *Index*, 1936, page 348.

271.

Clown in Green Pantaloons

H. 40″ W. 30″

EXHIBITED: MHG,1932

272.

Clown with Red Wig

H. 30″ W. 36″   Signed and dated lower right.

COLLECTIONS: Mr. and Mrs. Otto L. Spaeth, New York, 1955; Mrs. Eugene McDermot, Dallas, Texas.

EXHIBITED: Fine Arts Associates, Otto Gerson, "Collectors—Their Faces—Their Favorites,"1958, illustrated; World House, New York, 50th Anniversary of the American Federation of Arts, "Trustee's Choice," 1959, number 15; CAM, 1960, number 46, illustrated page 45; U of A, 1966, number 61, illustrated in color page 9, and on jacket.

273.

Fox Farmer

H. 24″ W. 20″   Signed and dated lower left.

EXHIBITED: MHG, 1932, number 12, illustrated; CAM, Saint Louis, 1933.

PUBLISHED: Frank E. Washburn Freund, "Walt Kuhn," *Creative Arts*, May 1932, pages 347-49, illustrated in color page 340; *Index,*1936, page 348.

The model was Henry Borton, a Maine farmer, or a self-portrait in make-up.

274.

The Guide

H. 24″ W. 30″   Signed and dated lower left.

COLLECTIONS: University of Nebraska Art Galleries, F.M. Hall Collection, Lincoln, Nebraska.

EXHIBITED: MHG, 1932, number 6, illustrated; Studio Club, Phillips Memorial Gallery, Washington, D.C.,1932; MOMA, "American Painting and Sculpture, 1862—1932," 1932—33; Cleveland Museum of Art, "13th Exhibition of Contemporary American Painting,"1933, illustrated in *Bulletin,* June 1933, page 103; Nelson, Kansas City, 1934; MHG, 1939; Metropolitan Museum of Art, April 1941; CAM, Saint Louis, 1942; Phillips Memorial Gallery, Washington, D.C.,1944, number 2; CAM, 1960, number 48, illustrated page 46; U of A, 1966, number 62.

PUBLISHED: *New York Evening Post*, 9 January 1932, illustrated; *New York Sun*, 9 January 1932, illustrated; *Salt Lake Tribune*, Utah, 27 February 1932, illustrated; *Chicago Evening Post,* 12 January 1932, illustrated; *Creative Arts*, February 1932, illustrated page 136; *Town ancountry*, February 1932, illustrated page 33; *Washington News*, 7 July 1934, illustrated; *Index,* 1936, page 348; Philip R. Adams, "Art at American Crossroads," *Harper's Bazaar*, August 1951, illustrated page 183.

The model was Jim Ames, a Maine guide, or a self-portrait in make-up.

275.

The Mysterious Stranger

H. 24″ W. 20″

Never exhibited.

The model was Vittorio Falconi.

276.

Plumes

H. 40″ W. 30″   Signed and dated lower right.

COLLECTIONS: Phillips Collection, Washington, D.C. (*Show Girl with Plumes*).

EXHIBITED: MHG, 1932, number 7, illustrated; Phillips Memorial Gallery, 1932; Phillips Memorial Gallery, 1944, number 9 (*Show Girl with Plumes*); CAM, 1960, number 47.

PUBLISHED: *Detroit Free Press*, 17 January 1932; Freund, "Walt Kuhn," *Creative Arts*, May 1932, pp. 347–49, illustrated page 346; *Index*, 1936, page 348; *50 Paintings by Walt Kuhn*, number 19, illustrated; *The Phillips Catalogue*, page 59.

277.

Top Man

H. 72″ W. 32″   Signed and dated lower right.

EXHIBITED: MHG, 1932, number 9, illustrated *(The Topman)*; Whitney, "1st Biennial," 1932–33, number 26, illustrated; Nelson, Kansas City, 1934; CAM, 1960, number 50; U of A, number 63, illustrated in color page 5 (Maynard Walker Gallery); KG, 1967, number 1, illustrated page 18; Heckscher Museum, Huntington, New York, "The Image in Twentieth Century America," 14 September to 27 October 1968, number 24, illustrated page 13; Montclair Art Museum, New Jersey, "The Post Armory Decades," 9 February to 2 March 1969, number 28; "Walt Kuhn, 1877–1949," 1 to 18 March 1972; KG, "A Selection of 20th Century American Masterpieces," 7 November to 1 December 1973, number 11, illustrated.

PUBLISHED: *Studio News*, April 1932, illustrated page 5; *Creative Arts*, May 1932, illustrated page 349; *Art News*, 9 January 1936, illustrated on cover; *Index*, 1936, page 348; *Art Quarterly*, Winter 1961, illustrated page 407; *Arts Magazine*, November 1967, illustrated page 58; *Arts*, December 1973, illustrated page 18.

The model was Vittorio Falconi, who also posed for *The Blue Clown*. A developed watercolor sketch, H. 22″ W. 11″, survives.

278.

Trude

H. 68″ W. 33¼″   Signed and dated lower right.

COLLECTIONS: Santa Barbara Museum of Art, California, Gift of Mrs. Walt Kuhn in Memory of Walt Kuhn.

EXHIBITED: MHG, 1932, number 11; CSFAC Traveling Show, 1947, number 4, illustrated page 14; CAM, 1960, number 49, illustrated page 47; U of A, 1966, number 60, illustrated page 110.

PUBLISHED: *Studio News*, April 1932, illustrated page 4; *Creative Arts*, May 1932, illustrated page 348; *Index*, 1936, page 348; *50 Paintings by Walt Kuhn*, number 18, illustrated.

The model was Gertrude Lower, a chorus girl in the road company of *Show Boat*.

279.

Trees on a Ridge

H. W.
COLLECTIONS: Mrs. Ruth Pratt.

1932

280.

Apples on a Black Cloth
H. 30″ W. 40″   Destroyed

281.

Apples in the Hay
H. 30″ W. 40″   Signed and dated lower right.

COLLECTIONS: Museum of Modern Art, New York, given anonymously.

EXHIBITED: Nelson, Kansas City, 1934; CGFA, 1935; Dayton AI, 1935; Boston Museum of Modern Art, March 1938; CAM, 1960, number 55, illustrated page 49; U of A, 1966, number 68, illustrated page 65.

PUBLISHED: *Art News Annual*, 1948, illustrated page 36.

282.

Apples from Maine   Painted from apples grown near the Kuhn family cottage, Ogunquit, Maine.
H. 30″ W. 40″   Signed and dated lower right.

COLLECTIONS: Metropolitan Museum of Art, New York, George A. Hearn Fund, 1950.

EXHIBITED: MHG, "7 Paintings by Walt Kuhn," 1932, number 4, illustrated; CAM, 1960, number 53; U of A, 1966, number 67.

PUBLISHED: *New York Sun*, 19 November 1932, illustrated; *Index*, 1936, page 348; *50 Paintings by Walt Kuhn*, number 21, illustrated.

283.

Boy with Straw Hat
H. 20″ W. 16″   Signed and dated lower right; destroyed in 1944.

EXHIBITED: MHG, "7 Paintings by Walt Kuhn," 1932, number 5, illustrated; CAM, Saint Louis, 1933; CGFA, 1935; Dayton AI, 1935.

PUBLISHED: *Index*, 1936, page 348.

284.

Clown with Drum
H. 64″ W. 48″   Destroyed in 1938

285.

Head of Joyce
H. 15″ W. 12″
The model was Joyce Powers.

286.

Kansas (Portrait of the Artist as a Clown, title stipulated after the artist's death.)
H. 32″ W. 22″   Signed and dated lower left.

COLLECTIONS: Broadmoor Hotel, Colorado Springs, Colorado, purchased 27 March 1951.

EXHIBITED: MHG, "7 Paintings by Walt Kuhn," 1932, number 1, illustrated.

PUBLISHED: *Atlantica*, December 1932, illustrated; *Town and Country*, 15 March 1933, illustrated on cover; *Index*, 1936, page 348; *50 Paintings by Walt Kuhn*, number 20, illustrated; *Art News* April 1956, illustrated page 27.

The model was Ralph "Kansas" Osgood, or a self-portrait in make-up. A watercolor without the pointed hat over the skullcap survives, H. 21½″ W. 14½″.

287.

Miss X
H. 30″ W. 25″   Signed and dated lower right.

EXHIBITED: MHG, 1934, number 5, illustrated; Denver Art Museum, Colorado, 1937; CSFAC Traveling Show, 1947, number 5; CAM, "An American Show," 1948, number 45; CAM, 1960, number 56; U of A, 1966, number 65.

PUBLISHED: *Index*, 1936, page 348; *50 Paintings by Walt Kuhn*, number 24, illustrated.

288.

Rose Clown
H. 24″ W. 20″   Signed and dated lower right.

EXHIBITED: MHG, "Exhibition of Paintings by Walt Kuhn," February 1934, number 7, illustrated; Phillips Memorial Gallery, Washington, D.C., 1937; Cornell U, 1942, number 5; Dayton AI, 1943; CSFAC Traveling Show, 1947, number 6: U of A, 1966, number 69.

PUBLISHED: *Index*, 1936, page 348; *Art Journal*, Summer 1967, illustrated page 397.

289.

Sibyl
H. 68″ W. 33″   Signed and dated lower right.

EXHIBITED: MHG, "Paintings by Walt Kuhn," 1932, number 6, illustrated; Whitney Biennial, December 1934 to January 1935.

PUBLISHED: *Index*, 1936, page 348.

The model was Margaret Manly, whose stage name was Dixon.

290.

Studio Corner
H. 40″ W. 46″   Signed lower right.

EXHIBITED: MHG, "7 Paintings by Walt Kuhn," 1932, number 2, illustrated; CAM, Saint Louis, 1933; KG, 1967, number 4, illustrated page 21.

PUBLISHED: *Index*, 1936, page 384; *Connoisseur*, October 1967, illustrated page 1.

291.

Tiger Trainer
H. 40″ W. 30″   Signed and dated lower right.

EXHIBITED: MHG, "7 Paintings by Walt Kuhn," 1932, number 3, illustrated; University of Nebraska Art Galleries, 1932, number 55; Nelson, Kansas City, 1942; U of A, 1966, number 66.

PUBLISHED: *Art News*, 29 October 1932, illustrated, page 4; *Index*, 1936, page 384; *50 Paintings by Walt Kuhn*, number 22, illustrated; Johnson, *American Artist*, December 1967, illustrated page 55.

The model was Joanne Douglas.

292.

Young Clown

H. 30" W. 25" Signed and dated lower right.

COLLECTIONS: Denver Art Museum, Denver, Colorado.

EXHIBITED: MHG, 1934, number 13, illustrated; Nelson, Kansas City, 1934; Denver Art Museum, Colorado, 1935; University of Iowa, Iowa City, Iowa, 1936; Santa Barbara Museum of Art, California, 1941, number 69; CGFA, 1942, number 5; CAM, 1960, number 54; U of A, 1966, number 64.

PUBLISHED: *Art News*, 27 January 1934, illustrated page 14; *Studio News*, April 1934, illustrated page 8; *Index*, 1936, page 384; Marchal E. Langran, *Years of Art: The Story of the Art Students' League* (McBride, 1930), illustrated; *50 Paintings by Walt Kuhn*, number 23, illustrated.

1933

293

Acrobat in White

H. W. Signed and dated lower left.

EXHIBITED: MHG, 1934, number 9, illustrated.

PUBLISHED: Sheldon Cheney, *Expressionism in Art* (New York: Liveright, 1933), illustrated page 240; "Kuhn Digresses from Acrobats to Flowers," *Art Digest*, 1 February 1934, illustrated page 19; *Index*, 1936, page 347.

The model was Ben Benson, an acrobat who also posed for *Theatre, Trio,* and *Musical Clown*.

294.

Apples

H. 20" W. 24" Signed and dated lower right near center.

COLLECTIONS: Mr. and Mrs. Sol A. Davidson, Scranton, Pennsylvania.

EXHIBITED: CAM, 1960, number 58.

295.

Apple Basket

H. 30" W. 40" Signed and dated lower left.

COLLECTIONS: Mrs. Charles C. Rumsey, New York.

EXHIBITED: MHG, 1934, number 8, illustrated.

PUBLISHED: *Art News*, 24 February 1934, illustrated page 5; *Index*, 1936, page 347.

296.

Apples and Pineapple

H. 25" W. 30" Signed and dated lower right.

COLLECTIONS: W. Averell Harriman.

EXHIBITED: MHG, 1934, number 2, illustrated; MOMA, "5th Anniversary Exhibition," 20 November 1934 to 20 January 1935, number 97, illustrated; Albany, 1958, number 8; CAM, 1960, number 57, illustrated page 50; National Gallery "Harriman Collection," 1961, illustrated page 44.

PUBLISHED: *Parnassus*, February 1934, illustrated page 8; *New York Times*, December 1934, illustrated; *Index*, 1936, page 347; *50 Paintings by Walt Kuhn*, number 27, illustrated.

297.

Apples and Red Watering Can

H. 30" W. 40" Signed and dated lower right.

EXHIBITED: KG, 1967, number 5, illustrated page 22.

PUBLISHED: *Burlington Magazine*, October 1967, illustrated page xxxviii; *Art Quarterly*, Autumn 1969, illustrated page vii.

298.

Bouquet

H. 30" W. 25" Signed and dated lower right.

COLLECTIONS: W. Plunkett Stewart.

EXHIBITED: MHG, 1934, illustrated.

PUBLISHED: *Art News*, 3 February 1934, illustrated page 5; *Index*, 1936, page 348.

299.

Carlo

H. 20" W. 24" Signed and dated lower right.

COLLECTIONS: Mr. Sydney M. Shoenberg, Jr., Clayton, Missouri, 1959.

EXHIBITED: MHG, 1934, number 3, illustrated; Museum of Art, Ogunquit, Maine, "Group Memorial Exhibition of Artists of the Area," 15 July to 7 September 1953; U of A, 1966, number 75.

PUBLISHED: *Art News*, 27 January 1934, illustrated page 5; *Art News*, 3 February 1934, in advertisement; *Index*, 1936, page 348.

300.

Chorus Girl

H. 30" W. 25" Destroyed in 1938.

EXHIBITED: MHG, 1934.

301.

Dog

H. 30" W. 40" Signed and dated lower center.

PUBLISHED: *50 Paintings by Walt Kuhn*, 1940, number 41, illustrated.

302.

Pears

H. 25" W. 30" Signed and dated lower right.

COLLECTIONS: William E. Lord, 1967.

EXHIBITED: KG, 1967, number 8, illustrated page 25.

PUBLISHED: Johnson, *American Artist*, December 1967, illustrated page 57.

303.

Pears in the Barn

H. 25" W. 30" Signed and dated lower left.

EXHIBITED: MHG, 1934, number 14, illustrated; Nelson, Kansas City, 1934; U of A, 1966, number 72.

PUBLISHED: *Index*, 1936, page 348.

304.

Pine, Tall

H. 45" W. 30" Signed and dated lower right.

EXHIBITED: MHG, 1934, number 10, illustrated.

PUBLISHED: *Index*, 1936, page 348.

305.

Roses

H. 15" W. 11¼"   Signed and dated lower right.

COLLECTIONS: Mrs.J. Mueller, New York,1966.

EXHIBITED: U of A, 1966, number 71, illustrated page 66.

306.

Theatre

H. 72" W. 32"   Destroyed in 1942.

EXHIBITED: MHG, 16 February to 13 March 1937, number 1; Springfield Museum of Art, Massachusetts, "1st Biennial Exhibition of Contemporary American Painting," 1939.

PUBLISHED: *New York Sun*, 20 February 1937, illustrated; *Art News*, 35th Anniversary Number, 1 May 1937, illustrated in color page 138.

The model was Ben Benson, who also posed for *Trio, Musical Clown,* and *Acrobat in White.*

307.

Three Apples

H. 8" W. 10"   Signed and dated lower right.

COLLECTIONS: Mr. and Mrs. Gregory H. Doherty, North Tarrytown, New York.

EXHIBITED: MHG, "Small Paintings by Walt Kuhn" 8 to 27 February 1934, number 1; CAM, 1960, number 59; U of A, 1966, number 70 (lent by Mr. George H. Doherty).

308.

White Peonies

H. 30" W. 40"

COLLECTIONS: Mr. Harry B. Spalding, Buffalo, New York.

EXHIBITED: MHG, 1934, number 6, illustrated; Albright-Knox Art Gallery, Buffalo, New York, "Art of To-day," 1936.

PUBLISHED: *Index*, 1936 ,page 348.

309.

Woodsman

H. 20" W. 16"

EXHIBITED: MHG, 1934, number 1, illustrated; CGFA, 1935; Dayton AI, 1935; Denver Art Museum, Colorado, 1937; Phillips Memorial Gallery, Washington, D.C.,1937; U of A, 1966, number 74; KG, 1967, number 7, illustrated page 24.

PUBLISHED: *New York Times*, 4 February 1934, illustrated; *The Art of To-day*, March 1935, illustrated page 4; *Index*, 1936, page 348; *Art and Artists of To-day*, 7 June 1938; *50 Paintings by Walt Kuhn*, number 26, illustrated; Johnson, *American Artist*, December 1967, illustrated page 54.

310.

Wrestler

H. 40" W. 30"   Signed and dated lower right.

EXHIBITED: MHG, number 11, illustrated; CSFAC Traveling Show, 1947, number 7, illustrated page 15; KG, 1967, illustrated page 23.

PUBLISHED: *Index*, 1936, page 348; *50 Paintings by Walt*

Kuhn, number 6, illustrated; Johnson, *American Artist*, December 1967, illustrated page 54.

The model was Clevio Massamo, vaudeville partner of Ben Benson, who also posed for *Clown with Ball.*

311.

Yellow Apples

H. 25" W. 30"   Signed and dated lower right.

COLLECTIONS: Mr. Peter Carleton, 1966.

EXHIBITED: MHG, 1934, number 12, illustrated, CGFA,1935; Dayton AI, 1935; U of A, 1966, number 73.

PUBLISHED: *Index*, 1936, page 348.

312.

Zinnias

H. 25" W. 30"   Signed and dated lower right.

COLLECTIONS: W. Averell Harriman, New York; National Gallery of Art, Washington, D.C., Gift of the Averell Harriman Foundation in Memory of Marie N. Harriman.

EXHIBITED: Phillips Memorial Gallery, Washington, D.C.,1944, number 1; CAM, "An American Show," 1948, number 32; Albany, 1958, number 9; CAM,1960, number 60, illustrated page 51; National Gallery "Harriman Collection," 1961, illustrated page 46, Nasson College, 1964, number 8.

PUBLISHED: National Gallery of Art, *Annual Report,*1972, number 2603.

1934

313.

American Beauty

H. 33" W. 65"   Signed and dated lower right.

EXHIBITED: Denver Art Museum, Colorado, 1941; Carnegie Institute, Pittsburgh, 1946; KG, 1967, number 10, illustrated page 27.

PUBLISHED: *Rocky Mountain News*, Denver, 13 July 1941, illustrated.

The model was Mildred Mansfield. There are many drawings of the same pose.

314.

Apples in Bowl

H. 25" W. 30"

COLLECTIONS: Mr. and Mrs. Harry Daniel, Bristol, Tennessee, 1958.

EXHIBITED: CGFA, 1942, number 6; CAM,1960, number 64.

315.

Apples with Leaves

H. 15½" W. 12½"

COLLECTIONS: Mrs. Charles Payson, New York, 1958.

EXHIBITED: CAM, 1960, number 63.

316.

Athlete in White Face

H. 40" W. 30"   Signed and dated lower left.

COLLECTIONS: Philadelphia Museum of Art, Philadelphia, Pennsylvania, 1962.

261

EXHIBITED: Durand-Ruel, 1944, number 11; American Federation of Arts Tour of India, sponsored by the Ford Foundation, "Synthesis of Arts in America," 1953–54, number 20; CAM, 1960, number 62; Kalamazoo Institute of Art, Michigan, 1961.

PUBLISHED: *Statesman*, New Delhi, India, 5 May 1953, illustrated; *Times of India*, New Delhi, India, 6 May 1953, illustrated.

317.
Bread and Knife
H. 12" W. 15"   Signed and dated lower left.
COLLECTIONS: Phillips Collection Washington, D.C.
PUBLISHED: *Phillips Collection Catalogue*, page 59.

318.
Clown with Winged Collar
H. 15" W. 12"
COLLECTIONS: Allan Blunestein, 1963.
EXHIBITED: University of Nebraska Art Galleries, Lincoln, 1939.
The model was George Silverette, who also posed for *Juggler* and *Clown with Mandolin*.

319.
Flowers in a White Vase
H. 25" W. 30"
COLLECTIONS: John N. Irvin, 1964.
EXHIBITED: CGFA, 1935; Dayton AI, 1935; The Detroit Institute of Arts, 1940 *(Flowers)*; MHG, 1940; Phillips Memorial Gallery, Washington, D.C., 1942; U of A, 1966, number 76 (anonymous loan).
PUBLISHED: *Art Digest*, 15 April 1940, illustrated page 22; *Art Journal*, Fall 1964, illustrated page 51.

320.
Fruit Basket
H. 25" W. 30"   Destroyed.
COLLECTIONS: Mrs. Johnston Redmond

321.
Hydrangeas
H. 30" W. 40"   Signed and dated lower right.
COLLECTIONS: Mrs. Samuel Goldwyn; Samuel Goldwyn, Jr., Beverly Hills, California.
PUBLISHED: *50 Paintings by Walt Kuhn*, number 29, illustrated.

322.
Juggler
H. 30" W. 25"   Signed and dated lower left.
COLLECTIONS: William Rockhill Nelson Gallery of Art—Atkins Memorial Museum, Kansas City, Missouri, Friends of Art Collection.
EXHIBITED: MHG, 1937, number 2; Phillips Memorial Gallery, Washington, D.C., 1937; Bennington College, Vermont, 1937; Whitney, "This Is Our City," 1941, number 45, CGFA, 1942, number 7; CAM, 1960, number 61, illustrated page 52; U of A, 1966, number 77, illustrated pages 67 and 111.
PUBLISHED: *Travel*, February 1937, illustrated; *Spur*, February 1937, illustrated; *Art Digest*, 15 February 1937, illustrated on cover; *Washington Post*, 4 April 1937, illustrated; *New York Times*, 17 December 1937, illustrated; *Art News*, 25 December 1937, illustrated page 18; *Kansas City Journal Post*, 30 January 1938, illustrated; *Kansas City Star*, 30 January 1938, illustrated; Martha Chandler Cheney, *Modern Art in America* (New York: McGraw-Hill, 1939), number 7, and on jacket; *50 Paintings by Walt Kuhn*, number 30, illustrated; *Kansas City Star*, 15 June 1941, illustrated; *Kansas City Star*, 5 December 1941, illustrated; *PM's Weekly*, 16 March 1941, illustrated; *Guide to the Permanent Collections* (Kansas City: William Rockhill Nelson Gallery, 1940), illustrated page 158.
The model was George Silverette, who also posed for *Clown with Mandolin* and *Clown with Winged Collar*.

323.
Mysterious Stranger
H. 20" W. 16"   Signed and dated left center.
EXHIBITED: KG, 1–18 March 1972, number 9, illustrated.

324.
Pink Roses in Blue Pitcher
H. 30" W. 25"   Signed and dated lower right.
EXHIBITED: KG, 1967, number 9, illustrated page 26.

325.
Red Roses
H.   W.
COLLECTIONS: Mrs. Mary A. H. Rumsey

326.
Rose Basket
H. 28" W. 38"
COLLECTIONS: Mrs. Paul V. Shields, New York

327.
Salute
H. 72" W. 32" (H. 68" W. 33")
Never exhibited.
The model was Elsie Ricardo. A pen drawing titled under the signature and date, both lower left, survives, H. 18" W. 11".

328.
Waiting for the Robert E. Lee
H. 48½" W. 45" Signed and dated lower right.
EXHIBITED: U of A, 1966, number 86 (dated 1938); KG, 1967, number 11, illustrated page 28.
PUBLISHED: *Burlington Magazine*, December 1967, illustrated page 728.

329.
White Roses
H. 25" W. 30"
COLLECTIONS: Mr. and Mrs. Paul V. Shields, New York.
EXHIBITED: Albany, 1958, number 10.

1935

330.

Apples with Salmon Cloth
H. 25″ W. 30″
COLLECTIONS: Philip Sills, New York, 1967.
EXHIBITED: MHG, 1936, shown with Cézanne, Derain, Matisse, Picasso, Renoir, Van Gogh; Denver Art Museum, Colorado, "Chardin and the Modern Still Life," November 1936; Phillips Memorial Gallery, Washington, D.C., April 1937; Brooklyn Museum, 1937-41, on loan; Cornell U, 1942, number 7; U of A, 1966, number 80.

331.

Clown with Mandolin
H. 20″ W. 32″ Signed and dated lower right.
COLLECTIONS: Mr. and Mrs. Gary Cooper, Beverly Hills, California; Mrs. John Converse, New York.
EXHIBITED: CAM, 1960, number 60.
The model was George Silverette, a juggler, dancer, and boxer, who also posed for *Juggler* and *Clown with Winged Collar*

332.

Clown Musical   Smaller version of *Clown with Mandolin*.

H. 12″ W. 15″
EXHIBITED: Newport, Rhode Island, Art Association, 1938; MWG, 1939.

333.

Dryad
H. 34″ W. 23″ Signed and dated lower right.
COLLECTIONS: W. Averell Harriman, New York, 1961; National Gallery of Art, Washington, D.C., Gift of the W. Averell Harriman Foundation in Memory of Marie N. Harriman.
EXHIBITED: MHG, 1937, number 4; Phillips Memorial Gallery, Washington, D.C., 1937; MOMA, "Paintings for Paris," 1937; Musée du Jeu de Paume, Paris, "American Art in Paris," 1938; Albany, 1958, number 1 (lent by Kuhn Estate); CAM, 1960, number 65, illustrated page 53; National Gallery, "Harriman Collection," 1961, illustrated page 48; U of A, 1966, number 78, illustrated page 68.
PUBLISHED: *American Magazine of Art*, March 1937, illustrated page 34; Martha Davidson, "American Art at Home and Paris," *Art News*, 13 November 1947, illustrated page 14; *50 Paintings by Walt Kuhn*, number 31, illustrated.

334.

Flower Piece
H. 20″ W. 16″
COLLECTIONS: Mr. William J. Killea.
Never exhibited.

335.

Red Roses
H. 25″ W. 30″ Signed and dated lower left.
EXHIBITED: MHG, number 3.
PUBLISHED: *50 Paintings by Walt Kuhn*, number 32, illustrated.

336.

Talisman Roses
H. 30″ W. 25″ Signed and dated lower right.
EXHIBITED: Phillips Memorial Gallery, Washington, D.C., 1937; KG, 1967, number 12.

337.

Yellow Roses
H.   W.
COLLECTIONS: Mrs. Marshall Field, Chicago.

1936

338.

Carnival Girl
H. 40″ W. 30″ Signed and dated lower left.
EXHIBITED: MHG, 1937, number 7; Phillips Memorial Gallery, Washington, D.C., March 1937 to 25 April 1937; CGFA, 1942, number 8; CAM, 1960, number 69, illustrated page 54; KG, 1967, number 14, illustrated page 31.
PUBLISHED: *New York Post*, 2 February 1937, illustrated; *Art News*, 27 February 1937, illustrated on cover; *50 Paintings by Walt Kuhn*, 1940, number 33, illustrated; *Art News*, October 1967, page 13.
The model was Ruth Johnston, later Mrs. John Runger. She was one of the artist's favorite models, who also posed for *Miss R.*, *Fancy Dress*, and several other paintings. She was an acrobatic dancer in cabarets.

339.

Clown with Long Nose
H. 40″ W. 30″
EXHIBITED: MHG, 1937, number 8; Nasson College, 1964, number 6.
PUBLISHED: *New York Times*, 21 February 1937, illustrated.
The model was George Fitzgerald.

340

Copper Kettle and Oranges
H. 25″ W. 30″ Signed and dated lower left.
EXHIBITED: Denver Art Museum, Colorado, 1941; KG, 1967, number 16, illustrated page 33.

341.

Fancy Dress
H. 40″ W. 30″
EXHIBITED: MHG, 1937, number 9; Studio House, Phillips Memorial Gallery, Washington, D.C., April 1937.
PUBLISHED: *Washington Daily News*, 3 April 1937, illustrated.
The model was Ruth Johnston.

342.

Fruit Platter
H. 25″ W. 30″ Signed and dated lower right.
EXHIBITED: MHG, 1937, number 6; Phillips Memorial Gallery, Washington, D.C., 1937; KG, 1967, number 18, illustrated page 35.

PUBLISHED: Alfred M. Frankfurter, "Kuhn, Master of the Painting Language," *Art News*, 27 February 1937, pages 11 and 20, illustrated page 11.

343.

Girl in Uniform
H. 40″ W. 30″

EXHIBITED: Whitney, "3rd Biennial," 1936, number 112; Denver Art Museum, Colorado, January 1937; Studio House, Phillips Memorial Gallery, Washington, D.C., April 1937.

PUBLISHED: *New York Herald Tribune*, 10 November 1936, illustrated; *Denver Post*, 10 January 1937, illustrated; *Washington Daily News*, 3 April 1937, illustrated.

The model was Agnes Fox, a fan dancer.

344.

Green Apples on White Cloth in Basket
H. 25″ W. 30″

COLLECTIONS: Joseph H. Hirshhorn Foundation; Hirshhorn Museum and Sculpture Garden, Washington, D.C.

EXHIBITED: U of A, 1966, number 79.

345.

Indian of the Chorus
H. 30″ W. 25″

EXHIBITED: MHG, 1937, number 5.

The model was Katherine McCarthy, who played "cheap" nightclubs.

346.

Lassie
H. 30″ W. 25″

EXHIBITED: Phillips Memorial Gallery, Washington, D.C., 1937.

The model was Katherine McCarthy.

347.

Portrait of Mrs. C. C. Rumsey
H. 20″ W. 16″

348.

Miss R.
H. 30″ W. 25″   Signed and dated lower left.

COLLECTIONS: Mrs. Charles MacArthur (Helen Hayes), Nyack, New York; Mr. James MacArthur, Honolulu, Hawaii.

EXHIBITED: MHG, 1936; Albany, 1958, number 12; CAM, 1960, number 67.

PUBLISHED: *Index*, 1936, page 348; *Art News*, June 1958, illustrated page 8.

The model was Ruth Johnston.

349.

Spanish Plate
H. 16″ W. 20″ Destroyed.

EXHIBITED: MHG, 1937, number 10.

350.

Wisconsin.
H. 20″ W. 16″   Signed and dated lower right.

COLLECTIONS: National Gallery of Art, Washington, D.C., Gift of Brenda Kuhn

EXHIBITED: MHG, 1937, number 11; CAM, 1960, number 68; Nasson College, 1964, number 10; U of A, 1966, number 81, illustrated page 70; KG, 1967, number 17, illustrated page 34.

PUBLISHED: Alfred M.Frankfurter, "Kuhn, Master of the Painting Language," *Art News*, 27 February 1937, pages 11 and 20, illustrated page 11; Margaret Breuning, *Parnassus*, March 1937, illustrated page 34; *Art Quarterly*, Winter 1957, illustrated page 490.

The model was George Fitzgerald.

351.

Yellow Roses
H. 30″ W. 25″   Signed and dated lower left.

EXHIBITED: KG, 1967, number 13, illustrated page 30.

1937

352.

Acrobats in Dressing Room
H. 12″ W. 15″   Signed and dated lower right.

EXHIBITED: KG, 1967, number 20, illustrated page 37.

PUBLISHED: *Art News*, October 1967, illustrated page 4; *Arts*, November 1967, illustrated page 4, advertisement; Johnson, *American Artist*, December 1967, illustrated page 51.

353.

Apples from Dorset (Vermont)
H. 25″ W. 30″   Signed and dated lower right.

EXHIBITED: KG, 1967, number 21, illustrated page 38.

354.

Eight Point Buck
H. 45″ W. 30″

EXHIBITED: MHG, 1939, number 12.

355.

Elm at Dorset   Painted at Dorset, Vermont.
H. 16″ W. 15″
Never exhibited.

356.

Girl with Turban
H. 30″ W. 40″

EXHIBITED: Cornell U, 1942, number 8.

The model was Ruth Johnston.

357.

Golden Horn
H. 40″ W. 30″
Never exhibited.

A fully developed watercolor signed and dated lower left, H. 17½″ W. 10″, survives. It is titled *Horn of Plenty.*

358.

Hibiscus
H. 24″ W. 20″

EXHIBITED: Museum of Modern Art Gallery, Washington, D.C., "Flowers and Fruits," 1938.

PUBLISHED: *Washington Sunday Post*, 3 September 1938, illustrated; *Art News*, 2 April 1938, illustrated page 11.

359.

Pine, Vermont   Painted at Rutland, Vermont.
H. 40" W. 30"   Signed and dated lower right.
EXHIBITED: MWG, 1957, number 6; Durand-Ruel, 1945, number 2.

360.

Poplars, Vermont
EXHIBITED: MWG, 1957, number 7.

361.

Red and Yellow Roses
H. 30" W. 40"   Signed and dated lower left.
EXHIBITED: CAM, Saint Louis, "Development of Flower Painting from the 17th Century to Present," 1937, illustrated; U of A, 1966, number 83, illustrated pages 71 and 113; KG, 1967, number 19, illustrated page 36.

362.

Rose Basket
H.   W.
COLLECTIONS: Mrs. Paul V. Shields, New York.

363.

Trees — Vermont
H. 30" W. 40"   Signed and dated lower right.
COLLECTIONS: Edith Gregor Halpert, 1967.
EXHIBITED: MHG, 1939; Grace Horne Gallery, Boston, 1941; MHG, "An Exhibition of Landscape Paintings by Walt Kuhn," 7 December 1957, number 1, illustrated; CAM, 1960, number 70, illustrated in color, page 15; American Federation of Arts, Traveling Show, "Realism and Reality," 1965-66, number 22.
PUBLISHED: *New York World Telegram*, 8 July 1939, illustrated; *50 Paintings by Walt Kuhn*, number 34, illustrated; *Boston Evening Transcript*, 19 April 1941, illustrated; Edith Gregor Halpert Sale, Sotheby Parke Bernet, 16 May 1973, number 138, illustrated in color.

364.

Trio
H. 72" W. 50"   Signed and dated lower left.
COLLECTIONS: Colorado Springs Fine Arts Center, Colorado, Gift of the El Pomar Foundation.
EXHIBITED: MHG, 1940; Whitney Annual, 1940, number 61; CGFA, "One Painting Exhibition," 5 to 20 March 1940; Nelson, Kansas City, 1940; Worcester Art Museum, Massachusetts, "A Decade of American Painting, 1930–1940," 1942; Milwaukee Art Institute, Wisconsin, "Masters of Contemporary Painting," 1943, number 29, illustrated; CSFAC Traveling Show, 1947, number 8, illustrated page 9; CAM, 1960, number 71, illustrated in color page 16; U of A, 1966, number 82, illustrated in color page 9.
PUBLISHED: *Art News*, 13 January 1940, illustrated on cover; *Art Digest*, 15 January 1940, illustrated on cover; *50 Paintings by Walt Kuhn*, number 35, illustrated; *Art News*, 19 October 1940, illustrated page 9;

Art News, 14 March 1942, illustrated page 8; *Art Digest*, 15 March 1951, illustrated page 9; *Time*, 12 January 1953, illustrated page 62; Alexander Eliot, *Three Hundred Years of American Painting*, (New York: Time, Inc., 1957), pages 284 to 286, illustrated in color page 285.

The models were, from left to right, Frank Landy, Mario Venendi, a professional acrobat who also posed for *Mario* and *Veteran Acrobat*, and Ben Benson, a professional acrobat who also posed for *Theatre* and *Acrobat in White*.

365.

Water Butt
H. 25" W. 30"   Signed and dated lower right.
COLLECTIONS: Mr. and Mrs. Ralph S. O'Connor, Houston, Texas, 1968.
EXHIBITED: Whitney, "Annual Exhibition of Contemporary American Painting," 1937; Baltimore Museum of Art, Maryland, "200 years of American Art," 1938; Grace Horne Gallery, Boston, 1941; CAM, 1960, number 72, illustrated page 55; KG, 1967, number 22, illustrated page 39.
PUBLISHED: *50 Paintings by Walt Kuhn*, number 36, illustrated.

366.

Young Boy (Circus Performer)
H. 9¼" W. 6"   Initialed and dated lower left.
EXHIBITED: KG, 1972, number 20, illustrated.

1938

367.

Apples in Wooden Boat
H. 25" W. 30"
COLLECTIONS: University of Nebraska Art Galleries, F. M. Hall Collection, Lincoln, Nebraska.
EXHIBITED: University of Nebraska Art Galleries, Lincoln, March 1940.
PUBLISHED: *Art Digest*, 1 April 1940, illustrated page 10.

368.

Dragoon
H.   W.
PUBLISHED: *Art News*, Supplement, 26 March 1938, illustrated page 108; *Art News*, November 1948, illustrated page 3.

369.

Girl in Pink Tights
H. 14½" W. 8"   Initialed and dated lower right.
EXHIBITED: KG, 1972, number 5, illustrated.

370.

Girl with Turban Zuluka
H. 30" W. 40"   Signed and dated lower left.
EXHIBITED: KG, 1972, number 25, illustrated.

371.

Grenadier
H. 40" W. 30"   Signed and dated lower right.

265

EXHIBITED: CGFA, 1942, number 12; Dayton AI, 1943; CAM, 1948, number 38, illustrated page 14; CAM, 1960, number 75, illustrated in color page 24; U of A, 1966, number 84.

PUBLISHED: *50 Paintings by Walt Kuhn*, number 38, illustrated.

372.

Lavender Plumes

H. 40″ W. 30″   Signed and dated lower right.

COLLECTIONS: Dr. John I. McDonough, Youngstown, Ohio, 1968.

EXHIBITED: Dayton AI, 1943; CSFAC Traveling Show, 1947, number 9; CAM, 1960, number 77, illustrated page 58; KG, 1967, illustrated in color on cover.

PUBLISHED: *50 Paintings by Walt Kuhn*, number 43, illustrated; *Art in America*, September 1967, illustrated in color on back cover, advertisement; "A Panorama of American Painting: The John I. MacDonough Collection," number 28, illustrated in color page 113; New Orleans Museum of Art, 1975; Fine Arts Gallery of San Diego, 1975; Marion Koogler McNay Art Institute, San Antonio, 1975; Arkansas Arts Center, 1975; The Westmoreland County Museum of Art, Greensburg, Pennsylvania, 1976; The North Carolina Museum of Art, Raleigh, 1976; Oklahoma Art Center, Oklahoma City, 1976; The Butler Institute of American Art, Youngstown, Ohio, 1976.

The model was Ruth Johnston.

373.

Maine Pines

H.   W.

COLLECTIONS: Mr. Charles H. Lorms, purchased 15 November 1965.

EXHIBITED: MWG, 1957, number 3.

374.

The Mandolinist

H.   W.

COLLECTIONS: Mrs. John Irwin II, New York.

EXHIBITED: Durand-Ruel, "Circus Subjects, Small Clowns," 1943.

PUBLISHED: Rosamund Frost, "Walt Kuhn Clowns in a Great Tradition," *Art News*, 1 May 1943, page 11, illustrated page 11.

375.

Mario

H. 34″ W. 23″   Signed and dated lower right.

COLLECTIONS: Edna St. Vincent Millay (Mrs. Eugene Boissevain), bought back by Walt Kuhn in the mid 40s.

EXHIBITED: CGFA, 1942, number 11; CAM, 1948, number 43; CAM, 1960, number 74, illustrated page 57; U of A, 1966, number 85, illustrated pages 74 and 114.

PUBLISHED: *50 Paintings by Walt Kuhn*, number 37, illustrated; *Art Journal*, Winter 1964-65, illustrated page 153.

376.

Moist Forest

H. 30″ W. 40″   Signed and dated lower left.

EXHIBITED: Cornell U, 1942, number 9; Durand-Ruel, 1945, number 3; CSFAC Traveling Show, 1947, number 10, illustrated page 10; Carnegie Institute, Pittsburgh, Pennsylvania, February 1948; CAM, 1948, number 31; MWG, 1957, number 5; CAM, 1960, number 76; Nasson College, 1964, number 5.

PUBLISHED: John O'Connor, Jr., "Paintings by Walt Kuhn," *Carnegie Magazine*, January-February 1948, illustrated page 208.

377.

Musical Clown

H. 40″ W. 30″   Signed and dated lower right.

COLLECTIONS: Whitney Museum of American Art, New York.

EXHIBITED: CGFA, 1942, number 10; Whitney Annual, 13 December 1943 to 1 January 1944; CAM, 1948, number 34; CAM, 1960, number 73, illustrated page 56.

PUBLISHED: *50 Paintings by Walt Kuhn*, number 40, illustrated; *Brittanica Book of the Year*, 1945, illustrated.

The model was Ben Benson.

378.

Orange Roses

H. 24″ W. 30″

COLLECTIONS: Mrs. Mary A. H. Rumsey.

Never exhibited.

379.

Pink Roses

H. 30″ W. 25″   Signed and dated lower right.

EXHIBITED: Grace Horne Gallery, Boston, 14 April 1941.

PUBLISHED: *50 Paintings by Walt Kuhn*, number 44, illustrated.

380.

Pitcher and Apples

H. 25″ W. 30″

EXHIBITED: University of Nebraska Art Galleries, Lincoln, 1940.

381.

Plumed Head

H. 30″ W. 25″

EXHIBITED: Albright-Knox Art Gallery, Buffalo, New York, 1939.

The model was Ruth Johnston.

382.

Red Roses

H.   W.

COLLECTIONS: Mrs. Mary A. H. Rumsey

383.

Sunlit Pine   Painted in Ogunquit, Maine.

H. 40″ W. 30″   Signed and dated lower right.

EXHIBITED: Phillips Memorial Gallery, Washington, D.C., 1944, number 13; Durand-Ruel, 1945, number. 4

PUBLISHED:*50 Paintings by Walt Kuhn*, number 42, illustrated.

384.

Veteran Acrobat

H. 24″ W. 30″ Signed and dated upper left.

COLLECTIONS: Columbus Gallery of Fine Arts, Ohio, Purchased by Special Subscriptions, 1942.

EXHIBITED: Grace Horne Gallery, Boston, 1941; Denver Art Museum, 1941; CGFA, 1942, number 9, illustrated on cover of *Bulletin*, April 1942; Dayton AI, 1943; CAM, 1960, number 78, illustrated page 59.

PUBLISHED:*50 Paintings by Walt Kuhn*, number 39, illustrated; *Denver Post*, 6 July 1941, illustrated; *Art News*, June-July 1942, illustrated page 28; "Sensitive Kuhn Acrobat Goes to Columbus," *Art Digest*, 1 August 1942, illustrated page 7; *Art News*, 1 January 1943, illustrated page 25.

The model was Mario Venendi.

385.

Clown Making Gestures

EXHIBITED: MWG, 1954, number 7.

385A.

Five Clown Heads

H.   W.   Signed and dated upper right.

386.

Girl in White Tunic

H. 30″ W. 25″

Never exhibited.

387.

Green Apples and Scoop

H. 30″ W. 40″ Signed and dated lower right.

COLLECTIONS: W. Averell Harriman, New York; National Gallery of Art, Washington, D.C., Gift of the W. Averell Harriman Foundation in Memory of Marie N. Harriman.

EXHIBITED: Durand-Ruel, "Paintings by Walt Kuhn," 6 to 30 November 1946, number 1; Albany, 1958, number 13; CAM, 1960, number 79, illustrated in color page 25; National Gallery, "Harriman Collection," 1961, illustrated page 47; U of A, 1966, number 89, illustrated page /16.

PUBLISHED: *Art News*, May 1961, illustrated page 30; National Gallery of Art, *Annual Report*, 1972, number 2600.

388.

Hat with Blue Ribbon

H. 30″ W. 25″ Signed and dated lower right.

COLLECTIONS: Mr. and Mrs. Merritt Cutler, South Norwalk, Connecticut; Mr. Spencer Samuels, New York.

EXHIBITED: CAM, 1960, number 80, illustrated page 60.

389.

Lancer

H. 45″ W. 26″ Signed and dated lower left.

COLLECTIONS: Currier Gallery of Art, Manchester, New Hampshire, 1958.

EXHIBITED: Grace Horne Gallery, Boston, 1941; CGFA, 1942, number 13; Cleveland Museum of Art, "17th Exhibition of Contemporary American Oil Paintings," 1946; CSFAC Traveling Show, 1947, number 11; CAM, 1948, number 81; Museum of Art, Ogunquit, Maine, 1955; CAM, 1960, number 81, illustrated page 63; U of A, 1966, number 88.

PUBLISHED:*50 Paintings by Walt Kuhn*, number 45, illustrated; *Cleveland Plain Dealer*, 1946, illustrated; *Currier Gallery of Art Bulletin*, 1958, illustrated page 95.

The model was Lorraine Roe.

390.

Pine Reaching

H. 30″ W. 40″

EXHIBITED: University of Nebraska Art Galleries, Lincoln, 1940.

391.

Ramirez

H.   W.

COLLECTIONS: Joseph Hirshhorn, Greenwich, Connecticut, 1954; Hirshhorn Museum and Sculpture Garden, Washington, D.C.

EXHIBITED: MWG, 1954, number 15.

391A.

Rehearsal

Oil on board. Signed and dated upper right.

EXHIBITED: MWG, 1954, number 16.

392.

Still Life with Apples

H. 24⅝″ W. 29½″ Signed and dated lower right.

COLLECTIONS: Mrs. John W. Ames; Milch Galleries, New York; Joseph Hirshhorn, Greenwich, Connecticut; Hirshhorn Museum and Sculpture Garden, Washington, D.C.

PUBLISHED: *Catalogue of the Hirshhorn Museum and Sculpture Garden*, illustrated in color, number 489.

393.

Tree in a Field

H. 30″ W. 40″ Signed and dated lower right.

EXHIBITED: Durand-Ruel, 1944, number 12.

394.

Tricorne

H. 27″ W. 21″ Signed and dated lower left.

COLLECTIONS: Whitney Museum of American Art, New York; Cincinnati Art Museum, Ohio, Edwin and Virginia Irwin Memorial.

EXHIBITED: Whitney Annual, 1944, number 75; CAM, 1948, number 40; CAM, 1960, number 82, illustrated in color page 27; U of A, 1966, number 87, illustrated pages 75 and 115.

PUBLISHED: *50 Paintings by Walt Kuhn*, number 47, illustrated; Philip R. Adams, "Tricorne," *Cincinnati Art Museum Bulletin*, October 1958, pages 27-28, illustrated page 27.

The model was Eleanor Knapp, actress.

395.
White Vase
H.   W.
PUBLISHED: *Art News*, 13 April 1940, illustrated page 13; *Art Digest*, 15 April 1940, illustrated page 22.

396.
Young Girl
H. 30" W. 25"   Signed and dated lower left.
PUBLISHED: *50 Paintings by Walt Kuhn*, number 46, illustrated.
The model was Martha Skillings, a Martha Graham dancer.

1940

397.
Cabaret
H. 40" W. 30"
The model was Ruth Johnston.

398.
Chair with Apples
H. 40" W. 30"   Signed and dated lower center.
EXHIBITED: Cornell U., 1942, number 10; Durand-Ruel, 1946, number 2; CSFAC Traveling Show, 1947, number 12, illustrated page 8; World House, New York, 56th Anniversary of the American Federation of Arts, "Trustee's Choice," 1959, number 16, illustrated.
PUBLISHED: *50 Paintings by Walt Kuhn*, number 50, illustrated.

398A.
Clowns Waiting
H.   W.

399.
Dancing Clown
H. 12" W. 9"   Signed and dated upper right.
COLLECTIONS: Mr. and Mrs. Frank Winton, Birmingham, Michigan, 1960.
EXHIBITED: MWG, 1954, number 13; CAM, 1960, number 88.

400.
The Flautist
H.   W.
EXHIBITED: Durand-Ruel, April 1943.

401.
Girl – Cabaret
H. 40" W. 30"
EXHIBITED: Whitney, "Contemporary American Painting," December 1940 to January 1941.
PUBLISHED: *PM*, 1 December 1940, illustrated.

402.
Girl in Pierrot's Hat
H. 40" W. 30"   Signed and dated lower right.
EXHIBITED: KG, 1972, number 16, illustrated.

403.
Girl, Night Club
H. 18" W. 16"
The model was Ruth Johnston.

404.
Potatoes
H. 30" W. 40"   Signed and dated lower right.
EXHIBITED: CSFAC Traveling Show, 1947, number 13; CAM, 1960, number 84, illustrated page 64; U of A, 1966, number 90, illustrated pages 77 and 117.
PUBLISHED: *50 Paintings by Walt Kuhn*, number 48, illustrated.

405.
Raggedy Pants Comedian
H. 11¼" W. 8"   Signed and dated lower right.
COLLECTIONS: Los Angeles County Art Museum, California.
PUBLISHED: Sotheby Parke Bernet, Los Angeles, 1977, number 370, illustrated.

406.
Stumps   Painted in Great Barrington, Massachusetts.
H. 30" W. 40"   Signed and dated lower right.
EXHIBITED: Durand-Ruel, 1945, number 5; KG, 1967, number 23, illustrated page 40.
PUBLISHED: *50 Paintings by Walt Kuhn*, number 49, illustrated.

407.
The Twins
H.   W.   Two white horses and riders.

408.
Two Clowns (Two Veterans)
H. 14" W. 16"   Signed and dated lower right.
COLLECTIONS: Mr. and Mrs. Sol A. Davidson, Scranton, Pennsylvania.
EXHIBITED: Durand-Ruel, "Circus Subjects, Small Oils," 1943; CAM, 1960, number 85.
PUBLISHED: Rosamund Frost, "Walt Kuhn Clowns in a Great Tradition," *Art News*, 1 May 1943, illustrated page 11.

409.
Two Veterans
H.   W.   Signed and dated lower left.
EXHIBITED: Durand-Ruel, April 1943.
PUBLISHED: Rosamund Frost, "Walt Kuhn Clowns in a Great Tradition," *Art News*, 1 May 1943, illustrated page 11.

410.
Zinnias with Black Crock
H. 30" W. 25"   Signed and dated lower left.
EXHIBITED: KG, 1967, number 24, illustrated page 41.

1941

411.

Bananas Painted in Great Barrington, Massachusetts.

H. 40″ W. 30″ Signed and dated lower right.

EXHIBITED: Durand-Ruel, 1946, number 3; CSFAC Traveling Show, 1947, number 14, illustrated page 6; CAM, 1960, number 86; U of A, 1966, number 25, illustrated in color page 73; KG, 1967, number 25, illustrated page 42.

PUBLISHED: Marion Summers, *Daily Worker*, 14 November 1946, illustrated.

412.

Peaches

H. 25″ W. 30″ Signed and dated lower left.

EXHIBITED: Phillips Memorial Gallery, Washington, D.C., 1944, number 5; KG, 1967, number 27, illustrated page 44.

413.

Pumpkins Painted in Great Barrington, Massachusetts.

H. 40″ W. 50″ Signed and dated lower left.

COLLECTIONS: National Gallery of Art, Washington, D.C., Gift of the Avalon Foundation.

EXHIBITED: CSFAC Traveling Show, 1947, number 15, illustrated page 13; KG, 1967, number 26, illustrated page 43.

PUBLISHED: *Apollo*, December 1968, illustrated page 497; *Gazette des Beaux Arts*, February 1969, Illustrated page sup. 89.

414.

Red Bananas in Iron Dish

H. 20″ W. 24″

COLLECTIONS: Purchased by U.S. Department of State, 1946; Public School System, Owego, New York.

EXHIBITED: CGFA, 1942, number 14; Metropolitan Museum of Art, "State Department Exhibition, Europe," 1946; Musée d'Art Moderne, Paris, "Exposition Internationale d'Art Moderne," 18 November to 28 December 1946; Whitney, "War Assets Sales," May 1948, number 44.

PUBLISHED: *New York Journal American*, 26 November 1946, illustrated.

415.

Summer Glow

H. 25″ W. 30″ Yellow flowers against green background, pine table.

416.

Three Clowns

H.   W.

417.

White Zinnias

H. 29″ W. 24½″

COLLECTIONS: Mrs. Stephen Smith, New York, 1964.

1942

418.

Acrobat in Red and Green

H. 24″ W. 20″ Signed and dated lower right.

COLLECTIONS: Metropolitan Museum of Art, New York, George A. Hearn Fund, 1950.

EXHIBITED: Phillips Memorial Gallery, Washington, D.C., 1944, number 4; CSFAC Traveling Show, 1947, number 16, illustrated page 12; CAM, 1960, number 90, illustrated in color (detail) page 44.

PUBLISHED: *Art News*, 15 November 1944, illustrated in color, plate 1; *Art News*, November 1946, illustrated on cover in color; *Art News Annual*, 1949, illustrated in color page 42.

The model was Joe Pascucciello, known as Pasco, an exhibition bag-puncher, who also posed for *Veteran Clown* and *Clown with Drum*.

419.

Clown with Beret

H. 11″ W. 7½″ Signed and dated lower left.

COLLECTIONS: Dr. Arnold Emch, Chicago, Illinois.

EXHIBITED: CAM, 1960, number 87.

420.

Clown with Drum

H. 60″ W. 40″ Signed and dated lower right.

COLLECTIONS: Mr. Philip Sills, Riverdale-on-Hudson, New York.

EXHIBITED: Whitney Annual, 24 December 1942 to 6 January 1943; CAM, 1960, number 92, illustrated in color page 61; U of A, 1966, number 95, illustrated page 119.

The model was Joe Pascucciello.

421.

Clown with Rooster

H. 5½″ W. 8½″ Initialed and dated upper right.

COLLECTIONS: Mr. and Mrs. George R. Brown, Texas, 1961.

EXHIBITED: CAM, 1960, number 89; U of A, 1966, number 93.

422.

Clowns Dressing

H.   W.

EXHIBITED: Durand-Ruel, April 1943.

PUBLISHED: Rosamund Frost, "Walt Kuhn Clowns in a Great Tradition," *Art News*, 1 May 1943, illustrated page 11.

423.

Confab

H.   W.

EXHIBITED: MWG, 1954, number 9.

424.

Girl with Cocked Hat

H. 30″ W. 25″

COLLECTIONS: Mr. and Mrs. Otto L. Spaeth, New York; Hirshhorn Museum and Sculpture Garden, Washington, D.C.

269

EXHIBITED: Albany, 1958, number 14.

The model was Georgia Wayne

425.

Girl from Madrid

H. 40" W. 30" Signed and dated lower right.

EXHIBITED: CAM,1960, number 91, illustrated page 66; KG, 1967, number 28, illustrated page 45.

The model was Margo Gaynor.

426.

Girl Reading

H. 30" W. 25" Signed and dated lower right.

EXHIBITED: Dayton AI, 1943; Durand-Ruel, 1946, number 4; U of A, number 96.

427.

Hand Balancer

H. 40" W. 30" Signed and dated lower left.

COLLECTIONS: Mr. Fred L. Palmer, New York, 1959; Galley of Modern Art, including Huntington Hartford Collection, New York; Huntington Hartford, New York; Mr. Herbert Allen, Jr., New York.

EXHIBITED: Albany, 1958, number 15 (lent by Kuhn Estate); MWG, "Collector's Finds," 1959, number 1; CAM, 1960, number 8, illustrated page 65 (lent by Mr. Fred L. Palmer); U of A, 1966, number 94, illustrated pages 78 and 118 (lent by the Gallery of Modern Art, New York).

428.

Lily Cushing

H.   W.   Signed and dated lower right.

EXHIBITED: CSFAC Traveling Show, 1947, number 17, illustrated page 17.

429.

Lily with Feathered Hat

H. 15½" W. 16" Signed and dated lower left.

EXHIBITED: Phillips Memorial Gallery, Washington, D.C., 1944, number 12; KG, 1967, number 29, illustrated page 46.

The model was Lily Cushing.

430.

Seated Clown

H.   W.

431.

Self Portrait

H. 20" W. 14" Dated center right.

EXHIBITED: U of A, 1966, number 92, illustrated in color page 12.

PUBLISHED: Johnson, *American Artist*, December 1967, illustrated page 51.

432.

Teal

H.   W.   Signed and dated lower right.

EXHIBITED: Dayton AI, 1943; CSFAC Traveling Show, 1947, number 18, illustrated page 8; Carnegie Institute, Pittsburgh, Pennsylvania, 8 January to 15 February 1946.

PUBLISHED: John O'Connor, Jr., "Paintings by Walt Kuhn," *Carnegie Magazine,* January-February 1948, illustrated page 210.

433.

Veteran Clown

H. 24" W. 20" Signed and dated lower right.

COLLECTIONS: Mr. and Mrs. Henry Sears, New York.

EXHIBITED: U of A, 1966, number 97, illustrated in color, page 76.

PUBLISHED: *Connoisseur,* March 1966, page LXII, advertisement.

The model was Joe Pascucciello.

1943

434.

Clown with Dogs

H. 14½" W. 19" Initialed lower right.

COLLECTIONS: Mr. Henry Strater, Palm Beach, Florida, 1966.

EXHIBITED: Norton Gallery, West Palm Beach, 1944; MWG, 1954, number 17; U of A, 1966, number 99, illustrated page 79 (lent by Maynard Walker).

434A.

Clown with His Dog

H. 10" W. 12" Signed lower left center.

COLLECTIONS: University of Nebraska Art Galleries, Lincoln, Sheldon Bequest.

435.

Clown in His Dressing Room

H.   W.   Signed and dated lower left.

EXHIBITED: Durand-Ruel, 1944, number 5; CSFAC Traveling Show, 1947, number 19, illustrated page 3; Carnegie Institute, Pittsburgh, Pennsylvania, 8 January to 15 February 1948.

PUBLISHED: *Pictures on Exhibit,* November 1944, illustrated page 17; John O'Connor, Jr., "Paintings by Walt Kuhn," *Carnegie Magazine,* January–February 1948, illustrated page 209; *Art Digest,* 15 May 1951, illustrated page 12; "Painting in the United States," *Carnegie Magazine,* 1945, illustrated page 209.

436.

Clowns Dressing

H.   W.

EXHIBITED: Durand-Ruel, 1943.

PUBLISHED: *Art News,* 1–14 May 1943, illustrated page 11.

437.

Dimitri

H.   W.

EXHIBITED: MWG, 1954, number 12.

438.

Girl in White and Silver

H. 40" W. 30" Signed and dated lower right.

COLLECTIONS: Metropolitan Museum of Art, New York, George A. Hearn Fund, 1950.

EXHIBITED: Durand-Ruel, 1944, number 8; Phillips Memorial Gallery, Washington, D.C., 1944, number 3; CAM, 1960, number 96.

439.

Green Apples on Blue Cloth

H. 30" W. 40"   Signed and dated lower right.

COLLECTIONS: Mrs. Otto L. Spaeth, New York.

EXHIBITED: Durand-Ruel, 1944, number 4; Phillips Memorial Gallery, Washington, D.C., 1944, number 8; CAM, 1960, number 93, illustrated page 67.

PUBLISHED: *Art News*, 15 November 1944, illustrated page 22; *Art News*, 1 January 1945, illustrated page 27.

440.

Green Apples with Gray Curtain

H. 25" W. 30"   Signed and dated lower left.

COLLECTIONS: Indianapolis Museum of Art, Gift of Mr. and Mrs. Henry Hope, Given in Memory of William Ray Adams.

EXHIBITED: CAM, 1960, number 95.

PUBLISHED: Robert O. Parks, *John Herron Art Institute Bulletin*, April 1949, illustrated.

441

Head of Young Girl

H. 17" W. 14"   Signed and dated left center.

EXHIBITED: U of A, 1966, number 98.

442.

Ladies of the Ensemble

H. 6" W. 20"   Signed upper left.

EXHIBITED: Durand-Ruel, 1943; KG, 1972, number 25, illustrated.

443.

Mandolinist

H.   W.

EXHIBITED: Durand-Ruel, 1943.

PUBLISHED: *Art News*, 1-14 May 1943, illustrated page 11.

444.

Peaches

H. 7" W. 19"   Signed and dated lower right.

COLLECTIONS: Mr. and Mrs. Philip R. Adams, Cincinnati, Ohio.

EXHIBITED: Dayton AI, 1943; CAM and Milwaukee Art Institute, Wisconsin, "Still Life Painting since 1470," 1956, number 32, illustrated page 23; CAM, 1960, number 94, illustrated page 68.

445.

Self Portrait with Beard

H. 15" W. 12"   Signed and dated lower right.

EXHIBITED: KG, 1972, number 12, illustrated.

446.

Show Girl in Armor

H. 30" W. 25"   Signed and dated lower right.

447.

Smokey

H. 9" W. 5½"

COLLECTIONS: Mrs. Grace Arnold, Columbus, Ohio; Mr. H. Bartley Arnold, Columbus, Ohio.

EXHIBITED: Dayton AI, 1947; CAM, 1948, number 36.

448.

Two Veterans

H.   W.

PUBLISHED: *Art News*, 1-14 May 1943, illustrated page 11.

449.

Zinnias

H. 30" W. 24"   Signed and dated lower right.

COLLECTIONS: Mr. and Mrs. David Workman.

EXHIBITED: Dayton AI, 1943; KG, 1967, number 30, illustrated page 47.

1944

450.

Acrobat in Red

H. 24" W. 20"   Signed and dated lower left.

EXHIBITED: KG, 1967, number 33, illustrated page 50.

PUBLISHED: Johnson, *American Artist*, December 1967, illustrated page 54.

451.

Acrobat in White and Silver

H. 30" W. 25"

COLLECTIONS: Wichita Art Museum, Kansas, Roland P. Murdock Collection.

EXHIBITED: Durand-Ruel, 1944, number 9; CAM, 1948, number 42.

PUBLISHED: *Art News*, August 1946, illustrated page 55; *Art Digest*, 15 December 1946, illustrated page 55.

The model was Frank Landy, who also posed for *Trio*.

452.

Ax

H.   W.

EXHIBITED: Durand-Ruel, 1944, number 6.

453.

Brook and Trees

H.   W.

EXHIBITED: MWG, 1957, number 4.

454.

Clown in Beaver Hat

H. 24" W. 20"   Signed and dated.

COLLECTIONS: Mrs. David Levy, New York; Dr. and Mrs. Marion Sulzberger, New York, 1948.

PUBLISHED: Sotheby Parke Bernet, "Important 20th Century American Paintings, Drawings, Watercolors, and Sculptures," 13 December 1972, number 157, illustrated in color; Arts, November 1972, illustrated page 9, advertisement.

455.
Clown with Folded Arms
H.   W.
COLLECTIONS: Pennsylvania Academy of the Fine Arts, Philadelphia.
EXHIBITED: Durand-Ruel, 1944, number 7.
PUBLISHED: Margaret Bruening, "Walt Kuhn's Austere Modern Classics," *Art News*, November 1944, illustrated page 22; *Art Digest*, 15 November 1944, illustrated page 8.

456.
Elizabeth Bliss Parkinson
H.   W.   Signed and dated center right.
EXHIBITED: CSFAC Traveling Show, 1947, number 21, illustrated page 5.

457.
Gladys
H. 12″ W. 9″

458.
Goose Cronin—Clown
H. 12″ W. 9″   Signed and dated lower right.

459.
Green Pompom
H. 30″ W. 25″
EXHIBITED: Whitney, "Annual Exhibition of Contemporary American Painting," 16 December 1947 to 25 January 1948; CAM, 1948, number 41.
The model was Ruth Ester.

460.
Man in Green Opera Costume
H. 20″ W. 16″   Signed and dated lower right.
EXHIBITED: CSFAC Traveling Show, 1947, number 22, illustrated.
The model was the painter Frank di Gioia.

461.
Murph
H. 12″ W. 9″

462.
Oak
H.   W.
EXHIBITED: Durand-Ruel, 1945, number 6.

463.
Old Wharf, Cape Neddick River
H. 24″ W. 20″   Signed and dated lower right.

464.
Peaches on Blue Cloth
H. 20″ W. 24″   Signed and dated lower right.
COLLECTIONS: Mrs. Catherine S. Carleton, Morristown, New Jersey.

465.
Peaches on Red Cloth
H. 20″ W. 24″   Signed and dated lower right.
COLLECTIONS: I. Stetson Haverstick, 1964.

EXHIBITED: CAM, 1948, number 39; KG, 1967, number 31, illustrated page 48.

466.
Pending Storm
H. 13″ W. 16″   Signed and dated lower left.
EXHIBITED: Durand-Ruel, 1944, number 3; KG, 1967, number 34, illustrated page 51.

467.
Pine by a Road   Pine on Chase's Pond Road, York County, Maine.
H. 30″ W. 25″   Signed and dated lower right.
EXHIBITED: Durand-Ruel, 1946, number 7; CSFAC Traveling Show, 1947, number 23; MWG, 1957, number 2.

468.
"Pop" Pendleton—Juggler
H. 12″ W. 9″
COLLECTIONS: Hirshhorn Museum and Sculpture Garden, Washington, D.C.
EXHIBITED: MWG, 1954, number 6.

469.
Portrait of a Young Man
COLLECTIONS: Mr. and Mrs. Sol A. Davidson, Scranton, Pennsylvania.
EXHIBITED: CAM, 1960, number 96.
The model was Mr. Sol A. Davidson.

470.
Portrait of a Young Woman
H.   W.
COLLECTIONS: Phillips Memorial Gallery, Washington, D.C.
EXHIBITED: Phillips Memorial Gallery, Washington, D.C., 1944, number 7.

471.
Red Apples
H.   W.   Signed and dated lower right.
EXHIBITED: CSFAC Traveling Show, 1947, number 24, illustrated page 4.

471A.
Red Apples and Copper Kettle
H. 25″ W. 30″   Signed and dated lower right.
COLLECTIONS: Mrs. Seherr-Toss.

472.
Rock and Sea   Painted at Cape Neddick, Maine.
H. 30″ W. 25″
EXHIBITED: Durand-Ruel, "Exhibition of Paintings by Walt Kuhn," 8 November to 2 December 1944, number 1.

473.
White Cockade
H. 36″ W. 25″   Signed and dated lower right.
EXHIBITED: KG, 1967, number 32, illustrated page 49.
PUBLISHED: Johnson, *American Artist*, December 1967, illustrated page 55.

1945

474.

Bridge Painted at Cape Neddick, Maine.
II. 39" W. 40" Signed and dated lower left.
EXHIBITED: Durand-Ruel, 1945, number 8.

475.

Clown
H. 20" W. 16" Signed and dated lower right.
COLLECTIONS: Encyclopedia Britannica Collection, Chicago, Illinois.
PUBLISHED: *Catalogue of the Encyclopedia Britannica Collection*, 1945, number 67, illustrated; *Art Digest*, 1 April 1945, illustrated page 22.

476.

Girl with Brown Hair
H. 12" W. 10"
EXHIBITED: U of A, 1966, number 100.

477.

Joe Gomez
H. 10½" W. 7½" Initialed and dated lower right; oil on academy board.
COLLECTIONS: Mr. Stanley Barbee, 1947.
EXHIBITED: School for Art Studies, "Living Art in the New York Galleries," December 1945; Durand-Ruel, 1946.
PUBLISHED: Parke Bernet, "Barbee and Others," 16 February 1961, number 79.

478.

Green Bananas and Oranges In white bowl.
H. 20" W. 15" Signed and dated lower right.
COLLECTIONS: Mr. and Mrs. Fred L. Palmer, New York, 1956.
EXHIBITED: U of A, 1966, number 101, illustrated page 80; Hofstra University, "Eats: An Exhibition of Food in Art," 1972; Westmoreland County Museum of Art, Greensburg, Pennsylvania, "Art and the Kitchen," number A-23, 1975; Hirschl and Adler Galleries, New York, "American Painting 1876—1963," 1975, illustrated page 22.
PUBLISHED: *Apollo*, August 1969, illustrated in color page ix.

479.

Oak Painted on road to the Yorks, York County, Maine.
H. 30" W. 40" Signed and dated lower right.
EXHIBITED: Durand-Ruel, 1945, number 9; Nasson College, 1964, number 4; KG, 1967, number 35, illustrated page 52.

480.

Pine at 5 O'Clock
H. 30" W. 25"
EXHIBITED: Durand-Ruel, 1946, number 10; Metropolitan Museum of Art, 1946, "Advancing American Art," State Department, South American Section; Whitney, 1948.
PUBLISHED: *Art News*, October 1946, illustrated on cover.

481.

Pony
H. 30" W. 25" Signed and dated lower right.
EXHIBITED: Whitney Annual, 1945-46; CAM, 1948, number 35; Nasson College, 1964 (*The Pony*); KG, 1967, number 36, illustrated page 53 (*The Pony*).
PUBLISHED: *Art News*, 1 December 1945, illustrated page 13.

482.

River Bank Cape Neddick River, Maine.
H. 30" W. 40"
EXHIBITED: Durand-Ruel, 1945, number 10.

483.

River Bank
H. 30" W. 40" Signed and dated lower left.

484.

Shore Road Painted near Lake Manson, beyond Sanford, Maine.
H. 25" W. 30" Signed and dated lower left.
EXHIBITED: Durand-Ruel, 1945, number 12.

485.

Sextet of Clowns
H. 9" W. 12" Canvas on masonite, initial and dated lower right.
EXHIBITED: KG, 1972, number 21, illustrated.
PUBLISHED: Sotheby Parke Bernet, "American 19th & 20th Century Paintings, Drawings, Watercolors & Sculpture," 27 October 1977, number 179, illustrated.

486.

Smiling Clown
H. 9" W. 7" Signed and dated lower right.
COLLECTIONS: Mr. and Mrs. Walter L. Wyckoff, Seattle, Washington.
EXHIBITED: MWG, 1954, number 8, illustrated on cover; CAM, 1960, number 98.
PUBLISHED: Sotheby Parke Bernet, "Twentieth Century American Paintings," 13–14 December 1973 (ca. 1940–45).

487.

Star Performer
H.   W.
EXHIBITED: Durand-Ruel, 1946, number 5.
PUBLISHED: *Daily Worker*, 14 November 1946, illustrated in review by Marion Summers.

488.

Watching the Act
H.   W.

1946

489.

Acrobat in White and Silver
H.   W.
COLLECTIONS: Wichita Art Museum, Kansas, Roland J. Murdock Collection.

PUBLISHED: *Art News,* August 1946, illustrated page 55; *Art Digest,* 15 December 1946, illustrated page 15.

490.

Athlete in Green

H. 30" W. 25"   Signed and dated lower right.

COLLECTIONS: Mr. William Inge, 1964.

EXHIBITED: Carnegie Institute, Pittsburgh Pennsylvania, "Painting in the United States, 1947," 1947, illustrated; U of A, 1966, number 102, illustrated page 81 (anonymous loan).

The model was Vernon Sanderson, "Sandy," a singer in Gilbert and Sullivan operettas.

491.

Black Butterfly

H. 72" W. 32¼"   Signed and dated lower right.

EXHIBITED: Arts Center Gallery, Indiana University, Bloomington, Indiana, April 1946; KG, 1967, number 39, illustrated page 56.

The model was Charlotte Sanger, Mrs. William Ward.

492.

Clown with White Tie

H. 20" W. 16"

COLLECTIONS: Mrs. Alfred Starr.

EXHIBITED: Durand-Ruel, 1946.

PUBLISHED: *Art Digest,* 15 November 1946, illustrated.

493.

Country Girl

H.   W.

EXHIBITED: Corcoran Gallery, Washington, D.C., "20th Biennial Exhibition of Contemporary American Oil Paintings," 30 March to 11 May 1947, number 246.

494.

Fruit Dish

H.   W.

EXHIBITED: Durand-Ruel, 1946, number 7.

495.

Gold and Blue Bolero

H. 24" W. 18"   Signed and dated left center.

496.

Golden and Blue Bolero

H. 24" W. 20"   Signed and dated left center.

EXHIBITED: KG, 1972, number 6, illustrated.

497.

Green Bananas

H. 24" W. 20"   Signed and dated lower right.

COLLECTIONS: Des Moines Art Center, Des Moines, Iowa, Edmundson Collection.

EXHIBITED: Durand-Ruel, 1946, number 8; MWG, 1954, number 14; CAM, 1960, number 103, illustrated page 70; U of A, 1966, number 104.

498.

Joady—Clown

H.   W.

EXHIBITED: MWG, 1954, number 10.

PUBLISHED: *Newsweek,* 7 March 1955, illustrated page 85.

499.

Loaf of Bread

H. 16" W. 20"   Signed and dated lower right.

COLLECTIONS: Mrs. Otto L. Spaeth, New York.

EXHIBITED: Durand-Ruel, 1946, number 6 (*Bread*); CAM, 1948, number 44, illustrated page 16; CAM, 1960, number 100, illustrated in color page 62; Nasson College, 1964, number 9.

500.

Miss D

H. 26" W. 19"   Signed and dated lower right.

EXHIBITED: CAM, 1960, number 101; U of A, 1966, number 108.

PUBLISHED: *Time Magazine,* 22 November 1948, illustrated page 52; *Art Digest,* 1 November 1948, illustrated page 15.

501.

Oak   Painted in York County, Maine.

H. 30" W. 40"   Signed and dated lower right.

EXHIBITED: Durand-Ruel, 1946, number 9; MWG, 1957, number 10; Albany, 1958, number 16; CAM, 1960, number 102; U of A, 1966, number 105.

502.

Peaches

H. 30" W. 40"   Signed and dated lower right.

COLLECTIONS: Helen and David P. Pall, Roslyn, New York.

EXHIBITED: Durand-Ruel, 1946, number 10; Pennsylvania Academy of the Fine Arts, January–February 1947; U of A, 1966, number 106; KG, 1967, number 41, illustrated in color page 58.

503.

Peaches on Red Cloth No. 2

H. 18" W. 24"   Signed and dated lower right.

504.

Pine

H.   W.

EXHIBITED: Durand-Ruel, 1946, number 11.

505.

Rider with Blue Sash

H. 40" W. 30"   Signed and dated lower left.

EXHIBITED: KG, 1967, number 38, illustrated page 55 (*The White Rider*).

506.

Roberto

H. 40" W. 30"   Signed and dated center right.

COLLECTIONS: Mr. and Mrs. Harry Daniel, Bristol, Tennessee; Mr. and Mrs. Henry Sears, New York.

EXHIBITED: Durand-Ruel, 1946, number 12; CAM, 1960, number 99, illustrated page 69; U of A, 1966, number 103, illustrated page 120.

PUBLISHED: *Art News*, November 1946, illustrated page 39; Marion Summers, *Daily Worker*, 14 November 1946, illustrated; *Art Digest*, 15 November 1946, illustrated page 12; *Connoisseur*, May 1969, illustrated page iii in color, advertisement; Johnson, *American Artist*, December 1967, illustrated page 56.

The model was Robert Camilieri.

507.

Sandy

H. 30″ W. 25″

COLLECTIONS: Minneapolis Institute of Arts, Minnesota.

EXHIBITED: Whitney Annual, 10 December 1946 to 16 January 1947; Toledo, Ohio, Museum of Art, "34th Annual Exhibition of Contemporary American Painting," 15 May–31 August 1947; Pennsylvania Academy of the Fine Arts, Philadelphia, Pennsylvania, "143rd Annual Exhibition of Oils and Sculpture," 1 January–29 February 1948; U of A, 1966, number 107.

PUBLISHED: *New York Herald Tribune*, 27 July 1947, illustrated; *Art Quarterly*, Summer 1961, illustrated page 8; Carl J. Weinhardt, Jr., "Recent Accessions," *Minneapolis Institute of Arts Bulletin*, illustrated page 8.

The model was Vernon Sanderson, who also posed for *Athlete in Green*.

508.

Sparrow   Head of a clown.

H. 8¾″ W. 6½″   Oil on academy board, signed and dated lower right.

PUBLISHED: Sotheby Parke Bernet, "Saltonstall and Others, American Paintings, etc.," 14 October 1970, number 126, illustrated.

509.

Tri-Color Cockade

H. 24″ W. 20″   Signed and dated lower right.

EXHIBITED: KG, 1967, number 37, illustrated page 54.

PUBLISHED: Johnson, *American Artist*, December 1967, illustrated page 55.

1947

510.

Acrobat in White and Blue

H. 29¼″ W. 24¼″   Signed and dated lower right.

COLLECTIONS: Joseph H. Hirshhorn, Greenwich, Connecticut, 1954; Hirshhorn Museum and Sculpture Garden, Washington, D.C.

EXHIBITED: CSFAC Traveling Show, 1947; Durand-Ruel, 8 November to 4 December 1948, "Walt Kuhn, Fifty Years a Painter"; National Gallery of Canada, Ottawa, 1957, "Some American Paintings from the Collection of Joseph H. Hirshhorn," number 40, illustrated page 13; American Federation of Arts Tour, 1962–65, "Paintings from the Joseph H. Hirshhorn Foundation Collection: A View of the

Protean Century," number 41, illustrated page 11; MWG, 1954.

PUBLISHED: *New York Times*, 9 October 1960, illustrated; *Pictures on Exhibit*, November 1962, illustrated on cover; Emily Genauer, "75 Choice Hirshhorn Paintings," *New York Herald Tribune*, 4 November 1962, illustrated; Emmet John Hughes, "Joe Hirshhorn, the Brooklyn Uranium King," *Fortune*, November 1965, illustrated in color, page 157; Alonzo Lansford, "State of the Union," *Art Digest*, interview, 1 November 1948, illustrated page 15; *Boston Herald*, 13 December 1964; *Catalogue of the Hirshhorn Museum and Sculpture Garden*, illustrated number 538.

511.

Bert Lahr

H. 20″ W. 16″   Signed and dated lower right, with copyright symbol.

COLLECTIONS: Mr. Richard A. Manoogian, Grosse Pointe, Michigan, 1968.

EXHIBITED: Durand-Ruel, 1947; Carnegie Institute, Pittsburgh, Pennsylvania, 1948; U of A, 1966, number 10; KG, 1967, number 43, illustrated page 60 (*Portrait of Bert Lahr, Comedian*).

PUBLISHED: New York World Telegram, 31 May 1947, illustrated; *Art Digest*, 1 June 1947, illustrated page 22; *Art News*, June 1947, illustrated page 8; *New York Times*, 1 June 1947, illustrated; Fayetteville, North Carolina, *Observer*, 6 June 1947, illustrated; *Pittsburgh Sun Telegraph*, 10 February 1948, illustrated; *Pittsburgh Post Gazette*, 10 February 1948, illustrated; *Pittsburgh Press*, 10 February 1948, illustrated; cover of playbill for Broadway show *Burlesque*.

512.

Bobby Barry, Comedian

H. 19″ W. 15″   Signed and dated lower right.

EXHIBITED: Durand-Ruel, 1948, "Walt Kuhn, Fifty Years a Painter," U of A, 1966, number 111; KG, 1967, number 42, illustrated page 59.

PUBLISHED: *Art Digest*, 1 November 1948, illustrated page 2, advertisement; *Time Magazine*, 22 November 1948, illustrated page 52.

513.

Butternut Squash

H. 20″ W. 24″   Signed and dated lower right.

EXHIBITED: KG, 1967, number 40, illustrated page 57.

514.

Cannoneer

H. 30″ W. 25″   Signed and dated center left.

EXHIBITED: KG, 1967, number 45, illustrated page 62.

515.

Challa

H. 12″ W. 14″

COLLECTIONS: Mr. and Mrs. Henry R. Hope.

EXHIBITED: CAM, 1960, number 106.

516.
Clown in Red and Green against Blue
H.   W.
EXHIBITED: MWG, 1954, number 5.
PUBLISHED: *Art Digest*, 15 February 1954, illustrated page 18.

517.
Dominique
H. 10″ W. 8″
COLLECTIONS: Mr. and Mrs. R. L. Sergel, Chicago, Illinois, 1957.
EXHIBITED: MWG, 154, number 11; CAM, 1960, number 105.

518.
Dragoon
H. 36″ W. 22″   Signed and dated lower right.
EXHIBITED: KG, 1967, number 44, illustrated page 61.

519.
Ed Hennessey
H. 12″ W. 8″
COLLECTIONS: Mr. and Mrs. R. L. Sergel, Chicago, Illinois, 1958.
EXHIBITED: MWG, 1954, number 14; CAM, 1960, number 104.

520.
Frightened Horses
H. 6¾″ W. 12″
COLLECTIONS: Mr. and Mrs. Henry, Sears, New York.
EXHIBITED: U of A, 1966, number 112.

521.
Rocks in Landscape
H.   W.
EXHIBITED: MWG, 1957, number 8.

522.
Sap Bucket and Apples
H. 30″ W. 40″   Signed and dated lower right.
COLLECTIONS: Mr. Richard A. Manoogian, Grosse Pointe, Michigan, 1967.
EXHIBITED: KG, 1967, number 46, illustrated page 63.

523.
Sliced Loaf
H. 12″ W. 15″
Never exhibited.

523A.
Zinnias in Blue Vase
H. 9″ W. 8½″
COLLECTIONS: Mr. and Mrs. Frank X. Gina, New York.

1948

524.
Apples on Green Cloth
H.   W.
EXHIBITED: MWG, 1954, number 3.

525.
Apples on Red Cloth
H. 25″ W. 30″   Signed and dated lower left.
COLLECTIONS: Mrs. Stephen Smith, 1962.
EXHIBITED: CAM, 1960, number 109, illustrated page 74.

526.
Apples on White Cloth
COLLECTIONS: Mrs. Charles Dougherty, Saint Paul, Minnesota.

527.
Apples in a Wooden Bucket
H. 20″ W. 24″   Signed and dated lower right.
EXHIBITED: KG, 1967, number 48, illustrated page 65.

528.
Bread
H. 16″ W. 20″   Signed and dated lower right.
EXHIBITED: KG, 1967, number 47, illustrated page 64.
PUBLISHED: *Art Digest*, 1 October 1952, illustrated page 14.

529.
Bread with Knife (Bread and Bread Knife on White Cloth)
H. 16″ W. 20″   Signed and dated lower left.
COLLECTIONS: Wichita Art Museum, Kansas, Roland P. Murdock Collection.
EXHIBITED: MWG, 1954, number 2, CAM, 1960, number 108.
PUBLISHED: *Art News*, February 1954, illustrated page 43.

530.
Chico in Silk Hat
H. 40″ W. 30″
COLLECTIONS: Mr. and Mrs. Henry Sears, New York, 1965.
EXHIBITED: U of A, 1966, number 115, illustrated page 83.

531.
Chico in Top Hat
H. 23″ W. 21″
EXHIBITED: U of A, 1966, number 116; KG, 1967, number 50, illustrated page 67.
PUBLISHED: *Apollo*, June 1967, illustrated page 467; Johnson, *American Artist*, December 1967, illustrated page 57.

532.
Clown
H. 20″ W. 16″   Signed and dated lower right.
EXHIBITED: KG, 1967, number 49, illustrated page 66.

533.
Clown with Blue Shirt and Green Vest
H. 20″ W. 16″   Signed and dated lower right.
EXHIBITED: U of A, 1966, number 114.

534.

Clown in Red Tights

H. 30" W. 25"

COLLECTIONS: Mrs. Jacob M. Kaplan, New York, 1965; Brooks Memorial Gallery, Memphis, Tennessee.

EXHIBITED: U of A, 1966, number 113.

535.

Lion

H.   W.   Signed and dated lower left.

EXHIBITED: Durand-Ruel, 1948, "Walt Kuhn, Fifty Years a Painter."

PUBLISHED: *Time Magazine*, 22 November 1948, illustrated page 52; Alonzo Lansford, "State of the Union," interview, *Art Digest*, 1 November 1948, page 15.

536.

Lioness

H. 13" W. 11"   Signed and dated lower left.

EXHIBITED: KG, 1972, number 8, illustrated.

537.

Still Life of Rib Roast on Table

H.   W.

EXHIBITED: Durand-Ruel, 1948, "Walt Kuhn, Fifty Years a Painter."

PUBLISHED: *Time Magazine*, 22 November 1948, page 52.

538.

Still Life of a Turkey

H.   W.

EXHIBITED: Durand-Ruel, 1948, "Walt Kuhn, Fifty Years a Painter."

PUBLISHED: *Time Magazine*, 22 November 1948, page 52.

539.

White Riders

H.   W.

PUBLISHED: "Spotlight on Kuhn," *Art News*, 19 November 1948, page 18.

540.

Winter Apples

H. 20" W. 24"

COLLECTIONS: Hirshhorn Museum and Sculpture Garden, Washington, D.C.

541.

Zinnias   Probably the last painting.

H.   W.

COLLECTIONS: Mrs. Ruth King Adams, Cape Neddick, Maine; Mr. George S. Hutchins, Jr., York, Maine.

Undated

542.

Apples in Barn

H.   W.

PUBLISHED: *Art in America*, September 1969, illustrated page 2.

543.

Beryl Plays the Guitar

H.   W.

544.

Broken Doll

H. 22" W. 34"   Oil on burlap, signed.

PUBLISHED: Parke Bernet, "American Paintings, Various Owners," 16 March 1967, number 111.

545.

Circus Performer with Mustache

H. 10" W. 7¾"

EXHIBITED: KG, 1972, number 2, illustrated.

546.

The Clown

H. 8" W. 6"   Canvas mounted on board, initialed.

PUBLISHED: Parke Bernet, "American Paintings, Various Owners," 15 November 1967, number 111.

547.

The Clown

H. 8½" W. 6"   Canvas mounted on board, initialed.

COLLECTIONS: Schneider Galleries, 1970.

PUBLISHED: Sotheby Parke Bernet, "Saltonstall and Others, 19th Century American Painters, etc.," 1 October 1970, number 95.

548.

Clowns

H. 12" W. 15"   Signed upper left.

PUBLISHED: Parke Bernet, "Campbell and Others," 20 November 1956.

549.

Two Clowns   1935-40?

H. 9½" W. 12½"

EXHIBITED: KG, 1972, number 22, illustrated.

PUBLISHED: Sotheby Parke Bernet, "Important 18th, 19th and 20th Century American Paintings, 23 May 1974, number 83, illustrated.

550.

Flowers

H. 12" W. 10"   Signed lower right.

COLLECTIONS: A. William Bahr.

PUBLISHED: Parke Bernet, "Ingres and Others, Modern Paintings, Drawings and Prints," 12 November 1953, number 35.

551.

Flowers of the Season: Set of Three Panels

H. 31½" W. 11¾"   Unframed.

PUBLISHED: Parke Bernet, "American Paintings, Various Owners," 16 March 1967, number 66a.

552.

Girl in Green Costume

H. 14" W. 6½"

EXHIBITED: KG, 1972, number 19, illustrated.

553.
Green Apples with Watering Can
H.   W.
EXHIBITED: CAM, 1948, number 33.

554.
Green and Red Clown
H. 8½" W. 5¾"   Initialed lower right.
EXHIBITED: KG, 1972, number 10, illustrated.

555.
Happy Clown with Mustache (Smiling Clown)
H. 12" W. 8"

556.
Head of a Smiling Clown   1940-45?

H. 9" W. 7"   Initialed lower left.
PUBLISHED: Sotheby Parke Bernet, "20th Century American Paintings, etc.," 14 December 1973, number 119, illustrated.

557.
Kitchen Interior
H. 15" W. 12"
COLLECTIONS: Private collection, New York.
PUBLISHED: Parke Bernet, "Foster and Others," 22-23 February 1957, number 38.

558.
Light Blue Clown
H. 12" W. 9"

559.
Mean Circus Performer
H. 8¾" W. 6½"
EXHIBITED: KG, 1972, number 11, illustrated.

560.
Red Wig
H.   W.
COLLECTIONS: Mr. Philip Isles, 1947.

561.
Show Girl
H. 24" W. 13¾"   Oil on paper mounted on canvas.
COLLECTIONS: Mr. Philip Sills, New York.
PUBLISHED: Parke Bernet, "American Paintings, Various Owners," 16 March 1967, number 100, illustrated.

562.
The Show Is On
H. 16" W. 18"

563.
Smiling Clown
H. 12" W. 8"
EXHIBITED: KG, 1972, number 13, illustrated.

564.
Still Life with Peaches
H. 10" W. 15"   Signed lower right.
PUBLISHED: Sotheby Parke Bernet, "American 18th, 19th & 20th Century Paintings, Drawings and Watercolors," 17 April 1975, number 113, illustrated.

565.
Still Life – Zinnias, Fresias, Cornflowers
H. 7¾" W. 7"
EXHIBITED: KG, 1972, number 29, illustrated.

566.
Summer in Ogunquit
H.   W
EXHIBITED: Nasson College, 1964, number 7.

567.
White Faced Clown
H. 8" W. 5¾"   Initialed upper right.
EXHIBITED: KG, 1972, number 1, illustrated.

568.
White Faced Clown with Full Head of Hair
H. 8¼" W. 6½"
EXHIBITED: KG, 1972, number 18, illustrated.

569.
White Faced Clown in Green Shirt
H. 9" W. 6"
EXHIBITED: KG, 1972, number 15, illustrated.

570.
White Clown in Rust Shirt
H. 8" W. 6¼"   Canvas on board, initialed upper right.

571.
Young Man   (Circus Performer)
H. 12" W. 8¾"
EXHIBITED: KG, 1972, number 4, illustrated.

Appendix

Exhibitors in the Armory Show

Abenschein, Albert
Aitken, Robert
Alger, John J.
Anderson, Karl
Archipenko, Alexandre
Ashe, Edwin Marion
Barclay, Florence Howell
Barnard, George Gray
Beach, Chester
Bechtejeff, W. von
Becker, Maurice
Beckett, Marion H.
Bellows, George
Berlin, H.
Bernard, Joseph
Bickford, Nelson N.
Bjorkman, Olaf
Blanchet, Alexandre
Bluemner, Oscar
Bolz, Hans
Bonnard, Pierre
Borglum, Solon
Boss, Homer
Bourdelle, E.A.
Brancusi, Constantin
Braque, Georges
Brewer, Bessie Marsh
Brinley, D. Putnam
Brown, Bolton
Brown, Fannie Miller
Bruce, P.H.
Burroughs, Mrs. Bryson
Butler, Theodore Earl
Camoin, Charles
Carles, Arthur B.
Carr, Mrs. Myra Mussleman
Casarini, A.
Cassatt, Mary
Cesare, O.F.
Cézanne, Paul

Chabaud, Auguste
Chaffee, O.N.
Chanler, Robert W.
Charmy, Emilie
Chavannes, Puvis De
Chew, Amos
Churchill, Alfred Vance
Cimiotti,Jr., Gustave
Coate, H.W.
Cohen, Nessa
Coleman, Glenn O.
Coluzzi, Howard
Conder, Charles
Corot, J.B.C.
Cory, Kate
Courbet, Gustave
Crisp, Arthur
Cross, Henri Edmond
Crowley, Herbert
Currie, Frank
Cutler, Carl Gordon
Dabo, Leon
Dasburg, Andrew
Daumier, Honore
Davey, Randall
Davidson, Jo
Davies, Arthur B.
Davis,Charles H.
Davis, Stuart
Degas, Edgar
Delacroix, Eugene
Delaunay, Robert
Denis, Maurice
Derain, Andre
Dimock, Edith
Dirks, Rudolph
Dolinsky, Nathaniel
Donoho, Ruger
Doucet, Henri
Dreier, Katherine

Dresser, Aileen
Dresser, Lawrence
Dreyfous, Florence
Du Bois, Guy Pene
Duchamp, Marcel
Duchamp-Villon, Raymond
Duffy, Richard H.
Dufrenoy, Georges
Dufy, Raoul
Dumoyer de Segonzac, A.
Eberle, Abastinia
Eddy, H.B.
Eells, Jean
Engle, Amos W.
Epstein, Jacob
Este, Florence
Everett, Lily
Flandrin, Jules
Foote, Mary
Frazer, James Earle
Frazier, Kenneth
Fresnaye, Rogert de la
Freund, Arthur
Friesz, Othon
Fuhr, Ernest
Gauguin, Paul
Gaylor, Wood
Gibb, Phelan
Gimmi, Wilhelm
Girieud, Pierre
Glackens, William
Gleizes, Albert
Glintenkamp, H.
Goldthwaite, Anne
Goya, Francisco
Guerin, Charles
Gussow, Bernard
Gutmann, Bernhard
Hale, Philip L.
Halpert, Samuel

Harley, Chas. R.
Hartley, Marsden
Hassam, Childe
Haworth, Edith
Helbig, Walter
Henri, Robert
Hess, Julius
Higgins, Eugene
Hoard, Margaret
Hodler, Ferdinand
Hone, Nathaniel
Hopkinson, Charles
Hopper, Edward
Howard, Cecil
Humphreys, Albert
Hunt, Mrs. Thomas
Huntington, Margaret
Ingres
Innes, J.D.
Jansen, F. M.
John, Augustus
John, Gwen
Johnson, Grace M.
Junghanns, Julius
Kandinsky, Wassily
Karfiol, Bernard
Keller, Henry G.
King, Edith L.
Kirchner, T.L.
Kirstein, Alfred
Kleiminger, Adolph
Kleinert, Herman
Kramer, Edward Adam
Kroll, Leon
Kuhn, Walt
Lachaise, Gaston
Laprade, Pierre
Laurencin, Marie
Lawson, Ernest
Lee, Arthur
Lees, Derwent
Leger, Fernand
Lehmbruck, Wilhelm
Levy, Rudolph
Lie, Jonas
Londoner, Amy
Luks, George
Lundberg, A.F.
McComas, Francis
McEnery, Kathleen
McLane, Howard
McLean, Hower
Macknight, Dodge
MacRae, Elmer L.
Mager, Gus
Maillol, Aristide
Manet, Edouard
Manigault
Manolo, Manuel
Manquin, Henri
Marin, John
Maris, Matthew
Marquet, Albert
Marval, Jacqueline
Mase, C.C.
Matisse, Henri

Maurer, Alfred
Mayrshofer, Max
Meltzer, Charlotte
Miestchaninoff, Oscar
Miller, Kenneth Hayes
Milne, David B.
Monet, Claude
Monticelli, A.
Mowbray-Clarke, J.
Munch, Edward
Muhrmann, Henry
Murphy, Herman Dudley
Myers, Ethel
Myers, Jerome
Nadelman, Eli
Nankivell, Frank A.
Niles, Helen J.
Oppenheimer, Olga
Organ, Marjorie
Pach, Walter
Paddock, Josephine
Pascin, Jules
Pelton, Agnes
Pepper, Charles H.
Perrine, Van Dearing
Phillips, H.S.
Picabia, Francis
Picasso, Pablo
Pietro
Pissarro, Camille
Pleuthner, Walter
Pope, Louise
Prendergast, Maurice
Preston, James
Preston, May Wilson
Pryde, James
Putnam, Arthur
Rasmussen, Bertrand
Redon, Odilon
Renoir, Pierre Auguste
Reuterdahl, H.
Rhoades, Catherine N.
Rimmer, Dr. William
Robinson, Boardman
Robinson, Theordore
Rodin
Rogers, Mary C.
Roine, E.
Rohland, Paul
Rook, Edward T.
Rouault, Georges
Rousseau, Henri
Roussel, K. X.
Rumsey, Charles C.
Russel, Morgan
Russell, George W.
Ryder, Albert P.
Salvatore, Victor W.
Schamberg, Morton L.
Sheeler, Charles
Schumacher, Wm. E.
Serret, Charles
Seurat, Georges
Seyler, Julius
Shannon, Charles H.
Shaw, Sidney Dale

Sickert, Walter
Signac, Paul
Sisley, Alfred
Slevogt, Max
Sloan, John
Sousa-Cardozo, Amadeo
Sprinchorn, Carl
Steer, Wilson
Stella, Joseph
Stevens, Frances S.
Stinemetz, Morgan
Tarkhoff, Nicolas
Taylor, Henry Fitch
Taylor, William L.
Tobeen, Felix E.
Toulouse-Lautrec, Henri de
Toussaint, Gaston
Tucker, Allen
Twachtman, Alden
Twachtman, John H.
Vallotton, Felix
Van Gogh, Vincent
Villon, Jacques
Vlaminck, Maurice de
Vonnoh, Bessie Potter
Vuillard, Edouard
Waishawasky, Alexander
Walkowitz, A.
Walts, F.M.
Ward, Hilda
Weber, F. William
Webster, E. Ambroise
Weinzheimer, Felix E.
Weir, J. Alden
Weisgerber, Albert
Wentscher, Julius
Whistler, J. McN.
White, Chas. H.
Wilson, Claggett
Wolf, Leon
Wortman, Denys
Yandell, Enid
Yeats, Jack B.
Young, Art
Young, Mahonri
Zak, Eugene
Zorach, William
Zorach, Marguerite

Index

283

287

Index of Artists